RUSSIAN

PHILOSOPHY

EDITED BY

JAMES · M · EDIE
Northwestern University

JAMES · P · SCANLAN
Ohio State University

MARY-BARBARA · ZELDIN
Hollins College

WITH THE COLLABORATION OF

GEORGE · L · KLINE
Bryn Mawr College

RUSSIAN
PHILOSOPHY

VOLUME III

Pre-Revolutionary Philosophy and Theology

Philosophers in Exile

Marxists and Communists

THE UNIVERSITY OF TENNESSEE PRESS

Russian Philosophy in three volumes.
Copyright © 1965 by Quadrangle Books, Inc.
Second printing, 1969.

Copyright © 1976 by The University of Tennessee
Press, Knoxville. All rights reserved. Manufactured in
the United States of America.

Paper: 1st printing, 1976; 2nd printing, 1984;
          3rd printing, 1992.

The paper in this book meets the minimum requirements of the American National Standard for Perma-
nence of Paper for Printed Library Materials.
∞
The binding materials have been chosen for strength
and durability.

This edition is reprinted by arrangement with
Quadrangle/The New York Times Book Co.

Library of Congress Catalog Card Number: 64–10928.
ISBN 0–87049–716–2

Acknowledgments

THE EDITORS WISH to thank the publishers who have granted permission to reprint material from the following books:

Alexander Radishchev, *A Journey from Saint Petersburg to Moscow*, Cambridge, Mass., Harvard University Press, 1958.

Alexander Herzen, *From the Other Shore*, New York, George Braziller Inc.; London, Weidenfeld & Nicolson Ltd., 1956.

Fyodor Dostoevsky, *Notes from Underground*, London, William Heinemann Ltd.

Fyodor Dostoevsky, *Summer Impressions*, London, John Calder Ltd., 1955.

Fyodor Dostoevsky, *The Brothers Karamazov*, New York, Random House, 1943.

Fyodor Dostoevsky, *Diary of a Writer*, New York, Charles Scribner's Sons, 1954.

V. V. Rozanov, *Solitaria*, London, Wishart & Co., 1927.

V. V. Rozanov, *L'Apocalypse de notre temps*, Paris, Plon, 1930.

Vladimir Solovyov, *A Solovyov Anthology*, London, Student Christian Movement Press Ltd., 1950.

Nicholas Berdyaev, "Marx versus Man" from *Religion in Life*, Nashville, The Abingdon Press, Inc., 1938.

Nicholas Berdyaev, *Dream and Reality*, London, Geoffrey Bles; New York, The Macmillan Co., 1950.

Nicholas Berdyaev, *Slavery and Freedom*, London, Geoffrey Bles, 1939; New York, Charles Scribner's Sons, 1944.

Nicholas Berdyaev, *The Beginning and the End*, London, Geoffrey Bles; New York, Harper and Brothers, 1952.

Nicholas Berdyaev, *Solitude and Society*, London, Geoffrey Bles, 1938.

Nicholas Berdyaev, *The Destiny of Man*, London, Geoffrey Bles; New York, Harper and Brothers, 1937.

Nicholas Berdyaev, *The End of Our Time*, London and New York, Sheed and Ward, 1933.

Nicholas Berdyaev, *The Divine and the Human*, London, Geoffrey Bles, 1949.

Leon Shestov, *Kierkegaard et la philosophie existentielle*, Paris, J. Vrin, 1936.

George Plekhanov, *The Role of the Individual in History*, New York, International Publishers, 1940.

George Plekhanov, *Fundamental Problems of Marxism*, New York, International Publishers, n.d.

We also wish to thank Professor Peter K. Christoff and Mouton & Co. of The Hague for permission to publish Professor Christoff's translation of Ivan Kireyevsky's "On the Necessity and Possibility of New Principles in Philosophy" prior to its appearance in the series of "Slavistic Printings and Reprintings" being published by Mouton & Co. We wish to thank Philip Rahv and the *Partisan Review* for permission to reprint Mr. Rahv's translation of Vissarion Belinsky's "Letters to V. P. Botkin" which appeared in the *Partisan Review* in the Fall issue of 1960 (pp. 728-736); Professor Marvin Farber, editor of *Philosophy and Phenomenological Research*, for permission to reprint George L. Kline's translation of Leon Shestov's "In Memory of a Great Philosopher: Edmund Husserl," which appeared in that journal in June, 1962 (pp. 449-471); Donald A. Lowrie for permission to use his translation of Nicholas Berdyaev's "Marx versus Man"; Mrs. Tatiana Frank and Victor Frank for permission to use selections from Simon Frank's *Reality and Man* prior to its publication in English, and Mrs. Natalie Duddington for permission to publish her translation of Simon Frank's "Of the Two Natures in Man" and Nicholas O. Lossky's "Intuitivism."

We thank the officials of the Northwestern University Graduate School, Goucher College, the Hollins College Faculty Research and Travel Fund, and the Ford Foundation for grants to the editors for research and the preparation of this work.

We wish to recognize the following libraries for special assistance given in research on this work: The Library of Congress, The New York Public Library, The Newberry Library, The University of Chicago Library, The Fishburn Library of Hollins College, The Columbia University Library, The Widener Library at Harvard University, The Library of the United States Information Service in Calcutta, The National Library of Calcutta, The Goucher College Library, and The Northwestern University Library.

Our special thanks go to Professor Jesse Zeldin of Hollins College for his substantial editorial advice on the work as a whole, to Professor Wallace Cayard of West Liberty State College for his help in making the Berdyaev selections, and to Leo Werneke for his help in preparing the index, as well as to Miss Dorothy A. Doerr, Librarian of the Fishburn Library, and Mrs. Sue Deaton Ross and Mrs. Marilyn Scanlan for their help in preparing the manuscript.

Finally, we are particularly indebted to Professor George L. Kline for his assistance in the preparation of this work. He not only contributed a number of original translations but also gave substantial help by revising several other translations, by suggesting selections to be included, by putting at our disposal his vast fund of general and specific knowledge in the field of Russian thought and Russian philosophy, and by giving us invaluable aid and advice in the preparation of this work as a whole and of each of its parts. Without his help and inspiration the publication of this historical anthology of Russian philosophy could have been neither successfully planned nor achieved.

J. M. E.
J. P. S.
M.-B. Z.

Preface

Russian speculation has always been decidedly *man-centered*. From the beginnings of philosophy in the seventeenth and eighteenth centuries, and into the post-Revolutionary emigration, certain themes have remained constant: the problem of good and evil in individual and social life, the meaning of individual existence, the nature of history. Russian thinkers turned late, and hesitantly, to such technical disciplines as logic, theory of knowledge, and philosophy of science. Even metaphysics and philosophical theology, as practiced in Russia, were intimately linked to ethics, social philosophy, and the philosophy of history. Indeed, the small group of Russian religious thinkers who might be called "theocentric" rather than "anthropocentric" made their most striking *philosophical* contributions in these same man-centered disciplines.

Furthermore, Russian philosophical thought has been uniquely non-academic and non-institutional. One could scarcely write a history of philosophy in Germany without including such professional academics as Kant, Fichte, Schelling, and Hegel; nor could one discuss philosophy in the twentieth century without reference to Professors Heidegger, Whitehead, Wittgenstein, and Carnap.

In Russia the situation was quite different: the original and influential thinkers (and originality of thought has not always coincided with influence) have almost without exception been non-academic. The professors of philosophy in the universities and theological academies, though competent, tended to be faithful disciples of one or another Western master rather than

ix

independent thinkers. Vladimir Solovyov is an exception, but even he left the academic world fairly early, as a result of differences with university and governmental authorities.

Thus the major Russian thinkers—until the twentieth century —were not university professors but, in a large sense, "critics." Their counterparts in Western Europe would be thinkers like Kierkegaard, John Stuart Mill, Nietzsche and Sartre (both of whom *began* as professors), the later Santayana and the later Wittgenstein. Most of these Russians made their living by writing book reviews; professionally they were literary critics. But "literature" in Russia has always been conceived very broadly—to include not just poetry, the novel, and the short story, but also political and philosophical commentary. In the current English sense of the terms, these Russians were political, social, and cultural critics as well as literary critics. (The untranslatable Russian word for such wide-ranging "literary" activity is *publitsistika*.)

In Russia, more than elsewhere, the major literary figures have been concerned with philosophical problems, or, more precisely, with philosophical formulations of the perennial "problems of men." Tolstoy, Dostoevsky, and Pasternak are the obvious examples; less well known in this regard are Gogol and, among the poets, Fet (who translated Schopenhauer), and the Symbolists, particularly Blok and Bely. At the same time, many Russian thinkers best known as literary, philosophical, and religious critics have been gifted and productive poets: for example, Skovoroda, Radishchev, Khomyakov, and, of course, Vladimir Solovyov.

Related both to its non-academic character and to its involvement with *belles lettres* is the fact that Russian philosophical thought has been marked by a special intensity and an impatience with moderation. A kind of personal risk, an "existential" decision or commitment, was involved in being an intellectual in Russia, a commitment to oppose the repressive aspects of "Russian reality" (and sometimes of Western theory) in the name of human freedom and dignity. This in turn is related to the almost monastic isolation of the nineteenth-century Russian *intelligentsia*, and the exclusion (after the Decembrist uprising of 1825) of free and creative thinkers from academic life. University instruction in philosophy was formally proscribed in Russian universities from 1850 until 1863. From 1884 to 1889, permitted instruction was officially limited to lecture-commentaries on selected texts of Plato and Aristotle.

From the 1830's on, the informal philosophical discussion group or "circle" (*kruzhok*, pl. *kruzhki*) was a major instrument of philosophical education among the most gifted of Russian university students, as well as a major channel for the penetration of German metaphysics and French socialist theory into Russian intellectual life.

For the reasons sketched above, philosophy in Russia was seldom "pure"—in the sense of non-committed or non-instrumental. Ideas, for the Russian intellectuals of the nineteenth century, were weapons. Most Russians viewed "pure" philosophy, in the Platonic sense of the "passion to know the truth," not merely as an abstruse exercise but also as an evasion of pressing moral and socio-political concerns. This attitude can be expressed in Russian by saying that they subordinated *istina*—theoretical truth—to *pravda*—practical "truth-justice." Russian thinkers conceived their central task as the *iskaniye pravdy*—the quest for truth-justice.

On this question it is possible to distinguish a "rationalist" and an "irrationalist" tradition in Russian thought. The rationalists (e.g., the "Men of the Sixties," Tolstoy, Solovyov, the Marxists) assumed that theoretical truth (*pravda-istina*) can and should serve as a support for practical justice (*pravda-spravedlivost*) in individual and social life. The irrationalists—inconsistently and hesitantly in the nineteenth century (e.g., Herzen and the Populists)—consistently and unhesitatingly in the twentieth century (Shestov)—assumed the priority of *pravda-spravedlivost*, in the sense of moral value, and were willing to bracket, or reject outright, the claims of *pravda-istina*, understood as theoretical truth. In Shestov's formulation: one must either absolutize theoretical truth and thus relativize moral values, or else relativize theoretical truth in order to absolutize moral values, thus "redeeming" the life of the existing individual.

This "either-or" echoes Kierkegaard's, although Shestov formulated it—under the influence of Dostoevsky and Nietzsche—long before he had read Kierkegaard. However, Shestov's "revolt against reason" is also in part a revolt against Kant's terminological assimilation (perpetuated by Hegel) of speculation to action, of "theoretical reason" to "practical reason." For Shestov the common term is a fraud: what the German philosophers, up to but not including Schopenhauer and Nietzsche, had called "practical reason" is not *reason* at all—is not cognitive, but instinctive, intuitive, emotive—a mode of value-appropriation, of decision, and action. In this sense, Shestov's "existentialism," even more than Berdyaev's, represents the culmination of one major tradition in Russian philosophy. The other major tradition—that of the "rationalists"—is today represented chiefly by the epigoni of Marxism-Leninism, who are, needless to say, unalterably opposed to every form of existential philosophy.

Russian Philosophical Terminology

Russian philosophical terminology was largely stabilized during the 1830's and 1840's, partly under the influence of Bakunin and Belinsky, partly under the influence of such Slavophiles as Kireyevsky and Khomyakov—all of them drawing heavily upon Hegelian models. Russian is the only European language that has a precise technical equivalent of Hegel's notorious *Aufhebung,* i.e., *snyatiye.* The term is sometimes (inadequately) rendered in English by the exotic "sublation." (The Russian *snyatiye* preserves the threefold sense—not suggested by the English—of "cancellation," "raising to a higher level," and "preservation.")

The Hegelian coloring of Russian philosophical terminology— fixed long before Marxism had appeared on the Russian scene— was doubtless a mixed blessing. It made possible distinctions which were often invidious and sometimes careless, e.g., the Slavophile opposition of "Reason"—*razum (Vernunft)*—to mere "Understanding"—*rassudok (Verstand).* And it preserved ambiguities which might better have been dissolved, e.g., *pravo (Recht):* meaning both "law" and "right"; *samosoznaniye (Selbstbewusstsein):* meaning both consciousness *of* self and consciousness *by* self, i.e., the self as, respectively, object and subject of awareness; *nauka (Wissenschaft),* in the broad sense which includes philosophy and scholarship as well as science. But this Hegelian terminology had the marked advantage of bringing Russian philosophical discourse into contact with a lively and powerful philosophical tradition.

The present work is intended as a comprehensive anthology of Russian philosophical writings, arranged in generally chronological order. It is designed for use by the student of Russian philosophy and intellectual history, as well as the general reader with an interest in Russian culture. Fortunately, there is almost nothing in Russian philosophical writing so technical as to be beyond the grasp of such a reader.

The selected bibliographies consist primarily of works in English, occasionally supplemented by French or German titles, and very occasionally (in the absence of appropriate non-Russian works) by Russian titles. This applies to primary as well as secondary sources.

The development of Russian philosophy through its various schools and "isms" is traced in the general introductions to each of the nine parts of the work. Detailed discussion of individual thinkers is to be found in the special introductions which precede selections from their work.

SELECTED GENERAL BIBLIOGRAPHY OF WORKS ON RUSSIAN AND SOVIET PHILOSOPHY

Acton, Harry B., *The Illusion of the Epoch: Marxism-Leninism as a Philosophical Creed*, London, 1955; Boston, 1957.

Berdyaev, Nicholas, *The Russian Idea*, trans. R. M. French, New York, 1948; paperback edition: Boston, 1962.

Bochenski, J. M., *Soviet Russian Dialectical Materialism*, trans. from the 3rd German edition by Nicolas Sollohub, Dordrecht, 1963.

Bubnoff, Nikolai von, ed., *Russische Religionsphilosophen. Dokumente*, Heidelberg, 1956.

Chyzhevski, Dmytro, "Hegel in Russland," in *Hegel bei den Slaven*, Bad Homburg vor der Hohe, 1961, pp. 145-396 (reprint of the 1934 edition).

Fedotov, George P., *The Russian Religious Mind*, Cambridge, Mass., 1946.

———, *A Treasury of Russian Spirituality*, New York, 1948.

Jakowenko, Boris V., *Filosofi russi: saggio di storia della filosofia russa*, trans. from the Russian, Florence, 1925.

Koyré, Alexandre, *Etudes sur l'histoire de la pensée philosophique en Russie*, Paris, 1950.

———, *La philosophie et le problème national en Russie au début du XIXe siècle*, Paris, 1929.

Lossky, Nicholas O., *History of Russian Philosophy*, London and New York, 1951.

Marcuse, Herbert, *Soviet Marxism: A Critical Analysis*, New York, 1958; paperback edition with new preface: New York, 1961.

xiv   *Preface*

Masaryk, Thomas G., *The Spirit of Russia: Studies in History, Literature and Philosophy*, trans. E. and C. Paul, 2 vols., New York, 1955.

Pascal, Pierre, "Les grands courants de la pensée russe contemporaine," in *Les grands courants de la pensée mondiale contemporaine*, ed. M. F. Sciacca, Milan, 1959, Pt. 1, Vol. 2.

Raeff, Marc, ed., *Russian Intellectual History: An Anthology*, New York, 1966.

Scheibert, Peter, *Von Bakunin zu Lenin: Geschichte der russischen revolutionären Ideologien, 1840-1895*. Vol. 1: *Die Formung des radikalen Denkens in der Auseinandersetzung mit deutschem Idealismus und französischem Bürgertum*, Leiden, 1956.

Schmemann, Alexander, ed., *Ultimate Questions: An Anthology of Modern Russian Religious Thought*, New York, 1965.

Simmons, Ernest J., ed., *Continuity and Change in Russian and Soviet Thought*, Cambridge, Mass., 1955. Especially Pt. IV: "Rationality and Nonrationality," pp. 283-377, with contributions by Theodosius Dobzhansky, Fr. Georges Florovsky, Waldemar Gurian, George L. Kline, and Herbert Marcuse, and a summary and review by Geroid T. Robinson.

Utechin, S. V., *Russian Political Thought: A Concise History*, New York, 1964.

Weidlé, Wladimir, *Russia Absent and Present*, trans. A. Gordon Smith, London and New York, 1952.

Wetter, Gustav A., *Dialectical Materialism: A Historical and Systematic Survey of Philosophy in the Soviet Union*, trans. from the 4th German edition by Peter Heath, London and New York, 1958.

Zenkovsky, V. V., *A History of Russian Philosophy*, trans. George L. Kline, 2 vols., London and New York, 1953.

Contents

VOLUME II

VOLUME III

Book Seven

PRE-REVOLUTIONARY
PHILOSOPHY
AND THEOLOGY

IT IS TEMPTING TO SAY that the controversy between the
Slavophiles and the Westernizers ended in the victory of the
latter. Certainly, Russian thought in the second half of the nineteenth century is primarily secular. This is the period of the
growth and flourishing of Nihilism, Populism, and, finally, of
Marxism. And if, as Berdyaev claims,[1] Nihilism is really religious,
it is religious in a non-spiritual sense. If among the Populists
there were men with a religious outlook, Populism is nevertheless not characterized by such an outlook. The concern of these
people was for a this-worldly Utopia and the means of achieving
it, for man-godhood perhaps, but not for Godmanhood. On the
other hand, the Slavophilism of the same period had decayed into
reaction and Pan-Slavism.

But in reality this description is true only of the 1850's and
1860's. It ignores the work of the great critics considered in the
last section. Moreover, it overlooks the fact that in the last three
decades of the nineteenth century, Russian philosophy, both religious and secular, was finally coming of age, and in these decades
the fully systematic world views of the twentieth century had
their beginnings. The religious philosophers of this period have
roots in common with their secular contemporaries in the philosophical views of the forties, and, before that, of Skovoroda,
Radishchev, and Chaadayev. Like the heirs of the Westernizers,
these philosophers had their own secular moments, both in their

1. *The Origin of Russian Communism*, trans. R. M. French, Ann Arbor,
1960, p. 45.

development and their concern. Almost all of them, at some point in their early intellectual development, were atheists or agnostics, and turned to a religious world view only after reaching an intellectual impasse or suffering a religious crisis. In this they resemble the generation that followed them, that of the dissatisfied Marxists, Nicholas Berdyaev (1874-1948), Serge Bulgakov (1871-1944), S. L. Frank (1877-1950), and P. B. Struve (1870-1944), who turned from Marxist revisionism to a spiritual philosophy. Like their secular counterparts, moreover, they were keenly aware of scientific developments and were eager to bring the fruits of science into their philosophical world outlook. Again like the sons of the Westernizers, these true heirs to the Slavophiles are remarkable for their lack of orthodoxy. Their orientation might, in contrast to that of their Populist and Marxist cousins, be religious, but like many of their cousins they asserted their personalities and refused to be doctrinaire or eclectic. Thus, although several trends are distinguishable among them, in no trend do we find an uncritical acceptance of the views either of their Russian fathers or of their Western tutors. In this sense the last two or three decades of the nineteenth century are distinguished from the period of the fifties and sixties, when the dominant philosophies were either doctrinaire Nihilism or decadent Slavophilism.

Unlike the Slavophiles, however, and, on the whole, unlike the Westernizers, the pre-Revolutionary philosophers were rich in resources. Whereas Schelling and Hegel were almost the only Western European philosophical influences on the thought of the forties, Slavophile or Westernizer, now other Western philosophical classics were studied, assimilated, and combined with native Russian ideas. It is tempting, indeed, to see this last period of nineteenth-century Russian religious philosophy as a unit, beginning with the highly original thought of NICHOLAS FYODOROV (1828-1903), reaching complete expression in the system of VLADIMIR SOLOVYOV (1853-1900), and ending with the elaborations of that system by the Princes Serge and Eugene Trubetskoy (1862-1905 and 1863-1920). But to do this would be to ignore other major trends, particularly the personalistic-Leibnizian philosophy of such writers as A. A. Kozlov (1831-

1901) or the neo-Kantian views of A. I. Vvedensky (1856-1925). Perhaps the most correct approach is to see in this period from 1870 to 1900 the development of the heritage on which the Russian émigré philosophers were to build—always, however, excepting Fyodorov and Solovyov, who had a rich enough philosophy to be considered in their own right as well as in relation to their successors.

Thus three major streams may be seen rising in this period: that started by Kozlov, that started by Vvedensky, and that which is completed by Solovyov only to be interpreted, elaborated, and modified by Serge and Eugene Trubetskoy.

The first stream has its source in Leibniz. Its concern, as with all religious philosophy of this period, is to provide Christianity, and specifically Eastern Orthodox Christianity, with a philosophical basis. In the case of the neo-Leibnizian school, this concern centers on an attempt to preserve the independence of the individual spiritual person on the one hand and to assert cosmic unity on the other. In this, Alexis Alexandrovich Kozlov is succeeded by the mathematician N. V. Bugayev (1837-1903), and by L. M. Lopatin (1855-1920). In the next generation he is followed by N. O. Lossky (1870-1965).

According to Kozlov, the world is an organic system of spiritual substances (active agents), their activities, and the content of their activities (ideas). Matter exists only as our representation of spiritual activity, of the interaction of spiritual substances. That other spiritual substances exist is inferred from our representations of other bodies: if matter is a result of the interaction of spiritual substances and if such activity can occur only where substantial agents act, we may conclude that such agents, like ourselves, exist. The root of the organic unity of the world is God, the Supreme Substance. The relation of God to the world is not clear, but would seem to be the same as in Leibniz.

In this system, time and space have no more objective reality than matter: they are results of our limited faculties, which find it necessary to coordinate phenomena in such terms. Timelessness does not exclude development, however, any more than development is excluded from an axiomatic system. Space is the symbol of the interconnection of substances, time of the activity involved in this connection and of the variety of the relations. Death is the suspension of our Ego's interaction with less developed substances (our organs), and it is probable that our Ego enters into new interactions after death, thus developing a new body.

In epistemology, Kozlov distinguishes two levels of cognition: consciousness and knowledge. Consciousness is immediate, knowledge is mediate. Cognition of the external world is knowledge; it is thus mediate and symbolic. It is, however, of reality: "Phenomena are not actual entities or things as they are in themselves; in dealing with them we do not deal directly with the activities of actual entities. Nevertheless, we make contact with their law-like *reflection* in consciousness." [2] This view is popular not only among the Russian Leibnizians; it is characteristic of Russian religious philosophy in contrast to the realism of Roman Catholicism.

Leo Mikhailovich Lopatin followed Kozlov in his metaphysics. He establishes the supra-temporality of the Ego on the basis of its awareness of time: "Time cannot be observed and understood by that which is itself temporal." [3] But the self does not wholly transcend its activities, rather the supra-temporal substance and its temporal processes form an indissoluble whole, its processes being its creations. Thus, substance is essentially creative. By arguing in this fashion Lopatin adds an ethical dimension to Kozlov's world view. The self is responsible for its actions which are indissolubly part of it: since the product of my creative activity is never alienated from me, I can never deny my responsibility. And, since the world consists of such creative self-subsisting substances, free causality not only exists but is prior to mechanical causality. Lopatin's pluralism has unity, how-

2. *A Personal Word*, Part V, pp. 85, 136, quoted in V. V. Zenkovsky, *A History of Russian Philosophy*, trans. George L. Kline, 2 vols., London and New York, 1953, p. 639.

3. "The Concept of the Soul According to the Data of Inner Experience," *Problems of Philosophy and Psychology*, XXXII, 1896, p. 288, quoted in Nicholas O. Lossky, *History of Russian Philosophy*, New York, 1951, pp. 160-161.

ever. This unity is possible because the world is "rooted" in God. Unfortunately, the exact relation of the world to God is never made clear.

The second stream evident in pre-Revolutionary Russian religious philosophy is Kantian, and its chief exponent is Alexander Ivanovich Vvedensky. By the late nineteenth century, Russian thinkers had long been familiar with the works of Kant. Chaadayev was an avid reader of Kant. So were the philosophers of the forties. The *Critique of Pure Reason* was not translated into Russian until 1867 (by Michael Ivanovich Vladislavlev), but Kant had by that time long been studied in the original German. The direct, obvious, and consciously accepted influence of Kant, however, is not apparent until late in the century.

Vvedensky's neo-Kantian philosophy starts out as remarkably faithful, even as to method. He establishes the possibility of synthetic *a priori* judgments, by arguing that without them no synthetic judgment and therefore no science is possible. But then he ignores Kant's first statement in the Introduction to the *Critique of Pure Reason*, that all knowledge begins with experience, as sensation, and argues that scientific inferences can be drawn from a combination of analytic judgments and general basic synthetic judgments. These inferences, he adds, returning to Kant, can hold only for experience which alone is subject to the law of contradiction. Thus metaphysics as a science is impossible.

So far, Vvedensky has not got beyond Fichte. But he is not satisfied with the situation. "It is intolerable for us to be prisoners in the world of phenomena," he exclaims.[4] Accordingly, he finds another kind of cognition, *a posteriori* cognition of the *content* of consciousness, i.e., of experience, and this knowledge, he tells us, proves that things-in-themselves, things, that is, *other* than my rational activity, exist. We can, however, know things-in-themselves only in this way, as, that is, they appear *a posteriori* in our consciousness. We are now back with Kant.

4. *An Attempt to Construct a Theory of Matter on the Basis of the Principles of Critical Philosophy*, St. Petersburg, 1888, p. 80, quoted in Zenkovsky, *op. cit.*, p. 682.

Now, like Kant, Vvedensky admits a third kind of cognition: faith. And Vvedensky's faith is much more capacious than that for which Kant "made room." In fact, faith for Vvedensky implies a special faculty, a "metaphysical sense" additional to the empirical senses. This faculty has only "moral" employment to be sure, but, under Vvedensky's guidance, it brings back into the realm of philosophy all that had been excluded from it and much more than Kant found room for in the *Critique of Practical Reason*.

Vvedensky's neo-Kantianism may not be wholly successful, but it is courageous. In finding in Kant a place for a special faculty for faith it permits "Kantians" of the next generation to combine the notion of "intuitive cognition" developed by the Slavophiles with critical philosophy, and thus to construct a critical metaphysics.

The third philosophical stream to be found in the pre-Revolutionary period is by far the most significant in itself as well as for its later influence. This is the philosophical system of Vladimir Solovyov, and the views of his friends, the Princes Serge and Eugene Trubetskoy.

Solovyov's philosophy will be discussed in the section devoted to him, and all that need be done here is to point out its general characteristics. Solovyov has been called Russia's first systematic philosopher. Although one may argue as to his being the first, there is no doubt about the elaborateness and breadth of his system. The philosophy of the Slavophiles is, in Solovyov, combined with critical philosophy and with Eastern religion; empiricism, rationalism, and mysticism are brought together; religion, philosophy, science, and poetry are all united into one tremendous edifice bound by the concept of the total-unity of all reality. Such total-unity may be more than we care to accept, but we cannot fail to admire it.

This philosophical system was wholeheartedly endorsed by Solovyov's younger friends, Serge and Eugene Trubetskoy. Indeed, such was the influence of Solovyov on the younger of the two brothers, Eugene, that the latter felt obliged to refuse to write an article in a volume in honor of Solovyov: he could, he said, "neither oppose my own viewpoint to his, nor expound his views as my own." [5] Nevertheless, with time, both brothers interpreted Solovyov in an original way.

Serge Trubetskoy emphasizes in his views the principle of *sobornost* [6] worked out by Kireyevsky and Khomyakov. All being is in essence relative, in interaction in all its spheres and levels, and in this interaction is one and yet diverse. This unity is the Absolute, which as such is not relative, while it is relative insofar as it is its own content. Our consciousness, like all being, is characterized by relativity. In consciousness we go beyond the limit of our individuality and "hold a conference with all men within ourselves." [7] This is not, however, to deny personality to consciousness but to broaden it: consciousness is collective. Every individual consciousness is, in fact, rooted in a cosmic consciousness which produces individual consciousness. This is remarkably like the views of Chaadayev, although it is unlikely that Serge Trubetskoy knew those views. What we have, rather, is an attempt to use the principle of *sobornost* within Solovyov's metaphysics of total-unity—to rescue, to some extent, the philosophy of Solovyov from its pantheistic tendencies.

Eugene Trubetskoy elaborates further his brother's views on the nature of consciousness, and, also, attempts wholly to avoid the pantheism latent in Solovyov's philosophy. The Absolute is timeless *consciousness*—only if this is the case can *any* judgment be universally valid; moreover, an Absolute Consciousness is broader than an Absolute Being, for consciousness includes non-being, the future and the past. The content of our consciousness is temporal, but the truth about it is eternal: thus we combine in our cognition human and absolute thought. Such a combination of the created and the divine, of freedom and dependence, can be explained in terms of the nature of Creation: Creation is an absolutely *free, real* act of God, a creation out of *nothing*; it is effected in accordance with a principle, Sophia, which is real in God but, for us who are temporal, only an ideal. Thus

5. *Vl. Solovyov's World View*, Moscow, 1913, I, vi, quoted in Zenkovsky, *op. cit.*, p. 804.
6. See above, Vol. 1, pp. 161-162.
7. *Works*, II, p. 12, quoted in Zenkovsky, *op. cit.*, p. 795.

we are independent of God and free to accept or reject the ideal.

These three streams of thought in Russian pre-Revolutionary philosophy all have Russian, as well as non-Russian, sources. They are characteristically Russian, however, in their concerns: the attempt to ground knowledge of reality in intuition, the attempt to preserve both unity and plurality—the freedom of the individual person in a spiritual-social order. It was as much owing to these epistemological and ethical concerns as to the religious orientation of these philosophies that, in the next generation, the men who expounded them found themselves compelled to go into exile.

NICHOLAS FYODOROVICH FYODOROV

[1828–1903]

NICHOLAS FYODOROV was born in 1828, the illegitimate son of Prince P. I. Gagarin and a peasant woman. He was given the surname of his godfather and lived in the household of Prince Gagarin until the latter's death in 1832, when he and his mother were required to leave. They were, however, well taken care of and Fyodorov received a good education, first in the *gymnasium* in Tambov and then in the Faculty of Law of the Lycée Richelieu in Odessa.

From 1854 to 1868 he taught history and geography in a series of elementary schools in various provincial towns. Zenkovsky calls this period of his life the "period of his wanderings." [1] Finally, in 1868, he received the position of librarian in the Rumyantsev Museum in Moscow where he lived until his death in 1903.

In the words of Nicholas O. Lossky, who calls him "an uncanonized saint":

> Living an intensive spiritual life and devoting himself entirely to public service, he reduced his own physical wants to the minimum. He occupied a tiny room and slept not more than four or five hours a day on a bare humpbacked trunk, resting his head on some hard object. His food consisted of tea with hard rolls, and of cheese or salted fish and often he would go for whole months on end without any hot food. Money was a nuisance to him.

1. Zenkovsky, *op. cit.*, p. 589.

Receiving an insignificant salary (less than 400 roubles a year) and refusing any increase, he used to give away the greater part of it, every month, to some "stipendiates" of his. He wanted to possess no property, and never had even a warm overcoat.

Fame and popularity he regarded as manifestations of immodesty. His articles appeared anonymously, and the majority of them were never published by him. . . .

In spite of his austere life he enjoyed excellent health and only fell ill when his friends compelled him to give up his habits. He never wore a fur coat and always walked; but in 1903, during severe December frosts, his friends made him put on a fur coat and take a cab. He contracted pneumonia and died.[2]

Fyodorov was renowned for his great erudition in his own day and is said to have known the exact location and the contents of every volume in the Rumyantsev Library. Vladimir Solovyov and Fyodor Dostoevsky knew him and considered him a man of great wisdom and holiness. Leo Tolstoy, despite the fact that Fyodorov was one of his more severe critics, once said: "I am proud to live in the same century with such a man."

After his death his friends, V. Kozhevnikov and N. Peterson, privately printed a collection of his writings under the title *Filosofiya obshchevo dela* (The Philosophy of the Common Task) and distributed the 480 copies free of charge to libraries, learned societies, and interested persons. A second edition was published by a group of Russian missionaries in Kharbin, Manchuria, in 1928, on the centennial of his birth.

It is from this work that the following selection is taken, *The Question of Brotherhood or Relatedness, and of the Reasons for the Unbrotherly, Dis-Related, or Unpeaceful State of the World, and of the Means for the Restoration of Relatedness*, which contains a discussion of the themes dearest to Fyodorov's heart.

It is noteworthy that when Russian philosophers first came into close contact with Western thought in the nineteenth cen-

2. Lossky, *op. cit.*, pp. 75-76.

tury, there was one point which they unanimously rejected. On this even the Slavophiles and the Westernizers were at one. From the time of Descartes onward Western philosophers had been "fascinated" with the epistemological problems surrounding solipsism, and consequently the need to demonstrate, if possible, or justify in some manner, the existence of the external world and of other persons. Russian philosophers, from the beginning, denounced this as a "false problem" which could only have resulted from the over-intellectualized and rationalistic Western approach to epistemology.[3] The most common experiences of affectivity, of love, friendship, brotherhood, community serve to establish the existence of "others" and our essential, emotional interrelationship with them at the very point of departure. Russian philosophers felt that it was only by restricting epistemology to the realm of "pure reason" or to the pure *cognition* of clear and distinct ideas, that it was even possible to begin to comprehend the odd, demonstrably false, and artificial status of Western epistemology as they encountered it.

Fyodorov continues this critique and makes his own specific contribution to it. The category of "Relatedness" is at the center of his thought, and in terms of it he discusses and criticizes Western (and the most recent Russian) thought. The great, even tragic, error of modern philosophy and science is that it has become too "objective," and has neglected the state of *man as a whole,* of mankind as a brotherhood. Mankind, according to Fyodorov, does constitute a *whole;* all men are sons of their fathers and, ultimately, of the Father of fathers. But through the gradual restriction of knowledge and science to a special "class," which has become more and more concerned with pure knowledge and less and less interested in using it for the amelioration of the "whole," mankind has entered a state of disharmony, disrelatedness, isolation. But even the extension of knowledge to everyone, universal education in science, would not remedy the

3. A significant exception is Solovyov, whose "Foundations of Theoretical Philosophy" is an examination of some of these epistemological problems in a style more typical of the Western approach. After Solovyov, Russian philosophy became more and more thoroughly "Westernized"—particularly in epistemological questions.

state of dis-relatedness into which mankind has fallen, since the attitude toward the use of knowledge itself must also be changed.

Here Fyodorov seems to express a kind of "pragmatism" or "meliorism," by demanding that those who possess this knowledge and science begin *to act* in the world to improve the lot of men as a whole and thus establish brotherhood. It is, he believes, fully within the power of man to make the universe gradually better, to control the blind forces of nature which threaten human life, to create the paradise of which Scripture speaks. For Fyodorov, Christianity is not something which has been accomplished; it is rather a promise, something which we must *begin to do*—and he identifies it with the establishment of "brotherhood" through the collective use of knowledge. This rather Utopian, and even naive, philosophy takes on an increased grandeur as we follow Fyodorov's arguments and feel his hopes for the possible future of the human race. He is a religious philosopher who interprets the teachings of Christianity in terms of the material and moral improvement of the world as a whole. The dogma of "the resurrection of the flesh" becomes, in Fyodorov's philosophy, a meditation on the scientific possibility of bringing our ancestors, "our fathers," back to life. He sets no bounds whatsoever to what humanity can accomplish if it will take human "brotherhood" seriously and use its collective knowledge in order *to act*. *Knowledge without action* (the characteristic sin of philosophers and scientists) is the gift of Satan. Salvation lies in actively overcoming scientific "disinterestedness." The Kingdom of God, i.e., the brotherhood of the human race, is a possibility which men have unconscionably neglected. Fyodorov is the apostle of this brotherhood.

Zenkovsky [4] is no doubt correct in tracing this concern to two basic motive-forces in Fyodorov's own experience: his sense of human isolation, of alienation, of the "unbrotherly" conduct which characterizes most human relationships, and, secondly, the refusal to resign himself to death, to abandon the "fathers" of the human race. Perhaps psychologists can analyze all this in terms of Fyodorov's own illegitimate birth, his lack of "legal" status in any family; but clearly in his own thought the ideal

4. Zenkovsky, *op. cit.*, p. 595.

is much greater than any of its possible psychological sources. It is a concern for the "race" as a whole, for the tragic isolation of men from one another when they possess the means to overcome this isolation. Thus we find in Fyodorov's thought a dialectical tension between a Utopian optimism and an extreme pessimism. He believes that the Kingdom of God is possible, that it is within the reach of men, but he is oppressed with the extreme unlikelihood of mankind's ever coming to realize this or achieve it. His philosophy is a program, a "projective" philosophy—the "philosophy of the common task"—and he attempts to offer both a vision of what can be achieved and a plan for its accomplishment. As has been remarked,[5] many of the projects which may have seemed chimerical when Fyodorov first advanced them, such as interplanetary colonization and the control of atmospheric conditions, are now recognized as within the possibility of human science. It is even possible that future science will recognize Fyodorov as a "prophet" of its own achievements. At the present time his thought is almost completely unknown, especially to Western philosophers.

SELECTED BIBLIOGRAPHY

Works:
Filosofiya obshchevo dela, ed. V. A. Kozhevnikov and N. P. Peterson, Verny, 1906.

Secondary Sources:
Nicholas Berydaev, "N. F. Fyodorov," *Russian Review,* Vol. 9 (1950).
V. V. Zenkovsky, *A History of Russian Philosophy,* trans. George L. Kline, 2 vols., London and New York, 1953, pp. 588-604.

5. Lossky, *op. cit.,* pp. 78-79.

[NICHOLAS FYODOROV]

The Question of Brotherhood or Relatedness, and of the Reasons for the Unbrotherly, Dis-Related, or Unpeaceful State of the World, and of the Means for the Restoration of Relatedness

(A memorandum from the unlearned to the learned, both religious and secular, and to unbelievers as well as believers.) *

I.

In the disastrous year of 1891, when there was a famine—brought on by an apparently chronic drought—in many of the provinces which make up the granary of Russia, when rumors were constantly springing up which tended to increase the tense expectation of war, we suddenly heard about experiments in inducing rain by means of explosive substances which had hitherto been used exclusively, one might say, in foreign and domestic wars—revolutions, bomb-throwers' plots, etc. The coincidence of our famine from drought with the discovery of a means to combat drought, the very same means which had previously served only for mutual destruction, could not fail to produce a profound impression, particularly upon those who were close to the famine or who had close relatives in the age group which would have to enter the army's ranks in the event of war; and yet not only upon them! Man had in fact plainly done

---

* Translated for this volume by Ashleigh E. Moorhouse and George L. Kline from "*Vopros o bratstve, ili rodstve, o prichinakh nebratskovo, nerodstvennovo, t. e. nemirnovo, sostoyaniya mira, i o sredstvakh k vosstanovleniyu rodstva: Zapiska ot neuchonykh k uchonym, dukhovnym i svetskim, k veruyushchim i neveruyushchim,*" Pt. I, included in *Filosofiya obshchevo dela: Stati, mysli i pisma Nikolaya Fyodorovicha Fyodorova*, ed. V. A. Kozhevnikov and N. P. Peterson, Verny, 1906, I, 5-30. A few footnotes have been omitted, others have been shortened.

all the evil he could, both to nature (the exhaustion, despoiling, and plundering of it) and to his fellow man (the invention of the most deadly weapons and of the means of mutual destruction in general). . . .

And suddenly here, like a consoling ray of light for those "sitting in the darkness and shadow of death," came tidings which changed everything, the good tidings that the means invented for mutual destruction had become a means of salvation from famine, bringing the hope that now there would be an end to both famine and war, an end to war without the disarmament which is in fact impossible. . . .

Our hopes rest not on the possibility of producing rain by a few [cannon] shots or explosions, but on the possibility of controlling the moist and dry currents of air over broad areas, the possibility of saving men not only from drought but also from destructive downpours. This is a task which requires the common action of the armies of all nations, and therefore it must not under any circumstances become an object of mere [financial] speculation. The discovery of the possibility of producing rain by means of explosives, even if it did not justify the hopes which it has raised, would nevertheless not lose its significance as an indication of a method of action for the whole of the human race taken in its totality. . . .

At the present time everything serves war. There is not a single discovery which the military do not study with a view to its application to war; there is not a single invention which they have not tried to turn to the purposes of war. If armies were charged with the duty of adapting everything which they now adapt to war to the control of the forces of nature, the task of war would in fact be converted into the common task of the whole human race.

2.

The crop failure and especially the famine of 1891 compel the unlearned to remind the learned of their own origins, and of the obligation they are under as a result of these origins: (a) the obligation to turn to the study of the forces which produce crop failure and fatal plagues, i.e., to turn to a study of nature as a lethal force, devoting themselves to this study as a sacred duty, but also as a simple, natural, and reasonable one; and (b) the obligation to unite all men, the learned and the unlearned alike, in the task of studying and controlling this blind force. There can be no other obligation, no other task for a conscious being. To expect that the blind force which has been put under the control of this conscious being—but is not controlled by him—should of itself begin to produce only blessings and good harvests is utter childishness. . . .

Having divided up science and scholarship into a multitude of separate disciplines, the learned are saying that the oppressive calamities which have overtaken us fall within the purview of specialized disciplines and do not represent a general question for all men, i.e., the question of the dis-relatedness of this blind force with respect to rational human beings; this force obviously asks nothing of us but what it itself lacks, i.e., guiding reason, regulation. Of course such regulation is impossible as long as we are divided, but then there is division because there is no common task. It is the regulation or control of the forces of blind nature which constitutes the great task that can and must become common to all.

3.

The regulation of meteorological processes is necessary not just to guarantee a good harvest, not just for the sake of agriculture, but also in order to take the place of the forced underground labor of miners who dig for coal and iron, upon which the whole of modern industry is based. Regulation is necessary for the replacement of this digging by the extraction of energy directly from the currents of the atmosphere, from the energy of the sun which originally created the supply of coal, since the miners' position is so miserable that it would be unforgivable to forget them; it is precisely the enemies of society, the socialists, who are taking advantage of the miners' miserable position to stir up revolt. Thus the solution to both the agricultural and the industrial question lies in regulation and control of meteorological processes.

Practical reason, which is equal in scope to theoretical reason, is controlling reason or regulation, i.e., the transformation of the blind course of nature into one that is rational. Such a transformation is bound to appear to the learned as a disruption of order, although this order of theirs brings only disorder among men, striking them down with famine, plague, and death.

4.

The unlearned, bearing as they do all the consequences of dis-relatedness, cannot avoid turning to the learned with the question of dis-relatedness, since the learned constitute the stratum or class which, on the one hand, is an extreme expression of dis-relatedness and, on the other, bears the obligation and has the ability and opportunity of restoring relatedness—the class in whose hands resides all knowledge and therefore also the solution to this question. However, they not only are not solving it but, having created and supported the manufacturing industry (the root of dis-relatedness) to satisfy an effeminate caprice, are now inventing destructive weapons for the defense of this industry, once again motivated by effeminate caprice.

The unlearned are obligated to turn to the learned with the question of dis-relatedness, and this obligation arises not simply out of the present relationship of the learned to the unlearned, but also out of the very origin of this former class. We would be untrue to history if we explained the origin of the learned as resulting from a temporary assignment or commission for some purpose, just as the philosophers of the eighteenth century were untrue to history when they explained the origin of the state as due to an agreement or contract. There is of course no juridical evidence of an assignment, but in history—understood in moral categories—the emergence of the urban out of the rural class, and of the learned out of the urban class must have the significance of a temporary assignment. Otherwise this amounts to a permanent disintegration, the complete negation of unity.

Thus while we may not be true to history in explaining the origin of the learned class as the result of a temporary assignment, while we may not agree on how this really took place, we are at least true to morality, i.e., to how things ought to be. A truly moral being has no need for compulsion, command, or force. He himself is aware of his obligation, revealing it in all its fullness. He himself issues an assignment to himself and indicates what must be done for those from whom he has been isolated, since the isolation (whether it be compulsory or voluntary) cannot be irrevocable. Indeed, it would be criminal to renounce those from whom one has sprung, to forget about their welfare.

Moreover, if the learned were to behave in this way it would mean that they would be renouncing their own welfare, too, that they would remain forever as prodigal sons, eternal hired servants, slaves of urban caprice, completely heedless of the needs of the rural population, which are the genuine needs, since the needs of those who are unspoiled by urban influences are limited to the daily necessities which offer security against famine and sickness, against those things which destroy not only life but also relatedness, substituting enmity and hostility for love. The rural question is, first, the question of the dis-relatedness among people who through ignorance have forgotten their relatedness; and second, the question of the dis-relatedness of nature to people, i.e., that dis-relatedness which is felt preeminently in the villages, standing as they do in direct relationship to this blind force. In the cities, which are remote from nature, one can only *imagine* that one lives a life that is one with the life of nature.

5.

The hostile dividedness of the world and all the misfortunes stemming from this also compel us—i.e., the unlearned, those who put work above thought (work that is common to all, and not simply strife)—to turn to the learned, and especially to the theologians . . . , to those who put thought above work, with this memorandum concerning dis-relatedness and the means of restoring relatedness. The separation of thought from work (both of which have become the property of special classes) is the greatest of all misfortunes, incomparably worse than the separation into rich and poor. Socialism and in general our whole age attach the greatest significance to the division into rich and poor, assuming of course that with the removal of this division the other will also disappear and everyone will become educated. But we are thinking not of popular education, which, with the elimination of poverty, will certainly be distributed more equally. We are thinking rather of an actual participation in the pursuit of knowledge, the common participation of all men, without which the division into learned and unlearned will not disappear. This cannot be brought about by the removal of poverty alone. So long as everyone does not participate in the pursuit of knowledge, pure science and scholarship will remain indifferent to conflict and destruction, and applied science will continue to further it, either directly by the invention of destructive weapons, or indirectly by lending a seductive appearance to objects of consumption, thus introducing hostility among men.

Science and scholarship, taking no direct personal part in conflict or war, and standing beyond the reach of natural misfortunes, shielded by the peasantry—who stand in an immediate relationship to nature—from these misfortunes, science remains indifferent to the exhaustion of natural energies and to the changes of weather which for townspeople may be rather pleasant, even though they produce a crop failure. Only when all people are participants in the pursuit of knowledge will pure science and scholarship (which now sees nature as a sphere in which the sentient is sacrificed to the insentient) cease being indifferent to such a perverted relationship between the sentient and the insentient. Applied science will cease to be the companion and ally of insentient forces and will convert weapons of destruction into instruments for the regulation of the blind death-dealing force of nature. . . .

The solution of the second problem—concerning the division into rich and poor—depends on the solution of the first—the problem of the division into learned and unlearned (men of thought and men of work). The problem of the division between men of thought and men of work has as its starting point such common misfortunes as sickness and death, and requires for its solution not wealth or luxury but a higher good, the participation of all in art and knowledge as applied to the solution of the problem of dis-relatedness and the restoration of relatedness—which means a quest for the Kingdom of God.

6.

In raising the question of "brotherhood and the reasons for the unbrotherly state of the world," we have in mind above all else the conditions under which brotherhood can and must be actualized, i.e., this is a practical question, a question in the sense that one speaks of an Eastern Question, a Question of Colonization, Emigration, etc. This is a question of what must be done to bring an end to the unbrotherly state. As such the question is obligatory for all sons of men and all the more so for those who have been baptized in the name of the God of all fathers. This is not a learned question, not a matter of research, even though it very much concerns the learned insofar as the question of knowledge, or science and scholarship (the theoretical question), is already a necessary, antecedent, and integral part of the practical question.

7.

By calling all that is involved in the title of this memorandum addressed by the unlearned to the learned a "question," by calling it all the raising of a question, we at once admit and wish to make clear our own weakness in comparison with those to whom we are addressing the question. Those who ask questions are not those who know the answers, but those who are conscious of their own weakness; and this is not an expression of the sort of modesty usually found in prefaces, but an inescapable humility in the face of the terrible power which causes non-brotherhood and thus forces us toward unity, compelling us to speak to those with whom we are not accustomed to speak. This is a humility before a power which causes all special interests to fall silent.

If Russia, or Russian science and scholarship, were to turn with this question to nations which stand above her intellectually and morally, there would be nothing in the question to offend the pride of such advanced nations.

8.

The unbrotherly state, of course, has its serious causes: we are all living in conditions which raise the question of non-brotherhood. Thus, in formulating this question we are not separating ourselves from the people but are expressing the common mind or spirit [*dukh*] of all. . . . Non-brotherhood is not rooted in caprice; it cannot be eradicated by words, and wishing alone is powerless to remove its causes. What is needed is the combined work of knowledge and action, since a stubborn sickness of this sort, having its roots both within and outside of man, is not to be healed in the wink of an eye, as those people think who are led only by feeling, whose statements about non-brotherhood may be called "treatises on the groundlessness of the unbrotherly state"; they forbid thought because thinking or reflection is a laying bare of reasons and conditions.

Belief in the groundlessness of the unbrotherly state leads not to real peace, to brotherhood, but only to playing at peace, to comedies of reconciliation which create a pseudo-peaceful state, a false peace that is much worse than open hostility, because the latter raises the question, while an imaginary reconciliation conceals and perpetuates enmity. Tolstoy preaches such a doctrine: having quarreled one day, he goes to make up the quarrel the next. Not only does he not take any steps to prevent clashes; he actually seems to seek them out, perhaps simply in order to conclude an unstable peace later on.

But causation, in the sense of determinism, can be admitted only for men taken in isolation, in division. The learned class accepts a fateful, eternal determinism precisely because it does not believe in combined action. The utter irremovability of the unbrotherly state is a fundamental dogma of the learned as a class, since an admission of the removability of the causes of the unbrotherly state by the combined effort of all people would require the transformation of the learned class into a commission or "task force."

9.

By "unbrotherly state" we mean all juridically fixed economic relations, social hierarchies, and international divisions. In speaking of the question of the causes of dis-relatedness we are using "dis-relatedness" to mean the "citizen-ship" or "civilization" which has replaced "brotherliness," we have in mind the "stateness" [*gosudarstvennost*] which has replaced "fatherland-ness" [*otechestvennost*]. Fatherland-ness is not the same as patriotism, which instead of loving one's forefathers makes them an object of one's pride, replacing love or virtue by pride and vice, love of one's forefathers by love of oneself, by self-love. People who are proud of the same thing may form an honorary society, but not a brotherhood of sons who love one another. However, as soon as pride in the exploits of one's forefathers is replaced by contrition for their death, as soon as the earth is seen as a cemetery and nature as a death-dealing force, just so soon will the political question be replaced by the physical question; and in this context the physical will not be separated from the astronomical, i.e., the earth will be recognized as a heavenly body and the stars will be recognized as other earths. The unification of all sciences under astronomy is the simplest, most natural, unlearned thing, required as much by the feelings as by the non-abstract intellect, since by such a unification mythical "patrolatry" is transformed into a real raising of the dead, into a regulation of all worlds by all the resurrected generations.

The question of the force which compels the two sexes to unite in one flesh as a transition to the being of a third by means of childbearing is the question of death: a man's exclusive adherence to his wife forces him to forget his forefathers and brings political and civil enmity into the world. At the same time it compels him to forget that the earth is a body located in space and that the heavenly bodies are earths. As long as historical life was only oceanic or coastal, as long as it embraced only a small part of the earth, with approximately the same conditions of life, it was a political, civil, or commercial history —a civilization, i.e., a struggle. But when the interiors of the continents enter into history, i.e., when the whole earth becomes historical, then the question of states and cultures will become a question of physics or astrophysics, a question of the earth as a heavenly body.

10.

By refusing to grant ourselves the right to set ourselves apart from the mass of people (the crowd), we are kept from setting any goal for ourselves that is not the common task of all, and so we cannot neglect the question of non-brotherhood. We did not raise it and we will not resolve it. We live constantly in conditions which provoke the question; it is as impossible not to think about it as it is to arrest the process of thought and reflection in one's head. There is only one doctrine which requires not separation but reunification, which has not artificial goals but a single, common, completely natural goal for all; this is the doctrine of relatedness. . . . Does this not point to the true goal of the human race? For it is not self-preservation but the restoration of life to our forefathers which must be our goal. The punishment of the confusion of tongues came precisely because the living generation wanted to raise a memorial to itself. . . .[1]

The question of the individual and the crowd is resolved only in the doctrine of relatedness. Unity does not engulf but rather exalts each unit, while the difference of individuals only strengthens the unity which includes them all first, in the awareness by each that he is a son, a grandson, a great-grandson, a descendant, i.e., a son of all his dead forefathers, and not a vagabond in a crowd having no sense of relatedness; and second, in the acknowledgment by each together with all others (not in diversity or separateness as in a crowd) of his duty toward them, toward all his dead forefathers, a duty the limitations of which proceed only from his sensuous nature or, more

1. "Life in and for another" (altruism) is the grossest distortion of the words of the Saviour "that they may be made one . . ." which speaks precisely about *all* men, while "life in and for another" can only refer to people taken in isolation. Christianity . . . is not altruism; it knows only *all* men. . . . Only a life "with all and for all" will be a fulfillment of the Son's prayer to his Father for all sons who are living and all fathers who have died. . . .

accurately, from the abuse of his sensuous nature, which •is fragmenting the mass of people (the rural population) and· turning it into a crowd.

The mass of mankind will be transformed from a crowd, a jostling and struggling throng, into a harmonious power when the rural mass or common people [*narod*] become a union of sons for the resurrection of their fathers, when they become a relatedness, "a psychocracy." The transformation of the "crowd" into a union of sons who find their unity in their fathers' work is precisely a fusion as opposed to a confusion. In this task of all the fathers, taken as one father, each will become a great man, a participant in the greatness of the task; he becomes incomparably greater than any of those who have been called "great." Only a son of man is a great man, a man who has entered into the measure of the stature of Christ. No so-called "great man" has attained this stature. The conception of a son of man includes the whole race, while the task which gives him this name is the transformation of blind, death-dealing forces into forces that will restore life to all fathers. To attain to the measure of the stature of Christ means to become in fact a son of man, for Christ called Himself the Son of Man.

The humanist who calls himself a *"man,"* and is proud of this name, has clearly not yet come to the measure of the stature of Christ, has not yet become a *son of man*. And all those who in our time have rejected the cult of the fathers have thereby deprived themselves of the right to be called sons of man. Instead of taking part in the common task they have become mere organs or instruments of various enterprises, mere cogs and valves, even though they think they are living for themselves. Such a situation makes it possible to understand that neither the eternal existence of these "x's and y's" (as Noire says: "No one would assert that the eternal existence of individual x's and y's has any exceptional significance") nor even their transitory existence can have any meaning, so that it would be better if they had not existed at all. But of course this is true only of x's and y's and cannot refer to the *sons of man, to those who restore life*, whose existence not only has an exceptional significance but also is absolutely inevitable if the goal of life is the transformation of the blind force of nature into a force controlled by the reason of all the resurrected generations. At that time, of course, *everyone*, down to the *last man*, will be necessary.

11.

The question which forms the subject of the present memorandum has a twofold significance:

1. When we compare the question of the causes of non-brotherhood to the Eastern Question, the Question of Emigration, etc., we mean that science must not be the knowledge of causes only without the knowledge of goals, must not be the knowledge of initiating causes only without the knowledge of final causes (i.e., must not be knowledge for the sake of knowledge, or knowledge without action); it must not be knowledge of *what is* without a knowledge of what *ought to be*. This means that science must be the knowledge not of causes *in general*, but precisely of the causes of non-brotherhood; it must be knowledge of the causes of the *division* which makes us instruments of the blind forces of nature, the displacing of the older generation by the younger, and the mutual crowding which leads to this displacement. Such is the general significance of the question of non-brotherhood. Hence it follows that the meaning of brotherhood is included in the unification of all men in the common task of transforming the blind forces of nature into an instrument of the reason of the whole human race for the restoration to life of those who have been displaced.

2. However, when those who acknowledge their ignorance (the unlearned) turn to the learned with the question of the causes of non-brotherhood, the question arises whether the learned should remain a class or school, whether the learned should refuse to answer this question, on the grounds that science is only an investigation of causes *in general (scholasticism)*, or whether they, the learned, ought to turn themselves into a commission or task force for the elucidation and critical explication of the question of the causes of division. The question arises whether the learned ought to look upon their separation from the mass of mankind as only a temporary assignment, or as a final goal. Whether they ought

to see themselves simply as "scouts" along the road that lies ahead or whether they are the best and highest class, the blossom and fruit of the whole life of the human race. The question arises about the learned and the intelligentsia, about the inner discord of the intellect deprived of feeling and will, the question of complete dis-relatedness as the essential characteristic of the learned, inevitably stemming from the separation of the intellect from feeling and will.

An inner discord is concealed in the external discord, in the separation of the learned and intelligent classes from the people. Knowledge deprived of feeling will be knowledge only of causes in general, and not the study of the causes of dis-relatedness; the intellect separated from the will will be knowledge of evil without the effort to eradicate it, and knowledge of good without the desire to establish it; i.e., it will be the acceptance of dis-relatedness rather than a project for the restoration of relatedness. Dis-relatedness is a consequence of the lack of feeling, a forgetting of the fathers, a falling out of the sons. (In its causes dis-relatedness involves all of nature, as a blind force not controlled by reason.) But as soon as intellect arrives at feeling there is remembrance of the dead fathers (in museums), together with the union of the sons of these dead fathers and of the fathers who are still living (the religious community—[*sobor*]) for the education of their sons (the school). But the fullness of feeling is the union of all living men (the sons), while the fullness of will or combined action of all the living is the raising to life of all who are the dead (fathers), the religious community of all the living, the union of those who have been born for the resurrection of those who have been put to death as a result of childbearing and child-rearing. What is needed now so that the museum and the community may attain this fullness?

If the subject of science is the resolution of the question of causes in general, this means that science is occupied with the question, "*Why does that which exists exist?*" Both of these questions clearly mean the same thing. But the question, "Why does that which exists exist?" is obviously an unnatural, completely artificial question. How unnatural it is to ask, "*Why does that which exists exist?"* and yet how completely natural it is to ask, *"Why do the living die?"* Both this question and the question of brotherhood would be raised by the philosophers and scientists if brotherhood existed among men; but in the absence of brotherhood they do not see the question, or at least they do not turn it into a task or make it the goal of their studies. Yet this purpose is really the only one which can give meaning to the existence of philosophers and scientists, not as a class, but simply as a temporary commission or task force.

12.

. . . In exchanging their position as an upper class for that of a commission or task force, the learned will be losing only their imaginary superiority and will be acquiring a real superiority. The world will then be not a mere representation (which it inevitably is for closeted scholars deprived of activity and condemned to contemplation and wishful thinking, without the means of bringing anything about). The representation of the world will then become a project for a better world, and the organizing and actualization of this project will be the commission's task. Pessimism will disappear but will not give way to that optimism which only seduces, striving to represent the world as better than it is. There will be no point then in concealing evil from ourselves; there will be no point then in trying to convince ourselves that death does not exist. Instead, while acknowledging the existence of evil in all its power, we shall not lose the hope that in uniting all rational powers we will find a way to give direction to the irrational power which brings evil and death and all that follows from the latter.

By acknowledging an immanent raising of the dead, we set a limit to that human curiosity which is directed toward the transcendent, toward thought without work. And yet by condemning spiritualism and in general the striving toward what is other-worldly, we are not laying a restraint upon man, since we are showing that the sphere of that which is accessible and immanent is so broad that the moral sense of relatedness, or all-embracing love, will find complete satisfaction therein.

Three vices inevitably result from the separation of the learned

into a special class: the first and fundamental one is the transformation of the world into an idea, a representation, or fiction.
That which in life constitutes egoism, solipsism, and all the
crimes stemming from them, has found its formula in the
philosophical expression, "The world is my idea or representation" (egoism), which is indeed the final result of all critical
[i.e., Kantian] philosophy. The transformation of the world into
an idea or a representation is the last word of the learned class.
Generated by idleness or external inactivity (if thinking is not
to be regarded as work or activity) and individualism, the
transformation of the world into an idea or representation is
the last offspring of idleness, which is the mother of vice, or
of solipsism (egoism), which is the father of crime. Two other
vices result from this major vice (the transformation of the
world into a representation): drug addiction and hypnosis. For
if the world is an idea or representation, then the transformation
of unpleasant ideas or representations into pleasant ones by means
of drugs would solve the world problem since this would eliminate all suffering, replacing it by pleasure. Hypnosis solves the
problem even more simply: it thinks that it can save people from
all sickness and vice simply by the power of wishing. . . .

13.

Positivism, the last word of European thought, is not a departure from the schools and hence from the learned class. Positivism too is based on the separation of theoretical and practical
reason. The impotence of theoretical reason is explained by its
inaction, the absence of any unification in a common task.
Positivism is only another form of metaphysical scholasticism
which in itself, by way of a similar transformation, grew out of
theological scholasticism. It too is a scholasticism, and positivists
constitute a school rather than a commission in the sense explained
above. However, if the positive movement were opposed not
to what is metaphysical or theological but to what is popular
[narodny] and religious (to what is not mere knowledge or
contemplation but also action, sacrifice, cult, although only a
mythical action, i.e., a miraculous, unreal, imaginary means
against evil)—then the positive school would convert this myth-

ical, miraculous, or fictitious action into a real and genuine means against evil. It would not remain an unsatisfied need which, as a result of ignorance of what is real, is satisfied with or rather is simply drowned in imaginary activity, in an imaginary means against evil.

If positivism (it makes no difference whether it is Western and European or Eastern and Oriental) were really to oppose everything mythical and fictitious, then there would be nothing arbitrary about it. But now positivism in fact prides itself on its limitations and denials; it does not replace the fictitious by the real but only negates the former. . . . Rejecting what is essential, positivism indulges man's artificial needs, needs which are satisfied, or rather stimulated, by industry. It is clear that as long as the learned form a special class which feeds on knowledge and lives the artificial life of the city, just so long will they be occupied only with the denial of fictions rather than their conversion into reality.

Criticism in philosophy is also a school, not a departure from it. Kantianism and neo-Kantianism are forms of scholasticism. The *Critique of Pure Reason* can be called science or philosophy only within the narrow limits of the artificial and un-unified experience of the study and laboratory. In the same way the *Critique of Practical Reason* can be called life only in the sense of life set within the narrow bounds of individual concerns, of division that is not regarded as a vice. It is a system of morality for the immature, according to which all crimes are simply pranks, which is just what the Russian people call them. The *Critique of Practical Reason* knows nothing of a united mankind; it gives no rules for the common action of the whole human race, just as the *Critique of Pure Reason* knows no experience other than that which is had *in some particular place, at some particular time, by some particular person.* It does not know the experience which is had *by all people everywhere and always,* as it will be when armed peoples (armies) convert their weapons into instruments for the regulation of atmospheric phenomena.

In the *Critique of Pure Reason* everything good, i.e., God, constitutes an ideal; in the *Critique of Practical Reason* it is an extra-worldly reality, while reality consists of: (a) the soulless world, an irrational and insentient power, for which "chaos" is a more appropriate term than "cosmos," while its study is more appropriately called "chaos-ography" than cosmology; and (b) the impotent soul, the study of which may be called psychology —in the sense of "psychocracy," but only a projective psychocracy, since apart from God and the world the soul is only the capability of feeling, knowing, and acting—it is a soul without any real power or will. Herein lies the separation of the soul from power and the world from reason and feeling; their unification can only be a project—something which is not to be found in Kant. If for idealists there is peace only beyond this world, while for materialists there is no peace either in this world or beyond it, for critical philosophy (Kant) peace exists only in our thought, and·not in reality at all. When the illegitimacy of the separation of the intelligentsia from the common people is recognized, thought will become ·projective. Are we not justified in saying, therefore, that critical philosophy, like positivism, is a school, and that both positive and critical philosophy are forms of scholasticism belonging to the years of immaturity? . . .

The happiness in this life which Kant was able to give man was bought at a very great price: forget about the perfection which is unattainable (God is only the ideal) and your imperfection will not disturb you; don't think about death and you will not fall into the paralogism of thinking that immortality is real; be concerned only with the visible and don't think about the future: you cannot decide whether the world is finite or infinite, eternal or not eternal. This is Kant's position in the *Critique of Pure Reason.*

However, the whole negative doubt of the *Critique of Pure Reason* is based on the presumed inevitability of division among men and the impossibility of their unification in a common task. This presupposition is a prejudice completely unrecognized by Kant himself, one which the great philosopher evidently did not even suspect; and he did not suspect it precisely because he was a great philosopher and consequently was unable to set anything above thought. What Kant believed to be inaccessible to knowledge is the object of a task, but a task which is only within the reach of people taken together, in the combining of independent persons and not in their separateness and diversity. The *Critique of Practical Reason* is also based on the unconscious acknowledgment of the inevitability of division; the vice of division (not recognized as such, of course) is at the heart of Kant's ethical system. This philosopher belongs to the epoch of what has been called enlightened absolutism, and he has transferred the principles of this absolutism into the moral world; it is as if he was making God say: "Everything for people and nothing through people." The principle of division and inaction is asserted by Kant in all three of his critiques.[2] The philosophy of art, which he calls the critique of judgment, speaks not of how to create but only of how to judge objects of art and works of nature from the viewpoint of aesthetics. This is a philosophy for art critics and not for artists or poets, not even for artists taken separately, to say nothing of the time when they will be regarded as executors of a single work in contrast to the division and even hostility which exists among them now. In the critique of judgment, nature too is regarded not as the object of a task, of an action involving the transformation of blind force into a force governed by reason, but only as a subject of judgment and contemplation, and then only from the aesthetic rather than the moral viewpoint, in which it would appear as a destructive and death-dealing force.

14.

In limiting man to what is necessary, to existence itself, in reconciling itself with loss and death, positivism in all its forms

2. It would be truer to say that the principle of division and inaction is preached by Kant not just in three but in all four of his critiques, since religion too is confined as in a prison within the narrow limits of pure reason. Having condemned religion to prison for having wished to save the world from final destruction through a fulfillment of the duty of raising the dead, Kant then ordered that it be stripped of the weapons (science and art) with which it wished to attain its good end (eutelism), and these too were condemned to solitary confinement. Having committed this crime (unconsciously, of course), the philosopher-king was then certain that he had secured for mankind a quiet and untroubled end. But supramoralism is breaking down the prison walls and releasing the prisoners.

shows that it is very sympathetic to the artificial demands which do not secure our existence but simply stir up our desires. Thus in China the moral sense (love of children for their parents) manifests itself in the form of ceremony and games and is becoming more and more fictitious. Even the things brought for sacrifice are replaced by models or figures, while amusements and diversions are elevated to the level of a real and serious task, i.e., priority is in fact given to artificial requirements—while hypocritically the first place is given to the satisfaction of the moral sense. In Europe, on the contrary, things are frankly and openly valued above the dead—while hypocrisy appears in the claim that the living are valued above things. But if the struggle for existence, i.e., the struggle among people for the sake of things, is accepted as the condition of progress, then things as ends must be preferred to people as means. Each person will value others only as allies in the business of acquiring things.

Not only that, but in contrast to the popular view which sees things as animate, philosophy converts animate beings into things. "Each being can be apprehended by another only as matter, as a thing endowed with the power of movement. It can exist as spirit only for itself; only to itself can it appear as a spirit endowed with consciousness, sensation, and will." From which it follows that every being, having applied this critique to himself, can accept as highly probable the idea that he alone is a spirit and that all other beings are things. "About the existence of conscious states outside myself, in other beings, I can draw conclusions only by way of analogy; I perceive directly only the movements of other beings and not their inner state." The acceptance (by each person) of all other persons only as things and of oneself alone as a sentient and conscious being, i.e., the acceptance of the soul in oneself alone, the acceptance of oneself alone as a man, and the non-acceptance of all others similar to oneself as one's relatives, is the complete negation of morality, brotherhood, and fatherland-ness, that is, if philosophy has in general ever recognized a fatherland; really it recognizes no fathers and ignores the reality of a fatherland. The practical expression of such a theoretical philosophy will involve the real acceptance of a soul only in oneself and the real negation of souls in all others; i.e., an utter contempt for morality. But if men were completely sincere and other souls were not darkness, if it were possible to define infallibly the psychic state of others by their external movements, and, on the other hand, if we ourselves did not lead others astray by movements of our own which do not correspond to our psychic states, i.e., if it happened not only that other souls were not darkness to us but also that our own souls were not a deception for others, then it would be impossible to consider others as being unlike ourselves. It is just here that we have the application of psychology to life and the organization of society, if psychology is to have any application at all.

15.

Leaving both initiating [efficient] and final causes out of its purview, positivism believes it impossible to know the meaning and goals of life. The scholastic positivism of the learned class is a distortion of life; for positivists the raising of the dead is not only not possible, it is not even desirable. But by not desiring the restoration of their own life, do they not prove that their life is not worth restoring? For the progressivists, everything that exists is bad, while all that was and has passed away is even worse; and only for unreflective progressivists can that which does not yet exist appear to be good, since even the future is becoming the present and the past, i.e., bad. Thus it is clear that a true progressivist is inevitably a pessimist. "*Progress*," says one well-known professor,[3] "is the constant raising of the level of universal human development. In this sense we find the prototype of progress in individual psychic development, which is not only an objective fact of observation, but also a subjective fact of consciousness. In our inner experience development appears in the form of a consciousness of a constant increase of knowledge and clarification of thought, and these processes are perceived in the form of an improvement or elevation of our reflective nature. This fact of individual psychology

3. N. I. Kareyev.—TRANS.

is repeated in collective psychology when the members of a whole society recognize their own superiority over their fore-fathers in the same society." But society is made up of a younger and an older generation, of fathers and sons; and if by the term "a whole society" the author has in mind both the old and the young, if he has in mind people of all ages without any differentiation, in other words, if he assumes the equal mobility of all members of society (denying the process of aging and weakening), then a superiority will be acknowledged only over the dead, in which case the remembrance of the dead (history) will be necessary only in order to have someone to whom one can be superior.

So then a whole society (all the living, both young and old) can recognize its superiority only over the departed generations. But how can one fail to see the culpability of such a view, fail to notice the egoism of the present generation? The life of a society consists in the fact that what is old grows older and what is young grows up; in growing up and realizing its superiority over the dead, the younger generation cannot, according to the law of progress, fail to realize also its superiority over those who are growing old, who are dying. If the elder says to the younger: "It is for you to grow up and for me to decrease," this wish is a good one, fatherly love is speaking here. But if the younger says to the elder: "It is for me to grow up and for you to be laid in the tomb," this is progress, and it is not love speaking here but hatred, the hatred, of course, of prodigal sons.

In the absence of an inner unification and an outer common task for the whole human race, progress is a natural phenomenon. Until there is full unity in the common task of transforming death-dealing forces into life-giving ones, man will be subjected to blind natural force, on a level with cattle and all other beasts, on a level with soulless matter.

Progress originates in the doctrine of redemption, but by way of a complete distortion of this doctrine. Prior to its ultimate distortion by Protestantism, redemption referred primarily to the dead, while progress is self-exaltation, the exaltation of oneself, that same sin which was punished by the confusion of tongues.

We have come close to this in our own time, when people are rejecting everything that is common and each person lives exclusively for himself, and this to such an extent that people cease even to understand one another. Progress consists in the sense of superiority, first, of a whole generation (the living) over their forefathers (the dead), and second, of the younger over the older generation, in which case this superiority—a matter of pride for the younger generation—will consist in the increase of knowledge, in the improvement and elevation of the thinking being. Even the development of moral convictions will be an occasion for the younger generation's self-exaltation over the older. "He (each member of the younger generation) feels his exaltation (his superiority over the older) when he is enriched with new knowledge, when he evolves a new idea, when he evaluates his environment from a new viewpoint, when in the collision of duty with habit and emotion victory is on the side of duty." [4]

But this is only the subjective, inner side of the sense of intellectual superiority over the forefathers; the professor is silent about the external side of this sense, about how this sense is expressed as an objective, observable fact for the forefathers who have not yet died. And yet the arrogant way that sons and daughters deal with their parents is sufficiently well known and has even found expression in the work of the author of *Fathers and Sons*, although this is not a very vivid representation of the situation.

It is impossible not to notice that if, in Western Europe, France and Germany are now the younger generation, nowhere has the antagonism of the younger against the older reached such an extreme as it has with us; hence for us it is easier than for others truly to evaluate the doctrine of progress. . . . Biologically, progress consists in the swallowing up of the old by the new, in the displacing of the fathers by the sons. Sociologically, progress is expressed in the attainment of the fullest measure of freedom accessible to man, not in the greatest

4. This quotation is from Kareyev; the parenthetical remarks are Fyodorov's.—TRANS.

participation of each person in the common filial task, since society as non-brotherhood requires a limitation of the freedom of each individual. Thus the demand of sociology will be a demand for the greatest freedom and the least unity and communion, i.e., sociology is the science not of association but of dissociation or enslavement [razobshcheniye ili poraboshcheniye], if society is allowed to swallow up the individual. As the science of dissociation for some people and the science of enslavement for others, sociology sins against both indivisibility and unconfusability [nesliyannost], against the Triune God.

:. . . Although stagnation is death and regression is no paradise, progress is a real hell, and the truly divine, truly human task is to save the victims of progress, to take them out of hell. As the negation of fatherland and brotherhood, progress is utter moral degeneration, the actual negation of morality. . . .

Thus progress consists in the sons' sense of superiority over their fathers, and in the sense of superiority of the living over the dead—a view which excludes the necessity and thus also the possibility of the unification of the living (sons) for the raising to life of the dead (fathers). However, the real superiority of the sons would be expressed in the task of raising the fathers to life, if indeed this could be called "superiority," while their self-exaltation over their forefathers is only an imaginary superiority. . . .

Progress transforms fathers and forefathers into accused prisoners, and gives judgment and dominion over them into the hands of their sons and descendants. Historians are judges over the dead, that is, over those who have already suffered the supreme punishment, the death penalty. The sons are also judges over those who have not yet died.

Of course, the learned are able to say that in former times the aged were killed while now they are only despised; isn't it progress to replace physical murder by spiritual murder?! The progress of progress itself, one might say! But in the future still greater improvements are to be expected of progress, i.e., contempt will gradually be decreased. And yet it is obvious that contempt can be eliminated only with the elimination of progress itself. Even with its improvement, that is, by its elimination, progress can only lead to a negative result, to the elimination of contempt, and not to love and respect for one's forefathers, not to feelings which elevate the descendants themselves. Can progress give meaning to life, to say nothing of purpose? For only that in which the highest degree of love and respect can be expressed gives both meaning and purpose to life.

Progress is the direct opposite of the raising of the dead. Progress consists in the critical attitude of the younger generation toward the older, in the condemnation of fathers by their sons, and in action which accords with such condemnation. "The goal of progress is the developed and ever-developing individual, or the fullest measure of freedom attainable by man." In other words, the goal of progress, as we have said, is not community but disunity, so that the lowest level of brotherhood is also the expression of the highest progress. Thus in condemning the human race to eternal division and non-brotherhood, the learned professor also signs a death warrant for the learned as a class, not, however, as a commission or task force for the investigation of the causes of nature's dis-relatedness with man, leading to the removal of these causes, to the controlling of nature's forces. As long as knowledge is regarded as an end in itself and the learned see themselves as the best and highest class, just so long will the question of dis-relatedness and of the restoration of relatedness fail to be set forth in all its force and meaning.

The specialization of the learned has its temporary significance; the conversion of the commission of the learned into a class is the same abuse which we see in the conversion of a dictatorship into a tyranny. The acceptance of knowledge as an end in itself, the replacement of work by *Weltanschauung*— "ideolatry" or the cult of ideas—is the legitimation of this abuse. Religion, in the Platonic sense of the raising of the dead without man's participation in this task, is the sanction of this abuse. . . . The learned professor ascribes the greatest significance to knowledge as an end in itself, to pure knowledge as a spiritual interest, and he even regards its inapplicability as a merit: "Man shall not live by bread alone," he (Kareyev) says, completely ignoring the all-embracing question of life and death, the question of the material conditions on which man's existence depends.[5] . . .

The raising of the dead is not progress, but it requires a real improvement, a true perfection. Nor is there any need for that which is self-generating or which proceeds out of itself, either in the reason or the will (if we avoid confusing the latter with appetite). The raising of the dead is the replacement of the lust to engender by conscious re-creation. Any other kind of progress is artificial, arbitrary, contrived—neither natural nor inevitable. When it is equated with development or evolution,

5. But there can be no knowledge without application; if knowledge has no application to work then it manifests itself in self-exaltation. Drawing conclusions from all that has been written about the philosophy of history, Kareyev thinks he finds a point on which all, or nearly all, philosophers are agreed. On the strength of this agreement he is now creating a new science under the not entirely new name of "Historiosophy." This science, which might more accurately be called "Historiosophistry," is in fact completely opposed to history, which has as its goal the unification of the living (sons) for the raising to life of the dead (fathers). The point on which the philosophers are supposed to be agreed is "progress," which in Kareyev's opinion is the very thing which gives meaning to history. Progress (forward movement, improvement) apparently has significance not only for future generations, but also for those that are past—"for all people in general, wherever they may be, whenever they may have lived," says our historiosophist. From history, as it is given to us in experience, he draws conclusions—by way of historiosophistry—not only about social progress but also about psychic progress in inter-personal relations, although psychology and sociology remain sciences sharply set apart one from the other. (But if the soul were to be improved there would be love, and society would be a brotherhood of sons, i.e., the full expression of love; and psychology and sociology would then be transformed into psychocracy.) For Kareyev, progress is the supreme criterion for judging history—the philosophy of history is, after all, judgment—and it is in progress that the significance of history is to be found. But if we take the raising of the dead as the criterion, then we shall see that insofar as it involves redemption it excludes judgment above all things. If it is adopted as a criterion, the raising of the dead need not be disputed, it can afford not to refute the assertion that the happiness of later generations is founded on the unhappiness of those who have gone before. But the raising of the dead cannot be limited to a negative good; it not only negates the unhappiness of preceding generations, it also demands their happiness.

progress is clearly a concept borrowed from blind nature and applied to human life. But if we accept the forward movement from worse to better as progress, if we accept the idea that the verbal animal is better and higher than the non-verbal, can we then take the latter as the model for the former, can we conceive of blind unconscious force as a model for that which has feeling and consciousness? As a transition from worse to better, progress of course requires that the inadequacies of blind nature be corrected by that nature which is conscious of them, i.e., by the combined power of the human race. It requires

---

Historiosophy is not historical wisdom, not a philosophy which teaches people what they must do together. If historical wisdom is unable to see a general plan in history, this is not for the same reason that historiosophistry fails to see such a plan. To see a plan means to ascribe a planned-ness to our actions, means not to admit the division in which we are living, not to admit our egoism, and at the same time it means to refuse to unite for the common task. Historiosophistry destroys the wheat with the tares, since it does not acknowledge or at any rate does not think about unity. The central thing in the philosophy of history is not unification, not the unity of persons, but their division, for, after all, the conceptual abstraction from all particular societies does not eliminate division. Only the raising of the dead can be a transition to a common, yet specific task. A subjective sympathy is powerless against reality and, most important, it is useless—unless it becomes a task. If it does become a task then the subjective is at once transformed into the projective. In acknowledging individuality as the central object of the philosophy of history, historiosophistry leaves unification to the operation of blind force. But history as wisdom, as a moral undertaking, is the unification in the common task of raising the dead. For the learned, history is the restoration of the past; for the people, it is *the raising of the dead,* although this is still only in the phase of mythical art, since the people still do not possess knowledge, since even today knowledge is separated from action. "History is made up of the actions of individuals (solitary individuals) and this must be the basic principle of historiosophy." However, the activity of individuals does not create history, but rather the comedy of world history. That history which is created, according to the principle of historiosophistry, by solitary individuals, is really the struggle of these individuals for the right to lead the crowd toward a goal or ideal which serves only as a decoy for ensnaring the people. The true wisdom of history consists not in being separated, or being freed from traditions, in replacing them by personal caprice, but in understanding them, with a view to remaining in harmony with the masses; it involves turning the mythical task into one that is actual and common to all.

that improvement through conflict and destruction be replaced by a restoration of the victims of this conflict. In this way progress will not be the improvement of goals only, but also of means. Such improvement would be not just an improvement or correction, but the eradication of evil and the planting of good in its place.

Progress itself requires the raising of the dead, but such a requirement consists of progress not in knowledge only, but also in action, a progress in knowledge not just of *what is* but also of *what ought to be*. Only with the passage of the learned class out of knowledge into work will progress pass from knowledge of *what is* to knowledge of *what ought to be*.

Nothing so clearly demonstrates the true nature of progress, of this hurried movement toward novelty and hasty negation of antiquity, of this unthinking replacement of the old by the new, than paleography, the science of ancient and modern forms of writing which bear the imprint of the transition from the old cult of the fathers to the new cult of the wives. The displacement of the former for the sake of the latter is reflected in these forms, for literature is simply the graphic representation of the progress of that being which has been endowed with speech. Although it is a humble science, paleography can therefore be the accuser of proud progress. As it studies the forms of letters, or literally, as it pursues its pedantry [*bukvoyedstvo* = "letter-eating"], this science is much despised by certain progressivists, and yet the forms of letters say much more than the words, and they speak more sincerely. The forms of letters cannot be corrupted as words can. The words of written script, for example, speak of progress, but the forms of the letters, as we shall see, show a regression. Pedantry actually gives paleography the opportunity to define the character of epochs, turning it into an art or skill which by tracing the changes in handwriting reveals the variations of mood which have occurred in the spirit of different generations, including variations in essential characteristics, such as shifts from faith and piety to doubt, unbelief, and secularness. Faith or piety is expressed in a reverence based on the awareness of one's imperfection, one's mortality, while doubt or unbelief is expressed in the feeling of contempt which begins with contempt toward past generations (toward the dead) and the forgetting of one's own mortality, and ends with the complete dis-valuing of life, i.e., pessimism, Buddhism. The goal of paleography is to define not the character of persons, but the character of societies, the level of their elevation or decline.

The name of the handwriting which prevailed in the Middle Ages is Gothic, the same name used for the architecture of those churches which united all the arts, and which were built up over many centuries, so that only the descendants of those who began the construction of these churches ever saw their completion. This name, as applied to all aspects of life, shows what a close connection there is between the forms of letters and the whole life of this period. Thus too in the case of ancient Russia, Byzantine Russia; the names used for the handwriting of that period [*Ustavny* or *Poluustavny*] use the same term which describes the established order [*ustav*] to which the whole life of the time, both religious and secular, was subjected. Gothic and "Ustavny" letters, traced out with deep reverence, with love, even with delight, and executed like works of art, like prayers (of course not like present-day prayer, concerned as it is with petitioning for a thousand and one benefits), and produced with the same feelings with which churches were built and ikons were painted in this epoch—these letters were something magnificent, like the Gothic cathedrals, and did not, of course, have that womanish beauty which prevails now in the epoch of the cult of woman. Sharply distinguished from one another, since they were produced neither hurriedly nor impatiently, they were produced as a labor which was viewed as a blessing, not a curse . . . to say nothing of a heavenly reward. Hoping for blessedness in the future, these copyists had a foretaste of it in the present in the delight they found in the labor itself. But now progressivists see in Gothic letters only the backwardness of a time when people traveled by ox-cart, or an immovability, so despised by progress, since progress is itself a change [*izmeneniye*], a movement, and in the moral sense a betrayal [*izmena*]. While in Ustavny letters they see not only what is hostile to progress (to what is moved by constant dissatisfaction and unrest), not only a hated backwardness, stagnation, unchangeability, but also slavery, the absence of freedom, i.e., the restraint of personal inclinations, the restraint of movement and action. . . .

In calling the letters of modern times "rapid," [6] by suggesting a property which belongs also to rapid-fire weapons, automatic printing presses, and can be applied to means of rapid transportation, this term catches the most essential feature or property of modern times. The concept of progress includes not simply the concept of change and movement but also that of constantly accelerating motion. "Rapid" can be applied to everything that exists in modern times. This definition may be applied even to literature, which is a speed-writing [*skoropisaniye* = "shorthand"], and thanks to speed [*skorost*] is also becoming a multiple-writing [*mnogopisaniye*], i.e., quantitatively but not qualitatively abundant. Present-day industry too may be called "rapid-making," but the rapidity in this case is leading to overproduction on the one hand, and to the impermanence of products on the other. This rapidity deprives all work, not only mechanical but also intellectual work, of artistic attractiveness, turning it into a means of profit without any goal whatever, unless sense pleasure is to be considered a goal. If Gothic and Ustavny lettering furnish pleasure, then cursive writing [*skoropis*], and everything to which the word "rapid" has been prefixed, can scarcely be taken as objects of pleasure. Thus the present generation is not only deprived of felicity in the present but also expects none in the future.

Moved by dissatisfaction, which is the enemy of immovability and unchangeability and therefore also of faith and dogmatism, progress can be nothing but criticism in thought and reform or revolution in life—that is, if it is not simply evolution.

In very recent times even cursive writing has seemed too slow, and shorthand has been created for the copying out of everything written in longhand. Cursive writing, in spite of its rapidity, still leaves a certain freedom to the copyist; now the

6. The Russian word here is *skory*, which in this context would normally be translated "cursive," except that this would destroy the sense of Fyodorov's play on words in the whole passage that follows.—TRANS.

stenographer, who is in complete dependence on the one who is speaking, is transformed into a machine or phonograph. To understand the essence of progress you have to see the whole path from painting [*zhivopis*] as the first form of writing, requiring artistic abilities and fullness of soul in the writer (as in hieroglyphics, a form of live writing [*zhivoye pismo*] which spoke primarily of the dead and as it were animated them) down to shorthand writing, in which there is no painting at all. Shorthand is "dead writing" [*mertvopis*] that speaks of the trifles of the living and is carried out by a man who has been turned into an automatic writing-machine.

Let us assume that speed is necessary because life is short, and the age of cursive writing or shorthand knows no other life, or acknowledges such a life less and less and denies it more and more. And yet speed does not fill the soul; instead, it empties it, since progress sacrifices the soul for the sake of increasing the size and number of objects of sense pleasure, for the sake of multiplying not the objects of necessity but the objects of luxury. The ideal of progress (according to the concept of the learned) is that all might share in both the production and use of objects of sense pleasure, while the goal of true progress can and must be only the sharing of all in the task or work of coming to know the blind force which brings famine, plague, and death, in order to convert it into a force which brings life. Instead of this, instead of transforming the blind force of nature into a force governed by reason, progress turns the soul itself into a blind force.

16.

The doctrine of raising the dead can perhaps be called positivism, but it is completely opposed to progress as the displacing of the older generation by the younger, as the exaltation of the sons over the fathers, and it is also opposed to positivism understood as knowledge only, as a school, as a form of scholasticism. The doctrine of raising the dead may be called positivism, but it is a positivism of action, since according to this doctrine mythical knowledge is not replaced by positive knowledge, but mythical, fictitious action is replaced by positive and real action.

At the same time, the doctrine of the raising of the dead does not set arbitrary limits to action and has in view a common action and not the action of separate individuals. The raising of the dead, as an action, is a positivism in the sphere of final causes; while positivism in the usual sense, i.e., positivism of knowledge, refers to the realm of initiating or efficient causes. However, the positivism of final causes does not exclude the positivism of efficient causes. . . . Positivism of action (the doctrine of the raising of the dead) has as its forerunner not mythology but mythical art, since mythology is the product of a special class of sacrificial priests, while the common people have their cult, their sacrifices, their mythical art, and the raising of the dead is the conversion of this into art that is actual.

Positivism of action is not something belonging to a class, but something belonging to all the people. Science will be its instrument. On the other hand, positivism of knowledge is nothing more than the philosophy of the learned as a special class or hierarchy. A positivism which does not set arbitrary limits to action, but which recognizes what were initiating or efficient causes in the final causes or results of action, has a different origin than the positivism which limits both knowledge and action. It does not stem from the loss of hope, nor from the desire to be reconciled with evil for the sake of enjoying the present, nor from the desire for repose in old age; or if it stems from a loss, it is the loss of superstition. The learned positivism, however, while it limits the task of the human race, does not consider it necessary to indicate the reasons for such a limitation. In this connection it is not only uncritical, it is positively superstitious. Positivism in theory has its foundation in the so-called positivity of life, and consists in the renunciation of the struggle against the fundamental evil which comes as a result of fatigue or feebleness, or as the result of the wish to surrender to pleasure instead of work. This is not humility before the Divine will (which they do not accept, or rather do not wish to know, and which in any case cannot be represented as making such an evil command), but simply a debased worship of blind force.

Since it is the opposite of progress considered as the sense of superiority of the young over the old and as the displacing of the older by the younger, the raising of the dead requires an education which does not arm the sons against the fathers, but rather establishes the raising to life of the fathers as the main task of the sons. It requires an education which would be the fulfillment of the prophecy of Malachi, the last Old Testament prophet, an education which would be a mutual turning of the hearts of the fathers to the sons and of the sons to the fathers. True education consists not in the sense of superiority over the fathers, but in the consciousness of the fathers in oneself, and of oneself in them. The raising of the dead is the full expression of maturity, it is the departure from school, and it requires a society of independent persons, of sons, who are participating in the common task of raising the forefathers from the dead. The task of the fathers or parents ends with the end of upbringing, and then begins the task of the sons, of those who restore life. In giving birth to their children and in raising them, the parents give up their whole life to them, while the restoration of life to the fathers (which is also the expression of maturity) begins with the task of raising the dead.

17.

Positivism was right in regarding knowledge critically and saying that it is incapable of resolving fundamental questions; but the knowledge it was criticizing was only a class knowledge, it was only knowledge and not action, which ought not to be and in fact cannot be separated from knowledge. Aristotle can be considered as the father of the learned class, and yet we ascribe to this philosopher such a saying as: "We know only what we ourselves do," a statement which clearly does not permit a separation of knowledge from action, i.e., the isolation of the learned as a special class. And yet, even though more than two thousand years have passed since Aristotle's time, there has not been one thinker who has placed this principle, this criterion, this testing of knowledge by action, at the heart of his doctrine. What then would one's own knowledge of the external world (nature—both past and present) signify, if not a project for the transformation of what is born or given in life into that which is earned by labor, together with the restoration of power and life to those who gave birth? This would be a project for the

transformation of blind force into rational force, and the actualization of this project would demonstrate that life is not an
accidental or useless gift.

Equally justified was the criticism of personal, individual
reason, the reason of people taken in isolation. This criticism
would have been completely justified if only it had involved the
demand for a transition out of class knowledge (consisting in
the clash of opinions out of which truth is supposed to proceed)
into all-embracing knowledge, to the unification of the individual
powers of all people in one common task. But instead of that
the learned positivism, by denying the necessity of universal
unification, has only led to a schism within the learned class
itself, has led to its division into positivists and metaphysicians.

The learned are right in saying that the world is an idea or
representation, since as learned people they have an exclusively
cognitive relation with the world. But such a concept of the
world belongs to one class only, and by no means to the whole
human race, and so the learned are not right when by speaking
this way they reject action, replacing it by knowledge, and
even reject the possibility of acting. The learned are not right
when they do not admit the projective within the subjective.

When contemporary monism says that it "reconciles spirit
and matter in a higher unity, as two manifestations of one and
the same hidden essence, apprehended subjectively (in inner
experience) as spirit and objectively (in external experience) as
matter," it is evident that such a reconciliation or unity is completely imaginary and has no real significance. "The anthropo-
pathic monism of primitive man, and the mechanistic monism of
modern science—here we see the point of departure and the
last word in the history of man's view of the world." But a
mechanistic world view can be a last word only for soulless
people, for the learned, for positivists, since the notion of the
world as a soulless mechanism inevitably invites attempts to make
the mechanism the instrument of will, reason, and feeling. If
primitive mankind stubbornly spiritualized matter and materialized spirit, the new man will strive no less stubbornly toward
the real control of blind force. Here we have the true conversion of the mythical into the positive.

If positivism, like knowledge in general, is still spoken of as an activity, this is not because progress in language lags behind progress in thought (can inactivity be perfection?!!), but because man is by nature a doer. The savage expresses himself and the world precisely as they ought to be—i.e., himself as active and the world as living. The mistake of the positivists consists in the fact that they consider themselves above the savage in every respect, and that they apprehend the world and themselves as they ought not to be, and thus are unable to eliminate the contradiction between language and thought. (When a learned person of this or that school speaks of his operations of thought or knowledge as actions, or of the restoration of the past in the realm of thought as the raising of the dead, he is speaking metaphorically.) . . .

18.

As long as the learned or the philosophers remain a class the question of morality or of a task will be for them a question of knowledge only and not of action, will be a subject of study only and not an application of knowledge to life, and the task will be something that happens of its own accord instead of something that *ought* to be done, and done not in isolation but by all together. If the learned are not yet able to transform themselves from a class into a commission or task force for the development of a general plan of action (and without this the human race cannot act as one man according to a general plan, i.e., will not attain its maturity), the contradiction between the reflective and the instinctive cannot be resolved. Not having accepted work as its own task, the learned class remains reflective, while the human race—not yet united for common action—remains the instrument of blind force, acting instinctively. Reflection can only have a destructive effect on the human race, and it replaces what is destroyed with nothing. "To be the conscious agent of the evolution of the universe" means to become a conscious instrument for mutual crowding (conflict) and displacing (death); it means to subordinate the moral to the physical. And yet man, even in the midst of his present division and ineffective knowledge, in some way expresses moral demands as he yields to necessity out of physical weakness.

As long as division and inaction are not accepted as being

temporary, we are in no position even to imagine the scope and significance of the highest good. That state which Spencer and in particular his followers are promising mankind in the future cannot be accepted as the highest, or even as the very lowest, good. On the contrary, such a state, as the conversion of conscious activity into instinctive, automatic activity, as the conversion of man into a machine (which is in fact the ideal of blind fatalistic progress), is to be viewed as the very greatest evil. "The day is coming," says Spencer, "when the altruistic inclination will be so well implanted in our organism that people will vie with each other for opportunities of sacrifice and death." But if such an altruistic inclination is implanted in everyone, how will there be an occasion for its application? Such a condition presupposes the existence of oppressors, torturers, tyrants; either that or the common need to sacrifice oneself must produce benefactors who will become torturers and oppressors simply to satisfy the terrible need of others to become martyrs. Or else, finally, nature itself will remain a blind force in order to fulfill the role of executioner. If life is a good, then its sacrifice will be the loss of a good for those who have given up their lives for others; but then will life be good for those who have accepted the sacrifice and preserved their life at the expense of another's death? How is altruism possible without egoism? Those who sacrifice their lives are altruists; but those who accept the sacrifice . . . what are they? And if life is not a good, then, from the viewpoint of the one giving his life, there is no sacrifice or good work involved in giving it up.

If knowledge is separated from action, as is the case in the science and scholarship of the learned class, then what is done instinctively, in becoming conscious, destroys itself: "if morality is the instinct which moves an individual to sacrifice himself for the sake of the species, then morality is the love of those who have been born for those who gave birth to them, then the consciousness of one's origin, connected as it is with the death of one's parents, will not stop at knowledge but will also pass on to the task of raising the dead."

19.

The question of non-brotherhood, of dis-unity, and of the means of restoring relatedness in all its fullness and power (to the point of visibleness, obviousness) and the question of the unification of sons (brotherhood) for the raising to life of the fathers (full and complete relatedness) are of course identical, and are both opposed to progress or eternal immaturity, i.e., to the inability to restore life to the fathers, the incapacity for attaining moral and not just physical maturity, the latter not really being maturity at all. The second formulation of this question, however, i.e., the question of unification for the raising of the dead, is the more definite of the two. To outline this question even more clearly it is necessary to add that this unification of sons for the raising to life of the fathers is the fulfillment not simply of our own will but also the will of the God of our fathers, who is also not alien to us. This gives a true goal and meaning to life; in it there is expressed precisely the duty of the sons of man; and it is the result of "knowledge of all things by all men" and not a class knowledge. In it—in re-creation, in the replacement of birth-giving by the raising of the dead, of upbringing by creativity—we are looking for the purest (immortal) felicity, and not for mere comfort. In this form the question of dis-relatedness is opposed also to socialism, which misuses the word "brotherhood" and openly rejects the concept of fatherland.

At the present time socialism has no opponents; religions, with their transcendence, their "not of this world," and their "the Kingdom of God is within you," are unable to withstand it. Socialism can even appear to be an actualization of Christian morality. It is precisely the question of the unification of sons in the name of the fathers which is needed to expose the complete immorality of unity in the name of progress and comfort, a unity which displaces the fathers. Unification in the name of comfort and for the sake of one's own pleasure is the worst abuse of life, intellectually, aesthetically, and especially morally. When fathers are forgotten by their own sons, art is transformed from the purest felicity experienced in the restoring of life to

the fathers into a pornocratic delight, while science is transformed from knowledge by all the living of everything non-
living (for the restoration of life to the dead) into the invention
of pleasures or fruitless speculation. Socialism is triumphing over
the state, over religion, and over science. The appearance of
state socialism, of Catholic, Protestant, and "academic" socialism,
bears witness to this triumph. It not only has no opponents, but
also does not even admit their possibility. Socialism is a lie; it
gives the name of relatedness, brotherhood, to the "comradely"
association of people who are strangers to one another and are
connected only by the external ties of utility, while real blood
relatedness connects people by an inner feeling. The feeling of
relatedness cannot be limited to representation of persons [*litse-
predstavleniye*], it requires insight into persons [*litsezreniye*].
Death converts insight into persons into representation of persons, and so the sense of relatedness requires the restoration of
the dead person. As far as it is concerned, the dead person is
irreplaceable, while as far as "comrades" are concerned, death
is a loss which can be made entirely good.

Unification, not for the achievement of comfort and material
satisfaction for all the living, but for the raising to life of the
dead, requires universal (compulsory) education which will
reveal the character and ability of each person and will show
each person *what* he must do and *with whom*—beginning with
marriage. He must bear his burden in the task of transforming
the blind force of nature into one controlled by reason, in the
work of converting it from a death-dealing into a life-giving
force. Is it possible, is it even natural to limit the "human task"
to the mere maintaining of the proper distribution of the products of industry, forcing each person to take care, unfeelingly
and dispassionately, that no one appropriate more than others or
that no one sacrifice anything to others? Although socialism has
been called into being artificially, socialists are careful to take
advantage of the natural weaknesses of man. Thus in Germany
they reproached the German workers for the limitedness of
their demands, pointing to the English workers who were much
more capricious; they also reproached them for their excessive
love of work, inciting them to demand a reduction of working
hours and days. Socialists, who think only about their own

advancement and not about the welfare of the people, pay no attention to the fact that a cooperative state must have not the vices which they are promoting but the virtues, the fulfillment of duty, even self-sacrifice. In modern industrial states the work in industry may be light for the most part, but the existence of factories is maintained by the forced labor of miners who dig coal and iron; they are the necessary condition for the existence of industry. Under such conditions it is not an economic reform that is needed, but a radical technological reform, or rather not just a reform, but a universal transformation involving a transformation of morality as well. The need for forced labor for the sake of universal comfort is an anomaly—even if this labor be equally distributed. Such a need may be thinkable for the sake of attaining brotherhood and fatherlandness, but only as a temporary measure.

With regulation of the meteorological process energy will be drawn from the atmosphere, coal will be replaced by that same energy out of which the supply of energy was derived in the form of coal, and to which it will in any case have to return, since the supply of coal is being steadily exhausted. The same energy that is taken out of the atmospheric currents will certainly produce a transformation in the process of obtaining iron in metallic form. Regulation is also necessary for the uniting of manufacturing and agriculture, since the excess of solar heat acting destructively in the air currents in gales and hurricanes can be utilized in the handcraft industry and will give an opportunity to spread this industry over the whole earth instead of concentrating it at certain points as it is today. The regulator also transforms agriculture from an individual into a collective work. In this way the regulator will mean not only (1) the end of war, but also (2) the replacing of the harsh forced labor of miners, (3) the unification of small handcraft industry with agriculture, (4) the transformation of agriculture from individual into collective production, and in addition it will be a general instrument for agriculture, and (5) it will be the transformation of agriculture from a means of obtaining a "maximum" income, something which leads to crises and overproduction, into the chance of obtaining a "true" income. The call for regulation is being raised therefore on all sides.

The nineteenth century is approaching its mournful and gloomy end; it moves neither toward light nor toward joy. It is already possible to give it a name. In contrast to the so-called age of enlightenment and philanthropy (the eighteenth century), in contrast also to the preceding centuries, beginning with the epoch of the Renaissance, it can be called the age of the revival of prejudices and superstitions, and of the denial of philanthropy and humanism. But it is not reviving those superstitions which in the Middle Ages alleviated life and aroused hope. Instead, it is reviving the superstitions which in those ages made life unbearable. The nineteenth century has revived faith in evil and renounced faith in goodness. It has renounced the Kingdom of Heaven and abandoned faith in earthly happiness or the Kingdom on Earth, which was an article of faith in the age of the Renaissance and in the eighteenth century. The nineteenth century is not only a century of revival of superstitions, but also, as we have said above, of the denial of philanthropy and humanism, something that is especially evident in the doctrines of contemporary criminologists. Having denied philanthropy and adopted Darwinism, the present century has accepted conflict as a legitimate task and instead of being simply a blind instrument of nature it has become its conscious instrument or organ. The armaments of the present day are completely in accord with the beliefs of the century, and only backward people who would like to appear advanced are—despite their Darwinism—denouncing war.

At the same time the nineteenth century is a direct descendant, a true son of the preceding centuries, the direct consequence of the dividing of what is heavenly from what is earthly, of the complete distortion of Christianity, whose Covenant involves precisely the uniting of the heavenly and the earthly, the divine and the human. The universal immanent raising of the dead, a task pursued with all one's heart, with all one's mind, with all one's actions—a raising of the dead accomplished by means of all the powers and capabilities of all the sons of man, such is the fulfillment of this Covenant of Christ, the Son of God and the Son of Man.

VLADIMIR SERGEYEVICH SOLOVYOV

[1853–1900]

V<small>LADIMIR</small> S<small>ERGEYEVICH</small> S<small>OLOVYOV</small> is widely regarded as the most original, systematic, and influential of the Russian philosophers of the nineteenth century. With the possible exception of Leon Shestov, there is no non-Marxist twentieth-century Russian philosopher who has not come under his influence. Moreover, just as Chaadayev at the beginning of the century can be seen as a source for both Slavophile and Westernizing tendencies, and as uniting the religious orientation of the former with the Western outlook of the latter, so Solovyov at its end can be viewed as the ultimate *re*union of the two tendencies, though purely on the religious plane. In both these philosophers Russia's geographical position between East and West finds its intellectual expression.

Vladimir Solovyov was the grandson of a priest and the son of Serge M. Solovyov (1820-1879), historian and professor of history at Moscow University, and of Poliksena Vladimirovna Romanova, a distant relative of Skovoroda. Brought up as one of nine children in a lively intellectual and religious atmosphere, Solovyov very early gave indication of the influences of this background. He was a highly imaginative child whose diverse interests ranged from poetry and myth to military parades and practical jokes, but whose central concern was religious and mystical. At the age of nine, at a service in the chapel of Moscow University, he had a vision—of a beautiful woman whom he was later to call "Sophia." The vision was to recur twice more in his lifetime and without doubt was both an effect and a cause of his mystical orientation. Solovyov was well aware that he was subject to hallucinations, but, as he said, the fact that something is a hallucination is not a reason for denying its meaning.

After a brief period of rebellion against religion, during which he became a devotee of science and professed complete atheism, Solovyov turned to philosophy, found in Spinoza his "first philosophical love," then moved on to Kant, Schopenhauer, Schelling, and Hegel. Solovyov was a voracious reader: he eventually acquired a thorough knowledge of almost every religious and philosophical world view—Buddhism, neo-Platonism, Gnosticism, Medieval Scholasticism. He studied science, history, and philology at Moscow University, was graduated in 1873, and then—an eccentric move in those days for an intellectual—spent a year at the Moscow Theological Academy at Sergiyev Posad (now Zagorsk) near Moscow. He published his master's thesis on *The Crisis in Western Philosophy* in 1874 and began a career of teaching at Moscow University. It was at this time that he met Dostoevsky, who was to have a lasting influence on him and who, it is said, modeled Alyosha in *The Brothers Karamazov* after him.

In 1875, on a leave of absence, Solovyov studied at the British Museum in London where he had a second vision of Sophia. This time she spoke and told him to go to Egypt, which he promptly did. There, in the desert at dawn, he had his third and last vision of Sophia.

Solovyov returned to Russia in 1876 but resigned from Moscow University over a matter of university politics the following year and moved to Saint Petersburg, where he lectured at the University. He received his doctorate there in 1880. During the five years that he spent in academic circles in Saint Petersburg he established himself as Russia's first really original professional philosopher. In addition to a series of public lectures, the *Lectures on Godmanhood* (published in 1878), which were attended by all the intellectual élite of the Russian capital, he published *The Philosophical Foundations of Integral Knowledge* (1877) and his doctoral dissertation, *A Critique of Abstract Principles* (1880). By this time he had formulated the philosophical views he was to retain for the rest of his life—among them the political philosophy of a free theocracy—and he saw Russia as embodying this ideal. Accordingly, when Alexander II was assassinated in 1881, Solovyov, in a public lecture, demanded that Alexander III live up to the Christian ideal which Russia embodied and pardon his father's assassins. Such an unprecedented demand could have but one result. Solovyov's academic career was ended.

For the rest of his life, Solovyov lived in a more and more eccentric fashion, a monk without a monastery, seeking to realize his Christian Utopia and ideal of unity. Since, he now saw, Russia by itself was not fit for this, he turned to the Roman Catholic Church, only to be disappointed, however, for he could not accept that church's demand of absolute obedience and it could not accept his doctrine of Sophia or his program of a theocracy under the administration of the Pope and the Tsar. In 1899, Solovyov made one more journey to Egypt. It seems likely that once again he had a vision—not of Sophia, however, but of something evil. In any event, he returned in a very different mood, his hopes for a Kingdom of God on earth abandoned. His last work, *War, Progress, and the End of History* (1899), is a study of the nature of evil and his views are now apocalyptic, that evil will be overcome only with the end of this world. Never strong, Solovyov was now considerably weakened by his ascetic life. He fell ill and died at the home of his friend, Prince Eugene Trubetskoy, in 1900.

Solovyov's writings cover an enormous field—philosophy proper, religion, sociology, political theory, history. Within philosophy, Solovyov was concerned with all its major aspects, metaphysics, ethics, aesthetics, epistemology, history of philosophy. The third selection below, from the *Foundations of Theoretical Philosophy* (1897-1899, unfinished), shows Solovyov's interest in the last two of these. The selection is a Cartesian meditation presenting an incisive analysis and critique of Descartes' derivation of the existence of the individual self. At the same time, it delimits the field of the indubitable—the level of pure consciousness where the thought coincides with its object —from that of the dubitable, and concludes that the duty of philosophy is to start with the former and to *seek* to establish truth in the latter. Near the beginning of the selection Solovyov points out that "the standard of truth includes the idea of *conscientiousness:* genuine philosophical thought must be a *conscientious quest for valid truth to the finish*." [1] The selection is itself an example of such conscientiousness.

But conscientiousness frequently leads to intricate distinctions and highly abstract concepts. Because of this, much of Solovyov's writing is difficult. In addition, Solovyov uses symbols which are frequently unfamiliar and which tend to be fluid and to vary slightly but significantly in their meaning in different contexts. The most notable such symbol is Sophia, which stands for the *Wisdom of God*, the *principle of creation* (the "Eternal Feminine"), the *world soul, Christ's body*, the *universal Church*, the *Bride of Christ*, the *Kingdom of God:* these notions are all related, but they are not identical. His fundamental and essential principle, however, is the notion of *Godmanhood*, fully developed in his *Lectures on Godmanhood* from which the first selection below was taken. Godmanhood provides Solovyov with the necessary link to achieve his philosophical aim, a philosophy of total-unity embracing all aspects of reality and uniting science and philosophy on the one hand and theology on the other in the ultimate synthesis which is reality. In Solovyov's system not only does religion receive a rational basis, but East and West come together, matter and spirit unite.

The central point of Solovyov's philosophy thus becomes the Incarnation, from which, with the Sacrifice of the Son of God, comes our salvation and the sanctification of all creation, including matter. According to Solovyov, we have a direct intuition of the existence of God, absolute reality. The exact nature of this intuition is described differently in Solovyov's works. This much, however, is clear: There are three sources of knowledge— experience, reason, and intuition ("the mystical realm")— to which correspond three kinds of knowledge—empirical, rational, and faith. Neither of the first two is adequate alone, but through faith, through, that is, the intuition of the Absolute, which is a *union* with the Absolute as the object of knowledge,

1. See below, p. 104.

reason receives content and experience receives form.[2] But although by intuition we know *that* God, the Absolute, exists, the nature of God is known only through reason and experience —a reversal of the position of Saint Thomas Aquinas. As Absolute Being, God is All. As All, God must be wholly actual. He must, therefore, have an actual content which, as such, is *other* than himself as *One*, but which is still God, since it is His content and since He is All. As God's content, the Other is a second positing of the One and is plural. God as the recognition that the content is really one with the One gives us a third positing. In this way, the Trinity is derived from the absolute unity of God.

The second Person of the Trinity, the second positing, is Christ and the Logos. Christ, as the active force of divine unity, produces a passive unity, the principle of humanity or the ideal man (called "Sophia"). This ideal man is the produced principle of the created world, the world's soul. Insofar as Christ participates in the produced unity—as a cause participates in its effect —Christ is a man. We now have a Triune God and a divine world caused by Him through the Logos. The world-soul, however, which, as divine, is now the Other of the Triune God, is made independent through the love of God (as Christ), so that God can have a real object for His love. Thus individual souls arise. And thus arises a third level of Divine Being, the real independence of the plural content of the world-soul. The natural world then comes to be in the standard theological way, by the self-assertion of the world-soul and hence its Fall. In the natural world we have *separation* from the divine and from one another—as evidenced by the externality of matter.

Salvation is possible through the longing for unity preserved in all being and especially in its highest natural manifestation, man. Man can, through love, unite more and more, in historical

2. For a more detailed discussion of Solovyov's epistemology, see Zenkovsky, *op. cit.*, pp. 518-522. The following interpretation is tempting: as reason's field is form and experience's is content, intuition's is existence. Thus, through intuition, knowledge of *existing* reality is possible and the knower simultaneously receives his own existence (see *ibid.*, p. 522, quoting Eugene Trubetskoy, *Vl. Solovyov's World View*, Moscow, 1913, II, p. 237).

time. This has been done in history, in one man, Jesus Christ, who *is* the unity of humanity. The history of the world is a history of evolution to greater and greater unity from the world's first Fall. Once the divine reunion is achieved in the one God-man, the door is opened for the transfiguration of all creation through love.

This pervasive role of love is examined in *The Meaning of Love* (published as a series of five articles in *Problems of Philosophy and Psychology* in 1892-1894). The essay, parts of which form the second selection below, is a late restatement of the metaphysics of the *Lectures on Godmanhood*. Here Solovyov's views are, however, expressed in a concrete, almost poetic form, in contrast to the abstract, discursive approach of the earlier work.

Solovyov's ethics is based on a religious metaphysics.[3] Man's goal is the unification of mankind in history, the realization of the one ideal mankind. This is possible because God is the energy within man, and since God works in each individual, it follows that each has absolute value, but also that free will exists only in the *irrational* choice of evil. Evil is, as we have seen, separateness—in man, selfishness. To exist in society and history is therefore man's duty and the means to his salvation: "Society is the completed . . . individual, and the individual is . . . concentrated society,"[4] and "if we can have no absolute moral solidarity with those who have *died*, there can be no ground for such solidarity with those who certainly *will die*."[5]

Solovyov has succeeded in achieving total-unity through Godmanhood. This is, however, at the expense of traditional Christian dogma—the world is not created *ex nihilo*, individual souls are not *really* independent. The system cannot escape pantheism.

In his philosophy of total-unity, Solovyov brings to its rational culmination the trend begun by Chaadayev, developed by Kir-

---

3. In *The Justification of the Good* (1897), Solovyov attempts to develop his ethics wholly independently of metaphysics. The result is never inconsistent with his general view, however.

4. *The Justification of the Good*, trans. Natalie Duddington, London, 1918, p. 204.

5. *Ibid.*, p. 422.

eyevsky, in the notion of "integral knowledge," and by Khomyakov in the concept of *sobornost*.[6] The two Slavophiles, however, demanded only a limited unity, a limitation which the rationalistic, Western side of Solovyov, straining for a fundamental first principle, could not accept. Thus, in the end, Solovyov's ultimate pantheism is, paradoxically, a result of the Western elements in his thought.

SELECTED BIBLIOGRAPHY

Works:

Vladimir Solovyov, *Lectures on Godmanhood*, Introduction by P. Zouboff, New York, 1944.

——————, *Russia and the Universal Church*, trans. H. Rees, London, 1948.

——————, *The Meaning of Love*, trans. Janet Marshall, New York, 1947.

——————, *The Justification of the Good*, trans. Natalie Duddington, London, 1918.

——————, *Three Conversations Concerning War, Progress, and the End of History, including a Short Story of the Antichrist*, trans. A. Bakshy, London, 1915.

——————, *A Solovyov Anthology*, arranged by S. L. Frank, trans. Natalie Duddington, New York, 1950.

Secondary Sources:

L. M. Lopatin, "The Philosophy of V. Soloviev" (1901), trans. A. Bakshy, *Mind*, XXV (1916), pp. 425-460.

Nicholas O. Lossky, "The Philosophy of Vl. Solovyev," "The Successors of Vl. Solovyev," trans. Natalie Duddington, *The Slavonic Review*, II (1923), pp. 346-358, and III (1924), pp. 92-109.

——————, *History of Russian Philosophy*, New York, 1951, pp. 81-133.

Thomas G. Masaryk, *The Spirit of Russia*, trans. E. and C. Paul, New York, 1955, II, 225-286.

V. V. Zenkovsky, *A History of Russian Philosophy*, trans. George L. Kline, 2 vols., London and New York, 1953, pp. 469-531.

N. Zernov, *Three Russian Prophets: Khomiakov, Dostoevsky, Soloviev*, London, 1944.

6. See above, Vol. 1, pp. 161-162.

[VLADIMIR SOLOVYOV]

Lectures on Godmanhood *

God is that which is; i.e., to Him belongs being. . . . [but] being
can be conceived only as a *relation* of that which is to its objective essence or content—a relation in which this content or
essence is asserted, posited, or manifested. Indeed, if we were
to suppose an entity which in no way asserted or posited any
objective content, which did not represent anything, and was
not anything either in and for itself or for another, we could
not logically admit that such an entity had any being at all. . . .

Should we wish to find an analogy for this relation [the
absolute's positing of its content or essence] in the world of our
own experience, the most appropriate one would be the artist's
relation to the artistic idea in the creative act. The artistic idea
is certainly not anything alien or external to the artist; it is his
own inner essence, the center of his spirit and content of his
life, that which makes him what he is. In striving to actualize or
embody this idea in an actual work of art, he wants merely to
have this essence, this idea, not only in himself, but also for
himself, or before himself as an object. He wants to represent
what is his own as an "other" in some specific form. . . .

When we plunge into the mute and motionless depths from
which the turbulent stream of our actual existence originates,
being careful not to disturb its purity and peace, we come
into inward contact, in this generic source of our own spiritual
life, with the generic source of universal life. We come to know
God essentially as the first principle or substance of the all. . . .

Since that which God actualizes in the act of His own self-
determination—the *all*, or the fullness of all [individuals]—is

* Translated for this volume by George L. Kline, from the Russian original,
"Chteniya o Bogochelovechestve" in V. S. Solovyov, *Sobraniye sochineni*
(2nd ed., St. Petersburg, 1911-1914), III. The selections are drawn from Lectures Six through Twelve: pp. 83-84, 86-88, 90, 92-95, 99-100, 103-104, 108-110,
112-115, 117-118, 120-122, 125-127, 131-133, 136-138, 140-141, 143-146, 149-152,
159, 162, 171-172.

his own content or essence, its actualization too is only the complete expression or manifestation of that to which this content or essence belongs, and which is expressed in it or by it in the same way as the subject is expressed by the predicate. Thus, to return to our illustration, the poet who gives himself wholly to creation, translating his own inner life, so to speak, into objective works of art, not only does not lose his own individuality thereby, but on the contrary asserts it in the highest degree and actualizes it more completely. . . .

We thus have three relations, or *positings*, of that which absolutely is, positings through which it determines itself with respect to its own content. First, it posits itself as possessing this content in immediate substantial unity, in non-differentiation, with itself; it posits itself as a single substance which essentially includes all things in its absolute power. Second, it posits itself as manifesting or actualizing its own absolute content, opposing the latter to itself, or separating it from itself, by an act of self-determination. Third, and last, it posits itself as maintaining and asserting itself in its own content, or as actualizing itself in an actual, mediated, or differentiated unity with this content or essence, i.e., with all things—in other words, as finding itself in its other, as eternally returning into itself, and remaining "at home with itself." [1]

Thus far we have encountered only the [objective] triadicity of relations, positings, or modes of existence. But our own spirit necessarily exhibits a similar triadicity, once we recognize it to have an independent existence, i.e., to be a genuine entity. . . .

First, there is our primordial, indivisible, and integral subject. This subject, in a sense, contains the peculiar content of our spirit, our essence or idea, and this in turn determines our individual character. If such were not the case, i.e., if this idea and character were no more than products of our phenomenal (manifested) life, or depended on our conscious actions and states, we could not explain why we do not lose that character and idea when we lose our vital consciousness [i.e., when we are asleep]; why our conscious life, in renewing itself each day, does not provide us with a new character, a new life-content.

1. *"U sebya"*: cf. Hegel's *"bei sich."*—TRANS.

In fact, the identity of our fundamental character, or individual idea, amid the flux of conscious life clearly shows that this character and idea are contained in a primordial subject which is deeper than, and prior to, our conscious life. Of course, it is contained only substantially [i.e., potentially], in immediate unity with [that subject] as its inner idea, an idea as yet undisclosed and unembodied.

Second, we have our differentiated conscious life—the manifestation or disclosure of our spirit. Here our content or essence exists *actually*, in a multiplicity of differing manifestations, to which it lends a determinate character, disclosing its own peculiar quality in and through them.

Third, and last, since these manifestations, for all their multiplicity, disclose a *single* spirit equally present in all of them, we can reflect upon, or return into, ourselves out of these manifestations or disclosures, asserting ourselves as actual, as a single subject, a determinate "I," the unity of which is not only not lost through its differentiation and manifestation in a multiplicity of states and acts of conscious life, but, on the contrary, even more firmly posited. This return into oneself, this reflection upon oneself, or assertion of one's self in its manifestations, is precisely what is called "self-consciousness." It appears whenever we not only experience certain states—feeling, thinking, etc.— but also linger over these states and, by a special kind of inner act, assert ourselves as the subject which experiences these states —which feels, thinks, etc. We inwardly declare: "I feel, I think, etc." In its second positing, our spirit manifests or discloses its content, i.e., separates that content from itself as other. In this third positing, in self-consciousness, our spirit asserts its content as *its own*, and by the same token asserts itself as that which has manifested this content.

Thus the triadic relation of the subject to its content corresponds to the relation—already discussed—of the absolute subject, or that which absolutely is, to its absolute content or universal essence. But the parallel between absolute being and ourselves goes no further. In fact, in the actuality of our spirit the three positings referred to above are only episodes of our inner life. . . .

Thus, these three positings or modes of existence cannot be co-present in a single subject at a given time; they can be present in it only at different times. . . . This is true only of finite creatures which live in time. In the case of the absolute entity, which—as its very concept indicates [2]—cannot be determined by the form of temporality, its three positings of, or ways of relating to, its essence or content cannot alternate in temporal sequence. The absolute must present these three positings simultaneously, in one single, eternal act. But [the co-existence of] three mutually exclusive positings in a *single* act of a *single* subject is utterly inconceivable. A single eternal subject cannot at the same time conceal all of its determinations in itself, manifest them for itself, separate them from itself as its other, and still remain "at home with itself. . . ." [3]

But if this is so—if, on the one hand, there cannot be, in the absolute entity, three acts which alternate in temporal sequence; and if, on the other hand, three eternal acts, which by definition are mutually exclusive, cannot be conceived as belonging to a single subject—we must assume that these three eternal acts belong to three eternal subjects (or hypostases), the second of which, being immediately generated by the first, is the direct image of its hypostasis, expressing the essential content of the first through its own actuality, and serving as eternal expression, or Word, for the first. The third, also proceeding from the first, as from something that has already manifested itself in the second, asserts it [the first?] as something expressed or something in its expression.

But it may be asked: If God, as the first subject, includes the absolute content, or the whole, what need is there for the other two subjects? [The answer is] that God as the absolute or unconditioned cannot be content with having the whole *in Himself*; He must also have it for Himself and "with Himself." [4] Without such fullness of existence, Deity cannot be perfect or absolute, i.e., cannot be God. Consequently, to ask, "Why does

---

2. "*Po samomu ponyatiyu svoyemu*": cf. Hegel's "*seinem Begriff nach.*"—TRANS.

3. Cf. fn. 1.—TRANS.

4. Cf. fn. 1.—TRANS.

God need this triadic positing?" is like asking, "Why does God need to be God?"

But, once having admitted three divine subjects, how can we keep from falling into conflict with the requirements of monotheism? Are not the three subjects three Gods?

We must first agree as to precisely what we mean by the word "God." If we designate by this term any subject which participates, in one way or another, in the divine essence, we will have to acknowlege not just three but a very large number of gods; for every entity participates in the divine essence in one way or another. . . . But if we take the term "God" as designating total, integral, and actual possession of the entire fullness of the divine content in all of its aspects, then . . . the term "God" can be applied to the three divine subjects only insofar as they necessarily exist in absolute unity, in unbroken inner union among themselves. Each of them is a true God precisely because each is inseparable from the other two. If one of them could exist in separation from the other two, clearly, in that separateness, it would not be absolute. Thus it would not, in the strict sense, be God. But such separateness is precisely what is ruled out. To be sure, each divine subject contains in itself the entire fullness of Deity. But that is because each exists in unbroken union or unity with the other two. The relation of each to the other two must necessarily be internal and essential, for there can be nothing external in Deity. God the Father, by His very nature, cannot exist without the Word which expresses Him and the Spirit which asserts Him. In the same way, Word and Spirit cannot exist without the first Subject, expressed by the one and asserted by the other, which is their common source and first principle. . . .

Still, there is a sense in which we must admit the Divine Tri-unity to be wholly unfathomable to reason, namely, as an actual and substantial relation among living subjects, as the inner life of that which is. This cannot be covered, fully expressed, or exhausted by rational determinations or definitions. The latter, as their very conception indicates,[5] express only the universal and formal, not the essential and material, side of existence.

5. Cf. fn. 2.—TRANS.

Rational definitions and categories express only what is objective and knowable about an entity—not its own inner, subjective existence and life. But, clearly, *this* kind of unfathomability—which springs from the very nature of reason as a formal faculty—cannot be charged to any limitation of human reason. *Any* reason, no matter whose, is limited, *qua* reason, to grasping the logical aspect of what exists, its concept (λόγος), its universal relation to all else—not the existent itself in its immediate, singular, and subjective actuality. . . . It is not just the life of the Divine being that is unfathomable in this sense, but the life of any being whatever. For no entity is, as such, exhausted by its formal, objective side, by its concept. As an existent it necessarily has its inner, subjective side, which constitutes the very act of its existence. As an existent it is something absolutely singular, unique, and wholly inexpressible. This side of the entity is always something "other" for reason, something which cannot enter the sphere of rationality, something irrational.

Thus, God in Heaven and the least blade of grass on earth are equally unfathomable, and equally fathomable, for reason. . . .

Returning to the truth of Tri-unity, it should be said that this truth is not only fully intelligible from the side of logic, but also is grounded in the universal logical form which determines or defines every actual being. If this form, as applied to Deity, seems more difficult to understand than the same form as applied to other objects [of thought], this is not because the divine life in its formal, objective aspect is less amenable than are other entities to logical determination or definition (there is no basis for such a supposition), but only because the realm of divine being is not a customary object of our thought. . . .

Determinate being is a certain relation of that which is, or the subject, to its essence or content. The modes of that relation are the modes of being. Thus, for example, at the present moment my being as a thinking [subject] is a relating of my "I" to an object, i.e., to the content or objective essence of my thought. This relation, which is called "thinking," constitutes a certain mode of my being. But if being is a relation between that which is, as such, and its essence, the essence cannot be that which is, as such. Rather, it is its other. But at the same time it belongs to it as its own inner content. Since that which is is also the positive principle of its own essence, it is the principle of its own other. But the principle of one's own other is *will*. In fact, that which I posit by my own will is mine insofar as I posit it. At the same time it is other, distinct from me. If it were not, I would not have posited it. Thus, the first mode of being—a mode in which the essence is not yet separated from what is, but is distinguished from it only potentially or by its [vectoral] tendency; a mode in which it is and is not, is itself and also its other—is revealed to us as *will*.

However, that which is, in positing essence as both itself and its other in a primordial act of will, distinguishes the essence not only from itself as such, but also from its own will. That which is cannot will its other unless that other is given or available in some sense, unless it already exists for that which is as an other, i.e., as present to it. Thus the being of that which is receives its determination not merely as will but also as *representation*.[6]

The represented essence, as other, is able to act upon that which represents it insofar as the latter also wills. In this interaction the object of will, separated by representation from that which is, is once again united with it. In this interaction, that which is finds itself in its essence, and its essence in itself. In acting upon each other, they become sensitized to, or capable of feeling, each other. Thus, this interaction, the third mode of being, is nothing other than *feeling*.

That which is thus *wills* its essence or content, *represents* it, and *feels* it. In consequence, its very being, which is nothing other than its relation to its essence, takes on the determinate forms of will, representation, and feeling. We know from our own immediate consciousness what these three modes of being are like, as actual, inasmuch as our own inner experience is entirely made up of various positings of will, feeling, and representation. . . .

Thus we have three distinctive subjects of being; and all three of the fundamental modes of being pertain to each of them, although in different respects. The first subject represents and

6. "*Predstavleniye*": cf. Hegel's "*Vorstellung*."—TRANS.

feels only insofar as it *wills;* this follows necessarily from its primordial significance. The second, which has the first before it, is dominated by the objective element of representation, of which the first subject is the determining cause. Here will and feeling are subordinated to representation; [the second subject] wills and feels only insofar as it *represents.* Finally, in the third subject, which already has "before" it both the immediately-creative being of the first and the ideal being of the second, distinctive or independent significance attaches only to real or sensuous being. The third subject represents and wills only insofar as it *feels* or *senses.*

The first subject is pure *spirit,* the second is *intellect* (Νοῦς); the third, as spirit actualizing itself or acting in its other, may, to distinguish it from the first, be called *soul.* . . .

Corresponding to the three divine subjects (and to the three modes of being) are three forms of essence, or three ideas,[7] each comprising the predominant object or content of one of the three subjects. Two questions arise at this point: first, what do these three ideas actually include, i.e., what precisely is willed as good, represented as truth, and felt as beauty? Second, how are these three ideas related to the general determination or definition of the divine essence as *single,* as one, i.e., to its determination or definition in the form of *love?*

The object of will, representation, and feeling on the part of that which absolutely is can only be the *all.* Thus, the content of good, truth, and beauty, as ideas of the absolute, is just this *all* or totality. The differences among these ideas are not differences in what they contain (material differences) but only in the form of containment (formal differences). What the absolute wills as good is the same as what it represents as truth and feels as beauty—namely, the *all.* But only as inwardly one and integral can the all be the object of what absolutely is. Thus good, truth, and beauty are only different forms or species of unity, forms under which the content of the absolute, the *all,* appears to the absolute itself—or three different aspects, starting from which that which absolutely is reduces the all to unity. However, generally speaking, every inner unity, every unification of the many

7. In a Platonic sense of the term.—TRANS.

from within, is *love* (in the broad sense of the term, the sense which coincides with "accord," "harmony," and "peace" [МИР], as well as "world" [MIP] or "cosmos"). In this sense good, truth, and beauty are only different forms of love. But these three ideas and the three modes of being which correspond to them are not inwardly unified to the same degree. . . .

The good is the unity of the all, or all individuals, i.e., love as the object of will or desire, i.e., the beloved. Hence love, in a special and pre-eminent sense, is the idea of ideas; its unity is *essential*. Truth is love, i.e., the unity of the all, but as objectively represented; its unity is *ideal*. Finally, beauty is love (i.e., the unity of all individuals), but as manifested or made available to the senses; its unity is *real*. In other words, good is unity in its positive potentiality, energy, or *power* (hence the divine will can be characterized as an immediately-creative principle or principle of *power*). Truth is this same unity as *necessary;* and beauty is this unity as *actual*. To express the relation of these terms concisely, we may say that the absolute actualizes the good in beauty, through truth. The three ideas, or universal unities, since they are only different aspects or positings of a single [subject], form, in their interpenetration, a new concrete unity, which constitutes the perfect actualization of the divine content, the integral totality of the absolute essence, the realization of God as *total-unity*. . . .

In its complete definition, the divine principle appears to us in Christianity. Here, at last, we come to the distinctively Christian revelation. . . .

If we examine the entire theoretical and moral content of Christ's teaching as set forth in the New Testament, we shall find that the only teaching which is both new and different from the teachings of other religions is Christ's teaching about Himself, His reference to Himself as living, embodied truth. "I am the way, the Truth and the life: he who believeth on Me shall have life eternal." . . .

How, then, is Christ as the life and the Truth to be conceived or represented to reason?

God as eternal actualizes Himself eternally by actualizing His content, i.e., by actualizing the *all*. This "all," in contrast to God as that which is and is absolutely one, is a multiplicity. But this multiplicity is the content of the absolutely one, and thus is dominated by oneness, reduced to unity.

Multiplicity reduced to unity is wholeness. Real wholes are living organisms. God, as that which is and actualizes its content, is a single being which contains all multiplicity—a living organism. We have already seen that the "all," as the content of the absolute principle, cannot be a mere sum of separate, undifferentiated entities, but that each of these entities represents a particular idea, expressed in a harmonious relationship with everything else, and that, in consequence, each is an essential organ of the whole.

Thus we may also say that the "all" as the content of the absolute or of God, as having actualized His content, is an organism. . . .

The elements of the divine organism exhaust the fullness of being; in this sense it is a universal organism. But this does not keep the universal organism from being, at the same time, perfectly individual. On the contrary, it logically requires such individuality.

We call that entity (relatively) universal which contains a larger number of different and distinctive elements as compared with other entities. Clearly, the more elements there are in any organism, and the greater the number of distinctive entities which enter into its composition—the more each of them will be conditioned by the others; consequently, the stronger and closer will be the union of all of these elements and hence the unity of the entire organism.

It is also clear that the more elements there are in an organism, the greater the number of combinations in which they occur, and the less likely this exact combination of elements is to occur in another organism—the more the given organism will be marked by distinctiveness and originality.

Furthermore, since every relation and *combination* is, at the same time, necessarily a *distinction*, the more elements there are in a given organism, the more distinctions it will have in its unity, and the more distinct it will be from all others, i.e., the larger the multiplicity of elements which the organism's principle of unity reduces to itself, the more this same principle of unity will assert itself; consequently, the more *individual* the organism will be. Thus, we arrive, from this point of view as well, at the proposition already stated, namely, that the universality of an entity stands in direct relation to its individuality: the more universal it is, the more individual it will be. Therefore, the absolutely universal entity will be an absolutely individual entity.

Thus, the universal organism, which expresses the absolute content of the divine principle, is pre-eminently a distinctive individual entity. This individual entity, the actualized expression of God as that which absolutely is, is Christ.

Every organism necessarily includes two [kinds of] unity: on the one hand, the unity of an active principle which reduces the multiplicity of elements to itself as unity; on the other hand, that multiplicity as reduced to unity, as a determinate form of the given principle. There is the unity which *produces* and the unity which *is produced* [8]—unity as the principle (in itself) and unity [as manifested in] the phenomena.

In the divine organism of Christ, the active, unifying principle, the principle which expresses the unity of that which absolutely is, is obviously the Word or Logos.

The second kind of unity, unity as produced, is, in Christian theosophy, called "Sophia" or Divine Wisdom. If we distinguish within the absolute in general between the absolute as such, i.e., that which absolutely is, and its content, essence, or idea, we will find the direct expression of the former in the Logos and of the latter in Sophia, as expressed or actualized idea. Just as that which is, in differentiating itself from its own idea, is at the same time one with it, so the Logos too, in differentiating itself from Sophia, is inwardly united with it. . . .

If the will predominates, the principle is *moral;* if representation predominates, it is *theoretical;* finally, there is the sensuous or *aesthetic* principle. Thus we have three orders of living forces, comprising the three spheres of the divine world . . .— the sphere of pure spirits, the sphere of minds or intellects, and the sphere of souls. All of these spheres are united in a close and

8. This is reminiscent of Spinoza's distinction between *natura naturans* and *natura naturata.*—TRANS.

unbreakable bond. . . . Thus a single unbreakable bond of love unites all the countless elements which make up the divine world.

The actuality of this world, which is necessarily infinitely richer than that of our visible world, . . . can obviously be fully accessible only to one who actually is a member of it. But since our natural world is also and necessarily connected in the closest way to this divine world (what the connection is, we shall see presently), and since there is not and cannot be any impassable gulf between them—individual rays and glimmerings of the divine world must penetrate into our actual world, constituting the ideal content, the beauty and truth, which we find in it. Man, as a member of both worlds, can and must establish contact with the divine world by an act of intellectual intuition.[9] While remaining in the world of struggle and dark anxiety, he [can and must] enter into communion with the clear forms of the realm of glory and eternal beauty.

This positive, though incomplete, knowledge of, or penetration into, the actuality of the divine world is especially characteristic of poetic creation. Every true poet must necessarily penetrate into the "fatherland of flame and word," to find there the archetypes of his own creations, as well as that inward illumination which is called "inspiration"—through which we may find, even in the actuality of nature, sounds and colors which will embody those ideal types. . . .

It is not the eternal divine world, but rather human nature, and the actual world factually given to us, that constitutes an enigma for reason. Reason's task is to explain this actuality, which is both factually indubitable and obscure to reason.

The problem is to derive the relative from the absolute, the conditional from the unconditional; to derive what is not in itself obligatory from the absolutely obligatory; to derive contingent reality from the absolute idea—the natural, phenomenal world from the world of divine essence.

This derivation or deduction would be impossible if there were not something which unites the opposed terms (one of which is to be derived from the other, i.e., from its opposite)—something belonging equally to both spheres, and therefore capa-

9. *"Umstvennoye sozertsaniye"*: cf. Schelling's *"intellektuelle Anschauung."*—TRANS.

ble of providing a transition between them. This uniting link between the divine and natural worlds is *man*.

Man contains within himself all possible oppositions; but they can be reduced to the one great polarity of absolute and relative, of unconditional and conditional, of absolute, eternal essence and transitory phenomenon or appearance. Man is at the same time deity and nothingness. . . .

In a particular organism of the natural world we distinguish the active unity, the principle which *produces* and maintains its organic wholeness—the principle which constitutes the living and active *soul* of the organism—from the unity of that which *is produced* or actualized by this soul—the unity of the organic *body*.

In the divine being of Christ the first or productive unity is Deity, strictly speaking, that is, God as the active force or Logos. . . . The second, produced, unity, to which we have given the mystical name "Sophia" is the principle of humanity, that is, man as ideal or norm. And Christ, as partaking, within this unity, of the principle of humanity, is man, or, to use the Scriptural expression, the second Adam.

Thus Sophia is ideal or perfect humanity, eternally contained in the integral divine being or Christ. Since it is beyond doubt that God, in order to exist in actuality and reality, must manifest Himself, manifest His existence, i.e., must act in an other, the existence of this other is thereby established as necessary. And since, in speaking of God, we cannot have in mind the form of temporality, because whatever we say about God presupposes eternity, the existence of this other, with respect to which God manifests Himself, must necessarily be acknowledged as eternal. This other is not *absolutely* other for God (that would be inconceivable), but is His own expression or manifestation, with respect to which God is called the Word. . . .

In order that God should exist eternally as Logos or as active Deity, it is necessary to assume the eternal existence of real elements which are objects of the divine action. It is necessary to presuppose an existing world which is patient of divine action, making room in itself for the divine unity. The specific, produced unity of this world—the world's center and at the same time the periphery of God—is mankind.

Every actuality presupposes an act, and every act presupposes a real object of that act—a subject which receives it. Consequently, God's actuality, based upon His activity, presupposes a subject which receives this activity, namely man, and presupposes him *eternally*, since God's activity is eternal. The objection that an eternal object for God's activity is already present in the Logos is not valid, for the Logos is God himself made manifest. This manifestation, too, presupposes the other, for which, or with respect to which, God manifests himself; i.e., it presupposes man.

Of course, in speaking of the eternity of man or mankind, we are not referring to natural man, or man as appearance; that would be a contradiction in terms and would also conflict with scientific experience. . . .

Individual man, as phenomenon, represents, from the physical point of view, only a spatial grouping of elements; and, from the psychological point of view, only a temporal series of separate states or events. Consequently, from the [physical-psychological] point of view, not just man in general, or mankind, but also separate human individuals, are only abstractions, not real units. Generally speaking, . . . it is impossible, from such a point of view, to find *any* real unit. For, on the one hand, every material element which enters into the composition of an organism, since it is spatially extended, can be divided *ad infinitum;* and, on the other hand, every psychic event, since it occurs at a determinate time, can be divided, *ad infinitum*, into infinitely small temporal moments. In neither case is there an ultimate unit; every assumed unit turns out to be conventional and arbitrary.

But if there are no real units, there is no real whole either; if there are no actually determinate parts, there is no actual whole. From this point of view, the result is complete nothingness, the negation of all reality—a result which obviously proves the inadequacy of the point of view. In fact, empirical realism, which takes the given phenomenon as the sole actuality, cannot find any ground either for an ultimate reality or for real units.

We are thus justified in concluding that the real units, without which nothing can exist, have their own independent essence beyond the limits of given phenomena, and that the latter are only the manifestations of those genuine essences. . . .

We must acknowledge ideal beings as fully actual—although they are not given in immediate external experience, and are neither material elements existing in space nor psychic events or states occurring in time.

From this point of view, when we speak of man, we have neither need nor justification for restricting ourselves to his given visible actuality. We may speak of an ideal man, a man, nevertheless, who is altogether essential and real—much more, incommensurably more, essential and real than the visible manifestation of human nature. There is in us an infinite richness of energies and of content, concealed beyond the threshold of our present consciousness. Only a certain portion of those energies and that content passes—a little at a time—over the threshold into our consciousness, never exhausting the whole. . . .

Although man as phenomenon is a temporal, transitory fact, man as essence is necessarily eternal and all-embracing. What, then, is an ideal man? In order to be actual, such a being must be both one and many. Consequently, it is not merely the universal common essence of all human individuals, taken in abstraction from them. It is a universal, but also an individual, entity— an entity which actually contains all human individuals within itself. Every one of us, every single human being, is essentially and actually rooted in, and partakes of, the universal or absolute man.

Just as divine energies constitute the single, integral, absolutely universal, and absolutely individual organism of the living Logos, so all human elements constitute a similarly integral organism, both universal and individual, the necessary actualization and receptacle of the first—a universally-human organism—as the eternal body of God and the eternal soul of the world. Since this latter organism, i.e., Sophia, in its eternal being, necessarily consists of a multiplicity of elements, constituting their real unity, each of the elements, as a necessary component part of eternal Godmanhood, must be recognized as *eternal* in the absolute or ideal order.

Thus when we speak of the eternity of mankind, we make implicit reference to the eternity of each separate individual who constitutes mankind. Apart from such eternity, mankind would be an illusion. . . .

It is the abnormal attitude toward everything else, the exclusive self-assertion, or egoism, which dominates our practical life, even though we deny it in theory—the opposition of the self to all other selves, and the practical negation of the other selves—that constitutes the radical *evil* of our nature. It is common to all that lives, since every natural entity—every beast, insect, and blade of grass—separates itself in its own peculiar being from everything else, strives to be everything for itself, swallowing up or repelling what is other (whence arises external, material being). Therefore evil is a property common to all of nature. All of nature is, on the one hand, in its ideal content, its objective forms and laws, a reflection of the totally-one idea; but on the other hand, in its real, separated, and discordant existence, it is something alien and hostile to that idea, something wrong or evil, and that in two senses. For if egoism, i.e., the striving to set up one's exclusive "I" in the place of everything else, to eliminate everything else, is evil in the strict sense (morally evil), the fateful impossibility of actually enacting such egoism, i.e., the impossibility of actually being everything while yet remaining in one's own exclusiveness, is radical *suffering*. All other kinds of suffering are related to this radical suffering as special cases to a general law. Indeed, the common basis of all suffering, physical as well as moral, reduces to the dependence of the subject upon something other than and external to itself, some external fact which coerces and oppresses it. Such external dependence would obviously be impossible if the given subject existed in an inward and actual unity with all else, if it felt itself in all beings. . . .

It will be clear from what has been said that evil and suffering have an inner, subjective significance. They exist in us and for us, i.e., in and for every entity. They are states of individual entities. Evil is the state of tension of a will which asserts itself exclusively, denying every other. Suffering is the necessary reaction of the other against such a will, a reaction which the self-asserting entity undergoes involuntarily and inescapably, and which it experiences as suffering. Hence suffering, which constitutes one of the characteristic features of natural being, is an inevitable consequence of moral evil.

We have seen that the actual being of the natural world is something improper, wrong, or abnormal, insofar as it is opposed to the being of the divine world (as an absolute norm). But this opposition and, consequently, evil itself, is, as has been shown, only a condition of individual entities and a certain relation which they bear to one another (namely, a negative relation). It is not an independent essence or specific principle. The world which, in the words of the Apostle, "lieth in evil," is not some new world, absolutely distinct from the divine world and composed of specific essential elements of its own. It is rather a different, improper interrelation of the very same elements which constitute the being of the divine world.

The wrong or improper actuality of the natural world is the discordant and hostile positing, with respect to each other, of the very same elements which, in their normal relation, namely in their inner unity and harmony, comprise the divine world. For if God, as the absolute or all-perfect [being], contains in Himself all that is, all entities that are, there cannot be entities which have the ground of their being outside of God, or have substantial being apart from the divine world. Consequently, nature, in contradistinction to Deity, can only be a different positing or *permutation* of given essential elements which have their substantial being in the divine world.

Thus these two worlds differ from one another not in essence, but only in their [mode of] positing. One of them represents the unity of all that is, a positing in which each finds itself in all, and all in each. The other, in contrast, represents a positing of all that is, in which each, in itself or through its own will, asserts itself apart from the others and in opposition to them (evil), and thereby undergoes the external actuality of the others as opposed to its own will (suffering).

This raises a question: how can we explain this wrong or improper positing within the natural world, this exclusive self-assertion of all that is? . . .

All entities, in their primordial unity with Deity, form a single divine world, [divided] into three principal spheres, according to which of the three basic modes of being—substantial, intellectual (ideal), or sensuous (real)—predominates in them, or by which of the three divine acts (will, representation, feeling), they are principally determined. . . .

Entities as pure spirits, in the first sphere, where they exist in the immediate unity of divine will and love, have only potential existence. In the second sphere, although the multiple entities are separated out by the divine Logos as determinate objective forms, having a stable, determinate relation to one another, and thus receive a certain specificity or individuality, this is a purely ideal individuality, for the being of this sphere is determined by intellectual intuition [10] or pure representation. But such an ideal individuation of elements is insufficient for the divine principle as unitary. It requires that the multiple entities should receive their own real individuality; for otherwise the energy of the divine unity or love would have no object upon which to manifest or disclose itself in its fullness. Therefore, the divine being cannot be content with the eternal contemplation of ideal essences. . . . It pauses with each of them separately, . . . asserting and fixing the independent being [of each], so that each in turn may itself act upon the divine principle. . . .

The unity of the [third] sphere, produced by the divine Logos, appears for the first time as an actual, independent entity, capable of acting upon the divine principle. Only here does the object of divine action become an authentic, actual subject, and the action itself a genuine interaction. This second, produced, unity—in contrast to the primordial unity of the divine Logos —is, as we know, the soul of the world or ideal mankind (Sophia), which contains within itself and unites with itself all particular living entities or souls. As the realization of the divine principle, its image and likeness, archetypal mankind, or the

10. "*Umstvennoye sozertsaniye*": cf. Schelling's "*intellektuelle Anschauung*."—TRANS.

world-soul, is at the same time all and one. It occupies a mediating position between the multiplicity of living entities which constitute the real content of its life, and the absolute unity of Deity which is the ideal principle and norm of its life. . . . The divine principle, which is present in [the world-soul] frees it from its creaturely nature, while this nature, in turn, makes it free with respect to Deity. . . .

Insofar as it takes the divine Logos into itself and is determined thereby, the world-soul is humanity, the Godmanhood of Christ, the body of Christ, or Sophia. . . . Through it, God is manifested as a living force, active throughout creation, or as Holy Spirit. . . .

When the world-soul awakens the separate will within itself, thus isolating itself from the whole, the particular elements of the universal organism lose the common bond which they had known in the world-soul. Left to themselves, they are doomed to discordant, egoistic existence, the root of which is evil, and the fruit suffering. Thus all of creaturely existence is subjected to the vanity and bondage of corruption, not by its own will, but by the will of the world-soul which—as the free and unitary principle of natural life—has subjugated it.

The natural world, having fallen away from divine unity, appears as a chaos of discordant elements. The multiplicity of disintegrated elements, alien and impenetrable to each other, finds its expression in real *space*, which is not limited to the form of extendedness. All being for another, all representation, has a "spatial" form; even the content of the inner, psychic world, as concretely represented,[11] appears extended or "spatial" in this sense, i.e., in a formal sense. But this is only an *ideal* space, and it posits no permanent or independent limits for our action. *Real* space, or externality, necessarily results from the disintegration and reciprocal alienation of all that exists, by virtue of which every entity finds in all other entities a permanent and coercive limit to its actions.

In the state of externality each singular entity, each element,

11. For example, when we are dreaming we undoubtedly picture ourselves in a certain space; everything that happens in a dream, all the images and scenes of dream experience, are represented in spatial form.

is excluded or displaced by all the others. Resisting this external action, each element occupies a certain determinate space, which it attempts to retain exclusively for itself. In so doing, it displays the forces of inertia and impenetrability. The complex system of external forces, impulses, and motions resulting from such a mechanical interaction of elements comprises the world of *matter*. But this world is not a world of absolutely homogeneous elements. We know that each real element, each singular entity (atom) has its own particular individual essence (idea). In the divine order, all of these elements, positively supplementing one another, form an integral and harmonious organism. In the natural order this organism is actually disintegrated but retains its ideal unity as a hidden potency and tendency. The gradual actualization of this tendency, the gradual realization of ideal total-unity, is the meaning and goal of the cosmic process. Just as, in the divine order, the all *eternally is* an absolute organism, so, following the law of natural being, the all gradually *becomes* such an organism through time. . . .

Thus the divine principle appears here (in the cosmic process) as the active energy of an absolute idea striving to realize or embody itself in a chaos of discordant elements. The divine principle thus has the same aim as the world-soul, namely, the incarnation of the divine idea, or the deification (*theosis*) of all that exists, by giving all that exists the form of an absolute organism. The difference is that the world-soul, as a passive force, a pure tendency, does not, primordially, know what to strive for, i.e., lacks the idea of total-unity; whereas the divine Logos as a positive principle, an active and formative energy, has the idea of total-unity within itself, and gives this idea to the world-soul as a determining form. . . .

But a question may arise at this point: Why does not the union of the divine principle with the world-soul, and the resultant generation of a universal organism as the incarnate divine idea (Sophia)—why do not this union and this generation take place at once, in a single act of divine creation? . . . The answer to this question is wholly contained in a single word, a word which expresses something without which neither God nor nature can be conceived: that word is "freedom." As a result of the world-soul's free act, the world which it had unified broke apart internally into a multitude of conflicting elements. That whole rebellious multitude must, by a long series of free acts, be reconciled to one another and to God; it must be reborn in the form of an absolute organism. . . .

In man the world-soul is inwardly united with the divine Logos in consciousness for the first time, as a pure form of total-unity. . . . In man nature grows beyond itself and passes (in consciousness) into the realm of absolute being. . . . Man is the natural mediator between God and material being, the carrier of the divine principle of total-unification into the multiplicity of natural elements; it is his task to order and organize the universe. . . .

Thus man is not limited to one principle. He has within himself, first, the elements of material being which bind him to the natural world; second, the ideal consciousness of total-unity, which binds him to God; and third, since he is not confined entirely either to the first or the second, he is a free self or "I," capable of determining himself with respect to the two sides of his being—free to move one way or the other, to assert himself in one sphere or the other. In his ideal consciousness man bears the *image* of God. His absolute freedom from both idea and fact, the formal limitlessness of the human "I," is his *likeness* to God. Man not only has the same inner essence of life—total-unity—as God; he is also free to will to possess it in the way that God does, i.e., he may spontaneously will or desire to be like God. . . . In order to possess [the divine essence as something springing] from himself, and not merely from God, man asserts himself in separation from God, apart from God, and falls away or isolates himself from God in his own consciousness, just as the world-soul primordially isolated itself from God in its total being. . . .

The principle of evil, i.e., the exclusive self-assertion which had thrown all that exists back into primordial chaos—a principle externally dominated in the cosmic process—now emerges in a new form, as the free conscious act of an individual man. The new and emergent process has as its aim the inner, moral overcoming of this evil principle. . . .

Thus, in order that the divine principle should actually overcome man's evil will and life, it was necessary for it to appear
to [man's] soul as a living, personal force, capable of penetrating
the soul and taking possession of it. It was necessary that the
divine Logos should not only act upon the soul from without,
but should also be born within the soul, not merely limiting or
illuminating it, but *regenerating* it. And since, in natural man, the
soul is actual only in the multiplicity of individual souls, the
actual union of the divine principle with the soul necessarily
assumed an individual form, i.e., the divine Logos was born
as an actual, individual, human being. . . .

The setting in which the divine principle assumed human
form [12] was determined by the national character of the Jews;
but the time was determined by the general course of history.
. . . And when outward truth-justice, the truth-justice of people
and state, was actually concentrated in one living person—the
Roman Emperor, as a deified man—then divine truth-justice
appeared, in the living person of God-made-man,[13] as Jesus
Christ. . . .

The proper or right relationship between nature and God in
humanity, a relationship attained in the person of Jesus Christ
as the spiritual center or head of all mankind, must be attained
by all of mankind, as His body.

Mankind as reunited with its divine principle through the
mediation of Jesus Christ is the *Church*. In the eternal, primordial world, ideal mankind is the body of the divine Logos. Similarly, in the world of natural becoming, the Church is the body
of the Logos incarnate, i.e., historically individuated in the person of Jesus Christ, as God-man.

This body of Christ, which made its embryonic appearance in
the form of the tiny communion of the first Christians, is growing and developing little by little, until at the end of time it will
encompass all of mankind and all of nature in one universal
divine-human organism. . . .

This revelation, this glory of the sons of God, which all of

12. *"Vochelovecheniye bozhestvennovo nachala"*: cf. Hegel's *"Menschwer-
dung des göttlichen Wesens."*—TRANS.

13. *"Vochelovechivshisya Bog."*—TRANS.

Creation awaits with hope, is the complete realization of the free, divine-human bond in mankind as a whole, in all spheres of man's life and activity. All of these spheres must be brought into harmonious divine-human unity, entering into that free theocracy in which the Universal Church will reach the full measure of Christ's stature. . . .

[VLADIMIR SOLOVYOV]

The Meaning of Love *

As a general rule to which there are hardly any exceptions, particular intensity of sexual love either altogether excludes reproduction or results in offspring the importance of which in no way corresponds to the power of the love feeling and to the exceptional character of the relations arising from it.

To find the meaning of sexual love in successful childbearing is the same as to find meaning where there is no love, and where there is love, to deprive it of all meaning and justification. This fictitious theory of love when put to the test of facts proves to be not an explanation but, rather, a refusal to explain anything.

Both with animals and with man sexual love is the finest flowering of the individual life. But since in animals the life of the genus is of far more importance than that of the individual, the highest pitch of intensity achieved by the latter merely profits the generic process. Although sexual attraction is not simply a means for the propagation or the reproduction of organisms, it serves to produce *more perfect* organisms through sexual rivalry and selection. An attempt has been made to ascribe the same significance to love in the human world, but, as we have seen, quite in vain. For in the human world individuality has an independent significance and in its strongest expression cannot be merely a means for the ends of the historical process external to it. Or, to put it better, the true end of the historical process does not admit of the human personality being merely a passive and transitory means to it.

The conviction that man has absolute worth is based neither upon self-conceit nor upon the empirical fact that we know of no other more perfect being in the order of nature. Man's unconditional worth consists in the absolute form (or image) of *rational* consciousness undoubtedly inherent in him. Being

* From "The Meaning of Love," *A Solovyov Anthology*, arranged by S. L. Frank, trans. Natalie Duddington, New York, 1950, pp. 154-160, 162-167, 169-174, 177-179.

aware, as animals are, of his experiences, detecting certain connections between them, and, on the basis of those, anticipating
future experiences, man also has the faculty of passing judgments of value on his own states and actions, and on facts in
general, in their relation not only to other particular facts but
to universal ideal norms; man's consciousness is determined not
only by empirical facts but by the *knowledge of truth*. Conform-
ing his actions to this higher consciousness man can infinitely
perfect his life and nature *without transcending the human
form*. This is why he is the highest being in the natural world
and the true end of the process of world-creation; for, next to
the Being which is Itself the absolute and eternal truth, comes
the being which is capable of knowing and realizing truth in
itself; it is highest not relatively but unconditionally. . . .

Man's privilege over other natural beings—his power of understanding and realizing the truth—is both generic and individual:
every man is capable of knowing and realizing the truth, everyone can become a living reflection of the absolute whole, a
conscious and independent organ of universal life. The rest of
nature also contains truth (or the image of God), but only in
its objective universality, unknown to particular beings; this
truth forms them and acts in and through them as the power
of fate, as the unknown-to-them law of their being to which
they involuntarily and unconsciously submit; in themselves, in
their inner feeling and consciousness, they cannot rise above
their given, partial existence; they find themselves only in their
separateness, in isolation from *all*—consequently outside of truth;
therefore, truth or the universal unity can only triumph in the
animal kingdom through the change of generations, the per-
manence of the species, and the destruction of the individual life
incapable of comprehending the truth. The human individuality,
however, just because it is capable of comprehending the truth,
is not canceled by it, but is preserved and strengthened through
its triumph.

But in order that an individual being should find in truth—
in the all-unity—its own affirmation and justification, it must be
not only conscious of truth but be *in* it. Primarily and immediately, however, an individual man is not in truth, any more

than an animal is: he finds himself as an isolated particle of the cosmic whole and in his egoism affirms this partial existence as a whole for himself; he wants to be all in his separation from the whole, outside of truth. Egoism as the real basic principle of individual life penetrates it right through, directing and concretely determining everything in it, and therefore a merely theoretical consciousness of truth cannot possibly outweigh and abolish it. Until the living force of egoism meets in man with another living force opposed to it, consciousness of truth is only an external illumination, a reflection of another light. If man could only in this sense accept the truth, his connection with it would not be inward and indissoluble; his own being remaining, like that of animals, outside truth, would be, like theirs, doomed to disappear in its subjectivity and would only be preserved as an idea in the absolute mind.

Truth as a living power taking possession of man's inner being and really saving him from false self-affirmation is called love. Love as the actual abolition of egoism is the real justification and salvation of individuality. Love is higher than rational consciousness, but without it it could not act as an inner saving power which sublimates and does not destroy individuality. Only thanks to rational consciousness (or, what is the same thing, to the consciousness of truth) man can distinguish himself, i.e., his true individuality, from his egoism, and therefore in sacrificing this egoism and surrendering himself to love, he finds in it both a living and a life-giving power; he does not lose, together with his egoism, his individual being, but on the contrary preserves it forever.

. . . The meaning of human love in general is the *justification and salvation of individuality through the sacrifice of egoism.* Starting with this general position, we can deal with our specific task and explain the meaning of sexual love. It is highly significant that sexual relations are not only called love, but are generally recognized as pre-eminently representative of love, being the type and the ideal of all other kinds of love (see *The Song of Songs* and the *Revelation* of Saint John).

The evil and falsity of egoism certainly do not consist in the fact that man prizes himself too highly or ascribes absolute significance and infinite dignity to himself: he is right in this, for every human subject as an independent center of living powers, as the potency of infinite perfection, as a being capable of embracing in his life and consciousness the absolute truth, has unconditional significance and dignity, is something absolutely irreplaceable and cannot prize himself too highly (in the words of the Gospel, what shall a man give in exchange for his soul?). Not to recognize one's absolute significance in this sense is tantamount to renouncing one's human dignity. The fundamental evil and falsity of egoism lie not in the recognition of the subject's own absolute significance and value, but in the fact that while he justly ascribes such significance to himself, he unjustly denies it to others; in recognizing himself as a center of life, which he is in reality, he refers others to the circumference of his being, setting upon them only an external and relative value.

Of course, theoretically and in the abstract every man who is in his right mind always admits that other people have exactly the same rights as he; but in his vital consciousness, in his inner feeling, and in practice, he makes an infinite, incommensurable difference between himself and others: he, as such, is all; they, as such, are nothing. But it is precisely this exclusive self-affirmation that prevents man from being in fact what he claims to be. The unconditional significance and absoluteness which, speaking generally, he rightly recognizes in himself, but wrongly denies to others, is in itself merely potential—it is only a possibility demanding realization. God *is* all, i.e., possesses in one absolute act all the positive content, all the fullness of being. Man (in general, and every individual man in particular), being in fact only *this* and not *another*, may become all only by abolishing in his consciousness and his life the inner limits which separate him from others. "This" man may be "all" only *together with others;* only together with others can he realize his absolute significance and become an inseparable and irreplaceable part of the universal whole, an independent, unique, and living organ of the absolute life. True individuality is a certain definite form of universal unity, a certain definite way of apprehending and assimilating the whole. In affirming himself outside of all else, man robs his own existence of its meaning, deprives himself of the true content of life, and reduces his individuality to an empty form. Thus egoism is certainly not the self-affirmation and self-consciousness of individuality, but, on the contrary, its self-negation and destruction. . . .

Through love we come to know the truth of another not in abstraction but in reality, and actually transfer the center of our life beyond the confines of our empirical separateness; and in doing so we manifest and realize our own truth, our own absolute significance, which consists precisely in the power of transcending our actual phenomenal existence and of living not in ourselves only but also in another.

All love is a manifestation of this power, but not every kind of love realizes it to the same extent or undermines egoism with the same thoroughness. Egoism is a real and fundamental force rooted in the deepest center of our being and spreading from there to the whole of our reality—a force that continually acts in every department and every detail of our existence. If egoism is to be undermined right through, it must be counteracted by a love as concretely determined as it itself is, penetrating and possessing the whole of our being. The "other" which is to liberate our individuality from the fetters of egoism must be correlated with the whole of that individuality. It must be as real, concrete, and objectivized as we are, and at the same time must differ from us in every way, so as to be really "other." In other words, while having the same essential content as we, it must have it in another way, in a different form, so that our every manifestation, our every vital act should meet in that "other" a corresponding but not an identical manifestation. The relation of the one to the other must thus be a complete and continual exchange, a complete and continual affirmation of oneself in another, a perfect interaction and communion. Only then will egoism be undermined and abolished, not in principle only, but in all its concrete actuality. Only this, so to speak, chemical fusion of two beings of the same kind and significance, but throughout different in form, can render possible (both in the natural and the spiritual order) the creation of a new man, the actual realization of the true human individuality. Such fusion, or at any rate the nearest approximation to it, is to be found in sexual love, and that is the reason why it has an exceptional significance as a necessary and irreplaceable basis of all further growth in perfection, as the inevitable and constant condition which alone makes it possible for man to be actually in truth.

Fully admitting the great importance and the high dignity of other kinds of love by which false spiritualism and impotent moralism would like to replace sexual love, we find nevertheless that only the latter satisfies the two fundamental conditions without which there can be no final abolition of selfhood through complete vital communion with another. In all other kinds of love there is absent either the homogeneity, equality, and inter- action between the lover and the beloved, or the all-inclusive difference of complementary qualities. . . .

Love is important, not as one of our feelings, but as the trans- ference of our whole vital interest from ourselves to another, as the transposition of the very center of our personal life. This is characteristic of every kind of love, but of sexual love pre- eminently; it differs from other kinds of love by greater intensity, greater absorption, and the possibility of a more complete and comprehensive reciprocity; that love alone can lead to the actual and indissoluble union of two lives made one, and only of it does the word of God say that the two shall be one flesh, i.e., shall become one real being. . . .

The task of love is to *justify in fact* the meaning of love which is at first given only as a feeling—to create such a union of two given limited beings as would make of them one absolute ideal personality. Far from containing any inner contradiction, or being at variance with the meaning of the world as a whole, this task is directly set to us by our spiritual nature, the dis- tinguishing characteristic of which is that man can, while remain- ing himself, comprehend the absolute content and become an absolute personality. But in order to be filled with absolute con- tent (which in religious language is called eternal life or the Kingdom of God) the human form itself must be reinstated in its wholeness. In empirical reality there is no man *as such*—he exists only in a one-sided and limited form as a masculine or a feminine individual (all other differences develop upon this basis).

The true human being in the fullness of its ideal personality obviously cannot be merely a man or merely a woman, but must be the higher unity of the two. To realize this unity or to create the true human being as the free unity of the masculine and the feminine elements, which preserve· their formal separateness but overcome their essential disparity and disruption, is the direct *task* of love. If we consider the conditions required for carrying it out, we shall see that it is only because those conditions are not observed that love invariably comes to grief and has to be pronounced an illusion. . . .

Everyone knows that in love there always is a special *idealization* of the object of love which appears to the lover in quite a different light than it does to other people. I am speaking of light not in a metaphorical sense only, not only of a particular moral and intellectual valuation, but of special sensuous perception as well: the lover actually *sees*, visually apprehends, something different from what others do. True, for him too this light of love soon disappears, but does that imply that it was false, that it was merely a subjective illusion?

The true being of man in general and of every man in particular is not confined to his given empirical expressions; no rational grounds to the contrary can be adduced from any point of view.
. . . We know that in addition to his material animal nature man has an ideal nature connecting him with the absolute truth or God. Besides the material or empirical content of his life every man contains the image of God, i.e., a special form of the absolute content. That image of God is known to us in the abstract and in theory through reason, and concretely and actually through love. The revelation of the ideal being, generally concealed by the material appearance, is not confined in love to an inner feeling, but sometimes becomes apprehensible by the outer senses; and this imparts all the greater significance to love as the beginning of the visible reinstatement of the image of God in the material world, of the incarnation of true ideal humanity. The power of love transforming itself into light, transfiguring and spiritualizing the form of external appearances, reveals to us its objective force, but it is for us to do the rest: we must understand this revelation and make use of it so that

it should not remain an enigmatic and fleeting glimpse of some mystery.

The spiritually-physical process of the reinstatement of the image of God in material humanity cannot possibly happen of itself, apart from us. Like all that is best in this world it begins in the dark realm of unconscious processes and relations; the germ and the roots of the tree of life are hidden there, but we must tend its growth by our own conscious action. The passive receptivity of feeling is enough to begin with, but it must be followed by active faith, moral endeavor, and effort in order to preserve, strengthen, and develop the gift of radiant and creative love and by means of it embody in oneself and in the other the image of God, forming out of two limited and mortal beings one absolute and immortal personality. Idealization, inevitably and involuntarily present in love, shows to us through the material appearance the far-off ideal image of the loved one—not in order that we should merely admire it, but that by the power of true faith, active imagination, and real creativeness we should transform in accordance with that true image the reality that falls short of it, and embody the ideal in actual fact. . . .

. . . The actual feeling of love is merely a stimulus suggesting to us that we can and must re-create the wholeness of the human being. Every time that this sacred spark is lit in the human heart, all the groaning and travailing creation waits for the first manifestation of the glory of the sons of God. But without the action of the conscious human spirit, the divine spark dies down, and disappointed nature creates new generations of the sons of men for new hopes.

These hopes will not be fulfilled until we decide fully to recognize and realize to the end all that true love demands, all that is contained in the idea of it. Given a conscious attitude to love and real determination to accomplish the task it sets us, we are first of all hindered by two facts which apparently doom us to impotence and justify those who regard love as an illusion. In the feeling of love, in accordance with its essential meaning, we affirm the absolute significance of another personality and, through it, of our own. But an absolute personality cannot be *transitory* and it cannot be *empty*. The inevitability of death and the emptiness of our life are incompatible with the emphatic affirmation of one's own and another's personality contained in the feeling of love. That feeling, if it is strong and fully conscious, cannot resign itself to the certainty that decrepit old age and death are in store both for the beloved and the lover. And yet, the indubitable fact that all men have always died and go on dying is taken by everyone, or almost everyone, to be an absolutely unalterable law of nature. True, many believe in the immortality of the soul; but it is precisely the feeling of love that shows best the insufficiency of that abstract faith. A discarnate spirit is an angel and not a man; but if we love a human being, a complete human personality, and if love is the beginning of that being's spiritualization and enlightenment, it necessarily demands the preservation, the eternal youth and immortality of this particular person, this living spirit incarnate in a bodily organism.

. . . But if the inevitability of death is incompatible with true love, immortality is utterly incompatible with the emptiness of our life. . . .

It is self-evident that so long as man reproduces himself like an animal, he also dies like an animal. But it is equally evident that mere abstention from the act of procreation does not in any way save one from death: persons who have preserved their virginity die, and so do eunuchs, and neither enjoy even particular longevity. This is quite understandable. Speaking generally, death is the disintegration, the falling apart of a creature's constituent elements. But division into sexes, not remedied by their external and transitory union in the act of reproduction, the division between the masculine and the feminine elements of the human being, is in itself a state of disintegration and the beginning of death. To remain in sexual dividedness means to remain on the path of death, and those who cannot or will not leave that path must from natural necessity tread it to the end. He who supports the root of death must necessarily taste its fruit. Only the whole man can be immortal, and if physiological union cannot reinstate the wholeness of the human being, it means that this false union must be replaced by a true union and certainly not by abstention from all union, i.e., not by a striving to retain *in statu quo* the divided, disintegrated, and consequently mortal human nature.

In what, then, does the true union of the sexes consist and how is it realized? Our life is in this respect so far from the truth that we regard as a norm what is in reality only the less extreme and outrageous abnormality. . . .

Exclusively spiritual love is obviously as much of an anomaly as exclusively physical passion or a loveless legal union. The absolute norm is the reinstatement of the wholeness of the human being, and in whatever direction that norm is violated, the result always is abnormal and unnatural. Pseudo-spiritual love is not merely abnormal but also utterly purposeless, for the separation of the spiritual from the sensuous for which it strives is in any case performed in the best possible way by death. But true spiritual love is not a feeble imitation and anticipation of death, but triumph over death, not the separation of the immortal from the mortal, of the eternal from the temporal, but the transformation of the mortal into the immortal, the reception of the temporal into eternity. False spirituality is the negation of the flesh, true spirituality is its regeneration, salvation, and resurrection.

. . ."So God created man in His own image, in the image of God created He him; male and female created He them."

"This is a great mystery, but I speak concerning Christ and the Church." The mysterious image of God in which man was created refers originally not to one separate part of the human being, but to the true unity of its two essential aspects, the male and the female. The relation that God has to His creation and that Christ has to His Church must be the relation of the husband to the wife. Those words are generally known, but their meaning is little understood. As God creates the universe, as Christ builds the Church, so must man create and build his feminine complement. It is, of course, an elementary truth that man stands for the active and woman for the passive principle and that he ought to have a formative influence upon her mind and character; we are concerned, however, not with this superficial relation, but with the "great mystery" of which Saint Paul speaks. That great mystery is essentially analogous to, though not identical with, the relation between the human and the divine.

. . . God's relation to the creature is that of everything to nothing, i.e., of the absolute fullness of being to the pure potency of being; Christ's relation to the Church is that of actual to potential perfection, which is being raised into actuality; but the relation between husband and wife is that between two differently acting but equally imperfect potencies which attain perfection only through a process of interaction. Or, to put it differently, God receives nothing, i.e., gains no increase from the creature, but gives everything to it; Christ receives no increase from the Church in perfection, and gives all perfection to it, but He does receive from the Church increase in the fullness of His collective body; finally, man and his feminine *alter ego* complete each other both really and ideally, attaining perfection through interaction only. Man can creatively reinstate God's image in the living object of his love only by reinstating that image in himself as well; but he has no power of his own to do it, for if he had, he would not need any reinstatement; and not having the power, he must receive it from God. Hence man (husband) is the creative and formative principle in relation to his feminine complement, not in himself, but as a mediator of the divine power.

. . . The work of true love is based first of all upon *faith*. The basic meaning of love, as already shown, consists in recognizing the absolute significance of another personality. . . .

If for me, standing on this side of the transcendental world, a certain ideal object appears as a product of my imagination, this does not prevent it from being fully real in another, higher realm of being. And although our actual life lies outside that higher realm, our mind is not quite a stranger to it, and we can have some speculative knowledge of its laws. And this is its first and fundamental law: while in this world separate and isolated existence is an actual fact, and unity is only a concept or idea, there, on the contrary, it is the unity, or, more exactly, the all-unity, that is real, and isolation and separateness have only potential and subjective existence.

It follows that the being of *this* person in the transcendental sphere is not individual in our sense of the term. There, i.e., in truth, an individual person is only a ray, living and actual, but an inseparable ray of one ideal light—of the one universal substance. This ideal person or personified idea is merely an individualization of the all-unity which is indivisibly present in each one of its individual expressions. And so when we imagine the ideal form of the beloved, the all-embracing unity itself is given us in that form. How, then, is it to be conceived?

God as one, in distinguishing from Himself His "other," i.e., all that is not He, unites that other to Himself, positing it before Him together and all at once, in an absolutely perfect form and consequently as a unity. This *other* unity, distinct, though inseparable, from God's primary unity, is in relation to God a passive, feminine unity, for in it eternal emptiness (pure potency) receives the fullness of the divine life. But though *at the basis of* this eternal femininity lies pure nothing, for God this nothing is eternally concealed by the image of absolute perfection which He bestows upon it. This perfection, which for us is still in the process of being realized, for God, i.e., in truth, actually *is* already. The ideal unity toward which our world is striving, and which is the goal of the cosmic and historical process, cannot be merely a subjective idea (for whose idea could it be?), but truly is the eternal object of divine love, as God's eternal "other."

This living ideal of the divine love, prior to our love, contains the secret of its idealization. The idealization of the lower being is the beginning of the realization of the higher, and herein lies the truth of love's exaltation. The complete realization, the transformation of an individual feminine being into a ray of the divine eternal feminine, inseparable from its radiant source, will be the real, both the subjective and the objective, reunion of the individual human being with the Deity, the reinstatement of the living and immortal image of God in man.

The object of true love is not simple but twofold: we love, first, the ideal entity (ideal not in an abstract sense, but in the sense of belonging to a higher realm of being) which we must bring into our real world, and secondly, we love the natural human entity which provides the real personal material for such realization. . . .

In sexual love rightly understood and truly realized this

divine essence finds a means for its complete and final embodiment in the individual life of man, for the deepest and at the same time most outwardly sensible and real union with him. Hence those glimpses of unearthly bliss, that breath of heavenly joy, which accompany even imperfect love and make it the highest felicity for men and gods—*hominum divumque voluptas*. And hence, too, the deepest suffering of love that is incapable of holding its true object and recedes from it further and further.

A legitimate place is thus provided for the element of adoration and infinite devotion which is so characteristic of love, but so meaningless if it refers solely to its earthly object apart from the heavenly. . . .

If the root of false existence is impenetrability, i.e., mutual exclusion of one another's being, true life means living in another as in oneself or finding in another positive and absolute completion of one's own being. The foundation and pattern of this true life is and always shall be sexual or conjugal love. But as we have seen, that love cannot be realized without a corresponding transformation of the whole external environment; the integration of the individual life necessarily requires the same integration in the domains of social and of cosmic life. . . .

The relations between the individual members of society must be brotherly (and filial with respect to past generations and their social representatives), and their connection with different social wholes—local, national, and, finally, universal—must be still more inward, many-sided, and significant. The bond between the active personal human principle and the all-embracing idea embodied in the social spiritual-bodily organism must be a living *syzygic* relation.[1] Not to submit to one's social environment and not to dominate it, but to be in loving interaction with it, serve for it as an active fertilizing principle of movement, and to find in it the fullness of vital conditions and possibilities—that is the relation of the true human personality, not only to its immediate social environment and to its nation, but to humanity as a whole. . . .

1. From the Greek *syzygia*—conjunction. I have to introduce this new term, for I cannot find another better one in the existing terminology.

. . . As the all-embracing idea becomes actually realized through the strengthening and greater perfection of its individually human elements, the forms of false separation or impenetrability of beings in space and time inevitably grow less pronounced. But in order that they should be abolished altogether, and all individuals, both past and present, should finally become eternal, the process of integration must transcend the limits of social or strictly human life and include the cosmic sphere from which it started. In ordering the physical world the divine idea threw the veil of natural beauty over the kingdom of matter and death; through man, through the activity of his universally rational consciousness, it must enter that kingdom *from within* in order to give life to nature and make its beauty eternal. In this sense it is essential to change man's relation to nature. He must enter with it too into the same relation of syzygic unity which determines his true life in the personal and social sphere. . . .

[VLADIMIR SOLOVYOV]

Foundations of Theoretical Philosophy *

II

In the realm of moral ideas, philosophical thought, for all its
formal independence, is in essence directly subordinate to the
life-interest of the pure will, which strives toward the good and
demands of the intellect a more precise and full elucidation of
true goodness, as opposed to everything that seems to be or is
considered good without in fact being so.

We wish first, by virtue of our moral nature, to live in accordance with true goodness and *for that reason* to know its true
essence and real demands. At the same time we simply wish to
know—to know the truth for its own sake. This second wish,
too, is undoubtedly approved by our conscience, which thus
antecedently affirms the root unity of goodness and truth—
obviously necessary because without that unity the very idea of
true goodness, on which all morality is based, would have no
meaning. If goodness as such must certainly be true, then it
is clear that in essence truth cannot be something contradictory
or alien to goodness. . . .

Life and knowledge are of one essence and are inseparable
in their supreme norms; but at the same time there remains a
distinction between the practical and the theoretical attitude
toward an object: the good will and true knowledge, for all
their inseparability, remain two different inner states, two particular modes of existence and activity. This is in keeping with
both the unity of and the distinction between moral and theoretical philosophy.

* Translated for this volume by Vlada Tolley and James P. Scanlan, from
V. S. Solovyov, "Osnovy teoreticheskoy filosofii," *Sobraniye sochineni*, 10
vols., 2nd ed., St. Petersburg, 1911-1914, IX, 90-111, 112-130.

III

Formally, the idea of goodness demands of every agent a *conscientious* attitude toward the object of his activity. This demand has universal significance and brooks no exceptions. On the strength of it a theoretical thinker is obliged first and foremost to investigate truth conscientiously. Even though he believes the truth is given or revealed, he feels a need and an obligation to test or prove his belief by independent thought. A philosopher differs from a non-philosopher not in the content of his convictions, but in the fact that he considers it impermissible to admit *any* assertion of principle into his theories finally without antecedent analysis and verification by rational thought.

Although, strictly speaking, philosophical interest has to do with nothing but truth, we cannot stop at this excessively broad general definition. Moralists expounding true goodness or theologians interpreting the true revelation of Deity are also occupied with truth, but they are not all philosophers. Similarly, interest in truth is by no means the distinguishing feature of philosophy as compared with mathematics, history, and the other special sciences, which all strive for truth. If, thus, the distinctive character of philosophy does not consist in the fact that it has to do with truth, it can only be defined by *how* it has to do with truth, from what quarter it approaches truth, and what it seeks in truth.

We call a mind philosophical which is not content even with the firmest assurance of a truth if that assurance is unanalyzed, but accepts only truth which is certified, which has answered all the demands of thought. All sciences, of course, strive for validity; but there is relative validity and absolute or unconditional validity. True philosophy can ultimately be satisfied only with the latter.

It should not be inferred from this that philosophy is certified in advance and is guaranteed of attaining absolutely valid truth. Philosophy *may* never find such truth, but it is *obliged* to seek it *to the finish*, halting at no boundaries, accepting nothing without verification, demanding an analysis of every assertion. If it found itself unable to give an affirmative answer to the question of absolutely valid truth, it would still have achieved a great though negative result—the clear knowledge that nothing which is represented as absolute truth does in fact have that significance. *Either* silence, by valid thinking, all possible doubts concerning accepted truth and in this way justify your confidence in it, *or* candidly acknowledge that in the last analysis everything known is doubtful and renounce theoretical certitude—here are two positions worthy of the philosophical mind, between which it is obliged to make a resolute choice.

It goes without saying, as Descartes has already noted, that an antecedent intention never to stop doubting is as repugnant to the essence of philosophical thought as an advance decision to eliminate all doubts at any price, if only by means of arbitrary limitations on investigation. Preconceived skepticism and preconceived dogmatism simply manifest two types of intellectual timidity: the skeptic is afraid of believing and the dogmatist is afraid of losing his faith (which apparently is not very strong); and both are afraid of the very process of thinking, knowing not to what end, desirable or undesirable, it may lead them. But for one whose calling is to be a philosopher there is nothing more desirable than a truth which has been comprehended, or verified by thought; that is why he loves the actual process of thinking, as the only means of achieving the desired end, and why he devotes himself to that end without any extraneous fears or apprehensions. To him still more than to the poet can be applied the commandment:

By a free road follow your free mind's bent.

IV

Thus the essential feature of philosophical speculation is that it strives for absolute *validity*, tested by thinking which is free and consistent, which proceeds to the very end. The particular sciences, as philosophers have long since noted, are content with relative validity, accepting one or another set of assumptions without verification. No physicist is impelled by his pursuits to raise and resolve the question of the true essence of matter or the validity—in the sense of real existence—of space, motion, or the external world in general. He *assumes* this validity on the strength of general opinion, the particular errors of which he corrects without, however, subjecting it to general revision. In the same way the most critical historian, in investigating the validity of events in the temporal life of mankind, accepts without justifying it the common conception of time as a real medium within which historical phenomena arise and disappear. This is not to mention a great number of other assumptions accepted without verification by all the special sciences.

The distinctive character of philosophy in this respect is clear and indisputable. The particular sciences in their search for valid truth base themselves upon given data, accepted on faith as unalterable limits not admitting of further intellectual scrutiny (as, for example, space for geometry). That is why the validity achieved by the particular sciences is certainly only conditional, relative, and limited. Philosophy, as an enterprise of free thought, by its very essence cannot confine itself within such limits, and strives from the very beginning for unconditional or absolute validity.

In this respect philosophy is like religion, which also sets great store by the unconditional validity of the truth it affirms. Religion, however, assigns this unconditionality not to the form of thought but to the content of faith. Religious faith, in its own element, is not interested in the intellectual verification of its content: it affirms it with absolute confidence as truth given from on high or revealed. The philosophical mind will not deny such revelation in advance—that would be a prejudice improper to and unworthy of sound philosophy; but at the same time, even if it finds provisional reasons *supporting* religious truth, it cannot, without repudiating itself, repudiate its right to subject these reasons to free examination, to give itself and others a clear and consistent account of why it accepts this truth. This right of the philosophical mind has not only subjective but objective significance, since it draws its main force from one very simple but amazingly neglected circumstance—namely, that not one but *several* religions affirm the unconditional validity of their truth, demanding choice in their favor and thereby (whether they wish to or not) exposing their claims to investigation by free thought

—since otherwise choice would be a blind, arbitrary matter which it would be unworthy to desire of others and senseless to demand of them. While remaining within the bounds of reason and justice, the most zealous representative of any positive religion can desire of the philosopher only one thing: that through the free investigation of truth he arrive at the full inner accord of his convictions with the dogmas of the given revelation—an outcome which would be equally satisfactory to both sides.

V

If, as has now been pointed out, philosophical thought cannot find firm support in either sensory or religious experience, which present themselves to it as something to be tested, not as the bases for testing or the criteria of truth—then the question is, on what is philosophical thought based? What supports it and guides it? Where is the guarantee of its correctness and consequently of the validity of its results? . . .

It is clear that a *preliminary* answer to this question can only be highly general and indefinite, so as not to be bound up with some arbitrary or unanalyzed assumption. For the present we can only say that the criterion of validity for thought does not consist in anything external to it but is inherent in thought itself, in its own nature. Thought can rest on some representation or concept of an object as a valid truth when all its questions have been exhausted, when the matter is completely clear to it and the knowledge obtained satisfies it fully and conclusively. But what if it comes to rest sooner, before the end is reached? That, of course, can happen and only too often does happen with the thinking of Ivan Ivanovich and Pyotr Petrovich. If this thinking, having ceased, declares ingenuously: I am tired, I can't go any further!—then such a private misfortune is nothing to the case, for to assist the weak is the task of practical philanthropy, not theoretical philosophy. If, however, through self-delusion or an inclination toward charlatanism, thought stops and announces: I have reached the end, there is nowhere else to go, I have come to rest against the wall by which the peasants hang their homespun coats to the sky—then nothing prevents another, more *conscientious* thought from probing this wall thoroughly to see whether it, the sky, and all these peasant coats are only paper scenery.

Thus the standard of truth includes the idea of *conscientiousness:* genuine philosophical thought must be a *conscientious quest for valid truth to the finish.*

In demanding conscientiousness from thought, however, are we not introducing a moral element into theoretical philosophy and subordinating the latter to ethics? But has theoretical philosophy really committed itself in advance not to admit the moral element in any case, in any sense, and from any side? Such a commitment would, on the contrary, be a *prejudice* repugnant to the very essence of theoretical philosophy. So long as the moral element is demanded by the logical conditions of thought themselves, it not only can but must be taken as a basis of theoretical philosophy. So it is in the present case.

Let us try mentally to eliminate from philosophical thought this demand that it be a conscientious quest for truth *to the finish;* let us try to assert seriously that philosophical thought need not be conscientious and consistent. What in fact would such an assertion mean? Permission to deceive oneself and others in the quest for truth—i.e., to strive for truth by means of falsehood— is utter nonsense so long as the aim is truth itself. Consequently, to eliminate the demand for conscientiousness from philosophy is possible only if we have admitted into philosophy *other interests* apart from and contrary to the interest in truth. Whoever allows his thinking to digress from the search for pure truth, whoever finds it possible to act against his conscience in this endeavor, has, of course, some motive for doing so, the significance of which for him outweighs his interest in truth; if he does not remain loyal to truth to the finish, needless to say it is only because something else is more important and more valuable to him. But philosophy differs from everything else and the philosophical mind from every other simply in that the interest in pure truth is here the most important and valuable interest, and can be subordinated to no other. Consequently, to reject the conscientious search for truth to the finish is to reject philosophy itself.

Thus our requirement or initial criterion of truth is in fact nothing more than an analytic judgment which can be reduced to a simple identity: philosophical thought must be true to itself, or, still more simply: philosophy is philosophy, $A = A$. Evidently in the requirement of intellectual conscientiousness the moral interest coincides with the theoretical.

The demand for conscientiousness of this sort, or an unswerving quest for truth on the part of the philosopher, not only is very often violated in practice but sometimes is contested in principle on various plausible grounds. That is why I found it necessary to point out the logical nature of this demand, at the risk of appearing pedantic. But it is better to be taken for a pedant than for a smuggler.

VI

To be concerned with pure truth alone from the beginning to the end of the thinking process, without any arbitrary assumptions or extraneous aims—such a basic demand can engender doubt from another quarter, even after it has been accepted in principle. Where is the *guarantee* of its actual fulfillment, and where is the proof of its non-fulfillment in each case? Here the question is one not of the internal course of thinking itself but of the *external signs* by which one can evaluate its quality, once it has expressed itself objectively.

But though such signs may exist it is neither necessary nor possible to define them in advance: before thinking can become an object of alien evaluation, from the outside, it must be subjected to direct internal self-evaluation. It is as autonomous (self-legislative) as the moral will: You are your own supreme judge!

Within the thinking mind itself there is knowledge of the essential goodness or badness of its thinking in each actual case, whereas from the outside there can be presented to it only some such general demand, with some such general sanction, as: think conscientiously, be true to yourself, remain steadfast to the finish in the pure quest for truth, *or else* your thinking will not produce anything sound and satisfying. In other words, only real, authentic philosophizing creates real, authentic philosophy, only he who goes toward truth reaches it, $A = A$. This is the only basic criterion, but by outward signs alone philosophical thought cannot be identified unerringly any more than horses at a market can: in both cases enough gypsies will be found to fool you with their smooth talk.

The whole duty of the theoretical philosopher *as such* is simply to have the determination and the ability to abstract himself, in his enterprise, from all possible interests but the purely philosophical, to forget from the outset any other will but the will to possess the truth for its own sake.

But although theoretical thought can and must ignore the relationship of its object to the practical will, this does not mean, however, that it can consider its object apart from *every* relationship. Such a demand to think the object in its absolute unrelatedness would have no meaning, for the very act of thinking the object is a kind of relation between it and thought, and to be abstracted from this relation would mean for thought to be abstracted from itself. Without this relation the object would be completely unknown and unthinkable, i.e., it would not be present at all, there would be nothing to talk about, and there would not arise the very question of the validity of thought as regards knowledge, or the question of whether and under what conditions one has the right to take the existence of the object in thought, or in relation to thought, as evidence of its real existence and nature.

VII

Theoretical philosophy, in response to a purely intellectual interest, poses the question of truth in its relation to *knowledge,* or in other words examines its object not from the moral side or the practical side in general but solely from the side of its intellectual merit, which consists first and foremost in validity; and since the object does not exist for us otherwise than through our knowledge of it, so the question of the validity of the object is actually a question of the *validity of our knowledge* of it.

There is a great deal of diverse everyday knowledge, scientific knowledge, religious knowledge, which has its own *relative* validity which is quite sufficient for practical purposes. But the basic question of theoretical philosophy concerns the validity of knowledge in itself, in its essence. What is called knowledge in general is the agreement of a given thought of an object with the actual existence and character of the object. *How in general is such agreement possible, and how is its presence in each case certified?*

Doubtless we possess a type of knowledge the validity of which is absolute and is not subject to conscientious disputation; such knowledge must be taken as the starting point in solving the epistemological problem. But at the same time we must be careful. We must not begin with some abstract definition of this type of knowledge, for to every such definition there undoubtedly attach preconceived ideas and views which would make our reasoning at best unsatisfying and at worst delusive. In beginning with a general definition we necessarily violate the basic demand of conscientious thinking—not to admit arbitrary or unverified assumptions. Every abstract formula has so extended a boundary that there is no chance of closing it against thought-smugglers, who are always ready to pass, along with unquestionably legal currency, currency which has not been proved in the intellectual customhouse of truth and even currency which is simply counterfeit—delusion. Thus we must begin with a simple descriptive indication of such basic and indisputable knowledge, having seized it *in concreto*.

Today, after an early dinner, I was lying on the sofa with my eyes closed wondering whether one could consider the Platonic "Second Alcibiades" authentic. Opening my eyes I saw, first, hanging on the wall, a portrait of a deceased woman writer, and then by the opposite wall an iron stove, a desk, and some books. I arose and walked to the window; I could see Turkish bean plants beneath it with red flowers on them, a garden path, farther on a road, and beyond it the corner of a park. A kind of painful sensation arose, indefinite at first, but quickly taking shape as a recollection of a fine young fir tree in the park which a neighboring peasant named Firsan had thievingly chopped down to serve his own ends; I felt very sorry that the poor tree had been destroyed and very angry at the stupidity of this Firsan, who could have obtained the money he needed for the Nikolsky pub easily and without any violation of divine or human law by asking me for it. "He has met me and knows my face, he has greeted me, the anathema!" I decided to urge the proprietor of the park to take effective measures to protect it. The sight of the radiant day soothed my emotional agitation somewhat and aroused in me a desire to walk to the park to enjoy nature, but at the same time I felt an inclination to write about the epistemological problem; after some hesitation the second desire won out, I walked to the desk, picked up my pen—and woke up on the sofa.

Having come to my senses I was surprised at the clarity and reality of my dream, and walking up to the window I saw, of course, the same things I had seen in my dream, had the same feelings again, and after some vacillation between two desires— to go for a walk or to occupy myself with philosophy—I resolved upon the latter and began to write (beginning with the words, "theoretical philosophy, in response to a purely intellectual interest") that with which the reader is now familiar. For the reader's reassurance I hasten to mention that I was wide awake the rest of the day and fell asleep again only that night after having gone to bed.

From the facts described here as accurately as possible, on careful examination it is easy to draw evidence of two sorts— evidence of the presence in our knowledge of an element of absolute, immediate, and indisputable *validity* and evidence of the unalterable *limits* of such validity.

VIII

If during the dream just described I had been asked whether I knew that I was really seeing something, thinking of something, experiencing a certain feeling and desire, making a certain decision, performing a certain movement—in a word, undergoing all the states described—I would, of course, have said: yes, I know, and moreover I know with absolute validity, which does not require proof and is not subject to dispute. And subsequently, after awakening, I would be conscience-bound to reaffirm this answer of mine concerning the past dream. Even if it was not *in reality*, still it *was*. What [*chto*] (*was, quid*) I saw was not a reality at the given moment, but *that* [*chto*] (*dass, quod*) I *saw* it is a real and absolutely valid fact. Of course this validity belongs to the dream only while it is occurring; subsequent recollection can, in fact, be quite deceiving; but in that case the very fact of recollection, even though objectively false, remains nevertheless absolutely valid in the indicated sense, i.e., as a present subjective state. In general, asleep or awake, when we experience certain inner states and actions—sensations, ideas, emotional agitation, desires, decisions, and so on—we at the same time *know* that we are experiencing them. And this knowledge of fact—immediately and inseparably connected with the fact itself, always found with it, beside it, and therefore justly called *con-sciousness* [*so-znaniye*], *con-scientia*, *Bewusstsein* (i.e., Bei-*wusstsein*)—must be acknowledged as absolutely valid because here knowledge directly agrees with its object, thought is a simple repetition of fact, judgment is the expression of pure identity: A = A.

So long as this immediate identity between consciousness and its object is not violated, we find ourselves on a foundation of absolute validity and cannot err. So long as knowledge covers only the present fact, it is party to all the latter's certitude; between such knowledge—i.e., *pure consciousness*—and its object, not the keenest shaft of skepticism can be thrust.

The absolute self-validity of immediate [*nalichnoye*] consciousness is the fundamental truth of philosophy, and every broad cycle of philosophical evolution begins by asserting it. It was proclaimed with infantile delight at the threshold of ancient philosophy, in some of the Upanishads. We find its clearest account in the father of medieval philosophy, the blessed Augustine. And with it, twelve centuries later, Descartes initiated modern philosophy.

Pure consciousness or *knowledge of psychic immediacy* [*nalichnost*] pays for its absolute validity by the extreme narrowness of its limits. For all its indisputability this knowledge is in itself very scanty and can in no way satisfy the intellect's quest for truth. What if I do know with absolute validity the fact that I am experiencing something or other, that objects of some sort are presented to me, when this indisputable knowledge not only does not reveal to me the true nature of what is experienced and presented, but cannot even answer the question of whether I am experiencing and representing all this in a dream or in reality, since the subjective reality, which alone consciousness guarantees, is *equally valid* in both cases? And as soon as we wish to extend this testimony of consciousness beyond the bounds of inner immediacy we lose its absolute validity at once, and with the possibility of error there arises a legitimate basis for every kind of doubt.

You see before you a burning fireplace and with indisputable right affirm the absolute validity of that fact, i.e., the presence of a certain visual representation with definite features of color, shape, position, and so on. To this, but only to this, your consciousness testifies, immediately repeating the fact itself. But if you go further and begin to assert that all the qualities of the fireplace you are now sensing, as well as other qualities and relations which you are not experiencing at this moment but of which you are nonetheless convinced, such as the hardness and weight of the marble from which the fireplace is made, its chemical composition, and so on—if you assert that all these qualities belong to some real body existing independently of your present representation which is testified to by immediate consciousness, then obviously you are moving from the sphere of valid fact to the sphere of disputable assumptions, about which pure consciousness as such—i.e., the actual fact of consciousness—provides no direct evidence, and the erroneous character of which can soon be discovered. Unquestionably you do see this fireplace, but perhaps only in a dream, as I in the dream I described unquestionably had the sensation of seeing various objects and walking up to a window and then to a desk, whereas all the while I lay motionless on a sofa with my eyes closed. Thus, in this case your assertion concerning the material hardness and the independent reality of the fireplace you see could prove to be manifestly mistaken, for everyone agrees that dreams do not create solid and impenetrable bodies, and no one has yet ascribed independent existence to these or other elements of dreams apart from the actual occurrence of the dream.

But, dreaming aside, even if you were awake, pure consciousness of the fact that you are seeing this fireplace still does not contain any evidence or guarantee of the existence of the object itself: it could prove to be an optical illusion or hallucination.

The unquestionable fact that a person who affirms the given presence of a certain object may, however, in some cases prove to be completely deceived—i.e., to be taking the illusion of an object (a fireplace, for instance) for its reality—this fact does not in the least destroy the absolute validity of pure consciousness within its own bounds. For *in any case* there remains here the indisputable existence, for the given consciousness at the given moment, of that presentation which is signified by the word "fireplace" and which has certain definite features of visual outline, position, and so on—features which are *the same* in dreams, hallucinations, optical illusions, and normal perception, for a fireplace is always a fireplace and not a chessboard or a samovar, whether I see it in a dream or when awake, in a mirror or directly in front of me. In all these cases the same valid fact is present: a given consciousness is directly occupied with a certain definite presentation. The testimony of pure consciousness is limited to this fact and consequently cannot err. To the question of the actual reality as opposed to the mere appearance of a given object, immediate consciousness *cannot* give an *erroneous* answer, first because it gives *no* answer to this question and second because it never raises it. While I am directly conscious of the presence of a fireplace before me I do not ask: what is it?

The very possibility of illusion of any kind is in fact created by the initial *directness* of immediate consciousness, i.e., by the fact that it does not antecedently distinguish the appearance of an object from its reality, being occupied solely by the presentation itself in its actual immediacy, which is *identical* in both cases. If this were not so, if in the immediate consciousness of actually experienced states there were already included some distinction of the seeming from the real, then obviously no mistakes on this score would be possible: having a dream, I should always immediately observe that it was a dream; undergoing a hallucination or an illusion, I should at once see that it was a hallucination or an illusion—and consequently would not even succeed in undergoing it in a psychological sense, but would experience only a physiological anomaly.

As a matter of fact, however, in pure consciousness there is no distinction between the seeming and the real: for it everything is equally actual. But when the reflection that accompanies consciousness takes this absolute self-validating character of subjective immediacy as an indication of an external reality, then there arise those errors of judgment which since ancient times have given cause for skepticism—a skepticism, however, directed not at the data of consciousness, which are in no way subject to doubt, but only at certain of the conclusions drawn from them.

We have no right to assert in advance that there are no bases or signs at all for distinguishing the seeming from the truly existing, dreams from reality, hallucinations from real occurrences; on the contrary, we are sure that such bases and signs must exist. But undoubtedly they are *not found in the immediacy of the fact we are conscious of*, and the direct self-validity inherent in this immediacy cannot extend to them. We know that the mental activity that accompanies actual consciousness is subject to errors, and if we can manage to free ourselves from these errors and attain complete validity, it will be a different kind of validity, which goes beyond the bounds of the elementary self-evidence of subjective fact. Simple consciousness (in the sense explained) is the basic and initial, but fortunately not the only, type of knowledge.

IX

If, as we have seen, actual and absolutely self-validating consciousness cannot guarantee in every particular case that the facts given in it have a reality separate and independent from it—facts such as sensory representations of extended bodies, spatial motions, and so on—then of course we have no right to assert that the reality of the external world in itself is given in immediate consciousness. Actually there is given a certain aggregate of facts sensed, represented, thought of—called "the world" —but it is impossible to find in primary consciousness, by its very nature, any epistemological evaluation of these facts, or of this fact. The very demand for such evaluation, or the question of the independent reality of the external world, cannot arise in immediate consciousness: it cannot be *given* but can only be *put*.

As soon as this question is raised in reflective thought, there also springs up within the latter a first, provisional answer: we *believe* in the reality of the external world, and the task of philosophy is to give this belief a rational justification, explanation, or proof.[1] To renounce this task on the pretext that the reality of the external world is *given in immediate consciousness* is to put an arbitrary and false *opinion* in the place of philosophy. The vagueness and groundlessness of this opinion, for all its prevalence, are already evident from the fact that it peacefully coexists with the initial assertion that we *believe* in the real existence of the external world. This assertion is accepted without objection and indeed one cannot sensibly say anything against it, whereas it would be a completely absurd assertion if the reality of the external world were given in immediate consciousness, for one cannot *believe* [*verit*] in something that is present, or found in immediacy. I would be uttering an absurdity if I were to maintain that I *believe* I am now sitting at a desk and writing this discourse: I do not believe it, I am conscious of it as an immediate reality, experienced rather than affirmed. I can believe, and in fact am quite certain, that this immediate fact is taking place not in a dream but in reality: *that* is an object of belief (subject, then, to rational justification) precisely because it is not given in immediate consciousness, which itself says nothing about the distinction between reality and appearance; and the extension of the inner self-validity of immediate consciousness to a question not subject to it—the question of external reality—leads, as we know, to errors. Even now my confidence that I am awake could, speaking generally, prove to be mistaken; and if this abstract possibility of error has no serious

1. Sometimes belief [*vera*] is called *immediate* knowledge, and comparatively speaking this is true, since the fact of belief is more basic and less mediated than scientific knowledge or philosophical meditation. Similarly, people speak of immediate feelings or sensations (of the infinite or of God, for example), again not in an absolute sense but only by opposition to reflection (see above). In theoretical philosophy, and particularly in epistemology, these expressions should be avoided and the word "immediate" reserved for the pure consciousness of given inner states as facts.

significance in the present case it is only because I can justify my confidence by various rational considerations, while it would never occur to me to cite immediate consciousness, which has neither a deciding nor an advisory voice in this matter since in its self-sufficing simplicity it does not know the difference between appearance and reality, between dreaming and waking.

Our immediate consciousness of a seeming world so little guarantees the reality of that world itself that so sober a thinker as Descartes considers doubt of that reality a necessary prerequisite for the philosophical investigation of truth. Such doubt would be quite impossible if within the immediate consciousness of the supersubjective actuality or immediacy of the facts constituting the world there were also to be given the independent reality of these facts. But Descartes understood that the former does not guarantee the latter, and the soundness of his preliminary doubt only underscores the unsuccessfulness of his subsequent attempts to cross to solid ground without a sturdy bridge.

X

The self-validity of immediate consciousness, as an internal fact, does not guarantee the validity of the objects of consciousness, as external realities. But is it not possible directly to infer from this consciousness the true reality of a *conscious subject*, as a particular independent being or thinking substance? Descartes thought such an inference possible and necessary, and many have followed him on this point right up to the present day. I myself once adopted this point of view, which I now regard as containing a very material misunderstanding. So as not to compound that misunderstanding with still another, I must first of all declare that now as before I am firmly confident of my own existence as well as of the existence of all the human beings of both sexes listed and even not listed on the census rolls of the various countries. But I am more interested than before in the rational grounds for such confidence, not only for the sake of their demonstrative force, but also for the sake of that accuracy and precision which rational investigation imparts to our actual understanding of the object of our confidence; for without such investigation a person can have the greatest confidence in the truth of his opinion without properly knowing *what* in fact he is confident of.

Thus the question is: do we have, in simple or direct consciousness, self-validating evidence of the existence of one who is conscious, as the true subject? Is the existence of one's ego or self a self-evident fact of consciousness, which can be expressed in logically binding form?

XI

In order to connect the validity of the existence of a subject with that simple self-validity of consciousness which is inherent in each of its states, Descartes ingeniously takes the very state of *doubting* consciousness. Though I may doubt, he says, the existence of everything, I cannot doubt the existence of the doubter himself, because it is present in the very fact of doubt. *Dubito ergo sum*, or, more generally, *cogito ergo sum*.[2] But is this the case?

The father of modern philosophy began his work soundly by starting from the immediate validity of direct or pure consciousness, i.e., knowledge of given psychic states as such. But was he right in extending this self-validity or self-evidence to the conviction of the existence of the subject himself? One can reproach Descartes, not, of course, for abandoning the preliminary skepticism of his method, but only for doing so too hastily.

By asserting the *indubitability* of the existence of a subject, Descartes at once makes his position *dubitable*. He actually has to insist that it is *impossible* to doubt the true existence of the subject. Yet such doubt in fact exists. Despite encountering it as a fact, a Cartesian would have to deny it, i.e., deny a real phenomenon on grounds of its impossibility, against which a skeptic could with full right advance the opposite argument: I actually doubt, consequently such doubt is possible—*ab esse ad posse valet consequentia*. In any case, Cartesianism must yield

---

2. Although the particle *ergo* makes this assertion look like a formal deduction, the assertion is in reality—as has long since been noted—simply an expression of an assumed self-evident fact. Descartes himself in one of his letters calls his principle *"une connaissance intuitive"* (*Oeuvres choisies de Descartes*, ed. Garnier, p. 414).

its first position to skepticism: the very fact of dispute proves that it is not a matter of *self-evident* truth; of such there is no disputing. To defend the Cartesian position it is necessary to prove that a skeptic who doubts his own existence is thinking incorrectly, that he lacks clear and distinct ideas of the terms of the question, and so on. Thus instead of a starting point for thought we now have a subject for investigation.

Are sufficiently clear and distinct ideas of the terms of the question found in Descartes? "I see very clearly," he says, "that in order to think, one must be." (*"Je vois très-clairement, que pour penser, il faut être." Discours de la méthode, 4-ème partie.*) However, for this position to be made objectively clear and distinct there would have to be the most exact explication of the meaning of the verb "to be" (*être*), which unquestionably can be used in various senses. Descartes refers to his "very clear" judgment that thinking presupposes being in explaining his fundamental principle, "I think, therefore I am," the intuitive character of which (see above) evidently does not secure it against unclarity. Thus it must be subjected to diligent examination.

XII

We have before us three terms: thinking (*cogito*, je *pense*), being (ergo *sum*, donc je *suis*), and that subject to whom each of them equally belongs, who thinks and thereby exists. Of these three terms Descartes actually clarified only the first—thinking. In various places in his philosophical works it is shown perfectly clearly and indisputably that by "thinking" he means any inner psychic state of which we are *conscious as such*, i.e., irrespective of its real or assumed objects and likewise independently of any kind of evaluation of this state from the standpoint of any theoretical or practical norms. The thinking from which Descartes proceeds is only *the observed fact of a psychic occurrence*, and nothing more—the same thing we identified above as *consciousness* in the narrow sense, as the direct, simple, or immediate *form* of consciousness which is identical with its content. Thinking in that sense is something self-validating and cannot give rise to any doubt, argument, or question. The same cannot be said of the *thinker* or subject.

Of course, our consciousness of ourselves is an indubitable fact, but *what* exactly are we conscious of when we are conscious of ourselves? We do not find a clear and definite answer in Descartes. He everywhere *assumes* that thinking belongs to some sort of special reality distinct from the body, which he indifferently calls "soul" (*âme*), "spirit" (*esprit*), a "thinking thing" (*res cogitans, chose qui pense*), finally an "intelligent substance" (*substance intelligente*). When it was objected that the true substratum of thinking can be found in the body and that therefore the incorporeality of the soul can be inferred from the fact of thinking only by assuming precisely what has to be proved, Descartes answered: I recognize in myself *thinking, to which I have given the name spirit, and by that name I do not wish to designate anything other than that which thinks (rien de plus qu'une chose qui pense)*; thus I did not assume that spirit is incorporeal, but proved this in my Sixth Meditation, and consequently I have not fallen into *petitio principii.*[3] Actually, in the Sixth Meditation the incorporeality of *thinking* is proved, but from this it is impossible to draw any conclusions about the thinker, as something *different* from thinking. If there is no such difference at all (which is very close to the meaning of the words cited) then why give two names with such different senses to the same fact?

Undoubtedly there is thinking (in Descartes' sense), as a fact of *observed* sensations, representations, emotions, and *formed* concepts, judgments, conclusions, decisions. One of the concepts that arises in thought is the concept of the ego or subject, which has the peculiarity of being connected with all other mental facts (or given states) as an attendant secondary act. Let us assume there appears or is seen a red circle on a square green field; the primary fact of consciousness in this case is simply that such a circle is observed on such a field: there it is! But at once there is superadded the act of attaching this particular fact to a whole series or group of such facts, connected by a single

3. *Oeuvres choisies de Descartes,* ed. Garnier, p. 180.

mental subject; and thus it comes out: *I see* a red circle on a green square. As a function of an indefinite series of psychic facts, this *I* naturally is singled out from the aggregate of these facts, is made a common denominator, so to speak, and takes on the aspect of something independent—i.e., the idea arises that the logical subject of the series of conscious phenomena is the expression of something more real than these phenomena. But what is it? . . .

XIII

. . . Thinking presupposes the existence of a thinker. We do not yet know, however, what being or existence is (except that which is given in pure consciousness and about which there is no question), but the main thing is that we still have not found out what this thinker himself is (aside from thought and the concept of a thinker appearing in pure consciousness). Clearly, however, there is no sense in raising or deciding the question of the existence of something when it is not known what that something is. When Descartes, to express the essence of the subject, calls it *res cogitans, substantia intellectualis, seu spiritualis,* we know (from inner experience or pure consciousness) only the import of the participles and adjectives, while the substantives remain obscure. The terms *res* and *substantia*—which must designate precisely the subject himself insofar as he is something more than the attribute of thinking—these principal terms are taken by Descartes, without any critical examination, from that very scholasticism which methodical doubt should have thrown overboard first of all and which our philosopher generally treats with great disdain. In his *Meditations* and the supplements to them, he gives no explanation or derivation of these terms. In the *Principia* there is only a scholastic definition of substance, without any indication of any real content which this concept might have.

Descartes' thinking subject is an impostor without a philosophical passport. Formerly he occupied a humble cell in a scholastic monastery, as some *entitas, quidditas,* or even *haecceitas.* Hastily changing clothes he escaped from the monastery, proclaimed "*cogito ergo sum,*" and held for a time the throne of modern philosophy. But not one of his followers could clearly explain whence this ruler of men's minds had come or who he was. . . .

XIV

From the indubitable and self-validating fact of thinking, the author of the *Discourse on Method* jumps directly to a metaphysical subject, inherited from the scholastics, but proving to have even less content in his works than in theirs. Two other different concepts of the subject escaped his attention, and this is the first distinction one must make who wishes *bene docere*.[4]

When one says, "I think," the *I* can mean either the pure subject of thought or the empirical subject, i.e., the given living individuality—in other words, the subject in either an abstract or a concrete sense. Failing from the very beginning to make this essential distinction with sufficient clarity and distinctness, Descartes fell into a fatal confusion, mixing together the characteristics of both concepts of the subject and illegitimately creating a third—an undoubted mongrel, for on the one hand Descartes' spiritual substance is so abstract that it becomes indistinguishable from *thinking in general* (see above), while on the other hand it is an individual being or thing (*res, chose*) seated in the middle of the brain of each separate person. I am not saying that aside from the Cartesian mongrel there could not be a true third concept of the subject. But to begin with we must clearly differentiate the first two.

The pure subject of thinking is a *phenomenological* fact no less but also no more valid than any other; i.e., it is absolutely valid, but only as part of the immediate content of consciousness, or as a phenomenon in the proper, strictest sense of the word. When the thought of the ego appears in consciousness, obviously this ego is a fact of psychic immediacy, or direct consciousness. The ego is actually given or appears, the same as everything else. When I am conscious of myself as seeing this portrait hanging on the wall, both terms of the given relation have, of course, the same validity. This is clear both to common opinion or naive realism, and to philosophical reflec-

4. An old rule: *qui bene distinguit bene docet.*

tion. From the former point of view, both the ego and that which is given in my visual presentation exist with equal reality and independently of each other, and if *I* remain myself and retain my reality unchanged whether I look at this object or at some other, or even do not look at anything at all, then indeed this wall with the portrait on it also will remain (for naive opinion) the same real object whether anyone looks at it or not. Such a naive opinion is eliminated by methodical doubt, which shows that indisputable reality belongs to this wall only as the content of a given presentation, which may not correspond to any other reality; but in precisely the same way the ego seeing this wall has self-validating existence only as the subject of the presentation or other given psychic state, and we have no philosophical right to ascribe to it an indisputable or evident reality *beyond the bounds* of such given states—all the more since we are even unable to say plainly what in fact this subject would be beyond the bounds of its phenomenological existence or immanent appearance.

There is, it is true, a difference between the pure ego and the psychic states with which it is correlated: the latter are diverse and changeable, while the mental subject accompanying them all is one and the same. But this undoubted difference between the mobile circumference of consciousness and its fixed center does not go beyond the bounds of the phenomenological or immanent sphere. From the fact that all sorts of psychic states are correlated with one and the same thought of an ego, it by no means follows that this ego is not a thought but something else. A permanent member of a court does not in that capacity represent a court of higher instance.

It would be another matter if there were a consciousness of creative activity on the part of our ego in the actual origination of its representations, feelings, desires, and so on; if they differed in that the ego appeared in consciousness as a creative energy or true act, while everything else was characterized only as its passive work; if, for example, now, in looking at this wall with the portrait on it, I were immediately conscious that *it is produced by me*, by my own inner action, and also were conscious of *how* this is done. But not only with respect to such representations, which are connected with the so-called "outer senses" and are taken by naive opinion for independent realities, but also with respect to the simpler inner phenomena such as desires and emotions, there is no consciousness of them as products of subjective creativity. Everyone is conscious of himself as desiring and feeling, but as far as is known no one, awake or even dreaming, has ever been conscious of himself as the creator of his desires and feelings, i.e., as their real cause or sufficient reason. Expressing this fact in scholastic terms it must be said that *I am conscious of myself always as only the subject of my psychic states or passions and never as their substance.*[5]

Thus on grounds of immediate actuality there is no reason to ascribe to the subject of consciousness *as such* another reality besides the phenomenological. We find the subject to be a constant form linking psychic states in all their diversity, a changeless but empty and featureless channel through which the stream of psychic existence flows. And if we nonetheless do not attribute to ourselves or to our ego such emptiness and featurelessness, it is only because for the self-validating subject of consciousness we substitute something else, namely our empirical individuality, which of course can be quite full of content but in return—alas!—does not embody the self-evident immediate reality which belongs to the pure ego or phenomenological subject. When I am thinking, I cannot doubt myself as a thinker or this ego as a phenomenological condition of the given process of thinking, but nothing prevents me from doubting the validity of that very empirical individuality which up to that point had represented the real and constant embodiment of this ego or had been identified with it. In this sense one can, and as a preliminary should, doubt one's own existence. There is no logical contradiction here, for the doubter and the object of doubt are not identical: the first is the constant and unchanging subject of consciousness—the pure ego—while the second is that concrete, "processing" (*werdende*) individual, changing in its outlines and content, from which unphilosophical *opinion* does not distinguish the thinking subject as such. Practically, the existence of this

5. The etymology of the two words *subjectum* and *substantia* corresponds to this: the first contains a passive participle, the second an active.

concrete ego or human individuality is assumed as indubitable, but to remove the question concerning it from the realm of theoretical or methodical doubt would be to make of philosophy, instead of verified knowledge of absolute truth, only correct rational opinion. . . .

XV

If the so-called deceits of sensation (illusions and hallucinations) entitle us to doubt the validity of sensation as evidence of the objective reality of the physical world, then the deceits of self-consciousness which are observed (though not so frequently) impel us equally to doubt its evidence as to the authentic reality of our psychic subject.

Not long ago it was reported in a professional publication that during an experiment in hypnotism in France a modest young working girl, under the influence of suggestion, imagined herself, judging by her expressions, gestures, words, and actions, to be first a drunken fireman and then the Archbishop of Paris. Without vouching, of course, for the complete validity of this fact, I cite it simply as an example of the many cases of split personality, disturbed personality, and the like to which competent observers have testified and in which science is interested. Clearly such facts do, and would even if there were not nearly so many of them, radically undermine the imaginary self-validity of our personal self-consciousness, or its ordinary confidence in the essential, and not merely the formal or phenomenological, identity of the ego. Needless to say, it was not the number of dreams but the very fact of dreaming itself that was significant for Descartes' doubt as to the reality of the external world. But if the fact that sleeping people take subjective illusions for external reality also shakes the philosopher's absolute confidence in the reality which we seemingly perceive when awake, then the fact of hypnotic false consciousness of one's own ego must also arouse preliminary suspicion concerning that self-consciousness which seemingly is not connected with any such aberration. Philosophically speaking, we simply cannot admit an absolute and external criterion for the normality of our states or a *ready-made* guarantee that we are not under hypnosis or something like it in a particular case. And even speaking from an everyday point of view, just as the sleeper ordinarily does not know that he is asleep but unthinkingly considers himself awake—more exactly, does not raise the question of the difference between these states—so a hypnotized subject is unaware of his situation and directly takes outside suggestions for his own self-consciousness. It should be noted that the formal or phenomenological subject does not change at all while this is going on: *I, me, mine* remain as if nothing had happened. Nor is this surprising: in the subject of consciousness as such there is nothing to change, since in itself the subject has no content. It is only a form, which can with equal ease accommodate the psychic material of any individuality —modiste, fireman, or archbishop.

XVI

The fact of imaginary self-consciousness suggests, first of all, that perhaps the ancient Romans were not mistaken when, instead of saying "person" [*litso*] or "personality" [*lichnost*] they said "mask" [*lichina*] ("*persona*" originally meant "mask"). If in one case such as that cited above, the persons forming the empirical self-consciousness of a given individual are acknowledged without question even by common opinion to be hypnotic masks involuntarily put on by a subject of another sex and calling, then philosophically we cannot deny, *a priori* and without investigation, the possibility of the same being true in any other case. Just as an empirical subject conscious of himself as a drunken fireman or even as the Archbishop of Paris can in fact be by common consent a young modiste, so it is possible that the Vladimir Solovyov now given in my self-consciousness, who is writing a chapter on theoretical philosophy, is in reality only a hypnotic mask put on somehow by Queen Ranavalo of Madagascar or by Madame Virginia Zucchi; and if I have no positive reasons or grounds for admitting such a metaprosopopoeia [trans-personification] as a fact, there is also no philosophical right to deny its possibility in advance and absolutely.

Let us assume that I do not seriously think I could be only the hypnotic mask of a strange woman or man; but in exactly the same way I do not seriously think at the present moment that this room I see around me and this garden I see through the window can be only subjective states of my consciousness. I am firmly confident of the manifest reality of these objects. But not long before this I myself was convinced that one cannot rely on such confidence absolutely and that methodical doubt of the reality of the external world is not an idle mental game. Of course, even Descartes did not seriously think that the whole world around him might be a dream, a product of his mind, or an illusion of the senses; still it was not in vain that he made this hypothesis the foundation of philosophy, and if we can reproach him for anything it is only for abandoning this foundation too hastily and, instead of erecting on it a solid edifice of verified thought, beginning to build dogmatic card houses on the shifting sands of half-naive and half-pedantic realism.

In any case, the living *force* of the conviction which in practice eliminates doubt, the logical *right* to demand an account of this conviction, and finally the philosophical *duty* not to deny this demand—all these things are entirely the same for both sorts of evidence: the evidence of empirical sensation for the real existence of external objects as well as the evidence of empirical self-consciousness for the true reality of our psychic subject. And the value of methodical doubt is also the same for both.

I should not like either to underestimate or to exaggerate the importance of such doubt. Philosophical thought must be sincere, and I frankly confess that I am convinced not only of the real existence of the natural world and of everything that dwells within it, and not only of the existence of my soul and body and of the identity of my personality, but furthermore am convinced that with God's help I can philosophically justify my conviction. But precisely for this reason provisional methodical doubt concerning both outer and inner reality is valuable, for this doubt not only initiates the philosophical process of verifying our opinions—it also determines the desired end of this process, which will never be a simple return to the old belief but must be expressed in a new, better understanding of the world, not only formally more fully comprehended but profoundly transformed in essence. I cannot guarantee such a result in advance for future philosophy, but I know that without provisional doubt of *all* dogmatic views it is quite impossible. Concerning the external world, however, the job is already half done. If at the present time the positions of subjective idealism, solipsism, and illusionism hardly seem tempting or dangerous to any philosopher, on the other hand of course no thinker will be found who would attribute to the elements and forms of the physical world, to matter, space, and time, that completely independent reality which they have for minds untouched by critical doubt. But the same kind of revolution or perhaps a much greater one must be effected by the consistent philosophical examination of our ideas concerning the elements and forms of the inner world; and the first condition for this is methodical doubt of propositions, taken on faith, concerning the psychic subject. This doubt is not a game of blindman's buff but is a necessary stimulus to the reformative work of thought.

XVII

If, in the ordinary course of life, doubt of one's own existence or of one's personal identity has no serious importance practically, still less can the pseudo-rational considerations currently advanced in opposition to such doubt be taken seriously philosophically. It is pointed out, for instance, that the hypnotic falsification of self-consciousness is a transient state of brief duration brought about by definite artificial causes, whereas normal consciousness of one's personal identity is continuous and is connected with the totality of past experience. But, not to mention that cases of split and disturbed personality sometimes are of long duration, recur regularly, and are independent of evident external hypnosis, by itself the view cited makes sense only because of our inveterate realism.

Of course it seems to me that I did not just begin yesterday to conceive of myself as this subject rather than some other, that my self-consciousness embraces a considerable sum of phenomena of the past. But what actually is this sum of the past? Is it in my pocket, or in a bank account? Actually it exists at this moment only as a *recollection*, i.e., as a state of consciousness inseparable from what I am experiencing *now*, and needless to say if there is an illusion of self-consciousness it can also include an illusion of memory: being conscious of myself as a doctor of philosophy and not as the Queen of Madagascar, naturally I can recollect, i.e., represent as past, university disputations, lectures, publications, and not scenes of some sort from African life. But instead of proof of my personal identity, this could be an association of illusions in time, just as in a dream there is such an association of illusions in space: transported to Scotland in a dream, I see Scottish lakes and hills. And of course if that modiste who imagined herself to be the Archbishop of Paris were led to recall her past, in all probability she would recall not how she was apprenticed to a milliner but how she was ordained to the priesthood.

XVIII

Confidence in the self-identity of the empirical subject is precarious even independently of the facts revealed by hypnosis and other abnormal conditions. Once we question the independent reality of external beings and objects (and not to do so would mean to give up philosophy), we cannot logically refrain from questioning the reality of the empirical subject, since the latter is inseparably linked with an indefinite multitude of facts of external experience in space, time, and causation, and cannot have greater validity than they. Of course the reality of particular facts of external experience with which my existence is linked can be doubted without marked damage to my confidence in my independent existence as *this* person; but it is another matter when doubt comes to bear on a whole group of facts, or even on the totality of all facts.

My confidence that I exist as one Vladimir Solovyov, i.e., as the subject of this particular life-content, undoubtedly includes the confidence that I was born in Moscow in 1853 and christened in the Church of the Resurrection on Ostozhenka Street by a priest named Dobrov. Of course, if it were proved to me that this is a mistake—that actually I was born somewhere else in another year and was christened by another priest—that would not seriously disrupt my consciousness, particularly since the facts mentioned are ones I have accepted through trusting the testimony of others and not through my own recollection. But pursuing methodical doubt I must indeed allow something more: not only that I was not born in Moscow and so on, but further that Moscow itself does not exist in reality, that this city with all its streets and churches as well as the whole priestly order and even the very ceremony of christening—that all this exists only in my dreams, which can vanish at once without a trace. At this thought, of course, my self-consciousness must be strongly shaken, and the question necessarily arises: and I myself—who am I? And since such doubt as to the reality of facts must be admitted without limit concerning everything found in the world around us, and since all the data of my physical, spiritual, and social life, by its very content or by the very conception of this life, are inseparable from the facts of the external world, then with the elimination of all these facts as doubtful there is nothing left in me, either, that is not doubtful; the self-validity of the subject is reduced to a blank. With the disappearance of all psychological reality the individual ego coincides with the undifferentiated phenomenological subject, and personal identity reduces to the form of identity in general, $A = A$. Descartes' *cogito ergo sum* can legitimately contain nothing more. For with the removal of the external content of life the correlative internal content is necessarily removed as well, and only an empty form remains.

XIX

Thus the true subject of the internal world still evades us: there is on the one hand a self-validating but completely empty form of consciousness, and on the other hand its rich but illusory content. It has been pointed out, it is true, that there is a plausible way out of this vicious circle, namely through understanding the subject as a *potentiality* for psychological existence capable of experiencing all those states—even if only deceptively made real or objective—which form our entire empirical reality. But even with such a concession to methodical doubt the concept of the soul as an abiding potentiality cannot be admitted without careful examination of its residence permit in the realm of theoretical philosophy.

We are dealing here not with a direct fact of consciousness but with a product of reflection, an abstract concept. It is abstracted from a number of factual relationships, external and internal. Thus, for example, we notice that an oak tree grows only from an acorn and not from any other kind of seed, but that the definite shapes and properties of the mature oak are just as absent from the acorn as from any other object. Finding it possible neither to affirm that the oak is contained in the acorn as a present object, for that contradicts what is evident, nor to assume that it is not there at all, for then it would arise out of nothing, we distinguish two states of existence—actual and potential (real and possible)—and say that the acorn is the potentiality of the oak. Nothing prevents us from putting our ideas in order in this way, but at the same time we should remember that oaks, acorns, and consequently also the necessary relation between them are simply parts of that external world, the real existence of which is still a matter of doubt for us.

Another source, closer to the goal and apparently more reliable, from which we get the idea of potentiality is inner experience. Waking up each morning, we find our psychic life to be the same in make-up and state as we remember it being at the moment of falling asleep. In view of this fact, and acknowledging on the one hand an actual interruption in our psychic life, while on the other hand not considering it possible to understand this interruption as a complete cessation of our psychic life for a time, for then it would begin again without any inner basis and awakening would be a creation out of nothing, we say that this life existed during sleep potentially or in a latent state. In the same way, concerning the psychic existence of those phenomena that we remember after having forgotten them temporarily, we say that they existed in our memory in a latent form, or potentially. In all such cases the concept of potentiality is abstracted from the facts of the relativity and inconstancy of our manifest or immediate consciousness. Generally to this abstraction from factual data there is joined a *representation* of potentiality as a special kind of real being which alternately draws in and lets out its actual states like the tentacles of some elementary animal.

XX

Perhaps the concept of potential reality [*sushchnost*] is not very far from the truth, but in any case it is a product of reflection, demanding philosophical verification, and not a direct datum of consciousness. It is also clear that the definition of the soul as a special potentiality can make sense only on the strength of the assumed identity of the individual subject, and consequently cannot itself serve as the basis for asserting that identity. As a matter of fact, *assuming* that I am really the same person today as I was yesterday according to my present recollection, I infer that there is something in me which cannot be eradicated by the intervening state of actual unconsciousness or hetero-consciousness. But the authenticity or real identity of the personality is precisely what requires proof. The only immediate guarantee of this identity is the given recollection, which, however, can be just as erroneous in time as sense perception is in space. From the fact that I distinctly remember now everything that happened yesterday, it by no means follows that this yesterday is not today's illusion.

To the question of in what and how the psychic life is preserved during sleep, no direct answer is binding from the standpoint of provisional doubt. Perhaps this life is not preserved in anything or in any way, for it is possible that I really was not asleep, just as it is possible that I am still asleep now. And this is not to mention that a question arises concerning the true nature and real existence of *time*—in which it is assumed that personal identity resides as its states change—as well as of space; and without philosophical resolution of this question nothing can be built upon data which make sense only in relation to time, which may prove to be a pure illusion.

Thus, the concept of the soul as a potentiality cannot serve as a firm support for philosophical convictions as to the valid or true existence of the psychic subject, for this concept itself, to be an index of anything that truly exists, is still in need of support and justification. Hence we are left with the necessity of extending provisional doubt equally to both sides of what is thought about—to the subject of one's own psychic life as well as to the objects of the external world.

XXI

In any case there is one thing that cannot be doubted: *immediate* reality, fact *as such*, that which is *given*. We are conscious of the presence of certain sensations, thoughts, feelings, desires; consequently they exist as such, as what we are conscious of, or as states of consciousness. Here ordinarily the question is asked: *whose* consciousness?—by which it is implied that this very question antecedently shows the real participation in the work of consciousness of our ego as a true subject, potentiality, substance, and the like.

I myself used to think so. . . . But returning lately to a review of the basic concepts of theoretical philosophy I saw that this point of view is far from having the self-evident validity I imagined it to have. The fact is that not only must every answer be examined by rigorous thought—the same is required for every question. In everyday life we can ask, without giving it a second thought: whose coat? or, whose overshoes? But by what right may we ask in philosophy: whose consciousness?— thereby assuming the real presence of various selves to which we must give consciousness as private or communal property? The very question is simply a philosophically inadmissible expression of dogmatic certainty as to the independent and self-identical existence of individual beings. But it is precisely this certainty that needs examination and justification by indisputable logical deductions from self-evident data. Such justification I did not find either in Descartes' presumption—*cogito ergo sum*—or in the monad hypothesis of Leibniz or in Maine de Biran's references to the active elements in consciousness.

In the present state of affairs, to the question *whose* consciousness is this or *to whom* do the given psychic facts (the facts which form the starting point of philosophical discussion) belong, one can and should answer: *it is not known;* perhaps to no one; perhaps to some empirical individual: Ivan Ivanovich, Pyotr Petrovich, a French modiste who takes herself to be the Archbishop of Paris, or an archbishop who takes himself to be a modiste; perhaps, finally, to that general transcendental subject who, for reasons which are completely unknown *a priori*, had lapsed into the illusion of consciousness and broken up into a multitude of imaginary persons, like those created in a dream. Which of these possibilities has the advantage of being valid cannot, of course, be decided simply by examination: for neither Ivan Ivanovich, the modiste, the Archbishop, nor even the transcendental subject itself is a simple, immediate, given fact of consciousness: they are all simply expressions of psychologically mediated certainty requiring their own logical justification.

XXII

The aim of the foregoing discussion has not been to affirm any positive truth or to refute anything erroneously taken for truth, but solely to delimit the *indisputable* sphere of *immediate* consciousness from the sphere of all affirmed and denied opinions, beliefs, and convictions, which may prove to be either true or false but are *disputable*. The sole interest here, for the present, has been to protect the very source of philosophical thought from every sort of outside influence. This was the interest that guided the fathers of modern philosophy, Bacon and Descartes, particularly the latter; and if the latter had remained thoroughly true to his principle of methodical doubt, subsequent thinkers would not have had to begin theoretical philosophy all over again.

The objections to Cartesianism raised in the present discussion are concerned not with any of Descartes' ideas but only with his abandonment of doubt in the face of a particular idea. Descartes' provisional skepticism proved to be one-sided, without any serious attempt to explain and justify this one-sidedness. With respect to external objects he distinguished very well the indisputable from the disputable, the immediate from the assumed. The desk with books on it I now see in front of me is something indubitable and immediate as regards the presence in consciousness of this representation with its distinguishing geometric and sensory features (it is indisputable; if I see a desk, it would not occur to me or to anyone else to assert that I see a camel). But then the question arises: what is this desk as regards reality? Is it a dream, a reality wholly conditioned by the nature of the subject experiencing it, or a real object or thing independent of the subject (and to what extent and in what respect independent)? Any of these answers might be true; in other words, provisionally (before investigation and proof) all these answers are only debatable assumptions: if any of them were indisputable there would be no question concerning it, and if it were not an assumption but a manifest immediacy, then the other assumptions which it excludes would contradict what is evident and would be inconceivable.

Here Descartes' methodical doubt stops. Yet we find the same distinction between the immediate and the assumed, the indisputable and the disputable, in relation to the subject, of which we are conscious as something distinct from other phenomena. As long as the mental distinction between the ego and the non-ego is present in a given consciousness, the ego must be regarded as an indisputable immediate fact—whether this distinction between ego and non-ego is made on the basis of a given representation of an external object, on the basis of feeling, desire, or endeavor, or even if it arises purely theoretically in abstract thought or reflection. In all these cases, as long as the distinction of the subject both from everything else and from its own states *is present* along with all these states, the ego must be regarded as an indisputable, immediate fact. This is beyond question. No one can doubt that he is *conscious of the ego* when he is conscious of it. But then the question arises: what *is* this ego? Is it exhausted by this same apparent or phenomenological existence concerning which there are no doubts? Is it only one among a multitude of psychic states, a thought like any other, a phenomenon among other phenomena (which is the *opinion* of the English psychological school)? Or is the ego something special and unique of its kind, not one phenomenon among others but a general formal condition of all of them, an *a priori* connecting act of thought, inherent *implicite*, though in an inconspicuous fashion, in all phenomena but not existing apart from this connecting function (Kant's position)? Or, finally, is the ego some supraphenomenal essence or substance, the real center of psychic life, having its own existence independently of its given states (the position vaguely taken by Descartes and defended with greater clarity and distinctness by later spiritualists . . .).

The interminable debate among these three opinions shows obviously enough that none of them can be regarded as indisputable. This is all that I am affirming for the present, without prejudging anything. Clearly the issue is one of the truth or falsity of a particular assumption, and not of the self-validity of an immediate fact. Let us assume, for example, that the existence of our ego or soul as a substance is directly given in immediate states of consciousness: clearly no question or doubt as to this existence could arise, just as no question or doubt arises concerning the presence in consciousness of any kind of representation, emotion, or desire when it is actually present there. And as soon as there is a question or dispute, it is clear at once that the matter may be one of the truth of an assumption, but not of the immediacy of a fact. *Truth* can be not given, can be concealed, can require investigation and discovery; but *immediacy* which is not given, which is concealed or discovered, is a *contradictio in adjecto*, i.e., an absurdity.

Thus everyone has the philosophical right to affirm and to argue that the soul is a real being or substance, that this is the truth; but no one without an outrage to logic can affirm and argue that this truth is an immediate fact, for if it really is given in immediate consciousness that would already be a full proof, and if it is not given it is senseless to argue that the non-given is given.

The psychic immediacy given [*dannaya*], or more precisely being given [*davayemaya*], in consciousness, or the psychic process as such, depends on no opinions; the fact of the presence or absence of something in consciousness is the same from all points of view. Obviously there follows from this no preference for that opinion which is more careful than others to stop at this immediacy and acknowledges nothing beyond it. From the fact that immediate facts exist it does not follow that there is nothing else, and from the fact that this immediacy is known to us in the form of pure consciousness it does not follow that there is no other way of knowing what exists.

We must begin by differentiating between what is given and what is posited, between immediacy and assumptions. But to discriminate one from the other does not mean to be confined to one. Only elementary minds live by psychic immediacy alone, just as only primitive economies exist solely on the products of nature.

On the soil of immediate consciousness there grows up a demand to go beyond its bounds; amid the shifting, kaleidoscopic diversity of empirical appearances there *appears* a quest for something more stable and dependable. We cannot yet tell where this quest will lead us, but clearly the quest itself is something valid. If we are not satisfied with the immediacy of consciousness, with the flow of psychic states and phenomena, clearly there is in us something beyond it: A plus B cannot equal A.

We have defined the sphere of pure consciousness or psychic immediacy. This sphere, representing *self-validating* data, must be the starting point of philosophy. As we see, truth is not given here but is only posited. If truth were a fact of immediate consciousness, it need not and could not be sought, and hence there could be no philosophy. But, to the distress of some and the delight of others, there *is* philosophy. There is immediate reality and there is a demand for something else which is greater: there is *consciousness of fact* and there is an *aspiration* for *cognition of truth*. Let us see where this aspiration will lead us.

Book Eight

PHILOSOPHERS
IN EXILE

In 1922 a large number—according to Lossky, more than one hundred [1]—intellectuals and philosophers unsympathetic to Marxism were banished from Russia and emigrated to Western Europe. This group does not constitute the totality of what has come to be known as the Russian émigré philosophers, but it constitutes their nucleus. Among them were NICHOLAS O. LOSSKY (1870-1965), NICHOLAS BERDYAEV (1874-1948), Father Serge Bulgakov (1871-1944), SIMON L. FRANK (1877-1950), I. A. Ilyin (1882-1954), I. I. Lapshin (1870-1952), B. P. Vysheslavtsev (1877-1954), and many others. They settled where they could. Lossky went to Prague, then, after World War II, to the United States. Berdyaev went to Berlin and then to Paris. Bulgakov joined Lossky in Prague, then settled in Paris. Frank went to Berlin, to Paris, and finally to London. On the whole, however, the center of Russian émigré philosophy may, until after World War II, be considered Paris. In Paris, as for two years in Berlin, the group had the assistance of the Y.M.C.A., which supported the Religio-Philosophical Academy founded by Berdyaev in Berlin and which named him head of the Y.M.C.A. Press. The Press, along with the journal, *Put* (The Way), came to be the chief medium of publication for these philosophers. Also in Paris the same group joined Metropolitan Evlogius, the Russian Orthodox Exarch for Western Europe, in founding the now famous theological seminary of Saint Sergius, which became the center of Russian émigré intellectual and theological activity for the next two decades.

1. Nicholas O. Lossky, *History of Russian Philosophy*, New York, 1951, p. 233.

These men may be considered the group of philosophers in whom Russian philosophy was at last finding independent systematic expression when World War I broke out. The long period of gestation which started with Skovoroda and culminated in the philosophical world view of Solovyov finally found its fruit in the philosophers who were to be exiled just as their mature work was beginning. As has been indicated, Solovyov can be —and has been—considered the first systematic Russian philosopher, the first to develop a complete world view. The following generation, which began to publish in the first decade of the twentieth century, can be thought of as the mature expression of Russian philosophical thought. Its coming of age has, indeed, been called Russia's "intellectual" Renaissance—although, in the sense of systematic philosophy, it was rather a birth than a re-birth.

Like the Russian philosophy of the 1840's, Russian philosophy of the twentieth century falls naturally into two groups. And as, for the 1840's, the classification can be made in terms of the secular or religious orientation of the philosophers concerned, so in the twentieth century the philosophers are divided into the Marxists, on the one hand, and, on the other, the religious philosophers who went into exile after the Bolshevik Revolution. But such a classification is a facile one. Marxism includes not only the official philosophy of the U.S.S.R., but a number of revisions. Similarly, the émigré philosophy, although consistently religiously oriented, is subdivided into several schools. To add to the confusion, the division between Marxists and non-Marxists in Russia is historically unstable: many of the émigrés began not as theologians or even as religiously oriented thinkers, but as Marxists. They were, in fact, revisionists whose revisions became so extensive that their views could finally no longer be classified as Marxist at all.

The first decade of the twentieth century in Russia was a period of social, political, and intellectual unrest. The accession of Nicholas II in 1894 came at a time when Marxism was already growing strong. And in the following decade Marxists developed a revolutionary party with underground contacts in all the major Russian cities, with its own newspapers (printed abroad), with a central organization (with headquarters abroad), with a defined theory in terms of which to evolve its program and to attack its major rival in revolution, the Populist-minded Socialist Revolutionaries. In 1903, final details of organization were clarified and the Bolshevik group obtained the leadership which it was to maintain henceforth.

Nicholas II, meanwhile, continued the reactionary autocratic regime of his father, Alexander III, unwilling to draw the implications of the changed social situation. Russia was becoming industrialized, a proletariat was growing, and a middle class was developing. But politically Russia remained an absolute monarchy. In an optimistic mood, the government embarked on what was to be "a successful little war" with Japan in 1904, confident as it had been some fifty years before when it plunged into the Crimean War, and with results even more disastrous.

The great empire lost the war, lost half of Sakhalin Island, lost the ice-free facilities of Port Arthur in Southern Manchuria, and gained a revolution. The revolution of 1905 was unorganized and unsuccessful, but it paved the way for the success of the revolutions of 1917.

It is not surprising, in the midst of this social, political, and economic turmoil, that many of the philosophers who were first publishing at the beginning of the century should have been concerned with this unrest and should have begun as Marxists. Such were Berdyaev, Bulgakov, Frank, and P. B. Struve (1870-1944). But these men were never really satisfied with Marxism—they were revisionists from the start. Paradoxically, it was their social and ethical concern, the concern which had first led them to Marxism, which led them at once to revision and ultimately was to lead them out of the Marxist fold altogether. Marxist ethics was, in their view, at best insufficient. Marx offers no objective ethical criterion. The stage of history which has been achieved is *right* and *good* for that stage. The previous one was *right* for the previous stage. What *is* is what *ought to* be. There is no objective right for all stages, except for the last stage, the right achieved by the final emancipation of the proletariat, and this stage is right and good because it is determined—as are all previous ones—and because it is desired. None of the philosophers who were later to be exiled could accept this ethical relativism. Accordingly, they tried to supplement Marx with the most objective ethics they knew, that of Immanuel Kant. In rapid stages, Kantian idealism led them to religion, to a return to Russian Orthodoxy, but in no case was this a return to academic, official Orthodoxy, but rather, in the tradition of Kireyevsky and Khomyakov and Solovyov, a creative reinterpretation. One of the most striking instances of such a reinterpretation is the philosophy of Bulgakov.

Serge Bulgakov was ordained a priest in 1918. After leaving Russia and settling in Paris, he was active in the founding of the Seminary of Saint Sergius and held the chair of Dogmatic Theology there from 1925 until his death in 1944. Nevertheless, his views, strongly influenced by Solovyov and Solovyov's follower, Father Paul Florensky, led him to be officially accused of heresy by the Moscow Patriarchate.

Like the philosophy of Solovyov and later that of Frank, Bulgakov's mature philosophy is a philosophy of total-unity. The created world is one, bound together by a world-soul, Sophia, acting as the principle of creation, as *natura naturans*. It is his conception of Sophia that brought the criticism of official theological circles. Although the world and the Absolute remain distinct for Bulgakov—as they do not for S. L. Frank—it is Sophia that relates them, and in order to do so, Sophia must participate in both divine and created nature. Insofar as Sophia is divine, Sophia is a "third being" between God and the world. It is but one step from here to positing a fourth person in the Trinity.

Nicholas Berdyaev's revision of Marxism started in terms of Kant but did not stop there. From Kant he took the notion of man as an end in himself, but rejected Kant's legalism. Instead, he turned to Nietzsche and developed an ethics of creativity. In his turning to Nietzsche, Berdyaev places himself alongside LEON SHESTOV (Schwarzman) (1866-1938). Although most of the émigré philosophers are to a greater or lesser extent irrationalists, Shestov outdoes them all. In Shestov there is none of Solovyov's "Western" rationalist side, nor is there any evidence of Solovyov's philosophy of total-unity. Rather, like D. S. Merezhkovsky (1865-1941), his Russian sources are in Dostoevsky—at least in his interpretation of Dostoevsky. In addition, Shestov was never a Marxist. Thus, although he has affinities with various aspects of Russian émigré philosophy, among them he stands alone.

N. O. Lossky was closely associated with Bulgakov and Berdyaev in pre-revolutionary Russia. With them he edited the journal *Voprosy Zhizni* (Problems of Life). After his exile, he went to Prague with a number of colleagues and students. His influence on the younger generation of Russian philosophers-in-exile is very strong, particularly in epistemology. It is because of this influence and because of the systematic nature of his many publications that he has rightly been called the dean of the émigré philosophers, although the direction of his philosophical views cannot be associated with that of any group of his contemporaries: where they follow Solovyov, or Kant, or Nietzsche, Lossky combines Leibniz and Platonic realism. In following Leibniz he is a successor of A. A. Kozlov.[2] In his intuitivist epistemology, on the other hand, he is closer to his compatriots, although even in this branch of philosophy he is much more a rationalist than most of the Russian religious thinkers.

Struve and Vysheslavtsev can be grouped as neo-Kantians who, like Solovyov in his theory of knowledge, went beyond critical philosophy to metaphysics by means of intuition. The latter, making use of modern science—especially mathematics and psychology—to support his views, interprets the problem of philosophy fundamentally as one of the dialectic of "system and infinity." The Absolute cannot be grasped by reason, it "is not given in concept"—it is revealed in intuition. Man, he argues, is dependent on the Absolute and it is in this that his freedom lies, for in his relation to the Absolute, and only in this relation, man can transcend his limitations and the chains of his self-consciousness, achieving "free movement into the vast freedom of the Absolute."[3]

The establishment of the Seminary of Saint Sergius in Paris,

2. See above, pp. 4-6.
3. *The Ethics of the Transfigured Eros*, Paris, 1931, quoted in V. V. Zenkovsky, *A History of Russian Philosophy*, trans. George L. Kline, 2 vols., London and New York, 1953, p. 818.

and, later, of Saint Vladimir in New York, provided centers for the philosophical and theological activity of these philosophers. Through these centers one side of Russian philosophy has been kept alive and developed. A younger generation, taught by these men, is now already mature. The 1917 Revolution thus did not put an end to the religious philosophy which was growing in Russia just as Lenin's version of Marxist philosophy was being implemented. Perhaps what is most striking in this situation is that the present official philosophy of the Soviet Union, although it has many native Russian roots, is nevertheless largely Western in origin, while the émigré philosophy, formulated for the most part in the West, is clearly an expression of a Russian world view. It is probably no more than a coincidence that this Russian philosophy, especially that of Berdyaev and Shestov, should appear just as existentialism began to assert itself in Europe, but it is a fortunate coincidence that the emigration of Russian philosophy to the West occurred at such a time, for both Western existentialism and Russian religious philosophy have profited from their association.

NICHOLAS ALEXANDROVICH
BERDYAEV
[1874–1948]

O<small>F ALL THE PHILOSOPHERS</small> who emigrated after the Revolution of 1917, and probably of all Russian philosophers, Nicholas Berdyaev is best known in the West. He was a prolific writer and most of his works have been translated into several languages. He is thought of as expressing the fundamental characteristics of Russian thought, as the spokesman of Russian Orthodoxy, as the philosopher of freedom. To what extent all this is true is debatable, but it can fairly be said that it was he who, in the decades immediately following the Revolution, introduced the West to major trends of Russian thought.

Berdyaev was born in 1874, in Kiev province. His family was of the military aristocracy, relatively liberal, not particularly religiously oriented. He studied law at the University of Kiev and soon, like many students of his time, joined Marxist circles there. His studies were interrupted in 1898, when he was arrested for his socialist activities and exiled for three years to Vologda. It was there that he wrote several articles for *Die Neue Zeit,* edited in Germany by Karl Kautsky. It was there also that he wrote his first book, *Subjectivism and Individualism in Social Philosophy,* published in 1901. The book is a critique of Mikhailovsky's "subjectivism." [1] In the selection from it which has been included in this volume, Berdyaev's dissatisfaction with orthodox Marxism is already evident.

Berdyaev very early found Marxism insufficient as a world

1. See above, Vol. 2, pp. 188-198.

view. He could not accept Marxist determinism: Berdyaèv has
been called the philosopher of freedom; his concern was ethical
and he placed the highest value on the dignity and worth of
the individual person. It was inevitable that with such an outlook
Berdyaev should try to supplement the relativistic ethics and
the determinism of Marxism. He did so from the first, seeking,
as many of his compatriots did, an answer in the ethics of Kant.
But Marxism cannot tolerate any form of idealism. In such
an impasse, Berdyaev broke with Marxism, retaining only the
critique of bourgeois capitalism and much of the dialectic—the
latter, however, purified of materialism and returned to its Hegelian form. In the second selection for this volume, Berdyaev
gives his evaluation of Marxism in terms of his mature philosophical view.

Turning more and more to mystical religion and to Nietzsche
—many of whose views he found highly congenial—Berdyaev
successively edited two periodicals, *Novy Put* (The New Way)
and *Voprosy Zhizni* (Problems of Life). By the time he published *The Meaning of Creativity* in 1916, his philosophy had
taken definite shape; after this it never substantially changed.

Berdyaev left Russia in 1922. He settled briefly in Berlin,
then moved to Paris where he wrote most of his major works.

Aside from his early Marxism, its Kantian revision, and the
influence of Nietzsche, Berdyaev mentions as authors whose
thought particularly affected his own, Jacob Boehme, Dostoevsky,
Solovyov, the major Slavophiles of the 1840's, and Merezhkovsky. Many of these influences are indeed evident in his
work.

Berdyaev characterizes his mature philosophical outlook as
existential and eschatological. It is thus a form of religious existentialism which has its roots in the philosophy of the Slavophiles and the main concern of which is for the person as a
creative spirit, in contrast to the socialized role-playing individual,
whom he finds "bourgeois" and banal. His philosophy thus centers on freedom, spirit, and their role in history. The majority
of the selections below are intended to give the reader the essential
features of this philosophy.

Berdyaev distinguishes two realms of reality—spirit and nature, or being.[2] Spirit is opposed to nature, it is living, personal, free, creative activity. Nature is object, thing; it is necessity, passivity. To put it in more familiar terms, there is a "noumenal realm" contrasted with a "phenomenal realm," but, unlike Kant, Berdyaev envisages both realms as knowable and both realms as ontologically real. The former is knowable through free, creative activity, which indeed takes place in that realm; the latter is also real and has come to be through original sin.

Taking his cue from Boehme, Berdyaev explains the world as follows: The world was created out of nothing, but this "nothing" is not empty, it is the *Ungrund*, comparable to a de-materialized Aristotelian pure potency. The *Ungrund*, as pure potency, is irrational and free. Out of it is born God, a Spirit, suprarational, as is all that is spiritual. We can describe God only by pairs of contradictories, but we *can* speak of His love, which is the irrational "meonic" freedom of the *Ungrund* in *Him*. God is really present in all creative activity and has power over all His creation. Longing for an "object" of His love, God creates the world and man out of nothing (the *Ungrund*). Thus the world is a combination of the one characteristic of the *Ungrund*, namely, irrational freedom, and of God as its maker. Since God does not *create* irrational freedom, He has no power over it and is not responsible for it. And it is irrational freedom which gives birth to evil. It does this by violating the proper hierarchy of the world—creator over creation—when the world asserts itself (its freedom) against God.

The result is the Fall—separation from the divine, the loss of spiritual primacy, disintegration, slavery, natural being, meaninglessness, the "phenomenal" world of objects and law. The freedom of this world is the mere "freedom" of obeying law, it is "the recognition of necessity." God cannot avert the evil of the Fall. He can, however, not as Creator, but as Redeemer, conquer evil born of *irrational* freedom, by descending into the world and enlightening it, by reawakening the spiritual element

2. Berdyaev's terminology is not always consistent. "Being" is normally used interchangeably with "nature," the objectified state, but sometimes it is used to include all realms of reality. In this introduction it will be used only in the former sense.

in the world, that element which the world cannot lose since the world is the creation of spirit. In the Incarnation, therefore, God, through love, delivers man from nature. By God's act a third type of freedom is born, man's free love of God. This freedom is creative, spiritual, and thus the source of the salvation of man and the world.

Man, who is created a person, i.e., a spirit, as fallen becomes an object in an "objectified world," and he knows the world only objectively. Original sin is thus the source of the world of objects and of objective knowledge, and has both an ontological and an epistemological effect. In this situation, object is alien to knowing subject, personality is submerged in the general, man is socialized, determined by natural laws, true communication of persons becomes impossible, and only mediated approximations through concepts are left. This is the world of science and common sense. It is the world of the Philistine and bourgeois, of facts, of substances, categories, logical laws, and all the trappings of metaphysics. In fact, it is Hell.

Fortunately, the divine in man remains. Insofar as man is a creative being, has creative activity, he is still spirit. In such activity, man is a citizen of the realm of spirit. He knows *instinctively* spiritual reality which, in contrast to fact, is value and meaning. For creative activity is love: it is the energy with which God created man, the force of Grace, and love is a capacity to fuse and yet to be a person; in love the relation is not one of I-to-it, but, to use Buber's terminology, of I-Thou.

And insofar as this is possible, man is *now* saved, a spirit; the Kingdom of God is *now* for anyone who would but look with the eyes of spirit. For time itself, as we know it, is a result of the Fall. Time is division into past and future.

Berdyaev's view of time is given in the last selection. He distinguishes three kinds of time: cosmic, the cyclical time of the objectified natural world; historical, in which man acts and in which, insofar as man acts creatively, spirit intrudes and the chain of necessity is *really* broken; existential, which is creative time, the time of the spiritual realm in which all creativity originates. The three kinds of time may be symbolized in geometric terms as a circle, a line, and a point. History, then, can be seen as a conflict between irrational freedom and its effects on the one hand, and the free love of God on the other. Thus it is a mixture of necessity and freedom, evolution and revolution.[3] It is a drama which starts with the Fall and which will end with the ultimate salvation of the world. And ever present behind it, in existential time, is "meta-history," which is simultaneously the goal of history, the meaning of history, and the end of history. Revolutions are breaks of meta-history into history, "little apocalypses," and with them history becomes a "revelation of noumenal reality."[4] The most significant break, after the start of history, is the Incarnation (an eighth day of Creation). After it the conflict of freedom and necessity becomes more and more evident as necessity becomes more and more pervasive at each historical stage. Man is freed from pure nature, but reacts by also freeing himself from God; his severance from God leads to the invention of the machine. The machine, in turn, mechanizes man. At present man, by his very attempt at salvation, is not only dehumanized, but de-natured; he is not even a mere natural thing, he is an artifact. In extreme contrast to the spiritual life of free communion and love (*sobornost*),[5] man is now subject to compulsory service to society for material needs. The process of history is thus dialectical and, Berdyaev feels optimistically, is rapidly reaching its final phase, when this world will necessarily end in an ultimate conflict and man, all men, will obtain emancipation from objectification.

3. *The Beginning and the End*, trans. R. M. French, New York, 1957, p. 167.

4. *The Origin of Russian Communism*, trans. R. M. French, Ann Arbor, 1960, p. 131; *The Meaning of History*, trans. George Reavey, New York, 1936, p. 16.

5. See above, Vol. 1, pp. 161-162.

SELECTED BIBLIOGRAPHY

Works:

Nicholas Berdyaev, *The Meaning of the Creative Act*, trans. Donald A. Lowrie, New York, 1955.

——————, *Dostoevsky, An Interpretation*, trans. Donald Attwater, New York, 1960.

——————, *The Meaning of History*, trans. George Reavey, New York, 1936.

——————, *The End of Our Time*, trans. Donald Attwater, New York, 1933.

——————, *Freedom and the Spirit*, trans. O. F. Clarke, London, 1935.

——————, *The Destiny of Man*, trans. Natalie Duddington, London, 1959.

——————, *Solitude and Society*, trans. George Reavey, New York, 1939.

——————, *Spirit and Reality*, trans. George Reavey, London, 1946.

——————, *The Origin of Russian Communism*, trans. R. M. French, Ann Arbor, 1960.

——————, *Slavery and Freedom*, trans. R. M. French, New York, 1944.

——————, *The Beginning and the End*, trans. R. M. French, New York, 1957.

——————, *The Russian Idea*, trans. R. M. French, New York, 1962.

——————, *The Divine and the Human*, trans. R. M. French, London, 1949.

——————, *Dream and Reality: An Essay in Autobiography*, trans. Katharine Lampert, New York, 1962.

Secondary Sources:

C. S. Calian, *The Significance of Eschatology in the Thoughts of Nicolas Berdyaev*, Leiden, 1965.

O. F. Clarke, *Introduction to Berdyaev*, London, 1950.

Nicholas O. Lossky, *History of Russian Philosophy*, New York, 1951, pp. 233-250.

Donald A. Lowrie, *Rebellious Prophet: A Life of Nicolai Berdyaev*, London, 1960.

Fuad Nucho, *Berdyaev's Philosophy: The Existential Paradox of Freedom and Necessity*, New York, 1966.

R. Rössler, *Das Weltbild Nikolai Berdjajews*, Göttingen, 1956.

S. Seaver, *Nicholas Berdyaev: An Introduction to His Thought*, London, 1950.

M. Spinka, *Nicholas Berdyaev: Captive of Freedom*, Philadelphia, 1950.

Subjectivism and Objectivism *

. . . Mr. Mikhailovsky wanted to give us a single "system of truth." We acknowledge [the validity of] this task. With its category of necessity, science cannot create the ideal nor is it even able to ground it; it is philosophy which must find the standpoint from which the scientific and ethical views of the world may be harmoniously combined. We have tried above to show that one half of *pravda* (truth-justice)—theoretical truth—is obligatory for all but not equally accessible to all. The other half of *pravda*—practical justice—also must be obligatory for all, otherwise it would not be *pravda*. The question we addressed to Mr. Mikhailovsky is not addressed to him alone, but to all who acknowledge only subjective morality and the subjective ideal but who deny what is objectively obligatory. Indeed this kind of "subjectivism" is a prevailing view in our time—even the social world view which we all share is not innocent of this "subjectivism." [1] But there must be some objective standard which would enable us to set one subjective ideal above others and would show us the *obligatory truth-justice which exists in the realm of morality*.

Social materialism is connected historically and psychologically

---

* Translated for this volume by Ashleigh E. Moorhouse, from *Subyektivizm i individualizm v obshchestvennoi filosofi*, St. Petersburg, 1901, pp. 62-81. Most of the footnotes to this text have been omitted. Berdyaev makes repeated reference in these notes to two books which obviously exercised a considerable influence on his thought: R. Stammler, *Wirtschaft und Recht nach der materialistischen Geschichtsauffassung*, 1896; L. Woltmann, *System des moralischen Bewusstseins*, 1898.—TRANS.

1. In its struggle with bourgeois ideology, Marxism has adopted a hostile attitude toward all ideologies. Historically this is completely understandable, but theoretically it is completely wrong. The theoretical elaboration and further development of Marxism ought to lead to the creation of an independent, higher ideology, which would give a philosophical-ethical basis to those idealistic calls for truth and progress, for justice and humanity, which so often accompany the practical activity of those who are fighting for this world view.

(but not, of course, logically) with a definite social ideal, with
the most sacred aspirations of contemporary man. How, then, does
it ground its social ideal? Its ideal has a double foundation. First,
this social ideal is *objectively necessary*, the tendencies of social
development are such that the social order which we regard as
ideal is bound to come; it will be the inevitable result of the
immanent conformity to law of the historical process. Thus the
ideal receives an objectively logical, scientific sanction, which
permits the Marxist to look to the future with confidence. The
modern proponents of this social ideal have therefore set themselves against the Utopians, and take pride not so much in their
ideal aspirations as in their scientific prognosis. Second, social
materialism gives the ideal a subjective psychological ground:
the ideal of social life does not simply conform to scientific
prediction, it is also something *subjectively desirable* for a given
social class, and this class is fighting for its actualization. While it
is more important practically, the second foundation is theoretically subordinated to the first, since the desires and ideals
of social classes are worked out in conformity with the laws
of the social process.[2] We say that this double foundation for
the ideal is absolutely inadequate; a third foundation is necessary,
one which we would call *objectively ethical*. It is necessary to
show that our social ideal is not only objectively necessary (the
logical category), not only subjectively desirable (the psychological category), but also that it is objectively moral and objectively just, that its actualization will be progress in the sense of
improvement; in a word, that it is binding on all, has unconditional value, is something *obligatory* (the ethical category).
For example, we take pride in using the expression "scientific
ideal," forgetting that this word-combination is no better than
"subjective method." Only our prediction of what is to come
can be scientific; the ideal of the future and our impulse toward
truth and justice are categories essentially different from the
categories of science.[3] Many of those who think as we do will

  2. This is why objectivism is regarded as the characteristic feature of
social materialism.
  3. In spite of its logical inconsistency, the expression "scientific ideal" can
still be retained, since for us it has a special significance.

not agree with the way we are putting the question here, and will regard our position as impermissible heresy. Nevertheless we shall venture to develop the ethical viewpoint, and shall attempt to show that it is very different from the usual ethical view of social phenomena, that view which we are all sick to death of hearing about from German "academic socialists" and Russian "subjectivists." What we are concerned with is the elimination of "subjectivism" from ethics, from the realm where it is particularly strong. . . .

. . . But why is the democratic ideal higher than the bourgeois ideal, why is it better that the heart should beat with joy at the words "justice" and "the welfare of the people" than at the words "knout" and "oppression"? Why is the subjective morality of that social group with which we sympathize higher and more humane than the morality of other groups which are in power now, but which do not arouse in us any special sympathy? On what grounds is Engels, who acknowledges only an empirical class morality, able to say that only now are we witnessing the birth of a truly humane morality? I may join a certain group in the social struggle because my feelings and sympathies attract me to this party; it is a *subjective* sanction which we encounter first of all. But can it be that there is no *objective* moral sanction?

In order to get out of this difficulty the materialistic view of history resorts to the following argument: One social ideal is higher than and morally preferable to another because it is supported by the historical process, because it is more progressive, better adapted to the demands of social development; the morality of one class is better and more just than that of another because it is more viable, because the future belongs to it. The bourgeois ideal is bad not only because it fails to arouse our sympathies but also because it has no future, because it obstructs the development of the progressive forces of contemporary society. All this is completely true, and the merits of historical materialism in this respect have not been given their due. But it does not give a satisfactory and exhaustive answer to the question we have been raising. It misses the point. From the argument we have been proposing we know that a certain ideal, for example, the democratic ideal, is not only subjectively desirable but also

objectively necessary, that social development will lead inevitably
to its triumph. It is very important, of course, for me to know
this, but this does not in any way increase the *ethical value* of
my ideal. It does not yet follow from this that it is better,
more just, more moral than any other ideal. Let us imagine a
situation of this kind: social development is leading in the most
obvious way to results which for me are repulsive, say, to new
and more refined forms of exploitation and slavery; and I understand this perfectly. The future contains only that ideal which
conforms to social necessity; but then in this situation the ideal
which conforms to life is possible only for the group that is
interested in the exploitation and enslavement of other groups.
By virtue of my ideal of justice, my democratic feelings, and
my hatred of exploitation and slavery, I part company with the
historical process—as it were flinging myself overboard. Does
this make my ideal lower, is it therefore reduced in ethical value,
am I then obliged to discard my ideal and embrace the predatory
ideal as one that is more viable? Surely not. I am an optimist
now, because I believe in a better future. In the situation just
described I would be a pessimist.

The whole of our world view rests on one idea—on the idea
of progress; but, as we shall try to show, the idea of progress
requires the acknowledgment of the teleological principle (objective and not subjective). Stammler formulated it as follows:
there must be a *universally obligatory* end of social life, an end
having objective moral value. In any case it is clear that the
objective necessity about which science speaks cannot be the
basis of the ideal, nor can it give it *ethical* value. I set an ideal
of social life for myself, I acknowledge this ideal as just and
consider that activity good which is directed toward its actualization, not at all because it is necessary. People who base their
ideal only on its subjective desirability fall into moral skepticism
and subjectivism, identifying ethics with psychology and morality
with mores. On the other hand, those who regard objective
necessity as the basis for the ideal are mixing different categories
in the most uncritical fashion.

It is most important to remember always that the ethical

category of justice has an independent significance, essentially different from the logical category of necessity. We shall try now to find the philosophical bases for the objective ideal and objective morality, in a word, for practical justice—as we have tried to do above in the case of theoretical truth.

As a theory of knowledge, ethics must take Kant's critical philosophy as its starting point. We have seen that the source of the objectively true is rooted in transcendental consciousness; but also rooted there is the source of the objectively moral, the objectively just. Objective morality is possible only if one accepts the *a priori* character of a moral law which distinguishes unconditionally between good and evil. Only in this case does good acquire a universally obligatory character. In the realm of ethics what is universally obligatory means: that which *ought to be*. All attempts to deduce the concepts of good and evil empirically from non-ethical elements, for example, from the constantly repeated experiences of pleasure and pain, have come to nothing and are just as unsatisfactory as the empirical theory of knowledge. We are interested here not in the question of the origin and development of morality, but in the question of value. For us morality is not a subjective illusion, as the empirical evolutionists would like to prove, it is rather an independent quality which cannot be broken down into a quantity of non-ethical molecules. The formal difference between good and evil or between the moral and the immoral precedes every sense experience; the category of justice is given *a priori* to our transcendental consciousness, and this ethical *a priori* is what makes moral experience and moral life possible. It plays the same role in the realm of morality as, say, the role played by the category of causality in the realm of knowledge. . . .

Man's consciousness has never risen above Kant's thought of man (or mankind) as an end in himself, an end which gives moral sanction to everything else and itself needs no sanction. Kant is the real founder of the religion of man, and not Comte, whose point of view is very superficial in comparison to Kant's. . . .

If mankind is that which is supremely sacred and an end in

itself, then we have no right to postulate something higher than mankind.[4] We acknowledge only one postulate of practical reason, the postulate of the moral world-order. But this moral order is located not in the intelligible world, nor in unknown things in themselves; it is found rather in the one real world of phenomena, in that progress which is being accomplished within the worldly and historical process and is actualizing the "realm of ends." We shall dwell later on the theory of progress, and will see progress as improvement sanctioned by the regulative idea of a universally obligatory end. Empirically it is just as impossible to arrive at the objective ethical norm that man is an end in himself as it is to arrive at the idea of the universal applicability of the principle of causality. A choice must be made: either moral good [blago] is something just as absolute and universally obligatory as truth [istina], or it is nothing more than a subjective illusion. The second conclusion is inevitable for empiricists, no matter what lengths they go to to prove the usefulness of this illusion of goodness and justice. . . .

Sociological ethics examines moral concepts and their crystallization in social mores, but we wish to pass on now from what people think is good to what really is good. Psychological moral consciousness (the source of subjective morality) is conditioned by the social being of people, their membership in this or that social group; and it may be found in the various attitudes toward transcendental moral consciousness, toward the ethical norm (the source of objective morality). In accordance with the general spirit of our world view, we believe that the harmonization of psychological and transcendental consciousness, of subjective and objective morality, can be observed only in the moral consciousness of the progressive social class. Why? Because, as we have already indicated, the psychology of the progressive class is the result of adaptation to the demands of universally human social

4. . . . The principle *fiat justitia, pereat mundus* is quite correct formally, and we subscribe to it, but in its content it is completely absurd. Justice must triumph come what may; it is the highest good. But then can the triumph of justice destroy the world? Never, because justice is precisely what promotes the growth of life in this world. Man cannot suffer because we subordinate him to this abstract norm—this norm is, rather, what deifies him.

progress. Consequently it is only in this psychology that we may observe that combining of the individual and particular with the *universal* which is the fundamental sign of morality. Morality, of course, cannot be class morality, any more than truth can be class truth, but historically it takes on a class form and is borne by the social class which is carrying the banner of universal human progress. Later we will try to show that historically the *avant garde* of society always works to elevate the value of man and leads him toward consciousness of absolute justice. In every epoch we see several moralities, but objectively only one of them is authentic and can be "the principle of universal legislation." This genuinely human morality is psychologically inaccessible to the exploiting classes of modern society, but ethically it is equally binding on all, as a norm. . . .

. . . Resting as it does on historical materialism, our whole argument is based—as we have said—on one fundamental presupposition: the presupposition of *universal progress*. If the latter falls, our argument too will inevitably collapse. The theory of progress is the bridge which joins together the two halves of *pravda*—theoretical truth and practical justice—and also joins the objective and subjective aspects within each of these halves.[5] . . .

. . . The difference between the worse and the better or between good and evil is given *a priori* to our transcendental consciousness; we ourselves bring into the historical process our own regulating idea of the universally obligatory end, and, on this firm foundation, we sanction this process as progress. Man as an end in himself, the kingdom of humanity and of human power and understanding—this is our guiding star. The validity of this idea cannot be proved, just as the universal applicability of the principle of causality cannot be proved; but without this *a priori* principle we would be morally blind and unable to separate what is just, humane, and progressive in the life around us from what is unjust, inhuman, and reactionary. . . .

5. Our examination of theoretical truth is related to Kant's *Critique of Pure Reason*, our study of practical justice to his *Critique of Practical Reason*, while our examination of progress will be related to his *Critique of Judgment*, or to the doctrine of teleology.

[NICHOLAS BERDYAEV]

Marx vs. Man *

Marxism aspires to becoming the predominant faith of the world's population: what does Marxism really mean for man, for human personality? Answering this question is not so simple as it may at first appear. That Marxism is anti-personal is easily demonstrated. Every purely sociological doctrine of man is anti-personal, every theory which considers man simply as a social entity, formed by the milieu in which he lives, limited to one plane of being, the social. For human personality has depth as well as mere extension. . . .

Personality . . . is a spiritual, a religious, category. Personality says that man belongs not only to the sociological and natural order but to another plane of being, the spiritual. Personality is an image of a higher form of being than either the social or the natural. It cannot be a part of anything else. Society has a tendency to consider personality as its creation, the individual as dependent upon society. From the sociological viewpoint, personality is a minute part of society, a small circle within the large one which is society itself. On the basis of sociology, personality cannot stand and defend itself against society.

But from the viewpoint of existence-philosophy, the reverse is true: society is a small part of personality, merely its social element. The world is only a part of personality. Personality is the existential center, rather than nature or society. The subject is existential, not the object. Personality realizes itself in social and in cosmic life, but it can do so only because within it is an element independent of both. Personality is not definable as a part of something else. It is "totalitarian," integral, central; it is essentially universal and cannot be a part of the world or society, of universal being or of divinity.

Personality in general does not belong to the realm of natural law: it cannot be ranked in the hierarchy of the natural. It is

* From "Marx vs. Man," trans. Donald A. Lowrie, *Religion in Life*, VI (Autumn, 1938), pp. 483-484, 486-496.

rooted in the realm of the spirit. Its existence presupposes the dualism of spirit and nature, freedom and determinism, the individual and the social, the kingdom of God and that of Caesar. . . .

. . . While personality is not determined by society, it is still something social. It can realize its own fullness only in communion with other personalities. The social projection of this view of personality demands a radical, a revolutionary revaluation of social values; it demands removing the center of gravity from society, the government, the state, the collective or social group, to the supreme value of the personality, of every human person. Thus, for instance, the socialization of economy, guaranteeing the right to labor and to a decent living for every human life, social legislation to prevent the exploitation of man by man, is a logical result of this theory of personality. Hence the only system which corresponds to the eternal truth of personality is that of "personalistic socialism." At the basis of this world outlook founded on personality, we have neither the idea of equality nor that of justice, but rather that of the supreme value of every human person, and his right to self-realization.

Marxism's attitude toward personality is full of contradictions. This is partly due to its vague ideas about anthropology. Marx's negative attitude toward personality is inherited from Hegel, with his recognition that the general is of greater importance than the individual. With Hegel, personality has no independent significance: it is only a function of the world-spirit. Hegel's anti-personalism was taken up by Feuerbach, whose humanism is racial, rather than personal. . . . Man realizes himself in, and in the last analysis is dissolved into, the racial, the collective life. Breaking into existence-philosophy, Feuerbach sought to release the "thou" as something other than object. But Hegel's stubborn materialism [determinism?] prevented Feuerbach's complete discovery of personality as real and original being.

Marx has a sort of medieval realism in his concepts. He follows both Hegel and Feuerbach and accepts the primacy of the racial man over the individual. The general, the racial, precedes and determines the partial, the individual. Society and class are more primitive realities than man or personality. Class is a reality which exists in the scheme of things, not merely in thought. It is human personality, not class, which is an abstraction. Class is something like *universalia ante rem*. It is the class which thinks, judges, evaluates, not the individual. The individual personality, as distinguished from the racial unit, is incapable of independent thought or judgment. Man is a social-racial being, a function of society. This determines in advance the totalitarian attitude of Communism toward state and society. . . .

Because he prefers the general to the individual, Marx's weakest point is his psychology. If we except Marx himself, with his occasional interesting psychological comments, the psychology of most Marxists is limited to vituperation. Not even the psychology of class has been thoroughly studied. The bourgeois type, instead of being analyzed, is simply presented as a bloodthirsty criminal engaged in instigating war. . . . With interest centered upon the general instead of the individual, and this interest conditioned chiefly by conflict, it is impossible to study psychology. Instead, we find moral judgment and denunciation.

This is a general defect in all Marx's doctrine of man. While Marx himself has certain prophetic elements, and in spite of his personal conflict with the society about him, the doctrine of man which has developed from Marx denies the prophetic which always means the elevation of human personality above the social collective, and conflict with the social in the name of justice. The call to this conflict is that of an inner voice, the voice of God. If Marxism were to be completely realized in human society, it would mean crushing out the prophetic element, which appears not in the religious sphere alone, but in philosophy, in art, even in social life. This annihilation of the prophetic would result from the final absolute conformity of man to society, complete adaptation, eliminating all possibility of conflict. This, the result of the anti-personal spirit of Marxism, is its most repulsive aspect. Marx himself was a personality battling against the world, but this Marxists cannot be. The socialization of Christianity in the past offers good examples of what takes place when the prophetic spirit is killed.

Anti-personalism is, however, only one side of Marxism. The

true sources of Marxist attacks on capitalism are personalistic and humanistic. The chief reason for Marx's hostility to the capitalist system was that it oppressed human personality, made man a thing. Marx used the German word *Verdinglichung*. In this he was right. The capitalist system dehumanizes both proletarian and capitalist. . . .

While he did not follow it through, this idea of *Verdinglichung* in Marx, especially in his younger years, is a bit of genius. Here are revealed the motives for his first hatred and denunciation of the capitalistic system. These motives are purely humanitarian: Marx proclaims revolutionary uprising against a social order in which human personality loses its integrity and part of it becomes a thing, an object of commerce. The proletarian is a man a part of whose personality has been taken from him by the oppressive economic system. (Among the Communists, this part of Marx's theory has been best developed by Lukacs in his *Geschichte und Klassenbewusstsein*.) Marx insists that if socialists expect the proletarian to play a great part in world history this is not because they regard the proletariat as something divine, superhuman, but just because it represents an abstraction of all humanity, because the proletariat has been robbed of its human nature and must find a way to recover it. It is the class which must struggle to regain that humanity of which it has been deprived. This idea, thoroughly dialectical, is of special importance in the study of Marxism, the idea that man is in the process of being robbed of part of himself, and that this process is most intense among the proletariat. This leads to the idea of class-consciousness: man mistakes his own activity for part of the objective world and hence subject to the same sort of immutable laws.

The influence of Feuerbach is noticeable on Marx's earlier years. What Feuerbach said of religion, Marx accepted and extended to other spheres. Feuerbach held that religion divided man's nature into parts: man makes God in his own image. What is really only man's own nature is presented to him by religion as something apart from and higher than himself. The poor man has a rich God, that is, all his property is taken from him and transferred to divinity. Belief in God thus "proletarianizes" man.

Once a man becomes rich, God becomes poor or vanishes altogether. Give man back his riches and he becomes an integral being, lacking no essential parts of his nature. These ideas of Feuerbach, Marx used as the basis for his brilliant criticism of capitalism and political economy. And it must be said that they apply much better to capitalism than to belief in God.

The doctrine of the fetishism of goods in Volume I of *Das Kapital* is perhaps Marx's most notable discovery. This fetishism is an illusory consciousness under which the product of human labor is seen as a thing, a material reality belonging to the objective world and subject to its fixed laws. Marx demolished the world of economics in which bourgeois political economy had been discovering its laws. Economics is not part of the world of things, it is only human activity, labor, man's attitude to man. Hence economics may be changed or controlled: man may rule economics. The riches man creates, alienated from him in the world of economics, considered as objective reality, may thus be restored. Man may become a rich, an integral being, may again have all that was taken from him. And this will be accomplished by the activity of the proletariat, just those people from whom the most wealth has been taken. . . .

Marx defined capital, not as a real thing but rather as the social relationship among men in the process of production. This definition was a great shock to bourgeois economists. It places the center of gravity of economic life in human activity and conflict. . . .

Even economic materialism may be comprehended in two ways. It gives the impression, first, of a logical and extremely sociological determinism. Economics determines the whole of human life, not only the structure of society, but all ideology, all spiritual culture. There is a definite set of laws for the social process. Both the Marxists and their critics have understood Marxism in this spirit of extreme determinism.

But this is only one interpretation, one side of Marxism. The fact that economics determines the whole of human life is due to past evils, to man's present slavery. The day will come when this slavish dependence on economics will be broken, when economics will depend on man, and man will become the master.

Marx proclaimed not only man's slavery, but the possibility of his liberation. Economic materialism by itself is a rather sad theory, incapable of arousing revolutionary enthusiasm. But Marxism possesses in a high degree the capacity to enkindle revolutionary zeal. . . .

Marx lived in a thoroughly capitalist society and saw how economics completely determined human life, enslaved human consciousness, and evoked illusory concepts. But Russian Communists today are living in the epoch of the proletarian revolution, and thus they see the world from another angle. Marx and Engels spoke of the leap from the realm of necessity to that of liberty. Russian Communists hold that they have already made the leap. Hence for them Marxism is turned inside out, although they insist upon remaining Marxists at all costs. Now it is not economics which determines consciousness, but the proletarian revolutionary consciousness which determines economics: not economics which determines politics, but the other way around.

Hence philosophizing Russian Communists try to construct a philosophy based upon the idea of auto-motivity. All the qualities of the spirit are attributed to the material: freedom, activity, reason, etc. Such a philosophy suits the revolutionary will. Mechanistic materialism is condemned: it is not in tune with the exaltation of the will to revolution, it is not a philosophy of heroic human conflict. Man is now discovered to be free from the power of the material, objective, economically determined world.

But it is the collective man, not the individual, who is free. The individual is not free from the human collective, from communist society. He attains liberty only in identifying himself with the collective life. This idea is found not only in Marx, but in Feuerbach as well. . . .

Marxism may be interpreted humanistically. It may be seen as struggle against depriving man of his human nature, struggle to restore man's integral being. And Marxism may also be interpreted as indeterminism: the proclamation of man's liberation from the power of economics, from the power of fate. Marxism exalts the human will. It tries to create a new man. But it has its fatalistic side also, an aspect which actually deeply degrades mankind. Marx's doctrine of man is completely dependent upon capitalist industry, upon the factory. The new Communist man is created in the factory: he is machine-made. The spiritual culture of the new man depends upon the conditions of life in heavy industry. This is the reason for the dialectic in Marxism. Good is born of an ever-increasing evil; light is kindled by an ever-deepening shadow. The conditions of life in capitalist industry exasperate the proletarian worker, unman him, deprive him of his human worth, make him a being torn by resentment, anger, hatred, desire for revenge. The process of proletarization dehumanizes, it robs man of his human nature. And in this the proletarian is the least to blame. But out of this progressive dehumanization, this terrible narrowing of man's consciousness, how can we expect a new type of man to emerge? Marxism expects a miraculous dialectical change of what it considers evil, into good, into the better life. But at the same time the proletariat is burdened with the "Fatum" of capitalist industry, exploiting, oppressing, robbing him of human dignity. According to Marxism the higher type of man will be the result of complete dehumanization.

Such a concept is thoroughly anti-personal. It fails to recognize the inherent value of human personality, its depths of being. According to this concept, man is a function of the world's social process, a function of the general, a means to an end, by which the new man is manufactured. Quantity of evil turns into quality of good. And in this process personal activity, human consciousness, creativeness, or conscience counts for nothing. Everything is wrought by "sly reason" (Hegel) which is general.

All this indicates the complex and contradictory make-up of Marxism. It not only declares war on the degradation of man by man, war against injustice and slavery, but also reflects the low levels to which bourgeois capitalist society has sunk, depressed by the spirit of materialism.

This is what both classical Marxism and Russian Communism fail to see. Feuerbach missed the point, also. One of the basic faults in Marxist humanism is that it involves subtracting from man his human nature. . . . Granted that man must recover his

full nature—is this really accomplished? Not in materialist Marxism. Man does not regain his spiritual nature: it is lost, together
with everything transcendental. Man is robbed of the spiritual,
he becomes nothing but a bit of matter.

But a bit of matter cannot possess human worth. It cannot
realize a complete, "totalitarian" life. Communism would give
back to the proletariat the means of production which have been
stolen from him, but has no idea of restoring the spiritual elements of which human nature has also been robbed. . . . Man's
true worth, just as his fullness of life, is bound up with the
fact that he belongs not only to the kingdom of Caesar, but
to the Kingdom of God as well. This means that man has higher
value, more completeness, if he is a personality. But neither in
Marxism nor in Communism do we find this idea of personality,
hence they cannot really defend man's best interests. At best,
Communism affirms only the individual, the socialized individual,
and demands for him an integral life. But personality is denied.
The individual is only a being formed by society, by a process
of training. Lenin said that after a period of dictatorship in
which there would be no liberty whatever, men would BECOME
ACCUSTOMED to the new conditions of social life and would feel
themselves free in a Communist society (Note: cf. Lenin, *The
State and Revolution*. In his book, *Materialism and Empirio-
criticism*, Lenin offers a rather ordinary defense of materialism
and naturalism. This is a philosophy much inferior to that of
A. Bogdanov, which deserves the name of socialist, while Lenin's
does not.) . . .

The very process of dehumanization which Marx denounced
in capitalism, takes place in materialistic Communism. Communist as well as capitalist industrialism may dehumanize man.
Both may turn man into a technical function. . . . The anti-
personalism of Communism is not a matter of its economic
system, but of its spirit, or, better, of its denial of the spiritual.
This must always be borne in mind in our thought of Communism. Personalism, on the other hand, demands the socialization of economics but cannot admit the socialization of spiritual
life, which means the death of the spirit, robbing man of his soul.

Again, the anti-personalism of Marx is due to its false attitude toward time. Marxism, and specially its practical application in Communism, considers the relationship between present and future to be that of means and end. The present is a means—no direct and definite end is achieved in the present. And means are approved which have no resemblance to the aim in view: violence and tyranny for the attainment of freedom, hatred and strife for the realization of brotherhood. An integral human life is realizable only in the future, perhaps in the distant future. In the present man remains denuded of all his inheritance, he is alienated from himself. Thus Marxist Communism affirms man, the whole man, only in the future, while denying him in the present. The man of the present is only a means to the man of the future: his condition at present only a means to that in some future epoch.

Such an attitude toward time is incompatible with the principle of personality, with the recognition of the value of each human personality in itself and its right to realize its own life. It is incompatible with man's consciousness of himself as a whole rather than a part, as an end and not merely a means. No man, regardless of the class to which he belongs, can be treated as a simple means to an end. No human person can be dealt with as an obstacle in the way. . . .

Philosophical anthropology teaches that a man is a personality. It is a personalist philosophy. There can be no personality without a spiritual element which makes man independent of the determinisms of external surroundings, natural or social. This spiritual element is no contradiction to the human body, to man's physical, material make-up, to everything that ties him up with the life of the whole natural world. Abstract spiritualism is powerless to construct a doctrine of man's essential integrity, oneness. The spiritual element embraces the human body, all the "material" in man. It postulates the control of man's body and spirit, the attainment of a complete image of personality, the entry of the whole man into another order of being. The body belongs to the human personality and the spiritual in man must not be alienated from it. The body is a form which demonstrates the victory of the spirit over formless matter. The old Cartesian dualism of "soul" and "body," "spirit" and "matter" is completely false and may be considered as already in the discard. The real dualism is that of spirit and nature, freedom and necessity, personality and thing. The human body, even the "body" of the world, can leave the sphere of "nature," of "necessity," of "things" and pass into the sphere of "the spirit," of "freedom," of "personality." This is the meaning of the Christian doctrine of the resurrection of the body. The resurrected body is no longer natural matter, subject to determinism, no mere thing. Neither is it bodilessness, abstract spirit: it is a new spiritual body. The doctrine of the resurrection thus differs from the immortality of the soul: the former postulates immortality for the whole, the integral man, and not for some separate part of him, like the soul. Hence it is a personalistic doctrine.

This independence of the spiritual in man from the power of society does not involve opposing the "spiritual" to the "social." It does not separate one from the other. It means, rather, that man should form society and be its master, should realize his fullness of life in society rather than being defined by society and becoming its slave or one of its functions. The spiritual governs the social in man and this involves the attainment of human completeness and integrity. Society is not an end in itself. The end is man, fullness and completeness of life. Even the most perfect organization of society is only a means. . . .

The basic error in Communism founded on Marxism is its belief in the possibility of realizing not only justice, but human brotherhood, by compulsion. Communism believes that not only society, but the communion of human spirits can be organized by force. Socialism derives from the word "society," Communism from the word "communion," the mutual communing of men, one with another. Socialism differs from Communism, but not on the plane of the social and economic organization of society—here they may coincide. But Socialism may be considered as only the social and economic organization of society, its aims limited to this one sphere. Communism, on the other hand, is totalitarian. It strives for a complete world-philosophy: it wants to build a new man, a new human brotherhood, a new attitude toward the whole of life. Communism cannot consent to be accepted partially. It demands complete adoption, a conversion, as to any religious faith. But to accept only the social and economic phases of Communism and attach these to some other world-philosophy—this does not produce Socialism. Socialism stands for the building of a classless society, which will realize social justice and will not permit the exploitation of man by man. But the building of a new man, of human brotherhood, is a spiritual, a religious task. It presupposes an inner rebirth. Communism will not admit this—it is a religion itself.

Thus a Christian may, and in my opinion must, be a Socialist, but he can hardly be a Communist since he cannot accept Communism's pretense to being a complete and all-embracing world-view. Christian personalism should not oppose the building of a classless society: it should aid in the task. . . .

But the socialization of society cannot by itself achieve the new man and the brotherhood of all men. It orders relationships and communication among men on the basis of justice, but it cannot bring about true communion, real brotherhood. Brotherhood has a personal character. It is always the meeting of personalities, of I and thou, the union of me and thee in us. This is not achievable by the external organization of society involving only a part of human personality and not reaching to its depths. . . .

But it may be that building a classless society, even if the effort be accompanied by materialist illusions and errors, will lead to a spiritual renaissance which is now hindered by class conflict and its concomitant evils. Once the classless society is attained, it will be clearly seen that materialism and atheism, the militant godlessness of Communism, all belong to the past, to the epoch of the conflict of classes. Then the new man will be face to face with the last secret of being, with the final problems of the spirit. Then will be clearly revealed the tragedy in human life, and man will long for eternity. And only then will men cease to mistake the partial for the integral. Only then can personality become truly whole.

Freedom *

Some have called me the philosopher of freedom, and a reactionary Russian bishop once said of me that I was "the captive
of freedom." I do indeed love freedom above all else. Man came
forth out of freedom and issues into freedom. Freedom is a
primordial source and condition of existence, and, characteristically, I have put Freedom, rather than Being, at the basis of
my philosophy. I do not think any other philosopher has done
this in such a radical and thoroughgoing way. The mystery of
the world abides in freedom: God desired freedom and freedom
gave rise to tragedy in the world. Freedom is at the beginning
and at the end. I might say that all my life I was engaged
in hammering out a philosophy of freedom. I was moved by
the basic conviction that God is truly present and operative only
in freedom. Freedom alone should be recognized as possessing a
sacred quality, whilst all the other things to which a sacred
character has been assigned by men since history began ought to
be made null and void.

I look at myself as pre-eminently an emancipator, and I am
in sympathy with every emancipation. Thus it was that Christianity presented itself to me and called upon my allegiance as
emancipation. From my early childhood I was wedded to freedom; already in the second form of the Cadet Corps I was
meditating on and dreaming of the miracle of freedom. Dependence on other things and other people offended me, and the
spirit of independence moved me in all my thinking and actions.
Even the slightest manifestation of servility aroused in me a
storm of protest and hostility. I could never agree to abdicate
freedom or even to curtail it, and never consented to anything
at the price of freedom. I found strength to renounce many
things in life, but I have never renounced anything in the name
of duty or out of obedience to precepts and prohibitions: I

* From *Dream and Reality; An Essay in Autobiography,* trans. Katherine
Lampert, New York, 1962, pp. 56-63.

renounced for the sake of freedom, and, maybe, also out of compassion. Nothing could ever tie me down, and this, no doubt, has to some extent weakened my efficiency and diminished my possibilities of self-realization. I always knew, however, that freedom gives birth to suffering, while the refusal to be free diminishes suffering. Freedom is not easy, as its enemies and slanderers allege: freedom is hard; it is a heavy burden. Men, as Dostoevsky has shown with such amazing power, often renounce freedom to ease their lot.

When I was young, people used to call me "the free son of the ether." This was true only insofar as I am certainly not a "son of the earth": I have always been a stranger to the stubborn and crushing element of earth; rather, I proceeded from and sought for freedom. If, however, the label "free son of the ether" denotes a kind of easygoingness, a lightness and lack of the sense of affliction and pain, then this cannot be true of me at all. I won freedom with difficulty and with untold pain. "Freedom led me to the crossing of the ways in the impenetrable darkness of night." All the things to which I have borne witness through my life spring from some initial experience of freedom and have been inspired by freedom. Freedom is not, as Hegel maintained, the creature of necessity; just the reverse: necessity is the creature of freedom, or, to put it differently, a certain tendency or orientation of freedom. I cannot agree to accept any truth otherwise than out of, and in, freedom. I am not, however, using the word "freedom" here in the sense current among professional philosophers, viz., not as denoting "free will," but in a much deeper, metaphysical sense. Truth can make me free, and yet I can accept truth only through, and in, freedom. Thus there are two kinds of freedom, and the problem of their relation has exercised my mind in most of my writings. The primordial, undetermined, and underived character of freedom has been expressed in the proposition that the "self" cannot receive the "non-self" unless it makes it (the "non-self") the content of itself, unless it takes it up into its own freedom.

The war for freedom which I have waged all my life was to me the thing of the greatest value and importance. But it also had its reverse and less fortunate side: it entailed opposition, estrangement, disunion, and even hostility. Sometimes freedom drove me into conflict with love. In contrast to the widespread opinion concerning these things, I have always held freedom to be aristocratic rather than democratic in character. The majority of men do not in the least love freedom and do not seek after it. The revolutions of the masses have never displayed any great love of freedom. . . .

All things in human life should be born of freedom and pass through freedom and be rejected whenever they betray freedom. The true meaning and origin of the fallen condition of man are to be seen in the primordial rejection of freedom. When I recall my whole life from the very first step into it I realize that I never knew or admitted any authority or extraneous power whatsoever. I could not recognize their admissibility for, and compatibility with, the dignity and freedom of man. I have not known authority either at home, or at school, or in my philosophical enquiries, or, most particularly, in my religious life. . . . I do not mean to say, of course, that I refused to learn from others, from all the great masters of thought, or that I was subject to no influences or not indebted to anyone. I was constantly stimulated by the minds of all those whom I had the privilege of meeting and reading, particularly of those whose universe of discourse was congenial to me. But all these influences and stimuli were received in freedom or, even more, were the outcome of the exercise of my own freedom. I cannot think of any intellectual influence which has not been assimilated by me in the very depths of freedom and self-determination. I have never complied with any philosophical tradition, and I am one of the most untraditional philosophers. I did not even need to break with authorities, since I never acknowledged any. There were, however, a number of thinkers and writers who nourished my love for the freedom of the spirit, who confirmed this love and attended to its fruition in me. The most important of these was Dostoevsky, particularly in his "Legend of the Grand Inquisitor." Among thinkers, the most important was Kant; his philosophy is a philosophy of freedom, although it is perhaps not sufficiently radical and consistent. At a later stage I discovered the great importance of Ibsen: I read him as one would read a prophet who is moved by a longing for the liberation of man.

All my differences and dissensions from individual people as well as from religious, social, and political movements had their origin in the matter of freedom. The struggle for freedom was for me not primarily a social struggle but one which concerned man standing over against society. Roger Secrétain says in one of the most remarkable books on Péguy (*Péguy, soldat de la verité*) that Péguy's secret passion in life was his anarchism and his repudiation of all authority. He also speaks of Péguy's solitariness, which made it impossible for him to have any followers: those who did follow him were encouraged by Péguy himself to break away. And, significantly enough, it was his very anarchism which brought him face to face with God—on condition, however, as Secrétain puts it, that God himself be *"un liberal, un libertaire, presque un anarchiste."*

It is perhaps characteristic of me that I never underwent what is known as conversion, neither did I know what it meant to be a complete unbeliever. I can only revolt against false and servile ideas about God in the name of another idea which is freer and nobler. But I shall try to explain this when I come to speak of my religious convictions.

I displayed great vehemence and passion in my fight for freedom, even when I was quite young. I have said before that our family did not uphold authoritarian principles, and I always succeeded in maintaining and defending my independence. Nevertheless, I broke with the social milieu into which I was born. . . . Everything which did not originate directly in spirit and in freedom repelled me, and I came to realize that all things belonging to the genus, class, family, were opposed to freedom. My dislike of the genus and of everything concerned with birth, as distinct from creation, should be seen in the light of an insensate love of freedom. Family has always appeared to me as the enemy and enslaver of personal freedom. Family is the order of "necessity" rather than of "freedom," and the struggle for freedom is the struggle against the power of the genus. The antithesis of birth and creativity is, in fact, at the center of my thought. I set out by placing freedom, personality, and creatorship at the basis of my whole outlook; but, in due course, my concern for freedom became more intense. When I broke with the life and traditions of the gentry and joined the revolutionary movement I began to struggle for freedom within that movement, among the revolutionary intelligentsia and in the midst of the Marxist world. I came to realize quite soon that the revolutionary intelligentsia did not really cherish freedom, and that its true inspiration was to be found elsewhere.

While still a Marxist I saw elements in Marxism which were bound to lead to despotism and the denial of freedom. Here as elsewhere I witnessed the clash of person and group, of person and society, of person and public opinion; and I invariably took the side of the person. I devoted many years of my life to fighting public opinion among the intelligentsia and, in doing so, failed to pursue the more creative and constructive work of philosophy. For a long time I was completely carried away by the task of solving the problem of the relation of socialism and freedom, and endured agonies of inner conflict and anxiety on this account. I considered the usual arguments provided by liberalism and individualism against socialism to be both unconvincing and hypocritical, and the defense of freedom put up by them altogether spurious. But it was clear to me that socialism may develop in different directions: it may lead to the emancipation of man, but it may also lead to the destruction of human freedom, to tyranny and to a system such as pre-figured by Dostoevsky in his "Legend of the Grand Inquisitor." In quite early days, while still active in Marxist circles, I had presentiments of the possibility of totalitarian communism and I endeavored to combat and to prevent this. But I was combating similar things in every ideological movement and circle with which I came into contact. All ideological groups, all gatherings of people in pursuit of "ideals" are known to encroach on, and to betray, the freedom, independence, and creativity of man. On becoming associated with ecclesiastical orthodoxy I experienced the same anguish which I felt amongst the nobility and the revolutionaries: I watched the same apostasy from freedom, the same hostility to the independence of the human person, and the same forfeiture of man's creativity. It was an identical phenomenon presenting itself on a deeper level, because religion touches the very depth of the human soul.

I persisted in my struggle for the freedom and dignity of man during the communist revolution, and this led to my exile from Russia. When I became an *émigré* and lived among the *émigrés*, I found myself, not unexpectedly, face to face with the same problem. I came to realize that the Russian "emigration" denied and hated freedom as much as and more than the Russian communists, with the difference, however, that the latter had more right to such hostility, seeing that the most monstrous crimes against freedom have been committed in the name of freedom. After the first World War a generation grew up which resolved to set itself against freedom and took to loving authority and force. This, however, in no way took me by surprise: I felt alone in my search for freedom and devotion to the human person as I had done all my life long. I could not discover any such searching or devotion either among the ruling classes of the old regime, or among the old revolutionary intelligentsia, or in historical Orthodoxy, or among the communists, or, and least of all, in the new generation of Fascists. Every mass of people banded together is hostile to freedom. I might put this more emphatically by saying that every society which has so far been organized or is in the process of organization is inimical to freedom and tends to deny human personality. This results from a fatal falsification of human consciousness misguided by a confusion in the hierarchy of values. Among the post-war (it should now be called the pre-war) generation there is no evidence of a single original thought: it lives entirely by the odds and ends and aberrations of nineteenth-century mentality. The realization of the value and primacy of freedom and personality sets man, alone and apart, over against society and the mass processes of history. The democratic age is an age of Philistinism. It is not conducive to the development of strong personalities. . . .

Freedom is the source of many misunderstandings and it has been found to denote many different and even contradictory things. Freedom is not a static concept but a living reality to be known dynamically through the exercise and the experience of it. There exists a dialectic of freedom, which is duly revealed in the destiny of man and of the world. Freedom can even turn into its opposite and issue in abject tyranny.

Philosophical textbooks generally speak of freedom as identical with "free will," that is to say, as the possibility of choice, of turning right or left. Such a choice, however, presupposes man's confrontation with a norm which determines a distinction between good and evil. Thus it is that the concept of free will became particularly useful as a basis for criminal law, guaranteeing man's accountability and hence his punishment or acquittal as the case might be. For me freedom has always meant something quite different. Freedom is first and foremost my independence, determination from within and creative initiative; its reality does not depend on any norm and its exercise is not a mere choice between a good and an evil standing over against me: rather, freedom is my own norm and my own creation of good and evil. The very condition of choice may result in a sense of repression, indecisiveness, or even in the complete disappearance of freedom on the part of man. Liberation comes when the choice is made and when I have begun to create. The problem of man and of human creativeness is indeed closely associated with that of freedom. I have always believed that life in God is freedom, untrammeled flight, anarchy in the true sense of the word. The real call of freedom is not to be thought of in moral or psychological but in metaphysical terms: God and freedom, evil and freedom, creative novelty and freedom. Freedom involves novelty.

The antagonists of freedom like to contrast it with truth, which commands the allegiance of man and forces recognition by him. But truth as an object which intrudes itself and wields authority over me—an object in the name of which it is demanded that I should renounce freedom—is a figment: truth is no extraneous thing; it is the way and the life. Truth is spiritual conquest; it is known in and through freedom. Truth which forces itself on me and in the name of which I am required to relinquish freedom is no truth at all but a temptation of the evil one. The dictum "Knowledge of the truth will make

you free" evidently and paradoxically entails two kinds of freedom—a final and an initial one. I come of my own freedom
to know the truth which (in its turn) liberates me. There is no
authority in the world which has the power to constrain me to
truth. I cannot be liberated by force.

I have never admitted and I do not now admit any orthodoxy
intruding itself on me and asserting its possession of truth apart
from my own free quest, my own asking and demanding. I
have always found myself resisting any orthodoxy, be it political
or religious, which has attempted to limit or destroy my freedom. It could not have been and cannot be otherwise. I am
even inclined to think that compelling orthodoxy has no relation at all to truth and, indeed, holds truth in abomination. The
greatest falsifications of truth have been brought about by the
orthodox. Orthodoxy has a social character and origin and
denotes the authority of an organized collective wielding power
over the free personality and the free spirit of man. I believe
in the scandal and stumbling block of freedom. Freedom itself
is a constituent and basic element of truth as it gradually reveals
itself in and to me. The freedom of my conscience is an absolute
dogma, in the face of which no mid-course and no compromise
are possible. . . . The whole value of Khomyakov's thought lay
in that he discovered *sobornost* as a reality belonging to the realm
of freedom. Yet he did not carry his discovery to its logical
conclusion. *Sobornost* can in no way be regarded as implying
an external authority, for here too absolute primacy belongs,
at each and every moment, to freedom. Khomyakov did not
take into account the possibility of a conflict between freedom
and *sobornost*, in which the ultimate decision must needs lie
with freedom. I cannot accept as truth that which is thrust
down my throat; I can accept as truth only that which is wrung
out from within myself. I cannot acknowledge as falsehood that
in which I see truth, and I cannot acknowledge as truth that in
which I see falsehood, merely because I am obliged to acknowledge them as such. In point of fact no one has really ever
consented to do this. If the Church wields authority by driving
me into conformity with the collective consciousness of ecclesiastical society, I find myself up against the same kind of

phenomenon as the ugly but very instructive Moscow trials of the veteran communists.

But *sobornost* signifies a quality of life which affirms the reality of freedom by widening the scope of freedom and by revealing its transcendent, universal dimension. The recognition of the absolute priority of freedom does not, therefore, denote, as some would like to make out, individualistic self-assertion. Freedom of the spirit has in fact nothing in common with individualism: to be free is not to be insulated; it is not to shut oneself up, but, on the contrary, to break through in a creative act to the fullness and universality of existence.

Personalism *

Man is a riddle in the world and, it may be, the greatest riddle.
Man is a riddle not because he is an animal, not because he is
a social being, not as a part of nature and society. It is as a person
that he is a riddle—just that precisely; it is because he possesses
personality. The entire world is nothing in comparison with
human personality, with the unique person of a man, with
his unique fate. Man lives in an agony, and he wants to know
who he is, where he comes from, and whither he is going.
Already in Greece man desired to know himself and in that
he saw the reading of the riddle of existence and the fountain
spring of philosophical knowledge. It is possible for man to get
knowledge of himself from above or from below, either from
his own light, the divine principle which is within him, or from
his own darkness, the elemental subconscious demonic principle
within him. And he can do this because he is a twofold and
contradictory being. He is a being who is polarized in the
highest degree, God-like and beast-like, exalted and base, free
and enslaved, apt both for rising and for falling, capable of
great love and sacrifice, capable also of great cruelty and
unlimited egoism. Dostoevsky, Kierkegaard, and Nietzsche recognized the tragic principle in man and the inconsistency of his
nature with peculiar distinctness. Before that Pascal had expressed
better than anyone this two-sidedness of man. Others have looked
at man from below and revealed the base elemental principles in
him, the impress of his Fall. As a fallen being, determined by
elemental forces, he appeared to be actuated solely by economic
interests, subconscious sensual impulses, and anxiety. But a sense
of need in suffering and martyrdom in the case of Dostoevsky,
horror and penitence in the case of Kierkegaard, and, with
Nietzsche, the will to power and cruelty also bear witness to
the fact that man is a fallen being, but that he suffers as the

* From *Slavery and Freedom*, trans. R. M. French, New York, 1944, pp.
20-25.

result of this Fall and that he desires to get the better of it. It is precisely the consciousness of personality in man which speaks of his higher nature and higher vocation. If man were not a person, albeit a personality which has not yet emerged into full view, or which has been crushed, albeit one struck down by disease, albeit a personality which exists only as potential or possible, then he would be like other things in the world and there would be nothing unusual about him. But personality in man is evidence of this, that the world is not self-sufficient, that it can be overcome and surmounted. Personality is like nothing else in the world, there is nothing with which it can be compared, nothing which can be placed on a level with it. When a person enters the world, a unique and unrepeatable personality, then the world process is broken into and compelled to change its course, in spite of the fact that outwardly there is no sign of this. Personality finds no place in the continuous complex process of world life, it cannot be a moment or an element in the evolution of the world. The existence of personality presupposes discontinuity; it is inexplicable by any sort of uninterruption; it is inexplicable by any sort of uninterrupted continuity.

Man, the only man known to biology and sociology, man as a natural being and a social being, is the offspring of the world and of the processes which take place in the world. But personality, man as a person, is not a child of the world, he is of another origin. And this it is that makes man a riddle. Personality is a breakthrough, a breaking in upon this world; it is the introduction of something new. Personality is not nature, it does not belong to the objective hierarchy of nature, as a subordinate part of it. And, therefore, as we shall see, hierarchical personalism is false. Man is a personality not by nature but by spirit. By nature he is only an individual. Personality is not a monad entering into a hierarchy of monads and subordinate to it. Personality is a microcosm, a complete universe. It is personality alone that can bring together a universal content and be a potential universe in an individual form. That universal content is not to be attained by any other reality in the world of nature or of history. Such other realities are always characterized as parts. Personality is not a part and cannot be a part in relation to any kind of whole, not even to an immense whole, or to the entire world. This is the essential principle of personality, and its mystery. To whatever extent empirical man enters as a part into any sort of natural or social whole, it is not as a personality that he does so, and his personality is left outside this subordination of the part to the whole. According to Leibniz, and Renouvier as well, the monad is simple substance entering into a complex organization. The monad is closed, shut up, it has neither windows nor doors. For personality, however, infinity opens out, it enters into infinity, and admits infinity into itself; in its self-revelation it is directed toward an infinite content.

And at the same time personality presupposes form and limit; it does not mingle with its environment nor is it dissolved in the world around it. Personality is the universal in an individually unrepeatable form. It is a union of the universal-infinite and the individual-particular. It is in this apparent contradiction that personality exists. The personal in man is just that in him which he does not have in common with others, but in that which is not shared with others is included the potentiality of the universal. The understanding of human personality as a microcosm is set in antithesis to the organic-hierarchical interpretation of him, which transforms man into a subordinate part of a whole, into a common, a universal.

But personality is not a part of the universe, the universe is a part of personality, it is its quality. Such is the paradox of personalism. One must not think of personality as a substance, that would be a naturalistic idea of personality. Personality cannot be recognized as an object, as one of the objects in a line with other objects in the world, like a part of the world. That is the way in which the anthropological sciences, biology, psychology, or sociology would regard man. In that way man is looked at partially: but there is in that case no mystery of man, as personality, as an existential center of the world. Personality is recognized only as a subject, in infinite subjectivity, in which is hidden the secret of existence.

Personality is the unchanging in change, unity in the manifold.

It strikes us unpleasantly, alike if there is the unchanging in man and not change, and if there is change and not the unchanging; if there is unity and not the manifold, or the manifold and not unity. Both in the one case and in the other the essential qualitativeness of personality is disclosed. Personality is not a congealed condition, it breaks up, it develops, it is enriched; but it is the development of one and the same abiding subject. That is its very name. The very change itself takes place for the preservation of this unchanging abiding thing, as Poulain correctly says.

Personality is not in any case a ready-made datum, it is the posing of a question, it is the ideal of a man. Perfectly accomplished unity and wholeness of personality is the ideal of man. Personality is self-constructive. Not a single man can say of himself that he is completely a person. Personality is an axiological category, a category of value. Here we meet the fundamental paradox in the existence of personality. Personality must construct itself, enrich itself, fill itself with universal content, achieve unity in wholeness in the whole extent of its life. But for this, it must already exist. There must originally exist that subject which is called upon to construct itself. Personality is at the beginning of the road and it is only at the end of the road. Personality is not made up of parts, it is not an aggregate, not a composition, it is a primary whole. The growth of personality, the realization of personality certainly does not mean the formation of a whole out of its parts. It means rather the creative acts of personality, as a whole thing, which is not brought out of anything and not put together from anything. The form of personality is integral, it is present as a whole in all the acts of personality, personality has a unique, an unrepeatable form, *Gestalt*. What is known as *Gestalt* psychology, which regards form as the primary qualitative value, is more acceptable to personalism than other systems of psychology.

The very breakup of the form of personality does not indicate its final disappearance. Personality is indestructible. Personality creates itself and exists by its own destiny, finding the source of its strength in an existence which surpasses it. Personality is potentially the universal, but quite certainly a distinct, unrepeatable, irreplaceable being with a unique form. Personality is the exception, not the rule. The secret of the existence of personality lies in its absolute irreplaceability, its happening but once, its uniqueness, its incomparableness. Everything individual is irreplaceable.

There is a baseness in the replacing of an individual creature which you have loved, permanently recognizing in it the form of personality, by another being. This irreplaceableness exists not only in reference to people, but also in reference to animals. One personality may have traits of resemblance to other personalities, which allow a comparison to be made. But these marks of similarity do not touch that essence of personality which makes it personality, not personality in general, but this personality.

In every human personality there is the common, the universal, not the inward universal as the creative acquisition of a qualitative content of life, but an outward, adherent universal. But personality, this concrete personality, exists by its non-common expression, not by the fact that it has two eyes, like all other people, and not by the common expression of those eyes. In human personality there is much that is generic, belonging to the human race, much which belongs to history, tradition, society, class, family, much that is hereditary and imitative, much that is "common." But it is precisely this which is not "personal" in personality. That which is "personal" is original, connected with the primary fountainhead, authentic. Personality must perform its self-existent, original, creative acts, and this alone makes it personality and constitutes its unique value.

Personality must be the exception, no law at all is applicable to it. Everything generic and hereditary is only material for the creative activity of personality. The whole burden which is laid upon man by nature and society, by history and the demands of civilization, confronts us in the form of difficulties which demand resistance and creative transformation into the personal, uniquely the personal. The typical members of a group, a class, or a profession may be clear individualities but not clear personalities. Personality in man is the triumph over the determination of the social group. Personality is not a substance but an act, a creative act. Every act is a creative act: a non-creative act is passivity. Personality is activity, opposition, victory over the dragging burden of the world, the triumph of freedom over the world's slavery. The fear of exertion is harmful to the realization of personality. Personality is effort and conflict, the conquest of self and of the world, victory over slavery; it is emancipation.

Personality is rational being, but it is not determined by reason and it cannot be defined as the vehicle of reason. Reason in itself is not personal, but universal, common, impersonal reason. The moral and rational nature of man with Kant is an impersonal common nature. The Greek understanding of man as a rational being does not fit in with personalist philosophy. Personality is not only rational being but also free being. Personality is my whole thinking, my whole willing, my whole feeling, my whole creative activity. The reason of Greek philosophy, the reason of German idealism is impersonal reason, universal reason. But there exist also my personal reason and especially my personal will. Personalism cannot be founded upon idealism, Platonic or German, and cannot be based on naturalism, on evolutionary philosophy, or on vital philosophy, which dissolves personality in the impersonal, cosmic, vital process.

Existentialism *

When, in opposing the subject and the object, philosophical theory abstracts them both from Being, it makes the apprehension of Being impossible. To oppose knowledge and Being is to exclude knowledge from Being. Thus the knowing subject is confronted with Being as an apprehensible but abstract object with which no communion is possible. The objective state is itself the source of this abstraction, which excludes any communion or, as Lévy-Bruhl puts it, any "participation" [1] in the object, although concepts may be formed about it. The nature of the object is purely general; it contains no element of irreducible originality, which is the sign of the individual. That is, indeed, the essential distinction between the subject and the object.

Objective processes transform Being into a superstructure of the subject, elaborated for philosophical purposes. It is precisely because the subject identifies himself with this objective superstructure that he discovers therein a more suitable expression of his own cognitive structure. Abstraction is one definition of knowledge; but this abstraction is the work of the subject, of the knowing spirit itself. When he is abstracted from his inner existence, the philosophical subject loses all contact with Being, and his existence becomes dependent on the objective processes he has set in motion. Thus intellection no longer affects or inheres in Being; on the contrary, it becomes an absolutely extrinsic and logical rather than a spiritual act.

This is the tragedy of knowledge as expounded by German Idealism, which reaches its highest expression in the neo-Kantian school. True, the opposition of knowledge and Being, of the subject and Being, is part of an older philosophical tradition; but the manifest superiority of the German post-Kantian philoso-

---

* From *Solitude and Society*, trans. George Reavey, New York, 1939, pp. 48-57.

1. Cf. Lévy-Bruhl, *Les fonctions mentales dans les sociétés inférieures.*

phies lay in their critical approach to the problem of objectification and in their recognition of the importance of the knowing subject. Pre-Kantian, and particularly Scholastic, philosophy had approached the problem realistically and had identified the concepts elaborated by the subject with Being itself. This was the origin of naturalist metaphysics with its doctrine of substance and its hierarchy of Being. In the light of these facts, the advent of Kant and of German Idealism marked a most important stage in the history of human self-consciousness. It was a step toward human emancipation, toward freeing man from the constraint and slavery of the objective world. The very fact of a critical awareness of the subject's participation in the objective processes implied the subject's deliverance from the external tyranny of the objective world. The work done in this sphere by Kant, and the German Idealists who followed on Descartes and Berkeley, precludes any return to the ancient metaphysical system of the substantialist type which identified Being with object. Henceforth Being could only be apprehended subjectively, and the subject accordingly assumed an ontological character. Philosophers like Kant, Fichte, Schelling, and Hegel have built up a metaphysical system on a subjective basis, but in the process they interpreted the subject in an objective and non-existential way. As a result, they have made no contribution to the problem of the human personality, but have tended rather to espouse the cause of universalism. They affirmed that the subject was neither human nor personal. Thus, after Kant and Fichte, Hegelian philosophy established itself on the whole, despite its irrational elements,[2] as a new type of objective rationalism. Actually, we can only transcend the tragic implications of Idealism by advancing in the direction of what is today called *Existenzphilosophie*, or existential philosophy, rather than by reviving any of the pre-Kantian metaphysical systems.

Kierkegaard laid the foundations of existential philosophy by challenging the Hegelian universal concept and its fatal effect on the individual. Kierkegaard's thought is not fundamentally new; it is very simple,[3] and is motivated by the sense of anguish

2. Cf. Kroner, *Von Kant bis Hegel.*
3. Cf. in particular, Kierkegaard's *Philosophische Brocken.*

to which the personal drama of his life gave rise.[4] His tragic experience led him to emphasize the existential character of the knowing subject, the initial fact of man's immersion in the mystery of existence. The philosophy most expressive of man's existential character is the most vital; for philosophers have too often tended to overlook the fact of their own existence as distinct from their power of intellection, and the fact that their philosophy is little more than the translation of their existence. We may therefore conclude, though not in Kierkegaard's own terms, that, from the existential standpoint, the philosopher is situated on the extra-natural plane, that is, in the inmost depth of Being; for the subject is himself a part of Being and, as such, communes with its mystery. Among the number of existential philosophers we may count Saint Augustine and Pascal, in a sense Schopenhauer and Feuerbach, Nietzsche and Dostoevsky. But Kierkegaard was the most significant exponent of this philosophy. In my book *The Philosophy of Freedom,* written some twenty years ago, I had already defined existential philosophy, though I did not use that term, as a philosophy which *represents* something in itself, which is a manifestation of Being, of existence, as opposed to the type of philosophy which treats of something extraneous, of the objective world.

On the basis of this affirmation, which has some affinity with Jaspers' conception, existential philosophy represents a mode of non-objective intellection. Ordinarily, the process of abstraction eliminates the mystery of existence, of concrete Being. There can be no worse aberration than to identify the object with reality. To know and to objectify or to abstract are currently regarded as synonyms. But the very opposite is true: effective knowledge involves familiarity, or, in other terms, a subjective approach, an identification of oneself with the subjective existence. It is our duty, therefore, to reject the naturalist, *objective* conception of Being in favor of the existential one. Even phenomenology may be interpreted as an experience transcending the objective state. Communion with men, animals, plants, or minerals is an extra-natural phenomenon revealing potential ways of knowing.

4. The same is true of Leon Shestov, whose philosophy consists in the self-negation of philosophy.

Heidegger and Jaspers are the two leading contemporary representatives of existential philosophy. Heidegger distinguishes between *essential* existence and *objective* existence, or the *Dasein*. The state of being-in-the-world, the *Dasein*, inspires anxiety and fear; it is above all a temporal state destined to become the One, *das Man*. The banality of everyday existence robs death of its tragic poignancy and obscures the fact that it is the direct outcome of the finite state, of the *Dasein;* but the sense of tragedy is intensified when the fact of existence is predominant. Existence is a state of Being, of which the *Dasein* is a part. *Seiende*, on the other hand, is essential Being, my own self, my own essential nature. The originality of Heidegger's philosophy lies in the importance he attached to the *In-der-Welt-sein*, the state of being-in-the-world, as one of the necessary but degraded aspects of Being. Human existence is substantial. Concrete existence has more importance for Being than essence. Thus philosophy should be concerned with existences rather than with essences. Heidegger's *Dasein* involves anxiety and fear of the degraded world as a constituent part of its ontological nature. Man's moral conscience requires him to experience this anxiety in a world where he is at the mercy of objectivity. The *Dasein* is a state of guilt, all that constitutes human anxiety and the oppressive sense of human insignificance.

In the light of Heidegger's philosophy, it is difficult to discover the genesis of the human conscience. His philosophy is anti-Platonic and anti-spiritual. Its pessimism makes it more purely a philosophy of "being-in-the-world" rather than an Existential philosophy. To use Heidegger's own expression, his ontology is that of nothingness, of being-nothing. He makes no attempt to explain the nature of extra-temporal existence. But Heidegger does set out to establish an Existential philosophy; and the essential problems with which he is concerned, such as the banality of everyday life, degradation, and death, are different from the problems usually treated by philosophy. . . .

The same problems are to be found in Jaspers,[5] with whom I have more in common than with Heidegger. The problem which preoccupies Jaspers most of all is that of man's "limit-

5. Karl Jaspers, 1st Bd. *Philosophische Weltorientierung;* 2nd Bd. *Existenzerhellung.*

situation," that of the communication between one Ego and another. He is particularly careful to point out that the Ego, as an entity, is distinct from universal Being. The Ego can never be an object, because the object is never existential.[6] Jaspers is much clearer on this point than Heidegger. He demonstrates that the existential Ego, as opposed to the empirical Ego, can transcend temporal existence because its entity is extra-temporal. The idea of transcendence is of capital importance in Jaspers' philosophy, and it dominates his "metaphysics.". . .

Both Heidegger and Jaspers have undoubtedly made an original contribution to thought, even though their philosophies are extremely tragic and pessimistic because they lead man to the brink of an abyss. The trend of modern philosophy, as manifest in Descartes and the Cartesians, in Kant and the neo-Kantians, and in the scientifically minded Positivists, was essentially naturalist. Existential philosophy, however, advances a stage further. That is its great and unquestioned merit; but its originality has so far been limited by its associations with Kierkegaard, who affirms that existence is the primary concern of the existential subject.[7] What then, we may ask, is existence? It is, in the first place, a very different thing from intellection. As Bergson has demonstrated, it is situated in time, but not in space. It is dynamic as contrasted with the immobility of logic. To formulate an idea of himself the intellectual subject is forced to deny his existential nature, to face the antagonism between abstract thought and existence. Existence excludes the idea of mediation: to exist is to be an entity. The *particular* is more deeply rooted in Being than the *general*. The world of eternal Ideas is not the image of existence, as the Platonic tradition would have us believe; this image is more truly reflected in human nostalgia, despair, unrest and dissatisfaction. Thus contradiction is more fruitful than identity. *Objective* thought conceals no mystery, but *subjective* thought does. Existence is synonymous with becoming. There may be a logical system behind it, but a system of exist-

6. Ideas of a similar nature may be found in Gabriel Marcel's *Journal métaphysique;* cf. notably the appendix which treats of the problem of objectification.

7. S. Kierkegaard, *Philosophische Brocken.*

ence is inconceivable. Objectively we treat of *things*, but subjectively our concern is with the *subject;* and even our preoccupation with objective truth is essentially *subjective*. This is, indeed, the very core of Kierkegaard's thought, which may be summed up as the *identification of the knowing subject with the existential subject:* the primary purpose of subjective thought is to manifest its existential nature. The essentially Christian character of Kierkegaard's "paradox" represents a departure from immanentism. For Kierkegaard, man's inner life, his existence, has nothing immanent about it. He interprets "phenomenon" to mean self-revelation, that is, transcendence. In this connection, we may recall the distinction established by N. Lossky between immanence in the consciousness and immanence in the conscious subject.

Despite a certain affinity between Kierkegaard's philosophy and that of Heidegger and Jaspers, there is yet an essential difference between them. For Kierkegaard, philosophy is itself existence rather than an *interpretation* of existence; whereas, for Heidegger and Jaspers, who are concerned with a particular philosophical tradition, philosophy is synonymous with interpretation. Their aim, especially Heidegger's, is to elaborate philosophical categories on an existential basis, to make categories of human anxiety or the fear of death. Heidegger's attempt to break away from the domination of rationalist and objective knowledge constitutes a very remarkable and in many ways original achievement. But actually, concepts and categories are only a means of apprehending the *Dasein*, the being-in-the-world, that is, objective or completely abstract Being. *The concept is only related to the object;* therefore, as Jaspers admits more clearly than Heidegger, the inner existence or primary Being can only be apprehended through the imagination, the symbol and the myth. The elaboration of concepts is an objective process leading inevitably to a hypostasis of the intellectual categories themselves. As a result, this type of philosophy is primarily concerned with essences, substances, objects; it makes God Himself an object, whereas a philosophy primarily concerned with the personality is able to apprehend existence. Thus Heidegger speaks with greater authority of the *Dasein* than of existence itself; in fact, although he considers the objective state a degraded one, his own philosophical approach contributes to maintain the world in its degraded state.

Existential philosophy cannot be based on concepts and ordinary categories even when it is ontological. *The concept is invariably concerned with something, it is never that something:* it is never existential. Vladimir Solovyov established an interesting distinction between abstract Being as the *predicate* and concrete Being as the *subject.* The notion *is* is an example of abstract Being; the notion *I am* is an example of concrete Being. Unfortunately, this distinction [8] is often ignored, and the predicates are converted into hypostases. In his criticism of German Idealism, Vladimir Solovyov would appear to have penetrated into the very heart of concrete Being. And yet his philosophy cannot really be called Existential, because it is still dominated by rationalist metaphysics; his most genuine expression lies in poetry rather than in philosophy. A judgment of existence is not simply a judgment of what exists; it is also a judgment made by the existing subject. Existence is not deduced from, but precedes, judgment; and logical Being is the product of intellection, of an objective process.

For this reason, Husserl's Phenomenology fails to be an Existential philosophy, although it exercised a considerable influence on Heidegger. Husserl affirms that real objects are inherent in the essences and need no mediation; he also contends that evidence is not a state of consciousness, but the presence of the object itself. Phenomenology is therefore a philosophy of the pure consciousness, a vision of essences (*Wesenheiten*).[9] But the vision of essences fails to reveal the mystery of existence. So does N. Hartmann's philosophy, with its idea of the "trans-objective," and its most interesting ontological conception of the relation between the subject and the object.[10] Dilthey is much nearer to Existential philosophy when he refuses to resolve the spiritual

8. V. Solovyov, *La Critique des principes abstraits* and *Les Principes philosophiques de la connaissance intégrale.*

9. Cf. Levinas, *La Théorie de l'intuition dans la phénoménologie de Husserl.*

10. N. Hartmann, *Metaphysik der Erkenntnis.*

life into its elements or to analyze it, and studies it, instead, as a whole in its synthetical aspects.[11]

I shall now come to my personal conception of the subject in relation to the object. By opposing subject and object, intellection and Being, philosophical theory reaches an impasse, for it inevitably eliminates the subject from Being and makes Being objective.

11. Dilthey, *Einleitung in die Geisteswissenschaften,* etc. *Die geistige Welt. Einleitung in die Philosophie des Lebens.*

[NICHOLAS BERDYAEV]

Objectification *

It is important to grasp, first of all, that the objective world
is a degraded and spellbound world—a world of phenomena
rather than one of existences. Objective processes *abstract* and
disrupt existence. They substitute society for community, general principles for communion, and the empire of Caesar for
the Kingdom of God. There is no participation in objective
processes; for, as we shall see more precisely hereafter, the
result of objectification in knowledge as elsewhere is not only to
isolate man but also to confine his activities to an essentially alien
world. Objective processes are a spiritual manifestation, but there
is no spiritual freedom in the resulting objective world. Reality
is originally part of the inner existence, of the inner spiritual
communion and community, but it becomes degraded in the
process of objectification and of having to submit to social necessities. Thus, although we are considering objectification only in
its relation to knowledge, we can affirm that there is no spiritual
mystery in the objective world. . . .

To objectify is to rationalize in the sense of accepting concepts—substances, universal ideas, and the rest—as realities.
Rational and objective thought is abstracted from the spheres of
the irrational and of the individual, of existence and of the
existing. We should distinguish above all between two types of
knowledge: there is, first of all, rational and objective knowledge
which is confined within the frontiers of reason and apprehends
only the general; and secondly, there is the knowledge immanent
in Being and in existence through which reason is enabled to
apprehend the irrational and the individual after transcending
the general; this knowledge is synonymous with *community* and
participation. Both these types of knowledge are to be found in
the history of human thought. Knowledge can thus be considered

* From *Solitude and Society*, trans. George Reavey, New York, 1939, pp. 61,
67-68, and *The Beginning and the End*, trans. R. M. French, New York,
1957, pp. 56-63.

from two different standpoints: from that of society, of communication between men by means of the objective and the general; and from that of community, of existential communion and
of penetration into the heart of the individual.

This is the very core of my thought. Objective knowledge is
invariably *social*, because it fails to apprehend the existential
subject; its essential nature, which is to be universally valid, is
social and depends on its degree of community. A sociology of
knowledge has still to be elaborated; . . . but it will have to be
interpreted in a different way from positivism, since it is a metaphysical discipline for which the problem of society, of communion, and of community is the ultimate problem of Being.
Being can be communion and participation; or it can be society
and communication. The idea that all the spheres of Being should
be rationalized and socialized is an erroneous and completely
anti-Christian one. It is the result of scientism rather than
science, of the attempt to universalize degrees and forms of
knowledge of which the validity is strictly limited. . . .

In my view the subject itself introduces objectification and
gives rise to the world of phenomena, and does so not only as
he who knows, but above all he who exists.

It is essential to grasp the mysterious process of objectification.
I live in two worlds, in a subjective world which is my own
proper world, and also in an objective world, the world of
objects, which exists for my sake and at the same time is alien
to me. This fact that I am cast into an objective world which
acts forcefully upon me has not merely an epistemological meaning, it has a metaphysical meaning also. Kant gave no explanation of why the world of appearances comes to be and why
reason is limited to the knowledge of this world of appearances,
which is not the true world. The true world of things-in-themselves is not open to perception. Does the thing-in-itself reveal
itself in appearance? In the phraseology that I use this means
that Kant does not explain the mystery of objectification. He leads
up to the subject, but does not himself deal with it.

The objectification of the world takes place through our agency
and for our sakes, and this is the fall of the world, this is its
loss of freedom, and the alienation of its parts. It might be

expressed by saying that the freedom of noumena passes into the necessity of phenomena. The world of appearances acquires a grandiose empirical reality which exercises compulsion and force upon us.

According to Hegel, "objectivity is a real concept which has moved out from its own inwardness and passed into existence." To him an idea is "an objectively true concept, something which is true, as such." Hegel makes the mistake of ascribing a sort of freedom to objectivity, whereas in fact it denotes the loss of freedom. He fails to understand that the self-alienation of spirit in objectivity is a fall. He is an optimist. He is mistaken in recognizing the existence of objective spirit instead of acknowledging only the objectification of spirit. It is along that line of thought that the Kantian dualism has been overcome and a transition made to monism. This comes near to Saint Thomas Aquinas and his ontologism again, though from the other direction.

In Hegel's view, objectivity, having passed through the critical act of knowledge, issues from the subject. According to Saint Thomas Aquinas, objectivity precedes this critical act. He teaches that the subject matter of knowledge is real and objective, that it does not depend upon the subject, but that it does not exist in nature in a universal form; it is thought which adds that to it. The abstraction of the mind converts thought into act.

Both in Hegel and in Saint Thomas Aquinas there is in principle the same ontologism which is unwilling to see in objectification the fall of the world. There is in each of them the same erroneous elimination of that dualism which is a picture of the tragic position of man in his effort to know. But it was more naively expressed in Saint Thomas Aquinas. In Hegel it was put more critically and it moves to a greater extent through a dialectic of thought. The logic of Saint Thomas Aquinas is static; Hegel's logic is dynamic. Aquinas starts from objectivity as a datum provided by nature and it remains with him unimpaired right to the end. Hegel, on the other hand, begins with subjective spirit and arrives at objectivity and objective spirit as the result of a dialectical process. To Saint Thomas there is in fact nothing irrational; the Latin mind illuminates the life of the world without any oncoming of night. But to Hegel the irrational does exist. His panlogism is not to be identified with objective rationalism. With him the irrational is rationalized and the rational becomes irrational.

Schopenhauer, the most inconsistent of philosophers, left the Kantian dualism by another route. What he teaches about the objectification of the will contains a greater element of truth than there is in Hegel's objective spirit, for he does recognize that the objectified world is not the true world and that it is a world which "lieth in evil."

My inward spiritual experience is not an object. Spirit is never object: the existence of that which exists is never an object. It is thought which determines the objectified phenomenal world. The primacy of the mind over being can be asserted. But this is not the final truth. The mind itself is determined by the noumenal world, by the "intelligible freedom" (in the Kantian sense) of that primary world. What also needs to be asserted is the supremacy of the primarily existent, of that which initially exists, over the mind. Idealism passes into realism.

Husserl remains within the limits of the conscious mind which in his view is more primary than subject and object. He should have arrived at a metaphysics of consciousness. But with him all consciousness is consciousness of something or other, the essence of consciousness is the transcending of self in "intention." Noesis is the subjective side of "intentionality" and Noema is that which the conscious mind recognizes. Phenomenology is the sympathetic descriptive science of the working of the mind.[1] But this would not justify a belief in the metaphysical roots of the conscious mind. The "intentional" character of consciousness is a doctrine which Brentano took over from scholasticism and it is obliged to give pre-eminence to objectivity over subjectivity. The transcending of the self in "intention" must needs be objectification and an onrush toward the objective world. But in the phraseology which I propose, the act of transcending follows a path which is diametrically the opposite of objectification. It is the path toward the noumenal world, to that which truly exists. There are two "intentions" of the conscious mind, one

1. See his *Ideen.*

which leads to the enslaving world of objects and to the realm
of necessity, the other which is directed toward the truly existent world, the realm of freedom.

The natural world of phenomena is symbolic in character. It
is full of signs of another world and it is a symptom of division
and alienation in the sphere of spirit. There is no natural objective
world in the sense of a reality in itself; the only world there is
is the world which is divinely and humanly free. The object
world is enslavement and fall. But the whole cosmos enters into
the true free world, whereas there is nothing of it in the world
of appearances, the world of objects. How the two stand to each
other may be put in this way: appearance is the objectified
world, the natural and social world of necessity, servitude,
enmity, and dominance; whereas the noumenal world is spirit,
freedom, and creative power; it is the world of love and sympathy; it is the whole cosmos. What is called the other world
is not an "other" world to me; it is pre-eminently my world.

There is a tendency in the reason to turn everything into an
object from which existentiality disappears. The whole of Kant's
critique is connected with this fact. The thing-in-itself is not an
object or "non-I," it is a subject, or "Thou." The subject is not,
as in Fichte, the Absolute or the Deity. The subject, the human
"I" and "Thou," are turned into objects and things as a result of
a fall in the relations between us. That fall is a matter of importance in the theory of knowledge. Objectification and the unau-
thentic character of the phenomenal world are by no means to
be taken as meaning that the world of men and women, animals,
plants, minerals, stars, seas, forests, and so on is unreal and that
behind it is something entirely unlike it—the things-in-themselves. It means rather that this world is in a spiritual and moral
condition in which it ought not to be, it is in a state of servitude
and loss of freedom, of enmity and alienation, of ejection into
the external, of subjection to necessity.

Objectification is the ejection of man into the external, it is
an exteriorization of him, it is the subjecting of him to the
conditions of space, time, causality, and rationalization. But in
his existential depth man is in communion with the spiritual
world and with the whole cosmos. The thing-in-itself can only

be the thing-for-my-sake, and it is only the thing-for-my-sake about which I can think. Objectification is the uprising of an exteriorized "not-I" in place of the "Thou" which exists interiorly. The subject matter of thought is the creation of thought itself; and that is the objectifying act.

To Kant, the way out of this situation is simply through the practical reason, which does not objectify and, therefore, breaks through beyond the world of phenomena. There is nothing, no things of the external world outside the subject which thinks them. Thus the impress of thought lies upon reality. But things-in-themselves do exist and in them the spiritual element in thought is inherent, and the irrational is inherent too. Objectification is not only a creation of thought, of the reason and its categories. At a deeper level than that is the fact that it is a result of a certain condition of the subject, with whom exteriorization and alienation are taking place. The object depends above all upon the will of the subject. There exists a transcendental will.

The most remarkable thing is that the objectification of the constructions of the mind begins to live an independent life and gives rise to pseudo-realities. In this respect the antidote should have been Kant, who showed that the existence of an idea does not imply the existence of a reality. This is a very strong point with him. Objectification is rationalization. But it is not merely a perceptual process, it is still more an emotional process, the socialization of feelings and passions. And rationalization may itself be a passion.

Lévy-Bruhl maintains that pre-logical, primitive thinking does not objectify, it is subject to the *loi de participation*, that is to say, the person who thinks and apprehends is united with the subject matter of his actual thought and knowledge.[2] Lévy-Bruhl himself is of the opinion that at the summit of civilization, to apprehend means to objectify, that is, makes the subject matter of knowledge into something alien, it does not unite with it nor become a partner with it. This throws a light upon the nature of objectification.

What we may for the time being call existential philosophy marks a transition from the interpretation of knowledge as objec-

2. See Lévy-Bruhl, *Les fonctions mentales dans les sociétés inférieures.*

tification, to understanding it as *participation*, union ·with the subject matter and entering into cooperation with it. The *loi de participation* among backward and pre-civilized peoples may denote a condition in which clear consciousness is not yet fully awake; it may denote the superstitious attitude to the world and the practice of magic in which mankind was steeped at its origin.

The awakening and development of the conscious mind was accompanied by division and alienation. Man had to pass through a stage in which he subjected his thought and reason to a critique. To pass through objectification is the fate of spirit in this world. Moreover, objectification has a positive significance also in a fallen world. It is capable of arming man and defending him. But at the summit of consciousness, where it comes into touch with the supra-conscious, the reverse process may be set in motion, and apprehension may become union and cooperation; yet in conjunction with all that has been gained by the conquests of criticism and enlightened reason. . . .

The problem of objectification, as I understand it, has nothing in common with the problem of perception, of sensation, or of the relation between the psychological and the physical, or even of the ordinary relation between the subjective and the objective. The problem of objectification lies in a different region from that of the criticism of naive realism and the defense of idealism. It is an existential problem and it is concerned with the disintegration and the fettering of the world, with estrangement and the chains of servitude. It is a problem which arises as a result of the fall of the existential subject, for whom everything is exteriorized and subjected to necessity.

What are the marks of objectification, and the rise of object relations in the world? The following signs may be taken as established: (1) the estrangement of the object from the subject; (2) the absorption of the unrepeatably individual and personal in what is common and impersonally universal; (3) the rule of necessity, of determination from without, the crushing of freedom and the concealment of it; (4) adjustment to the grandiose mien of the world and of history, to the average man, and the socialization of man and his opinions, which destroys distinctive character. In opposition to all this stand communion in sympathy and love, and the overcoming of estrangement; personalism and the expression of the individual and personal character of each existence; a transition to the realm of freedom and determination from within, with victory over enslaving necessity; and the predominance of quality over quantity, of creativeness over adaptation. This is at the same time a definition of the distinction between the noumenal and the phenomenal world. Phenomenon and noumenon are settled by the process of objectification. The fight against the power of objectification is a spiritual revolt of noumena against phenomena, it is a spiritual revolution.

Such an interpretation of the relation between the noumenal and phenomenal worlds is very different from Platonism, and moves out beyond the limits of Kantian dualism. The noumenon is spirit, personality, freedom; it is the creative energy which is active in this world. The task before man is to achieve liberation from his state of externality, and his subjection to necessity, from the violating power of "objectiveness" in nature and history. It is to discover spirituality and freedom as being the plenitude of real existence, which, at its highest point, is always personal: personal and at the same time experienced in common with other men. This is a sign of the transformation of enslaved nature by the power of the spirit. Spirit is the antithesis, not of nature, but of the enslaved state of nature which is in a disintegrated condition inwardly, while outwardly it is fettered and bound. If this world is my objectification which sets up idols and illusions of consciousness, I can in that case create a new and better world.

The Ethics of Creativity *

The Gospel constantly speaks of the fruit which the seed must bring forth if it falls on good soil and of talents given to man which must be returned with profit. Under cover of parable, Christ refers in these words to man's creative activity, to his creative vocation. Burying one's talents in the ground, i.e., absence of creativeness, is condemned by Christ. The whole of Saint Paul's teaching about various gifts is concerned with man's creative vocation. The gifts are from God and they indicate that man is intended to do creative work. These gifts are various, and everyone is called to creative service in accordance with the special gift bestowed upon him. It is therefore a mistake to assert, as people often do, that the Holy Writ contains no reference to creativeness. It does—but we must be able to read it, we must guess what it is God wants and expects of man.

Creativeness is always a growth, an addition, the making of something new that had not existed in the world before. The problem of creativeness is the problem as to whether something completely new is really possible. . . . Creativeness from its very meaning is bringing forth out of nothing. Nothing becomes something, non-being becomes being. Creativeness presupposes non-being, just as Hegel's "becoming" does. Like Plato's Eros, creativeness is the child of poverty and plenty, of want and abundance of power. Creativeness is connected with sin and at the same time it is sacrificial. True creativeness always involves catharsis, purification, liberation of the spirit from psycho-physical elements and victory over them. Creation is different in principle from generation and emanation. In emanation, particles of matter radiate from a center and are separated off. Nor is creation a redistribution of force and energy, as evolution is. So far from being identical with evolution, creation is the very opposite of it. In evolution nothing new is made, but the old is

* From *The Destiny of Man*, trans. Natalie Duddington, London, 1954, pp. 126-130.

redistributed. Evolution is necessity, creation is freedom. Creation is the greatest mystery of life, the mystery of the appearance of something new that had never existed before and is not deduced from, or generated by, anything. Creativeness presupposes non-being, μὴ ὄν (and not οὐκ ὄν) which is the source of the primeval, pre-cosmic, pre-existent freedom in man. The mystery of creativeness is the mystery of freedom. Creativeness can only spring from fathomless freedom, for such freedom alone can give rise to the new, to what had never existed before. Out of being, out of something that exists, it is impossible to create that which is completely new; there can only be emanation, generation, redistribution. But creativeness means breaking through from non-being, from freedom, to the world of being. The mystery of creativeness is revealed in the Biblical myth of the creation. God created the world out of nothing, i.e., freely and out of freedom. The world was not an emanation from God, it was not evolved or born from Him, but created, i.e., it was absolutely new, it was something that had never been before. Creativeness is only possible because the world is created, because there is a Creator. Man, made by God in His own image and likeness, is also a creator and is called to creative work.

Creativeness is a complex fact. It presupposes, first, man's primary, meonic, uncreated freedom; secondly, the gifts bestowed upon man the creator by God the Creator; and thirdly, the world as the field for his activity. Thus three elements are involved in human creativeness: the element of freedom, owing to which alone creation of new and hitherto non-existent realities is possible, gifts and vocations connected with them, and the already created world from which man can borrow his materials. Man is not the source of his gifts and his genius. He has received them from God and therefore feels that he is in God's hands and is an instrument of God's work in the world. Nothing can be more pitiful and absurd than to pride oneself on one's genius. There would be more excuse for being proud of one's holiness. The genius feels that he acts not of himself, but is possessed by God and is the means by which God works His own ends and designs. The "demon" of Socrates was not his self but a being that dwelt in him. A creator constantly feels himself possessed by a demon or a genius. His work is a manifestation through freedom of gifts bestowed upon him from above.

Man cannot produce the material for creation out of himself, out of nothing, out of the depths of his own being. The creative act is of the nature of marriage, it always implies a meeting between different elements. The material for human creativeness is borrowed from the world created by God. We find this in all art and in all inventions and discoveries. We find this in the creativeness of knowledge and in philosophy which presupposes the existence of the world created by God—objective realities without which thought would be left in a void. God has granted man the creative gift, the talent, the genius, and also the world in and through which the creative activity is to be carried out. God calls man to perform the creative act and realize his vocation, and He is expecting an answer to His call. Man's answer to God's call cannot entirely consist of elements that are given by and proceed from God. Something must come from man also, and that something is the very essence of creativeness, which brings forth new realities. It is, indeed, not "something" but "nothing"—in other words it is freedom, without which there can be no creative activity. . . . God's call is addressed to that abyss of freedom, and the answer must come from it. Fathomless freedom is present in all creativeness, but the creative process is so complex that it is not easy to detect this primary element in it. It is a process of interaction between grace and freedom, between forces going from God to man and from man to God. In describing it, emphasis may be laid either on the element of freedom or on the element of grace, of gracious possession and inspiration. But there can be no inspiration without freedom. Platonic philosophy is unfavorable to the interpretation of creativeness as the making of new realities.

Creativeness has two different aspects and we describe it differently according to whether we dwell upon one or the other. It has an inner and an outer aspect. There is the primary creative act in which man stands, as it were, face to face with God, and there is the secondary creative act in which he faces other men and the world. There is the creative conception, the primary creative intuition, in which a man hears the symphony, perceives the pictorial or poetic image, or is aware of a discovery or invention as yet unexpressed; there is such a thing as an inner creative act of love for a person, unexpressed in any way as yet. In that primary act man stands before God and is not concerned with realization. If knowledge is given me, that knowledge in the first instance is not a book written by me or a scientific discovery formulated for other people's benefit and forming part of human culture. In the first instance it is my own inner knowledge, as yet unexpressed, unknown to the world and hidden from it. This alone is real firsthand knowledge, my real philosophy in which I am face to face with the mystery of existence. Then comes the secondary creative act connected with man's social nature—the realization, namely, of the creative intuition. A book comes to be written. At this stage there arises the question of art and technique. The primary creative fire is not art at all. Art is secondary and in it the creative fire cools down. Art is subject to law and is not an interaction of freedom and grace, as the primary creative act is. In realizing his creative intuition man is limited by the world, by his material, by other people; all this weighs on him and damps the fire of inspiration. There is always a tragic discrepancy between the burning heat of the creative fire in which the artistic image is conceived, and the cold of its formal realization. Every book, picture, statue, good work, social institution is an instance of this cooling down of the original flame. Probably some creators never find expression; they have the inner fire and inspiration but fail to give it form. And yet people generally think that creativeness consists in producing concrete, definite things. Classic art requires the greatest possible adherence to the cold formal laws of technique.

The aim of creative inspiration is to bring forth new forms of life, but the results are the cold products of civilization, cultural values, books, pictures, institutions, good works. Good works mean the cooling down of the creative fire of love in the human heart just as a philosophical book means the cooling down of the creative fire of knowledge in the human spirit. This is the tragedy of human creativeness and its limitation. Its results are a terrible condemnation of it. The inner creative act in its fiery impetus ought to leave the heaviness of the world behind and "overcome the world." But in its external realization the creative act is subject to the power of "the world" and is fettered by it. Creativeness which is a fiery stream flowing out of fathomless freedom has not only to ascend but also to descend. It has to interpret to the world its creative vision and, in doing so, submit to the laws of art and technique.

Creativeness by its very nature implies genius. In his creative aspect man is endowed with genius; it is the image of God the Creator in him. This does not mean that every man has an outstanding talent for painting pictures, writing poems, novels, or philosophical books, ruling the state, or making inventions and discoveries. The presence of genius in man has to do with his inner creativeness and not with the external realization of it. It is a characteristic of human personality as a whole and not a specific gift, and it indicates that man is capable of breaking through to the primary source of life and that his spiritual activity is truly original and not determined by social influences. A man's genius may, however, be out of keeping with his powers of realization. The presence of genius and originality together with a great talent for realizing the products of creative activity makes a man a genius in the usual sense of the term. But there may be something of genius in a man's love for a woman, in a mother's love for her child, in a person's concern for other people's welfare, in inner intuitions which find no outer expression, in the pursuit of righteousness and the suffering of trying to discover the meaning of life. A saint may be a genius in his work of making himself into a perfect and transfigured creature, though he may have nothing to show for it. It is wrong to draw comparisons between the extent of men's genius and talent, for it means ignoring their individuality. Creativeness brings with it much sorrow and bitterness. It is a great failure even in its finest achievements, for they always fall short of the creative conception.

There is a tragic conflict between creativeness and personal perfection. The greatness of creative genius is not correlative to moral perfection. A great artist may be an idle pleasure-seeker, "of the world's worthless children the most worthless he may be." This problem has been stated in all its poignancy by Pushkin, who said the most remarkable things that have ever been said about artistic creation. Creative genius is bestowed on man for nothing and is not connected with his moral or religious efforts to attain perfection and become a new creature. It stands as it were outside the ethics of law and the ethics of redemption and presupposes a different kind of morality. The creator is justified by his creative achievement. We come here upon a curious moral paradox. Creative genius is not concerned with salvation or perdition. In his creative work the artist forgets about himself, about his own personality, and renounces himself. Creative work is intensely personal and at the same time it means forgetfulness of self. Creative activity always involves sacrifice. It means self-transcendence, overstepping the confines of one's own limited personal being. A creator forgets about salvation; he is concerned with values that are above man. There is nothing selfish about creativeness. Insofar as a man is self-centered he cannot create anything, he cannot abandon himself to inspiration or imagine a better world.

Philosophy of History *

There is a rhythm in history as there is in nature, a measured succession of ages and periods, alternation of diverse types of culture, ebb and flow, rise and fall. Such periodicity and rhythm are proper to all life. We can speak of epochs that are organic and of epochs that are critical, of those diurnal and nocturnal, of the sacred times and the secular. It is our lot to live historically in a period of transition. The old world, if I may call it so, or "modern times"—since from habit not less old times are still called modern when they are positively senile—have come to their end and are in decomposition. A new and unknown world is coming to birth. And it is worth noting that this end of one world and beginning of another appear simultaneously to some as a "revolution" and to others as a "reaction." The fact is that revolution and reaction are so inextricably mixed that neither the things nor the terms can well be distinguished from one another. Let us agree that our epoch is the end of modern times and the beginning of a new middle age. I certainly do not mean to foretell the exact course that history will take; I want only to try to point out the characteristics and tendencies which the renewed aspect of society and culture is likely to have.

My ideas are often misinterpreted and I know that people draw the most wrong conclusions from them. The explanation is that my thought is criticized according to current views and attempt is made to bring it into line with such and such a direction of modern thought: this is an essentially wrong way of considering it. The very substance of my philosophy is to have nothing at all to do with the thought of times which, so far as I am concerned, are over and done with. I look to the thought of a world which is to begin, the world of the new middle ages. Contemporary spiritual principles and forces are used up, the rationalist day of a past history declines: its sun

* From *The End of Our Time*, trans. Donald Attwater, New York, 1933, pp. 69-71, 79-81, 103-106.

sets and night is upon us. The means of research which are adequate to the sunlit day cannot be of any use for the examination and disentangling of events and phenomena in this eveningtide of history. Men of intuition perceive, all the signs and proofs show, that we have passed from an era of light to an era of darkness. Is it an evil, does this state appear as a misfortune, or are we perhaps pessimistic exaggerators? Such questions are meaningless for they are prompted by a rationalism that is at enmity with the true spirit of history. What is certain is that the veils of falsehood are torn away and we can see both good and evil in their plain nakedness. Night is not less wonderful than day, it is equally the work of God; it is lit by the splendor of the stars and it reveals to us things that the day does not know. . . .

When we write that some historical world or other is doomed to destruction, naturally we do not mean that nothing will be left of it, that it has nothing meet for eternity, that its very existence was futile. That may not be said of any epoch in history, and modern history was not brought about by chance. It experienced a great tension of human forces and it was a fine experiment in liberty. We do not want to ignore Leonardo or Michelangelo or Shakespeare or Goethe, or any of the other mighty heralds of human freedom. Humanist self-affirmation was a moment of value in the destiny of the human spirit, and the lived experience of this self-affirmation has not been wasted: man has gained much from it. The humanist heresy made by modern history contains a distorted truth. The new middle age will give a place to that experiment in liberty made by the modern world, with all the real benefits that we owe to it in the order of consciousness and the increased refining of the spirit that it has brought about. After the middle ages, men failed to effect a return to antiquity but instead accomplished the Renaissance, a very complex association of Christian and pagan elements; in the same way the experience of modern times does not allow us to go back to the old middle ages, but only forward to a new middle age. Léon Bloy used to say, "Suffering passes away, but to have suffered never passes away." Neither the ancient world nor the medieval world is perished forever, though the hour came for both to be superseded. It is just the same now: the world is undergoing a gigantic revolution; not the Communist revolution which, at bottom, is everything that is most reactionary, a mess of all the rotten elements of the old world, but a true spiritual revolution. The call to a new middle age is a call to this spiritual revolution, to a complete renewal of consciousness.

In all cultural and social life Humanism is giving way to its opposite, which leads us accordingly to the denial of man's image. The humanist system of ideas is now, to say the least, out of date and reactionary. But there still remain the anti-humanist deductions which the Communists have been able to draw from Humanism for adaptation to their own ends. We live in a time of stripping, things can be seen as they are. Look at Humanism stripped naked and observe its nature, which appeared so innocent and good to another age. *Where there is no God there is no man:* that is what we have learned from experience. Or look at the true nature of Socialism, now that we can see what it really looks like. But a truth that stands out and can be seen no less clearly is that there cannot be religious neutrality or absence of religion: to the religion of the living God is opposed the religion of Satan, facing the faith of Christ there is the faith of Antichrist. The neutral humanist kingdom that wanted to establish itself in an order intermediate between Heaven and Hell is in a state of corruption, and the two gulfs, of height above and of depth beneath, are disclosed. There rears up against the God-Man, not the man of the neutral intermediate kingdom, but the man-god, the man who has put himself in the place of God. The opposed poles of Being and of not-being are manifest and clear.

Religion cannot be "each man's private concern," as is enunciated nowadays. It cannot be autonomous any more than can any other category of culture. Real religion is in the highest degree generalized and collective, and holds the first place in a society. Communism proves it: it discards the modern independent and lay systems and demands a "sacred" society, the submission of all phases of life to the religion of Satan and Antichrist. What a colossal significance this has! For herein Communism goes beyond the boundaries of modern history to an entirely different sort of system which I am bound to characterize as medieval. The falling to pieces of the humanist "middle-way" lay-state, the emergence everywhere of opposed principles as far apart as the poles, clearly mark the end of the modern non-religious age and the beginning of a religious one, of a new medieval period. . . .

What will the new middle age look like to us? It is easier to catch its negative than its positive characteristics. It is before all, as I have already said, the end of Humanism, of individualism, of formal liberalism, and the beginning of a new religious collectivity in which opposing forces and principles will be defined and everything which is concealed in the underground or subconsciousness of modern history will be laid bare. The rotting humanist kingdom is dividing into two parts: an extreme Communism, anti-human and atheist, and that Church of Christ who is called to receive within herself all authentic being. There is the passage from the formalism of modern history which, after all, has chosen nothing, neither God nor devil, toward discovering the object of life. All the autonomous activities of civilization and social life are reduced to nothingness, the impetus of independent secular creation is spent, and longing is awakened in all spheres of activity for a religious choice, for a real existence, for a transfiguration of life.

None of the spheres of creation and aspects of culture and social life can remain neutral, which means definitely secular, in the matter of religion. Philosophy does not intend to be the handmaid of theology, or society to recognize the authority of an ecclesiastical hierarchy. But at the heart of knowledge and of social life a will to religion is quickening. Forms of knowledge and of society must spring from within, flowing from the freedom of a religious spirit, and a tendency toward theurgy has shown itself in art. There is no possibility of a revival of the old theocracy and of the former heteronomous relations between religion and the different aspects of life. In past theocracy the Kingdom of God was never actualized but only signified by outward symbols. Now there is everywhere a will *really* to attain the Kingdom of God, or the kingdom of Satan; a will, that is, for a free "rule-by-God," distinct from both "rule-by-self" and "rule-by-another."

Knowledge, morality, art, the state, economics, all must become religious, not by external constraint but freely and from within. No theology can regulate the process of my knowledge from outside and impose a norm: knowledge is free. But I cannot any longer realize the ends of knowledge without adverting to religion and undergoing a religious initiation into the mysteries of Being. In that I am already a man of the middle ages and no more a man of modern history. I do not look for the autonomy of religion, but for liberty in religion. No ecclesiastical hierarchy can now rule and regulate society and the life of the state, no clericalism is able to make use of external force. Nevertheless I cannot re-create the state and a decayed society otherwise than in the name of religious principles. I do not look for the autonomy of the state and of society in regard of religion, but for the foundation and strengthening of state and society *in* religion. Not for anything in the world would I be free from God; I wish to be free *in* God and *for* God. When the flight from God is over and the return to God begins, when the movement of aversion from God becomes a movement toward Satan, then modern times are over and the middle ages are begun. God must again be the center of our whole life—our thought, our feeling, our only dream, our only desire, our only hope. It is needful that my passion for a freedom without bounds should involve a conflict with the world, but not with God.

[NICHOLAS BERDYAEV]

Immortality *

Man aspires to integral immortality, not to the immortality of
the superman, or of the intellect, or of the ideal principle in
him; he aspires to the immortality of the personal, not of the
impersonal and the common. The problem of death has been
associated with the problem of sleep. Fechner thinks that death
is the transition from the half-sleep which is our earthly life, to
awakening and a state of vigilance.[1] A dream indicates the loss
of mental synthesis; what Fechner says means that we are still
living in a semi-conscious, half-dreaming state. Immortality then
will be the transition to full consciousness, which I prefer to call
super-consciousness. A full integral consciousness is super-consciousness, and this is also a spiritual awakening. Consciousness
which is directed to the phenomenal world is semi-consciousness;
it is only the liberation of consciousness from the sole power of
the phenomenal world which opens out the prospect of
immortality. . . .

The need of immortality lies in the very depths of human
nature. But the beliefs in immortality carry the impress of the
limitation of human nature. Into them there enter also the evil
human instincts which have created pictures of paradise and,
especially, of hell. It has been most difficult of all to speak about
paradise, for in spite of everything, hell was nearer to man;
there was less of the other world about it. But the picture of
paradise so easily gave rise to boredom. The subject of paradise
greatly disturbed Dostoevsky, and he gave expression to some
remarkable thoughts about it; for instance, in *The Dream of
the Ridiculous Man.* He always connected the subject of paradise
with the subject of freedom; he could not accept paradise apart
from freedom; but at the same time freedom might create hell
too. The repellent character of the picture of a paradise which

* From *The Divine and the Human,* trans. R. M. French, London, 1949,
pp. 158-159, 162-164.
1. See Fechner, *Das Büchlein vom Leben nach dem Tode.*

bears, by transference, the sensual marks of this world, in which the righteous even take pleasure in the suffering of sinners in hell, is due to the fact that nothing could be less apophatic than the way in which people were thinking about paradise. For kataphatic thought about paradise will always be intolerable to the more refined moral and aesthetic sense. Life is throughout infinite; but kataphatic thought about paradise has a finitude which is devoid of true creative life. Jaspers is fond of speaking about the *frontier-position* of man (*Grenzsituation*),[2] and in truth man finds himself on the boundary lines of various worlds; he is not present as a whole in one world only. Man is a being of many planes; at one time he is transported to the other world; at another he touches the edge of the abyss.

The metaphysical problem of immortality is connected most of all with the problem of time. Is his existence in this cosmic and historical time the only existence of man? Or does he exist in existential time as well, which comes into touch with eternity and plunges man into eternity? To deny immortality is to make the assumption that his existence in time is the final and only one; it is to say that he is crushed by time and the phenomenal world. The last word in the philosophy which Heidegger has up to the present propounded is the finite character of human existence. *Dasein* which with him replaces the real man is finite existence moving toward death. The nightmare idea of hell was due to a confusion between eternity and infinity. But the idea of an eternal hell is absolutely absurd. Hell is not eternity; there is no other sort of eternity than divine eternity. Hell is an evil infinitude, the impossibility of issuing out of time into eternity; it is a nightmare phantom born of the objectivization of human existence, which is submerged in the time of our aeon. If there were such a thing as an eternal hell it would be the final failure and defeat of God; and the condemnation of the creation of the world as a diabolical farce.[3] But there are many, many Christians to whom hell is very dear, though not for themselves, of course. The ontology of hell is the most evil

2. See K. Jaspers, *Philosophie*.
3. On this subject there are many admirable ideas in S. Bulgakov. See his *Bride of the Lamb*; this is the third part of his theological system.

form of objectivization, the most pretentiously exacting, the most inspired by feelings of vengeance and malice. But the psychology of hell is possible, and is associated with a real experience.

The legal interpretation of immortality is as base as the ancient magical conception. There is an educational element which plays a very large part in the traditional doctrines of immortality, and this is clearly of an exoteric character. Only a spiritual conception of immortality answers to the higher consciousness, but the spiritual conception by no means indicates that it is only the spiritual part of man which is immortal. The resurrection of the body must also be understood in a spiritual sense. "It is sown a natural body; it is raised a spiritual body." Man is immortal because the divine principle is in him, but it is not only the divine in man which is immortal; it is the whole organism of man of which the spirit has taken possession, which is immortal. It is the spiritual in man which also battles against the final objectivization of human existence, the definitive objectivization which issues in death for man by submerging him finally in the death-dealing stream of time. The objectivization of consciousness produces the illusion of an objective spirit which knows of immortality as impersonal only.

An intense consciousness of one's own vocation and one's mission in the world may bestow the sense of immortality, and that independently of a man's conscious ideas. Then there occurs an interlacement of personal eschatology and the historical eschatology of the whole world. My immortality cannot be separated from the immortality of other people and of the world. To be absorbed exclusively in one's own personal immortality or with one's personal salvation is transcendent egoism. If the idea of personal immortality is separated from the universal eschatological outlook, from the destiny of the world, it becomes a contradiction of love. But love is the principal spiritual weapon in the fight against the sovereignty of death. These two antitheses, love and death, are linked together. Love is revealed at its greatest strength when death is near, and love cannot but conquer death. He who truly loves is the conqueror of death. We ought to make superhuman efforts to secure that those whom we love—not only people but animals too—should inherit eternal life. Christ conquered death because He was the incarnation of the universal divine love and love cannot fail to desire universal salvation from death, and universal resurrection. Were there to be but one creature possessing an existential center, which was not resuscitated to eternal life, the world would have been a failure and a theodicy would be impossible. In such conditions my personal immortality would not only be lacking in some respect; it would, in fact, be impossible. I depend upon the destiny of the world and of those who are near to me, and the destiny of those who are near to me and of the world depends upon me.

[NICHOLAS BERDYAEV]

Time *

The problem of time occupies a position at the center of present-day philosophy. It is enough to name Bergson and Heidegger. This problem has a special significance for a philosophy of the existential type. The philosophy of history is to a considerable extent the philosophy of time. History is linked with time. To speak of time is not always to speak of one and the same thing. Time has a variety of meanings and it is needful to make distinctions. There are three times: cosmic time, historical time, and existential time, and every man lives in these three forms of time. Cosmic time is symbolized by the circle. It is connected with the motion of the earth round the sun, with the reckoning of days, months, and years, with the calendar and the clock. This is a circular movement in which a return is constantly taking place, morning comes and evening, spring and autumn. This is nature's time, and as natural beings we live in this time. The Greeks were primarily concerned with the apprehension of cosmic time; among them the aesthetic contemplation of the cosmos predominated, and they almost failed to apprehend historical time. Time is not by any means a sort of eternal and congealed form into which the existence of the world and of man is placed. Not only does change in time exist, but the change of time itself is possible. A turning back of time is possible, and also an end of time; there will be no more time. Time is a mode of existence, and depends upon the character of existence.

It is not true to say that movement and change take place because time exists; it is true to say that time exists because movement and change take place. The character of change is the origin of the character of time. Cosmic time is one of the effects of change in a world which is natural in an objectivized way. Cosmic time is objectivized time, and it is subject to mathematical calculation; it is subject to number, to division

* From *Slavery and Freedom*, trans. R. M. French, New York, 1944, pp. 257-265.

into parts, and to aggregation. Hours and days are divided into minutes and seconds and are aggregated into months and years. The second of cosmic time, which is at the same time mathematical time, is the atom of divisible time. Cosmic time is rhythmic time, but at the same time it is the time which is torn apart into present, past, and future. The objectivized world is the world to which time belongs, and this imprint of temporality which time has left upon it denotes also a malady of time. Time which is torn apart into the past, present, and future is time which is diseased, and it does an injury to human existence. Death is connected with the disease of time. Time inevitably leads on to death, it is a mortal disease. Natural life, cosmic life in natural cosmic time rests upon the alternating change of birth and death. It knows a periodic spring of the revival of life, but that revival takes place not for those whom death has carried away, but for others. Victory over death is impossible in cosmic time. The present, which cannot be seized because it falls between the past and the future, annihilates the past in order to be itself annihilated by the future. In cosmic time the realm of life is subject to death, although the engendering power of life is inexhaustible. Cosmic time is death-dealing not for the race but for personality; it desires no knowledge of personality and takes no interest in its fate.

But man is a being who lives in several dimensions of time, in several spheres of existence. Man is not only a cosmic natural being, subject to cosmic time which moves in cycles. Man is also a historical being. Historical life is actuality of another order than nature. History, of course, is subject to cosmic time also, it knows reckoning by years and centuries, but it knows also its own historical time. Historical time comes into being through movement and change of another sort than that which occurs in the cosmic cycle. Historical time is symbolized not by the circle but by the straight line stretching out forward. The special property of historical time is precisely this stretching out toward what is coming, this reaching forward to determine. In what is coming it waits for the disclosure of a meaning. Historical time brings novelty with it; in it that which was not becomes that which was. It is true that in historical time also there is return and repetition; resemblances can be established. But every event in historical time is individually particular, every decade and century introduces new life. And the very conflict against historical time, against the lure and slavery of history takes place not in cosmic but in historical time. Historical time has a closer connection with human activity than cosmic time. But personality is wounded and enslaved by historical time in a new way, and at times it even looks to a transition to the cosmic sphere of existence for deliverance from the captivity of history. The Divine figures in the cosmos more than in history, but in the cosmos into which man breaks through objectivized nature and objectivized time. The time of history is also objectivized time, but there is a breakthrough in it from a deeper stratum of human existence.

Historical time strains forward in determination toward what is coming. That is one region which brings it into being. But there is another region also. Historical time is also connected with the past and with tradition, which establishes a link between periods of time. Without that memory and that tradition in the inner sense of the word there is no history. "The historical" is constituted by memory and tradition. Historical time is at once conservative and revolutionary, but this fact does not reach down as far as the final deeps of existence, which do not belong to historical time. Historical time gives birth to illusions; the search in the past for what is better, truer, more beautiful, more perfect (the illusion of the conservative) or the search in the future for the fullness of achievement and the perfection of meaning (the illusion of progress). Historical time is time which is torn to pieces. It does not find completeness in any kind of present (the past and the future are always a kind of present at the same time). In the present man does not feel the fullness of time, and he seeks it in the past or in the future, especially in periods of history which are transitional and full of suffering. This is the seductive illusion of history. The present in which there is fullness and perfection is not a part of time, but an emergence from time, not an atom of time, but an atom of eternity, as Kierkegaard says. That which is experienced in the depth of this existential moment remains. The successive moments which enter into the sequence of time, and represent a less profound reality, pass away.

In addition to cosmic time and historical time, which are objectivized and subordinate to number, though in different ways, there is also existential time, profound time. Existential time must not be thought of in complete isolation from cosmic and historical time, it is a breakthrough of one time into the other. *Kairos*, about which Tillich is fond of speaking, is, as it were, the irruption of eternity into time, an interruption in cosmic and historical time, an addition to and a fulfillment of time. With this is connected the messianic prophetic consciousness which out of the depth of existential time speaks about historical time.

Existential time may be best symbolized not by the circle nor by the line but by the point. That is precisely what is meant by saying that existential time can least of all be symbolized by extension. This is inward time, not exteriorized in extension, not objectivized. It is the time of the world of subjectivity, not objectivity. It is not computed mathematically, it is not summed up nor divided into parts. The infinity of existential time is a qualitative infinity, not a quantitative. A moment of existential time is not subject to number, it is not a fractional part of time in a sequence of moments of objectivized time. A moment of existential time is an emergence into eternity. It would be untrue to say that existential time is identical with eternity, but it may be said that it is a participant in several moments of eternity. Every man knows from his own inward experience that he is a participant in several of his own moments of eternity. The protraction of existential time has nothing in common with the protraction of objectivized time, cosmic or historical. This protraction depends upon the intensity of experience within human existence. Minutes which are short from the objective point of view may be lived through as an infinity, and an infinity in opposite directions, in the direction of suffering and in the direction of joy and triumphant rapture. Every state of ecstasy leads out from the computation of objectivized mathematical time and leads into existential qualitative infinity. One moment may be eternity, another moment may be an evil and repellent endlessness. The fact that those who are happy do not keep a watchful eye upon the clock, indicates an emergence from mathematical time, a forgetfulness of clocks and calendars. The greater part of men's life is unhappy and is, therefore, chained to mathematical time. Suffering is a phenomenon of the existential order, but it is objectivized in mathematical time and appears to be infinite in the quantitative sense of the word. . . .

Every creative act is performed in existential time and is merely projected in historical time. The creative impulse and ecstasy is outside objectivized and mathematical time, it does not take place on a flat surface, on the level of the mediocrity of our life, it happens vertically, not horizontally. But the result of the creative act is exteriorized in the time stream of history. The existential breaks through in the historical and the historical in return acts upon the existential. Everything significant and great in history, everything authentically new is a breakthrough in the existential plane, in creative subjectivity. The emergence of every notable man in history is a phenomenon of that kind. In history, therefore, there is an interruption due to this break-through, there is no continuous uninterrupted process. Within history there is metahistory, which is not a product of historical evolution. There is the miraculous in history. The miraculous is not explicable by historical evolution and the reign of law in history; it is the breakthrough of events which belong to existential time into historical time, which does not contain these events to the full. The revelation of God in history also is this irruption of events belonging to existential time. The full significance of an event in the life of Christ moved in existential time; in historical time it only shines through the burdensome environment of objectivization. The metahistorical is never contained in the historical, history always distorts metahistory in adjusting it to itself.

The final victory of metahistory over history, of existential time over historical, would denote the end of history. In the religious scheme of things this would mean the coincidence of the first coming of Christ with the second. Between the first and the second metahistorical appearance of Christ lies the tense-ness of historical time in which man passes through all the lures and enslavements. This tense historical time cannot of itself come to an end, it streams out toward an infinity which is never converted into eternity. There are two ways out of historical time, in two opposite directions, toward cosmic time and toward existential time. The submersion of historical time in cosmic time is the way out for naturalism, which may take on a mystical color. History returns to nature and enters into the cosmic cycle. The other way is the submersion of historical time in existential time. This is the way out taken by eschatology. History passes into the realm of the freedom of the spirit. And a philosophy of history is always in the last resort either naturalistic, even though it makes use of the categories of spirit, or it is eschatological.

Historical time, with everything that happens in it, has a meaning, but that meaning lies outside the limits of historical time itself, it is to be seen in an eschatological perspective. History is the failure of spirit, the Kingdom of God is not realized or expressed in it. But that very failure itself has a meaning. The great testing trials of man and the experience of the seductive lures through which he lives have a meaning. Without them the freedom of man would not have been fully tested and proved. But an optimistic theory of progress is not to be relied upon, and it is in profound conflict with personalism. Progress remains entirely at the mercy of death-dealing time. Philosophy has never seriously faced the problem of the end of history and of the world; even theology has not given enough serious attention to it. The problem consists in the question, is time conquerable? It is conquerable only if it be the case that it is not an objective form, but is only the outcome of existence which is alienated from itself. In that case the breakthrough from the depth can put an end to time and overcome objectivization. But this breakthrough from the depth cannot be the work of man alone, it is also the work of God, it is the combined work of man and God, a divine-human action. Here we come face to face with the most difficult problem of the action of God's Providence in the world and upon the world. The whole mystery here lies in the fact that God does not act in the determined arrangement of things which belongs to objectivized nature. He acts only in freedom, only through the freedom of man.

Apocalypse is connected with the paradox of time, and in this lies the extraordinary difficulty of its explanation. And indeed, to tell the truth, the interpretation of the symbolism of apocalypse is to a large extent a futile occupation. I have not the smallest intention of giving an exposition of apocalypse, I only wish to state the philosophical problem of the end of history. In this connection the paradox of time consists in this, that the end of history is thought of as taking place in time, while at the same time the end of history is the end of time, that is to say the end of historical time. The end of history is an event of existential time. And at the same time we must not think of this event as being outside history. The end of history, which is accomplished in existential time, happens both "in the next world" and "in this world." The end of history cannot be objectivized, and that is what makes it difficult to understand and explain. Everything important which occurs in existential time appears in historical time as a paradox.

There are two ways of understanding apocalypse, a passive way and an active. In the history of Christian consciousness the former way has always been predominant. There has been a passive foreboding of and a passive waiting for the end of the world; it is determined exclusively by God, judgment upon the world is divine judgment only. In the other view, the end of the world is actively, creatively prepared by man; it depends upon the activity of man also, that is to say it will be a result of divine-human work. Passive waiting for the end is accompanied by the feeling of terror. On the other hand, the active preparation of the end is conflict and may be accompanied by the feeling of triumph. The apocalyptic consciousness may be conservative and reactionary and such it frequently has been; and it may be revolutionary and creative, and that is what it ought to be. Apocalyptic forebodings of the coming end of the world have been terribly misused. Every historical epoch which is drawing to a close, every social class which is coming to an end, readily connects its own demise with the coming of the end of the world. The French Revolution and the Napoleonic wars were accompanied by manifestations of such an apocalyptic frame of mind. The end of Imperial Russia, of which many people had a presentiment, was attended by signs of an apocalyptic state of thought. Solovyov and Leontyev represent the type of passive apocalyptic consciousness. Fyodorov represents the active type of apocalyptic consciousness. Fyodorov's active interpretation of apocalypse showed the audacity of genius, in spite of the fact that his philosophy was unsatisfactory. The conservative apocalyptic consciousness has a feeling of horror when faced by the ruin of things which present themselves as historical sanctities. The revolutionary apocalyptic consciousness actively and creatively turns to the realization of human personality and to the society which is linked with the principle of personality. An active relation to the end of history presupposes a more or less prolonged period of change in the structure of consciousness, a spiritual and social revolution even in historical time, which cannot be brought about by human efforts only, but also cannot be achieved without human effort or by passive waiting. The outpouring of the Spirit, which changes the world, is the activity of the spirit in man himself. The activity of man to which Fyodorov summoned men is an immense step forward in Christian consciousness. But with Fyodorov the structure of consciousness is not changed; he does not state the problem of the relation of the subject to objectivization. Spiritual revolution, which prepares the end, will be to a notable degree a victory over the illusions of consciousness. Active eschatology is the justification of the creative power of man. Man is liberated from the sway of the objectivization which had enslaved him. And then the problem of the end of history will present itself in a new aspect. The end of history is the victory of existential time over historical time, of creative subjectivity over objectivization, of personality over the universal-common, of existential society over objectivized society.

LEON SHESTOV
[1866–1938]

Leon shestov (pseudonym for Leo Isakovich Schwarzman) was born in Kiev on January 31, 1866. He received his early education in Kiev and then entered the Faculty of Law at the University of Moscow. After receiving his diploma in law he moved to Saint Petersburg where he lived until the Bolshevik Revolution, after which he emigrated to Western Europe, spending most of the rest of his life in Paris. He died in Paris on November 20, 1938.

Having been trained as a lawyer, Shestov came to philosophy rather late, in 1895, when, according to his friend and commentator Boris De Schloezer, he turned to the study of philosophy to find a way out of the inner "moral doubts" which were tormenting him.[1] We know little of Shestov's inner life beyond what can be gleaned from his works, but it seems that toward the year 1895 he underwent some kind of spiritual crisis. His first book was published in Saint Petersburg three years later, in 1898, under the title *Shakespeare and His Critic Brandes*. Shestov always considered Shakespeare as his "first master in philosophy" and writing this book helped him resolve his spiritual crisis in a positive manner. The book contains a violent attack on the positivism of Taine and the skepticism of Brandes. Shestov interprets the Brutus of Shakespeare's *Julius Caesar* as the embodiment of a moral ideal that is stronger than death. Morality, according to Shestov, is not a question of the transcendental idea of the *good* or the Kantian imperative of *duty*, but is to be found in every-

1. Boris De Schloezer, "Un Penseur Russe: Léon Chestov," *Mercure de France*, Paris, 1922, p. 86.

day, ordinary, natural life and action, in the ambiguous sphere in which men of great soul create their morality. Hamlet is the prototype of the *Platonist* who thinks too much, who disdains man; Brutus is a whole man and thus is able to act morally—"This was a man." This is Shestov's most "optimistic" book and also the only one in which he "teaches," "demonstrates," and "defends" a definite philosophical doctrine (a rather naive moral optimism, in the words of De Schloezer).

After completing this work Shestov turned to Tolstoy, Dostoevsky, Pascal, Luther, and Nietzsche, where he discovered the "other side" of morality, *the tragic*, and when he returned to the Brutus-Hamlet theme in his later writings, his judgment was reversed. After this first book, Shestov's style also changes, and, although there are a few long chapters of sustained argument in his later works, as in the critique of Etienne Gilson's conception of "Christian Philosophy" in *Athens and Jerusalem*, he gradually adopts an aphoristic, questioning, ironic, even skeptical style—not unlike that of Nietzsche or the later Rozanov. Moreover, he rarely defends or argues any particular philosophical position. His thought is a long, dialectical meditation on certain themes to which he returns again and again. As Boris De Schloezer remarks: after having in one book solemnly announced the death and burial of rationalism, he returns to it in the following book without giving any hint as to how it arose again in the interval. A large part of his writing is addressed (either directly or, more often, indirectly) to other contemporary philosophers such as Berdyaev, Gilson, and Husserl, and he is frequently at his best when commenting on their thought or defending himself against them.

Thus there is no system of philosophy to be found in Shestov. He is content to criticize, to suggest, to attack and dissect the views of others; he is reluctant to present any positive alternative of his own. The positive center of his thought is his belief in the Divine Revelation of the Old and New Testaments, and he believes in the possibility of a "Christian Philosophy," uncontaminated by rationalism, which would take the Bible as its point of departure. But he maintains his own independence from any specific creed and only sketches the *possibility* of such a Christian philosophy, without himself producing it. He was a man of profound religious faith and his philosophy consists of a series of reflections on the demands of this faith.

Shestov is a thoroughgoing irrationalist (which is not to say an anti-rationalist since, as Boris De Schloezer reminds us, he was not *weak in logic*). He emphasizes the "arbitrariness" of life and of the Divine interventions in life. He contrasts the Biblical faith of Jerusalem, which accepts contingency, arbitrariness, and "pure possibility," to the rationalism of Athens, which demands a fully comprehensible, necessary, clearly ordered cosmos—whose laws are universal and eternally necessary, beyond even God's power to alter. He is a kind of twentieth-century Peter Damian, who goes so far as to assert that God could make a past event not to have been. The "rationalists" are convinced, for instance, that Socrates drank the hemlock in 399 B.C. and that this is an unalterable, irreversible fact. Such "rationalism" overlooks the omnipotence of God, says Shestov, and he rejects it. No historical fact or scientific law is irreversible or eternally necessary.

As an apostle of irrationalism, Shestov can be considered one of the founders of "existentialism," but it must be recalled that he discovered Kierkegaard only late in life (in the 1930's—on the "insistence" of Husserl!) and that the term "existential philosophy" (by which he means almost exclusively the thought of Kierkegaard) occurs only in his last books. His critique of rationalism grew out of his own experience and antedated his reading of existential thinkers, except for Dostoevsky and Nietzsche. For Shestov, philosophy is not knowledge or the acquiring of knowledge; it is a lived "struggle," it teaches man to live in the uncertainty of faith. For a man of faith *anything* can happen, *anything* is possible, and thus a Christian philosophy precludes the establishing of final conclusions, the demonstration of ultimate truths. Consequently, Shestov himself delights in paradoxes and contradictions.

Truth, in the important sense of the word, does not lie in the systematic and "scientific" constructions of a Spinoza or a Husserl but in the contradictions of life. Shestov believes that "truth" always inherently involves contradiction, and thus he has no fear of contradicting himself. The only unity of his own writings lies in the coherence of his own personality and the continuity of his own dialectical meditations. In one place he writes *pro domo mea:* "People seem shocked when I enunciate two contradictory judgments at the same time. . . . But this is the difference between me and them: I speak frankly of my contradictions while they prefer to dissimulate theirs even to themselves. . . . They seem to think that contradictions are the *pudenda* of the human spirit . . . ," something to be hidden.[2]

In another place he addresses Berdyaev, who had "caught" him contradicting himself in his book *The Apotheosis of Groundlessness:*

> I must admit Berdyaev has caught me. But why should he want to catch me? . . . *Words* and ideas are only very imperfect means of communication. It is impossible to photograph the soul . . . so we are obliged to use words. . . . But now Berdyaev tries to catch me. Instead of coming to my aid by understanding how difficult it is to find adequate words, instead of helping me, he thrusts sticks into the spokes of the wheels. Truly, this is not acting as a comrade.[3]

We are thus not surprised to learn that Shestov especially loved the saying of Pascal: "Let us not be reproached for our lack of clarity, since we make it our profession."

The following selections are both taken from works which Shestov produced toward the end of his life. The first is from his major work, *Kierkegaard and Existential Philosophy*, written shortly after he had "discovered" Kierkegaard. It is a highly synthetic discussion of ideas which are typical of his thought as a whole and gives us as clear and concise a presentation of his own philosophical views (and of his appreciation of existential philosophy) as it is possible to find. The second selection gives his criticism of Husserl and the other major contemporary current of European philosophy, namely phenomenology, which in Shestov's day had not yet evolved in the "existential" direc-

2. As cited in De Schloezer, *op. cit.,* pp. 89-90.
3. As cited in De Schloezer, *op. cit.,* p. 93.

tion it has since taken. It is a valuable document from several points of view. It shows that these two men, Husserl and Shestov, true opposites, were strongly attracted to and impressed by the strength of each other's position and that there was in their friendship a true philosophical encounter which was nevertheless a total disagreement—especially on Shestov's side. Shestov's reaction to Husserl's attempt to make philosophy a *science* of absolute truth occasioned the most extreme statement of his own irrationalism.[4] Philosophy, for Shestov, is not a *Besinnung* but rather the recognition that there can be *no Besinnung* precisely because of the omnipotence of God and the total contingency of man and human science. Against Husserl's "revelation of the self-evidence of reason," Shestov intones the *De Profundis*, but at the same time he recognizes that in so doing he has not exorcized the human quest for rationality which the serpent of Genesis had insinuated into the soul of man and of which Husserl represented, to him, the greatest contemporary apotheosis.

4. Shestov's interpretation of Husserl as a "pure rationalist" is, of course, open to serious question. J. Héring has shown in his response to Shestov's article on Husserl (which appeared under the title "Memento Mori" in the *Revue philosophique de la France et de l'étranger*, 1926, pp. 5-62) that Husserl's goal was not a science of *reason* but of *consciousness* and of the structures of *experience*. (Cf. J. Héring, "Sub Specie Aeterni," *Revue d'histoire et de philosophie religieuses*, 1927, pp. 351-364). Husserl considered himself closer to Hume than to Kant and, at least when compared with the traditional rationalisms of classical philosophy, Husserl appears more as an empiricist than as a rationalist.

SELECTED BIBLIOGRAPHY [5]

Works:
Leon Shestov, *Anton Tchekov and Other Essays*, trans. S. S. Koteliansky and J. M. Murry, London, 1916.
——————, *Penultimate Words and Other Essays*, London, 1916.
——————, *All Things are Possible*, trans. S. S. Koteliansky, with a foreword by D. H. Lawrence, London, 1920.
——————, *In Job's Balances*, trans. Camilla Coventry and C. A. Macartney, London, 1932.
——————, *La nuit de Gethsémani, Essai sur la philosophie de Pascal*, Paris, 1923.
——————, *L'idée de bien chez Tolstoi et Nietzsche*, Paris, 1925, reprinted in 1949.
——————, *La philosophie de la tragédie: Dostoevski et Nietzsche*, Paris, 1926.
——————, *Le Pouvoir des clefs (Potestas Clavium)*, Paris, 1928.
——————, *Kierkegaard et la philosophie existentielle (Vox clamantis in deserto)*, Paris, 1936, reprinted in 1948.
——————, *Sola Fide, Luther et l'église*, Paris, 1957.
——————, *Athens and Jerusalem*, trans. with an introduction by Bernard Martin, Athens, Ohio, 1966.

Secondary Sources:
Boris De Schloezer, "Un Penseur Russe: Léon Chestov," *Mercure de France*, Paris, 1922, pp. 82-115.
V. V. Zenkovsky, *A History of Russian Philosophy*, trans. George L. Kline, 2 vols., London and New York, 1953, pp. 780-791.

5. Since all of Shestov's important works have been translated into Western languages, we shall list first those which are available in English and then those which exist in French (which were most frequently published prior to the Russian versions).

Kierkegaard and Dostoevsky*

I

You certainly do not expect me to exhaust the extremely complex and difficult subject of the work of Kierkegaard and Dostoevsky in the space of an hour.[1] Therefore I will limit myself to an examination of just one question: how did Kierkegaard and Dostoevsky conceive original sin? In other words—for it is the same thing—I will speak of speculative truth and of revealed truth. But I must warn you that with so little time at my disposal it will doubtless be impossible for me to elucidate as fully as you may desire what these two authors thought and said about the Fall of man. At the most I will be able to indicate—and that only schematically—the reason why original sin so strongly attracted the attention of two of the most remarkable thinkers of the nineteenth century. We should remark with respect to this problem that the Fall constitutes the pivot of Nietzsche's whole philosophical problematic as well, though he is generally regarded as being far removed from the Bible. His fundamental, essential theme is Socrates, whom he saw as a decadent man, or, in other words, as the fallen man *par excellence*. And Nietzsche saw Socrates' fall precisely in what history, and the history of philosophy in particular, had always believed, and taught us to believe, was Socrates' highest merit, namely, his unlimited confidence in reason and in the knowledge obtained by reason. As we read Nietzsche's reflections on Socrates, we constantly evoke, even against our will, the Biblical story: the forbidden fruit and

---

* Translated for this volume by James M. Edie, from Leon Shestov, *Kierkegaard et la philosophie existentielle (Vox clamantis in deserto)*, trans. T. Rageot and Boris De Schloezer, Paris, 1936, pp. 7-34. It was collated with the Russian edition (published slightly later), Lev Shestov, *Kirgegard i ekzistentsialnaya filosofiya (glas vopiyushchevo v pustyne)*, Paris, 1939, pp. 7-22, by James P. Scanlan for this volume.

1. This paper was originally read before the Russian Academy of Religion and Philosophy at Paris on May 5, 1935.

the seductive words of the tempter—*eritis scientes.* Kierkegaard speaks of Socrates even more and with greater insistence than Nietzsche. And this is the more striking in that Socrates, for Kierkegaard, is the most remarkable phenomenon in the history of humanity prior to the appearance on the European horizon of that mysterious book called "the Book," that is to say the Bible.

From the most distant times the Fall has troubled human thought. Men everywhere sensed that things were not going very well in the world, that they were even going very badly. "Something is rotten in the state of Denmark," to speak as Shakespeare. And they made enormous and the most intense efforts to understand why. Now it is necessary to say at once that to the question posed in this way Greek philosophy, like the philosophy of other peoples, including the peoples of the Far East, gave an answer which is the direct opposite of what we read in the first pages of Genesis. In a fragment which has come down to us, Anaximander, one of the first great philosophers of Greece, speaks in this way: "The source from which existing things derive their existence is also that to which they return at their destruction, according to necessity; for they give justice and make reparation to one another for their injustice, at the appointed time." This thought of Anaximander's pervades the whole development of Greek philosophy. The appearance of particular things, and primarily living beings, and above all of human beings, is considered as an impious audacity for which their death and destruction is just retribution. The idea of "birth" (γένεσις) and "destruction" (φθορά) is the point of departure of Greek philosophy (and I repeat that this same idea insistently asserted itself to the founders of the religions and philosophies of the Far East). At all times and among all peoples the natural thought of man stopped weakly, as if bewitched, before the fatal necessity which was introduced into the world by the terrible law of death ineluctably tied to the birth of man, of destruction which awaits everything which has appeared and will appear. Thought discovered within the very being of man something which ought not to be, a vice, a sickness, a sin, and, as a result, wisdom required that this sin be overcome at its roots. In other words, it required the renunciation of individual being which, having once begun, is irrevocably condemned to come to an end. The Greek catharsis or purification comes from this conviction that the immediate data of consciousness, which testify to the inevitable destruction of everything which is born, reveal to us a truth anterior to the world, eternal, unchanging, forever unconquerable. It is not among ourselves or for ourselves that true being, real being (ὄντως ὄν), should be sought, but there where the authority of the law of birth and destruction ends, i.e., there where there is no birth and, consequently, where there is no death. This has been the starting point of speculative philosophy. The law of the inevitable destruction of everything which has been born and created, this law discovered by intellectual vision, appears to us as forever inherent in being itself. Greek philosophy was as firmly convinced of it as the wisdom of the Hindus, and we who are separated from the Greeks and the Hindus by thousands of years are as little able to rid ourselves of the power of this most self-evident truth as those who first discovered it and showed it to us.

Only the Book of books is an enigmatic exception in this respect.

What is said there is directly opposed to what men have discovered by means of their intellectual vision.

Everything was created by the Creator, we read at the beginning of Genesis; everything had a beginning. But no lack or vice or sin in being follows from this. On the contrary, it is precisely this fact which conditions whatever good there can be in the universe. In other words, the creative act of God is the source, and what is more the unique source, of all good. At the evening of each day of creation, after contemplating His work, God said: *valde bonum*. And the last day, after looking over all He had created, God saw that it was good. Both the world and the men (whom God blessed) created by God—precisely because He had created them—were perfect, without any defect. Evil did not exist in the universe created by God and the sin from which evil came did not exist either. Sin and evil came afterward. From whence did they come? To this question Scripture also gives a definite answer. God had planted among the other trees of the Garden of Eden the tree of life and the tree of the knowledge of good and evil. And He said to the first man: "You may freely eat of every tree of the garden; but of the tree of the knowledge of good and evil you shall not eat, for in the day that you eat of it you shall die." But the tempter (in the Bible he is called the serpent, the slyest of all the animals created by God) said to Eve: "You will not die. For God knows that when you eat of it your eyes will be opened, and you will be like God, knowing good and evil." Man allowed himself to be tempted, tasted the forbidden fruit; his eyes were opened and he became wise. What was revealed to him? What did he learn? He learned what the Greek philosophers and the Hindu sages had seen: the divine *valde bonum* is not justified; all is not good in the created world. In the created world, and precisely because it is created, it is impossible that evil not exist, much evil, insupportable evil, as everything which surrounds us —the immediate data of consciousness—shows with irrefutable evidence. The man who looks at the world "with his eyes open," the man who "knows" cannot judge otherwise. From the moment at which men became *scientes*, that is to say "knowers," sin entered the world and, after sin, evil. Thus says the Bible.

The question is posed to us, men of the twentieth century, as it was posed to the ancients: whence comes sin, whence come the torments and horrors of existence tied to sin? Is there a vice in being itself which insofar as it is created, even though by God, insofar as it has a beginning must inevitably be marked by imperfection in virtue of an eternal law which is subject to nothing and to no one? Does this imperfection or sin or evil, which condemns being to destruction in advance, consist in "knowledge," in having "open eyes," and does it come thus from the forbidden fruit?

Hegel, one of the most remarkable philosophers of the last century, who had absorbed (this is the proper source of his importance and significance) the whole of European thought from its beginnings twenty-five centuries ago, affirms without the least hesitation: the serpent did not deceive man, the fruits of the tree of knowledge have become the source of philosophy for all times. And it is necessary to admit it. Historically Hegel is right. The fruits of the tree of knowledge have truly become the source of philosophy, the source of thought for all times. Not only the pagan philosophers, completely foreign to Sacred Scripture, but the Jews and the Christians who acknowledged the Bible to be a divinely inspired book, all the philosophers wanted to be *scientes* and did not want to renounce the fruits of the forbidden tree. For Clement of Alexandria (at the beginning of the third century), Greek philosophy was the "Second Old Testament," and he declared that if we could separate knowledge (γνῶσις) from eternal salvation, and if he had to choose between the two, he would choose knowledge and not eternal salvation. Medieval philosophy followed the same route; and the mystics themselves are no exceptions in this connection. The unknown author of the celebrated *Theologia deutsch* affirms that Adam could have eaten twenty apples and no harm would have come from it; sin did not come from the fruits of the tree of knowledge; no evil can come from knowledge. What is the basis of the assurance of the author of the *Theologia deutsch?* Where does he get his assurance that evil cannot come from knowledge? He does not pose this question; evidently it never occurred to him that one can search for and find the truth in Scripture. Truth can only be sought in one's own reason and what reason does not accept as true is not true. The serpent did not deceive man.

Kierkegaard and Dostoevsky were both born during the first quarter of the nineteenth century, though Kierkegaard, who died at the age of forty-four,[2] was ten years older than Dostoevsky and had already completed his literary career when Dostoevsky had only begun to write. They lived at the time when Hegel reigned over the minds of Europe and they obviously could not escape the power of Hegelian philosophy. There is reason to believe, it is true, that Dostoevsky never read a line of Hegel (as opposed to Kierkegaard who had an admirable knowledge of Hegel), but at the time he belonged to Belinsky's circle he certainly assimilated the fundamental ideas of Hegelian philosophy. Dostoevsky had an extraordinary flair for philosophical

2. Shestov is mistaken. Kierkegaard was only forty-two at his death, and only eight years older than Dostoevsky.—TRANS.

ideas, and what the friends of Belinsky who had been in Germany told him of Hegel sufficed for him to grasp clearly the problems which had been posed and solved by Hegelian philosophy. Moreover, not only Dostoevsky but Belinsky himself, "a student who had not finished his studies," and who was far from attaining the philosophical penetration of Dostoevsky, rightly sensed, and not only sensed but found the words necessary to express, everything that was unacceptable to him in Hegel's doctrine— and that Dostoevsky later found equally unacceptable.

I would remind you of this passage from a celebrated letter of Belinsky: "But if I should succeed in climbing to the highest rung of this ladder of development, even there I would ask you to render me an account of all the victims of real life and history, of all the victims of chance, of superstitions, of the inquisition, of Philip II, etc. Otherwise I should hurl myself head foremost from the top rung of this ladder. I do not want happiness even as a gift if my conscience is not easy with regard to each of my blood brethren." [3]

It is useless to say that if Hegel could have read these lines from Belinsky, he would have been satisfied to shrug his shoulders with contempt and would have called Belinsky a barbarian, an ignoramus, a savage. It is evident that Belinsky had not tasted the fruits of the tree of knowledge and did not even suspect the existence of an ineluctable law in virtue of which everything which has a beginning, and precisely the men whose side Belinsky takes with such ardor, must have an end. It is consequently vain to demand a reckoning (and there is nobody to whom to address such a demand) on behalf of beings which, because they are finite, cannot claim any protection or defense. Not only the first comers, the victims of chance, but even men like Socrates, Giordano Bruno, and many other great (the greatest) men, the sages, the just men, have no right to any protection or defense. The wheel of the historical process crushes them all without pity, with as much indifference as if they were inanimate objects.

The philosophy of the spirit is a philosophy of the spirit precisely because it can elevate itself above everything finite and passing. And, on the contrary, nothing finite and passing can be

3. From Belinsky's letter to Botkin of March 1, 1841.—TRANS.

integrated into the philosophy of the spirit unless it ceases pre-occupying itself with its mean interests which, because they are mean, are not deserving of any concern. Thus would Hegel have spoken, and he would have referred in this connection to the chapter of his *History of Philosophy* in which he explains that Socrates had to be poisoned and that this was not a catastrophe at all: an old Greek dies; is it worthwhile raising a din over such a trifle? Everything which is real is rational, that is to say that the real cannot and should not be other than it is. He who does not understand this is not a philosopher; he is not capable of penetrating to the essence of things by intellectual vision. And there is more: he who has not seen this—still following Hegel—cannot consider himself a religious man. For religion, all religion, and especially the absolute religion—this is what Hegel calls Christianity—reveals to men in images, that is to say in a less perfect manner, what the thinking spirit itself perceives in the essence of being. "The true content of the Christian faith," says Hegel in his *Philosophy of Religion*, "is thus justified by philosophy and not by history" (that is, by what is recounted in Sacred Scripture). This means that Scripture is acceptable only to the extent that the thinking spirit recognizes that it is in agreement with the truths which it obtains itself or, as Hegel puts it, that it extracts from itself. All the rest is to be rejected.

We already know what the thinking spirit of Hegel extracted from itself: whatever Scripture may say, the serpent did not deceive man, and the fruits of the forbidden tree have given us the best thing that there can be in life—knowledge. Similarly, the thinking spirit rejects as impossible the miracles of which Scripture speaks. The following lines testify clearly to the contempt which Hegel had for Scripture: "Whether the guests at the wedding feast at Cana had more wine or less is absolutely indifferent. Also, the fact that the paralyzed arm of a common man was cured is purely accidental. Millions of people have paralyzed arms and broken limbs and nobody heals them. The Old Testament says that at the time of the flight from Egypt the Jews marked their houses with red signs so that the angel of the Lord could recognize them. Such a faith has no meaning for the spirit. It was against faith of this kind that Voltaire directed his most venomous raillery. He says that God should have taught the Jews the immortality of the soul rather than teaching them to go to the toilet. Latrines thus become the content of faith."

Hegel's "philosophy of the spirit" scorns Scripture and makes fun of it; it accepts from the Bible only what it is able to "justify" before rational consciousness. Hegel has no need of "revealed" truth; more exactly, he does not accept it, or, if you prefer, he considers as revealed truth what his own spirit reveals to him. Certain theologians had no need of Hegel to realize this: so as not to trouble themselves and others with the enigma of the Biblical revelation, they declared that all truths are revealed. Truth in Greek is called ἀλήθεια. By making this term come from the verb ἀλανθάνω (to set ajar, to half-open), these theologians freed themselves from the obligation, so heavy for the cultivated man, to recognize the privileged status of the truths of Scripture. Every truth, precisely because it is a truth, reveals something which was hitherto hidden. From this point of view Biblical truth does not constitute an exception and enjoys no advantage over other truths. It is only acceptable to us when it can justify itself before our reason, when it can be seen by our "open eyes," and to that extent only. It is useless to say that under these circumstances we have to renounce three-fourths of the words of Scripture and interpret the rest in such a way that this same reason will not find anything offensive to itself. For Hegel (as for the medieval philosophers) the greatest authority was Aristotle. *The Encyclopedia of the Philosophical Sciences* ends with a long citation from Aristotle's *Metaphysics* (in Greek in the original) on this theme: ἡ θεωρία τὸ ἄριστον καὶ τὸ ἥδιστον, which means that contemplation is the best and highest beatitude. And in this same *Encyclopedia,* at the beginning of the third part, in the paragraphs on the "Philosophy of Spirit," Hegel writes: "The books of Aristotle on the soul are still the best and the only work of speculative character on this subject. The essential aim of the philosophy of spirit can consist only of introducing the idea of the concept into the knowledge of spirit, and thus gain access to the books of Aristotle." It was not in vain that Dante called Aristotle *il maestro di coloro, chi sanno* (the master of those who know). He who wants to "know" must follow Aristotle and consider his works—the *De Anima*, the *Metaphysics*, and the *Ethics*—not only as a second Old Testament, as Clement of Alexandria said, but also as a second New Testament, that is, as a Bible. He is the only master of those who want to know, who do know.

Still inspired by Aristotle, Hegel proclaims solemnly in his *Philosophy of Religion:* "The fundamental idea (of Christianity) is the unity of the divine nature and the human nature. God has become man." And in another place, in the chapter on "The Kingdom of the Spirit," he says again: "The individual should impregnate himself with the truth of the primordial unity of the divine and human natures, and he grasps this truth by faith in Christ; God is no longer for him something beyond." This is what the "absolute religion" taught Hegel. He joyfully cites the words of Meister Eckhardt (taken from his sermons) and the words of Angelus Silesius: "If God were not, I would not be; if I were not, God would not be." It is in this manner that the content of the absolute religion is interpreted and elevated to the level reached by the thought of Aristotle or of the Biblical serpent who promised the first man that "knowledge" would make him equal to God. And never for a moment does the idea enter Hegel's head that in this there lies a terrible, fatal fall, that "knowledge" does not make man equal to God but tears him away from God and hands him over to the power of dead and murderous "truth." We remember that Hegel had contemptuously rejected the "miracles" of Scripture, that is to say the almighty power of God, for, as he explains in another place: "One cannot require people to believe things which after a certain degree of education it is impossible for them to believe; such a faith is a faith in a finite and contingent, that is to say untrue, content; for true faith has no contingent content." In conformity with this, "the miraculous transgresses the natural connection of phenomena and thus does violence to the spirit."

II

I have had to dwell on the speculative philosophy of Hegel because both Dostoevsky and Kierkegaard saw their essential life's task (the first was not aware of it but the second was fully conscious of it) as the combating and overcoming of the system of ideas which Hegelianism, the culmination of the millennial evolution of European thought, incarnated. For Hegel, the break in the natural linkage of phenomena, the break which expresses the power of the Creator over the world and his omnipotence, was the most insupportable and terrible thought: it was a "violation of the spirit." He ridicules the stories of the Bible: they all belong to "history," they speak to us only of the "finite," of the finite which the man who wishes to live in the spirit and the truth must shake off. This is what Hegel called "reconciling" religion and reason. Religion is thus justified by philosophy, which sees in the diversity of its multiple religious conceptions a "necessary truth" and reveals in this necessary truth "the eternal idea."

Without any doubt reason thus obtains full satisfaction. But what remains of the religion which is justified in this way before reason? It is equally without doubt that, having reduced the content of the "absolute religion" to the unity of the divine nature and the human nature, Hegel and all those who followed him became *scientes,* as the tempter promised Adam when he lured him with the forbidden fruit. That is to say they discovered in the Creator a nature identical to what they saw in their own being. But do we go to religion to obtain knowledge? Belinsky demanded that he be given an "account" of all the victims of chance, of the Inquisition, etc. But does knowledge concern itself with accounting for these victims? Is knowledge even capable of it? On the contrary, he who "knows," and especially he who knows this truth that the nature of God and that of man is one, knows for certain that Belinsky is asking the impossible. And to demand the impossible is to show one's weakness of mind, as Aristotle said. Where the domain of the impossible begins, there all human claims must be silent; there, to speak the language of Hegel, all the interests of the spirit come to an end.

But when Kierkegaard, who had been raised on Hegel and who venerated him as a young man, came up against this reality which Hegel summoned men to shake off in the interests of the spirit, he suddenly sensed that the philosophy of the great master contained a perfidious, fatal lie, a dangerous temptation.

He recognized in it the *eritis scientes* of the Biblical serpent: the call to exchange faith in a living and free Creator, a fearless faith, for submission to the unchanging truths which have an absolute power over everything but which are indifferent to everything. Abandoning the celebrated philosopher, the illustrious thinker, Kierkegaard went, or rather ran, to his only saviour, to a "private thinker," to the Job of the Bible. And from Job he passed not to Aristotle, the master of those who know, but to Abraham, the man whom Scripture calls the father of faith. For Abraham he even quit Socrates. Socrates also "knew." Thanks to the γνῶθι σεαυτόν ("Know thyself"), the pagan god had revealed to him the truth of the unity of the divine and human natures five centuries before the Bible reached Europe. Socrates knew that for God, as for man, not everything is possible and that the possible and the impossible are determined not by God but by the eternal laws to which God is no less subject than man. This is why God has no power over history, that is to say over reality.

"In the domain of the sense world it is impossible to make what has once occurred not to have occurred. It is possible to do so only inwardly, in spirit." Thus speaks Hegel. And certainly he did not find this truth in Scripture which repeats so often and with such insistence that nothing is impossible for God, and which even promises man that he will have power over everything which exists in the world: "Nothing will be impossible to you if you have faith like a mustard-seed." But the philosopher of the spirit does not hear these words; he does not want to hear them. They make him indignant; the miracle, remember, is a violation of the spirit. But the source of the "miraculous" is faith, a faith which has the audacity not to attempt to justify itself before reason, which seeks no justification, which calls before its tribunal everything which exists in the world. Faith is above knowledge, beyond knowledge. When Abraham went toward the promised land, says the Apostle, he went without knowing himself where he was going. He had no need to know. He lived by the promise: the place he would reach—and because he would reach it—that would be the promised land. Such faith does not exist for the philosophy of the spirit. For the philosophy of the spirit faith is only imperfect knowledge, knowledge on credit, which will not become true until it obtains the recognition of reason. No one has the right to dispute nor the force to fight with reason and rational truths. Rational truths are eternal truths; it is necessary to accept and to assimilate them without reservation. The Hegelian formula— "Everything which is real is rational"—is the free translation of the Spinozist formula: *Non ridere, non lugere, neque detestari, sed intelligere* (Do not laugh, do not cry, do not damn, but understand). The Creator bows down before the eternal truths just like the creature. Speculative philosophy will not renounce this principle for anything in the world; and it defends it with all its resources. Gnosis—knowledge and comprehension are dearer to it than eternal salvation. To go still further, it sees eternal salvation in knowledge. And this is why Spinoza proclaimed with an unshakable assurance: Do not weep, do not damn, but comprehend.

Now it is precisely at this point, in this Hegelian "rational reality," that Kierkegaard realized that he had found the meaning of the mysterious link, so enigmatic for us, which the story of Genesis established between knowledge and the Fall.

However, Scripture does not reject knowledge in the proper sense of the word, nor does it forbid it. On the contrary, it is said in Scripture that man was called to name all things. But man did not want to; he did not want to rest content with naming the things created by God. This is what Kant expresses so well in the first edition of the *Critique of Pure Reason:* "Experience," he says, "shows us what exists, but it does not show us that what exists must necessarily exist in this manner (as it exists and not otherwise). This is why experience does not give us true generality. Thus reason, which avidly aspires to that type of knowledge, is rather irritated than satisfied by experience." Reason aspires avidly to deliver man to the power of necessity, and the free act of creation of which Scripture speaks not only does not satisfy it, but irritates it, troubles it, and frightens it. It prefers to abandon itself to the power of necessity with its eternal, universal, unchanging principles rather than to trust in its Creator. Thus it was with our first father, seduced or bewitched by the words of the tempter. Thus it continues to be with us all, including the greatest representatives of human thought. Aristotle twenty centuries ago, Spinoza, Kant, Hegel in modern times are possessed by the irresistible need to deliver themselves and humanity to the power of necessity. And they do not even suspect that in this is the greatest fall. They see in knowledge not the loss but the salvation of the soul.

Kierkegaard was also instructed by the ancients and he admired Hegel passionately in his youth. It was only after he felt himself to be, by the will of destiny, wholly in the power of necessity to which his reason aspired so avidly, it was only then that he understood the profound, upsetting meaning of the Biblical account of the Fall of man. We have exchanged the faith which determines the relation between creature and Creator and which is a promise of unlimited freedom and of infinite possibilities, for knowledge, for a slavish submission to eternal, petrified, and petrifying principles. Can we imagine a more terrible, more fatal fall? And then Kierkegaard realized that the beginning of philosophy is not wonder, as the Greeks taught, but despair: *De profundis ad te, Domine, clamavi.* He realized that we could find in Job, the "private thinker," what had never even entered the mind of the celebrated professor, the illustrious philosopher.

As opposed to Spinoza and those who before and after him sought in philosophy for "comprehension" (*intelligere*), and who made human reason the judge of the Creator himself, Job teaches us by his example that to discover the truth we should not refuse or prohibit ourselves from *lugere et detestari*, but take them as the point of departure. Knowledge, that is, the disposition to accept as true everything which appears self-evident, i.e., everything perceived with our eyes which, after the Fall, are "open" (Spinoza calls them *oculi mentis*, Hegel speaks of "spiritual" vision), leads man inevitably to his ruin. "The just man will live by faith," says the Prophet, and the Apostle repeats his words. "Everything that does not come from faith is sin." It is only thanks to these words that we can overcome the temptation, *eritis scientes*, to which the first man succumbed and to the power of which we are all subject. Job renders to the tears and cries (*lugere et detestari*) rejected by speculative philosophy their primordial rights: the right to judge where truth is to be found, where falsehood. "Human cowardice cannot bear what madness and death tell us," and men turn away from the horrors of life and are content with the "consolations" prepared by the philosophy of the spirit. "But Job," Kierkegaard continues, "bears witness to the fullness of his conception of the world by the solid steadfastness he opposes to the tricks and pitfalls of the ethical" (that is to say of the philosophy of the spirit—the friends of Job told him what later on Hegel proclaimed in his "philosophy of the spirit"). And again: "The greatness of Job consists in the fact that his pathos cannot be relieved or smothered by lying promises" (of this same philosophy of the spirit). And finally: "Job was blessed. Everything he had possessed was restored to him twofold. This is what is called repetition. When does repetition occur? It is difficult to explain with human words. When did it occur for Job? *When all humanly thinkable certitude and all probability says it is impossible*." And Kierkegaard noted in his *Journal:* "Only horror become despair develops man's highest powers."

For Kierkegaard and for his philosophy, which in opposition to speculative philosophy he calls existential philosophy, that is to say, a philosophy which gives man not "comprehension" but life ("The just man will live by faith"), the cries of Job are not merely cries, i.e., absurd, useless, fatiguing outbursts. According to Kierkegaard, a new dimension of thought is revealed in these cries; he feels in them an active force which, like the trumpets of Jericho, will bring down the walls of the fortress. This is the fundamental theme of existential philosophy. Kierkegaard knows as well as everyone else that from the point of view of speculative philosophy existential philosophy is the worst of absurdities. But that does not stop him; on the contrary, it inspires him. It is in the "objectivism" of speculative philosophy that he sees its essential vice. "Men," he writes, "have become too objective to obtain eternal beatitude, for eternal beatitude consists precisely in an infinitely passionate, personal interestedness." And this infinite interestedness is the beginning of faith. "If I renounce everything (as the speculative philosophy which 'frees' the human spirit by the dialectic of finitude demands), this is not yet faith; it is only submission," writes

Kierkegaard with reference to the sacrifice of Abraham. "I have accomplished this movement with my own powers. And if I do not do it, it is only out of cowardice and weakness. But in believing I do not renounce anything. On the contrary, by faith I gain all things. He who has faith like a mustard-seed can move mountains. A purely human courage is required to renounce the finite for the sake of the eternal. But a paradoxical and humble courage is required to grasp everything finite by virtue of the Absurd, and this is the courage of faith. Faith did not deprive Abraham of his son, Isaac, but by faith he got Isaac." We could cite any number of passages in Kierkegaard which express the same thought.[4] "The knight of faith," he declares, "is a truly happy man who possesses the whole of the finite."

Kierkegaard is perfectly aware that declarations of this kind defy all the promptings of natural human thought. Thus he seeks protection not from reason, with its necessary and universal judgments so avidly sought by Kant, but from the Absurd, that is, from faith which reason qualifies as Absurd. He knows from his own experience that "to believe against reason is a martyrdom." But only such a faith, a faith which does not look for and cannot find justification from reason, is the faith of Scripture, according to Kierkegaard. It alone gives to man the hope of overcoming this necessity which was introduced into the world and reigns there by reason. When Hegel transforms the truth of Scripture, revealed truth, into metaphysical truth, when instead of saying that God became man or that man was created in the image and likeness of God, he proclaims that "the fundamental idea of the absolute religion is the unity of divine and human nature," he kills faith. The meaning of the words of Hegel is identical to that of the words of Spinoza: *Deus ex solis suae naturae legibus et a nemine coactus agit* (God acts only according to the laws of his own nature and is constrained by no

4. As is customary in Shestov, the above quotations from Kierkegaard's *Fear and Trembling* are given quite freely and without exact references. Shestov read Kierkegaard in the German translations of Ketels, Gottsched, and Schrempf (*Gesammelte Werke*, Jena, 1923), Haecker (*Die Tagebücher*, Innsbruck, 1923), and Schrempf (*Erbauliche Reden*, Jena, 1924). In order to remain faithful to Shestov's own style, these and other quotations are given as they occur in *his* text rather than from the standard English translations of the works in question.—TRANS.

one). And the content of the absolute religion is reduced in the same way to Spinoza's principle: *Res nullo alio modo vel ordine a Deo produci potuerunt quam productae sunt* (Things could not be produced by God in any other manner or order than that in which they have been produced). Speculative philosophy cannot exist without the idea of Necessity. This idea is as indispensable to it as air to man, as water to fish. It is for this reason that the truths of experience irritate reason so much. They testify to the divine *fiat* and do not furnish true knowledge, that is, compelling, constraining knowledge. But for Kierkegaard, constraining knowledge is an abomination of desolation, the source of original sin; by means of the *eritis scientes* the tempter brought about the Fall of man.

As a result, according to Kierkegaard, "the contrary of sin is not virtue but freedom," and again, "the contrary of sin is faith." Faith and faith alone delivers man from sin. Faith alone can tear man away from the power of the necessary truths which took possession of man's consciousness after he had tasted of the forbidden fruit. And only faith gives man the courage and the strength to look straight into the eyes of death and madness and not to yield to them spinelessly. "Imagine," writes Kierkegaard, "a man who imagines, with all the strain of his frightened fantasy, something unspeakably terrible, something so terrible that it is absolutely impossible to stand it. And then suddenly this terrible thing appears before him, becomes his reality. According to human judgment his ruin is inevitable. . . . But for God all is possible. In this consists *the struggle of faith: an insane struggle for the possible*. For only possibility opens the way of salvation. . . . In the last analysis only one thing remains: *everything is possible for God*. It is only then that the path of faith is opened. Man does not believe until he finds no other possibility. God means that everything is possible, and that everything is possible means God. And only the man whose being has been so shaken that it becomes spirit and understands that everything is possible, only this man has come close to God." Thus Kierkegaard expresses himself in his books, and he repeats it constantly in his *Journal*.

III

On this point he comes so close to Dostoevsky that without fear of exaggeration we can call Dostoevsky the double of Kierkegaard. Not only their ideas but their methods of searching for truth are perfectly similar and equidistant from the whole content of speculative philosophy. Kierkegaard quit Hegel for the "private thinker" Job. Dostoevsky did the same. All the digressions interspersed in his great novels—Hippolyte's confession in *The Idiot*, the reflections of Ivan and Mitya in *The Brothers Karamazov*, those of Kirilov in *The Possessed*, his *Notes from Underground*, and the short stories which he published in the last years of his life in the *Diary of a Writer* (the *Dream of a Ridiculous Man*, *The Gentlewoman*)—are only, as in Kierkegaard, variations on the theme of the *Book of Job*. "Why has gloomy inertia destroyed everything that is most precious?" he asks in *The Gentlewoman*. "I shall shake it off. Inertia! O nature! Men are alone on earth, that is the misfortune!"

Like Kierkegaard, Dostoevsky "emerged from the general," or, in his words, from the "fullness." And suddenly he realized that it was not necessary, that it was impossible to return into the "fullness," that the fullness, i.e., what everyone, everywhere had always considered as true, is a lie, a terrible spell, and that all the horrors of being come from the fullness toward which our reason pushes us. In the *Dream of a Ridiculous Man*, Dostoevsky reveals with an unbearable clarity the sense of that *eritis scientes* by means of which the serpent seduced the first man and continues to this day to seduce us all. Our reason, said Kant, avidly aspires to universality and necessity. But Dostoevsky, inspired by Scripture, directs all his efforts toward tearing himself away from the power of knowledge. Just as Kierkegaard does, he fights desperately against the speculative truth and the human dialectics which reduce "revelation" to knowledge. When Hegel speaks of "love"—and Hegel speaks of love as much as of the unity of divine and human nature—Dostoevsky sees there only a betrayal. The divine word is betrayed. "I affirm," he says in the *Diary of a Writer*—thus in the last years of his life—"that the consciousness of our complete powerlessness to come to the help of suffering humanity or to be of any use to it whatever, while we remain fully convinced of the sufferings of mankind, can transform the love of humanity in your heart into the hatred of humanity."

Just like Belinsky, Dostoevsky demands that he be given an account of each of the victims of chance and of history, that is to say, of those who in the eyes of speculative philosophy do not, in principle, merit any attention as created and finite beings, and whom no one in the world can help, as speculative philosophy knows perfectly well.

Even more passionately, more impetuously, and with his unique boldness of style, Dostoevsky expresses the idea of the vanity of speculative philosophy in the following lines of *Notes from Underground:* "Confronted with the impossible, men resign themselves at once," he writes. "The impossible means the stone wall! What stone wall? Obviously, the laws of nature, the conclusions of natural science, of mathematics. Once they have proved that you have descended from the apes, it is useless to scowl; accept it as it is, because it is a mathematical deduction. Just try to dispute it! For goodness sake, they will shout, you can't dispute it; it is a case of two times two make four! Nature does not ask you; she does not care about your desires or about whether her laws please you or not. You are obliged to accept them as they are, and consequently to accept everything which follows from them. A wall is a wall, etc., etc."

You see that Dostoevsky was aware of the meaning and significance of universal and necessary judgments, of this constraining, compelling truth to which man's reason calls him, just as much as Kant and Hegel were. But, as opposed to Kant and Hegel, not only does he not stop, satisfied, before the "two times two make four" and the "stone walls," but the evidences of reason provoke in him, as in Kierkegaard, an extreme agitation. Who has delivered man to the power of Necessity? How does it happen that the fate of living men turns out to depend on "stone walls" and "two times two make four," which have nothing to do with men, which more generally have nothing to do with anyone or anything at all? The critique of pure reason does not raise such a question, and it would not have understood such a question had it been addressed to it. And Dostoevsky writes immediately after the passage I have cited: "My God! But what do I care for the laws of nature and arithmetic if, for some reason, these laws and two times two makes four displease me? It is evident that I will not be able to break through this wall with my head if I do not in fact have the strength, *but I will not resign myself to accepting it simply because it is a stone wall and I lack the strength. As if a stone wall really were an alleviation and really held within it some word of peace! O absurdity of absurdities!"* (Italics mine.)

Where speculative philosophy finds "truth," this truth to which our reason aspires so avidly and before which we all prostrate ourselves, Dostoevsky sees only the "absurdity of absurdities." He refuses to take reason for a guide and not only does not consent to accept its truths; rather he attacks our truths with all the violence of which he is capable. Whence do they come? Who gave them an unlimited power over man? And how did it happen that men accepted them and everything they have brought into the world, accepted them and even deified them? It suffices to pose this question—I repeat that the critique of pure reason did not and dared not pose it—in order for it to appear clearly that there is no answer and that there cannot be any answer. Or, to speak more exactly, there is only one answer: the power of the "stone walls," the power of "two times two make four," or, to employ a philosophical language, the power of the self-evident, eternal truths over man is only a phantom power even though it appears to us to pertain to the very foundation of being. And this brings us back to the Biblical story of original sin and the Fall of man.

The "stone walls" and the "two times two make four" are only the concrete expression of the meaning hidden in the words of the tempter: *eritis scientes.* Knowledge has not given man freedom; in spite of what we habitually believe, in spite of what speculative philosophy proclaims, knowledge has made us slaves. It has delivered us tied hand and foot into the power of the eternal truths. Dostoevsky saw it, as did Kierkegaard. "Sin," says the latter, "is the swooning of freedom. Psychologically speaking, sin always occurs in a syncope." "The state of innocence," he continues, "involves peace and repose; but at the same time it implies something else which is neither discord nor struggle, for there is nothing to fight against. What is it then? Nothingness. But what effect does Nothingness produce? It engenders Anxiety!" And again: "If we ask what the object of anxiety is, there is only one answer: Nothingness. Nothingness and anxiety always go together, but as soon as the reality of the freedom of the spirit is revealed, anxiety vanishes. What is the anxiety of paganism, ultimately, but Nothingness? It is called fate. Fate is the Nothingness of anxiety." The meaning of the Biblical story of the Fall has rarely been expressed with such clarity and force.

The Nothingness which the tempter showed to the first man awakened in him the fear of the omnipotent, unlimited will of the Creator, and, seeking to protect himself from God, Adam ran to knowledge, to the eternal, uncreated truths. And in this respect nothing has changed. We are afraid of God. We see our salvation in knowledge. Can there be a more profound or more dreadful fall? It is striking to what an extent the reflections of Dostoevsky on the "stone walls" and the "two times two make four" resemble what we have heard from Kierkegaard. Men efface themselves before the eternal truths and accept everything these truths bring them. When Belinsky "wailed," demanding an account of all the victims of chance and history, they answered that his words were completely senseless, that one could not dispute in this way with Hegel and speculative philosophy. When Kierkegaard countered Hegel as a thinker with Job, nobody listened. And when Dostoevsky spoke of the "stone walls," no one even guessed that this was the true critique of pure reason; all eyes were turned toward speculative philosophy. We are all persuaded that being itself hides within it a vice which the Creator himself is powerless to destroy. The *valde bonum* with which each day of creation ended signifies, to our way of thinking, that the Creator himself had not penetrated sufficiently profoundly the essence of being. Hegel would have counseled Him to taste of the fruit of the forbidden tree in order to elevate Himself to the proper level of "knowledge" and to understand that His nature, just like that of man, is limited by the eternal truths and is powerless to change anything at all in the universe.

And so the existential philosophy of Kierkegaard as well as the philosophy of Dostoevsky dares to oppose revealed truth to speculative truth. Sin is not in being; it is not in what came from the hands of the Creator. The sin, the vice, the lack are in our "knowledge." The first man feared the unlimited will of the Creator; he saw in it this terrible "arbitrariness" which is so terrifying to us and sought protection from God in knowledge which, as the tempter whispered, would make him the equal of God, i.e., which would place him in the same dependence as God with respect to the eternal, uncreated truths by revealing "the unity of the divine and human natures." And this "knowledge" flattened and crushed his consciousness by leading it to the plane of limited possibilities which now determine its terrestrial and eternal destiny. This is the way Scripture describes the "fall" of man. And only faith, which Kierkegaard, as always in conformity with Scripture, understands as the insane struggle for the possible (that is to say in our language, for the impossible, since it overcomes self-evidence)—only faith can lift from us the immense weight of original sin and allow us to "arise" and stand again. Faith, thus, is not confidence in what we have been told, in what we have been taught, in what we have heard. Faith is a new dimension of thought, unknown and foreign to speculative philosophy, and which opens to us the way which leads to the Creator of all things, to the source of all possibilities, to Him for whom there are no limits between the possible and the impossible. It is appallingly difficult not only to accomplish this but even to think it. Jacob Boehme says that when God withdraws His hand from him, he no longer understands himself what he has written. I think that Kierkegaard and Dostoevsky could have repeated these words of Boehme. It is not in vain that Kierkegaard said: to believe in spite of reason is a martyrdom. It is not in vain that the works of Dostoevsky breathe forth a superhuman tension. This is why we hear and understand Kierkegaard and Dostoevsky so poorly. Their voices were, and will remain, voices crying in the wilderness.

[LEON SHESTOV]

In Memory of a Great Philosopher:
Edmund Husserl *

I

Max Scheler, when last I saw him, two weeks before his death, suddenly asked me: "*Warum sind Sie mit so einem Ungestüm gegen Husserl losgegangen?*" Husserl himself, when I visited him in Freiburg, introduced me to a group of visiting American professors of philosophy with the words:

"No one has ever attacked me so sharply as he—and that's why we are such close friends." What astonishes one in Husserl's words is the clear expression of that "disinterestedness" which is so rare even in the great philosophers. His first interest was in the truth; and in the search for truth friendship with one's intellectual opponents is not only possible but essential. This is characteristic of Husserl in the highest degree.

But we are concerned for the moment with a different question: What could have been the cause of my harsh attack? To make intelligible a position as difficult and at the same time remarkable as Husserl's phenomenology, it seems to me useful to state not only the doctrine itself but also the reasons why I have found it, and still find it, unacceptable. Objections illuminate not only the views of the critic, but also those of the thinker criticized.

* Translated by George L. Kline from the Russian: "Pamyati velikovo filosofa (Edmund Husserl)," *Russkiye Zapiski*, Paris, No. 12 (1938), pp. 126-145; No. 1 (1939), pp. 107-116. This article, completed only a few weeks before Shestov's death, was first published in English, in the present translation, in *Philosophy and Phenomenological Research*, Vol. 22 (1962), pp. 449-471. The version here given is slightly abridged.

Shestov gives no explicit references for the many passages from Husserl's works which he cites. Where identification has been possible, the page references are given in footnotes.

I first encountered Husserl's works thirty years ago,[1] at a time when he had published only the *Logische Untersuchungen*. That book was and is enormously impressive. Among philosophers of the early twentieth century few indeed can rival Husserl in power, boldness, depth, and significance of thought. We did not meet until much later, after I had published two articles on Husserl in the *Revue Philosophique*.[2] I had been invited to Amsterdam to read a paper before a philosophical society. When I got there I was told that Husserl was coming later to read a paper and that he had asked if I could await his arrival so that we might meet. Of course, I gladly postponed my departure for a few days. I was pleasantly surprised by Husserl's desire to meet an outspoken intellectual opponent: such generosity of spirit is extremely rare.

Our first meeting took place at the philosophical society in the evening just before Husserl was to read his paper. At that time, of course, there was no philosophic discussion. Husserl was busy with his own paper, which lasted for more than two hours and which, incidentally, he read standing, with extraordinary ease, and with the artistry and vigor of a man of forty rather than seventy. Husserl asked the member of the philosophic society in whose home he and his wife were staying (it is the custom in Amsterdam for philosophers who are invited to read papers to stay with members of the philosophic society rather than in hotels) to invite me for dinner the following day. At dinner, of course, there was no talk of philosophy. But immediately after dinner, as soon as we had gone from the dining room into the study, Husserl began to raise philosophic issues, plunging directly *in medias res*. This was characteristic of him. I remember that when, a few days later, both of us had dinner with another member of the society, and after dinner our host,

1. That is, in 1908, when Shestov was still in Saint Petersburg. A Russian translation of Volume I of the *Logische Untersuchungen* was published in Saint Petersburg in 1909; "Philosophie als strenge Wissenschaft" appeared in the Russian edition of *Logos* in 1911-1912. Substantial Russian studies of Husserl's thought were produced by B. Jakovenko (1912) and G. Shpet (1914).—TRANS.

2. The two articles in question are: "Memento Mori," *Revue Philosophique*, *101-102* (1926), pp. 5-62, and "Qu'est-ce que la vérité?," *ibid.*, *103-104* (1927), pp. 36-74.—TRANS.

a very wealthy man and a passionate bibliophile, began showing Husserl some of his rare books—first editions of the *Critique of Pure Reason* and Spinoza's *Ethics*—Husserl, to the great chagrin of our host, cast only a perfunctory glance at these rare volumes, and in a few moments took me aside and began to talk philosophy.

This same concentration upon the questions which absorbed him was apparent on another occasion, when, at the request of Professor Andler, I began to sound Husserl out concerning his willingness to come to Paris at the invitation of the Sorbonne. He asked me only one question: "Do you think that I will find people in Paris who know German and are willing to reflect upon my problems?" Husserl's complete absorption in philosophy was evident in all of our conversations—first in Amsterdam, and then in Freiburg and Paris. "You were wrong," he began at our first meeting, throwing himself upon me sharply and passionately. "You have turned me into a stone statue, raised me onto a lofty pedestal, and then with hammer-blows you have shattered this statue to bits. But am I really so lapidary? You don't seem to have noticed what compelled me to formulate in such a radical way the question of the nature of knowledge, modifying the dominant theories of knowledge which previously had satisfied me as much an any other philosopher. The more deeply I probed into the basic problems of logic, the more I felt that our science, our knowledge, is shaking, tottering. And finally, to my own indescribable horror, I convinced myself that if contemporary philosophy has said the last word about the nature of knowledge, then we have no knowledge. Once, when I was giving a lecture at the university, expounding ideas which I had taken over from our contemporaries, I suddenly felt that I had nothing to say, that I was standing before my students with empty hands and an empty soul. And then I resolved both for myself and for my students to submit the existing theories of knowledge to that severe and unrelenting criticism which has aroused the indignation of so many people. On the other hand, I began to seek the truth precisely where no one had sought it before, since no one had admitted that it might be found there. Such was the origin of my *Logical Investigations*. But you did not want to see in my struggle, in my impetuous 'either-or,' an expression of what it in fact was—namely, the consciousness that, if the doubts which had arisen in me could not be overcome by the efforts of reason, if we are doomed merely to go on smoothing over—more or less thoroughly—the fissures and crevasses which have opened up in all of our epistemological constructions, then one fine day all of our knowledge will crumble and we will find ourselves standing amid the miserable ruins of former greatness."

It was in roughly these words, but with greater force and passion, with that extraordinary *élan* which one felt in all of his remarkable writings and addresses, that Husserl spoke to me of the sources of his bold and original philosophy, a philosophy which relentlessly swept away the fundamental ideas of the best contemporary thinkers. The *Logische Untersuchungen* and his other works were a "slaughter," not of the "innocent," of course (the innocent do not philosophize), but of the old men. At the same time they were a grandiose and magnificent attempt to find a support for our knowledge, a support which even the "gates of Hell" could not vanquish. Husserl spoke with sincerity, enthusiasm, and inspiration; I think even non-philosophers would immediately sense that the questions he raised were not theoretical ones—any proffered solution to which, being equally indifferent, would be equally acceptable—but questions, as he himself put it, of life and death. Husserl, like Shakespeare's Hamlet, raised the terrible and fateful question, "To be or not to be?" He saw with Hamlet (or with Shakespeare) that the time was out of joint. His words had a truly shattering impact. My first personal meeting with him, like my reading of his first works twenty years earlier, was truly memorable. One does not forget such human greatness.

I replied candidly—"You are right, of course. I have attacked your ideas with all the energy I could command. But this was only because I felt the enormous and incomparable power of your thought, and sensed what you have now told me about the motivations of your bold and original ideas. I have no doubt that in France—where you were almost entirely unknown before my articles appeared—people now realize that a neighboring country has produced a major philosopher who has opened up

horizons hitherto obscured by the thick haze of traditional com-
monplaces. The sharpness of my attack emphasizes, rather than
deprecates, the enormous significance of what you have done
for philosophy. To struggle with you one must marshal all of
his spiritual energies; every intense effort presupposes passion
and the sharpness of passion. I was faced by a fearful dilemma:
either to accept your whole position and its as-yet-unformulated
philosophical implications—or to rebel against you. And if in
the next world I am accused of betraying philosophy because
of my struggle against self-evidence,[3] I shall point to you, and
you will burn in my place. You have pursued and persecuted me
so persistently and inexorably with your intuitive self-evidence,
that I could find no other way out. Either I had to submit to
you in everything, or else steel myself for the desperate step of
revolt, not only against you but against everything that has always been considered the unquestioned foundation of philosophy
and of thought. I had to revolt against self-evident truth. You
were profoundly right when you said that the time was out
of joint. Every attempt to examine the least fissure in the foundation of human knowledge throws the time out of joint. But
must knowledge be preserved at whatever cost? Must the time
be put back in joint? Or rather, should we not give it a further
push—and shatter it to bits?"

This conversation—here given in brief and approximate outline—brought to a focus what united, and also what divided,
us. Strange as it may seem to some people, my first teacher of
philosophy was Shakespeare, with his enigmatic, incomprehensible, threatening, and melancholy words: "The time is out of
joint." What can one do, how can one act, when the time is
out of joint, when being reveals its horrors? From Shakespeare I
turned eagerly to Kant, who, with the incomparable artistry of
his *Critique of Practical Reason,* by means of his famous postu-

3. Shestov's term is *"ochevidnost,"* a close rendering of Husserl's *"Evidenz."*
Alternative English translations might be "obviousness," "certainty," or even
"intuition." Husserl himself characterizes *Evidenz* as "adequate perception
of truth," "knowledge," "incontestable certainty," and *"adaequatio rei et
intellectus"* (cf. *Logische Untersuchungen,* II, 118, 122, 225). He also speaks
of an "act of *Evidenz.*"—TRANS.

lates, attempted to gloss over, and for centuries succeeded in glossing over, the ontological fissures laid bare by his own critique of pure reason. But Kant had no answer for my questions. I next turned to a different source—the Scriptures. But surely the Scriptures cannot bear comparison with self-evidence? At that time I had not yet come to the point of asking this question. Even those who acknowledge papal infallibility have not come to the point of raising it. Men content themselves with the postulates of practical reason, using them to soften—or rather to forget, to fail to see—the all-destroying power of the truths of theoretical reason.

Almost all of my conversations with Husserl revolved about these themes. When he visited me at my home in Paris, immediately after dinner (which he seemed not even to have noticed), he took me into another room and immediately plunged into philosophic discussion. At that time I was working on the first part of my book *Athens and Jerusalem*—the section called "Parmenides Bound." Naturally, I tried to direct our discussion toward the topics which I was then treating. I said to Husserl, using almost the same words that I later used in "Parmenides Bound": In 399 B.C. Socrates was poisoned. Socrates left behind his disciple Plato, who, "forced by the truth itself" (in Aristotle's expression), did not, could not refrain from thinking and saying that Socrates had been poisoned. All of his writings elaborate a single central question: Is there any power in the world which can reconcile us to the fact that Socrates was poisoned? For Aristotle such a question would have been nonsensical. He was convinced that the "truth," "a dog was poisoned," like the "truth," "Socrates was poisoned," is permanently immune from human or divine objection. The hemlock makes no distinction between Socrates and dogs. Similarly, forced by the truth itself, we are obliged to make no distinction between Socrates and dogs, even mad dogs.

I expected Husserl to greet these remarks with a burst of indignation. But something else happened: He listened intently as though, in the depths of his being, he had already long since recognized that the Aristotelian "forced by truth itself" contained a kind of falsehood or betrayal. I was the more astonished in that we had previously disputed warmly as to what philosophy is. I had said that philosophy is a great and ultimate struggle; he had answered sharply, "*Nein, Philosophie ist Besinnung.*" But now our conversation took a different turn. It was as though he felt the Aristotelian certitude to be built upon sand. In any case, Husserl arranged to have my "Parmenides Bound" published as an article in the journal *Logos*, for which it was wholly unsuited both because of its length and, more importantly, because it challenged the conviction that men can never free themselves from such truths as, "Socrates was poisoned." Husserl's mind, I repeat, was open to everything. Soon after my article had appeared he wrote me: "Your ways are not my ways, but I understand and value your problems." [4] I then understood the strange fact that during my visit to Freiburg, learning that I had never read Kierkegaard, Husserl began not to *ask* but to *demand*—with enigmatic insistence—that I acquaint myself with the works of the Danish thinker. How was it that a man whose whole life had been a celebration of reason should have led me to Kierkegaard's hymn to the absurd? Husserl, to be sure, seems to have become acquainted with Kierkegaard only during the last years of his life. There is no evidence in his works of familiarity with any of the writings of the author of *Either—Or*. But it seems clear that Kierkegaard's ideas deeply impressed him.

II

On one view the aim of Husserl's phenomenology is purely methodological; such a view is profoundly mistaken and serves merely to veil the breadth and significance of Husserl's complex of problems. He himself writes: "Philosophy . . . is a science of the true principles, the sources, the ῥιζώματα πάντων." [5] Such a definition makes his aim clear. His long article, "Philosophy as a Strict Science," written with extraordinary *élan*, represents not the results but a kind of manifesto of the phenomenological school, a concise statement of the position which he had developed and was to develop further in his major works, *Logische*

4. Interestingly enough, he once said to me: "*Das, was Sie treiben, heisse ich auch Wissenschaft.*"

5. "Philosophie als strenge Wissenschaft," *Logos*, I (1910-1911), 340.— TRANS.

Untersuchungen (1900, 1901) and *Ideen zu einer reinen Phäno-menologie* . . . (1913). With the audacity of a man destined to do great things, Husserl declares:

> In the whole life of the modern period there is perhaps no idea more powerful, more irresistible in its advance, than the idea of science. Nothing will block its triumphant course. In the pursuit of its legitimate goals it is indeed all-encompassing. Conceived in its ideal perfection, it would be reason itself, admitting no other authority beside it or above it. . . . Science has spoken, from now on wisdom must learn from it.[6]

Husserl's forceful statement is reminiscent of the well-known saying, "*Roma locuta, causa finita.*"

However, we should not assume that Husserl repudiated the whole of earlier philosophy. On the contrary, he had a lively sense of his own continuity with the great thinkers of the past:

> A fully-conscious will toward exact science rules the Socratic-Platonic revolution in philosophy and also the scientific reactions against scholasticism of the early modern period, in particular the Cartesian revolution. Their impulse, carried over to the great philosophies of the seventeenth and eighteenth centuries, was renewed with the most radical energy in Kant's *Vernunftkritik*, and continued to exert controlling influence upon the philosophy of Fichte.[7]

It was only *contemporary* philosophy that Husserl condemned unconditionally, and here his attack was merciless:

> It lacks even the beginning of a scientifically rigorous doctrine, . . . it is at most a scientific semifinished product, or an undifferentiated mixture of *Weltanschauung* and theoretical knowledge.[8]

What Husserl calls *Weltanschauung* (or *Weisheit*) arouses his deepest indignation:

6. *Ibid.*, pp. 296, 334.—TRANS.
7. *Ibid.*, p. 292.—TRANS.
8. *Ibid.*, p. 335.—TRANS.

. . . we must remember our responsibility to mankind. We must not sacrifice eternity to time; we must not, in order to meet our own need, bequeath new needs to our posterity as an ultimately ineradicable evil . . . *Weltanschauungen* clash; only science is decisive, and its decisions bear the stamp of eternity.[9]

These challenging words are directed against the philosophy of the second half of the nineteenth century: Mill, Bain, Wundt, Sigwart, Erdmann, Lipps, Dilthey. He accuses them all of "psychologism," that is, relativism. Even the ancients had revealed the internal contradiction of relativism. Relativism, Aristotle declared—and not as a truth which he himself had discovered, but as a generally known truth—is self-destructive. For Husserl this proposition is the starting point for all of his investigations. Of course, his opponents reject Protagoras' thesis that "man is the measure of all things." But Husserl shows that, unconsciously or covertly, they are wholly in the power of Protagoras' idea; they fail to realize this only because they are not *absolute* relativists but what he calls "*specific*" (or "*species*") relativists.[10] They see the senselessness of the assertion that every man can have his own truth, but they do not see the equal senselessness of the assertion that man as a *species* has his own truth. In opposition to all such contemporary philosophers, Husserl declares with magnificent passion:

What is true is absolutely true, is true "in itself." Truth is identically one, whether it be apprehended in the judgments of men or of monsters [*Menschen oder Unmenschen*], of angels or of gods.[11]

All of Husserl is in these words, the whole enormous, almost superhuman task which he set himself and philosophy—the search for the principles, sources, and roots of all that is. After Kant— and especially after his *Critique of Pure Reason*—such a claim seems utterly fantastic. Who is willing to speak seriously of such

9. *Ibid.*, p. 337.—TRANS.
10. *Logische Untersuchungen*, I, 116ff.—TRANS.
11. *Ibid.*, p. 117.—TRANS.

a thing as absolute truth? Husserl, of course, knows very well that contemporary thought is afraid of approaching within cannon range of such a judgment. All epistemologists speak of self-evident truths, but for them self-evidence, our certainty of the existence of universal and necessary judgments, is only, in Sigwart's expression, "a postulate beyond which we cannot go," a certainty which is maintained only by subjective consciousness, "the feeling of certainty which accompanies a certain portion of our thought." This was the position of such an outstanding thinker as Erdmann. These thinkers seemed to want to assume that the feeling of self-evidence was a "sufficient reason" which would justify our confidence in the results of scientific investigation. But Husserl saw in such frivolous assumptions, whether conscious or unconscious, a fatal danger to philosophy. In answer to Erdmann and Sigwart he wrote:

> [On such a view] there might be creatures of a special kind, logical supermen [*Übermenschen*] so to speak, for whom not our fundamental principles, but quite different ones, would be valid; what is truth for us would be falsity for them. It may be true for them that they do not experience the psychic phenomena which they in fact experience. It may be true for us that we and they exist, but it may be false for them, etc. Of course, we ordinary logical creatures [*logische Alltagsmenschen*] would judge such creatures to be out of their senses: they speak of truth and at the same time destroy its laws; they claim to have their own laws of thought, and yet they deny the laws upon which the possibility of law in general rests. . . . In their thinking "yes" and "no," truth and error, being and non-being, would lose all distinctness.[12]

Husserl, of course, does not limit himself to such solemn pronouncements. The threat of the madhouse, which is implicit in the words just quoted, goes far beyond the limits of a simple pronouncement. The senselessness which is exhibited by the assertions of relativism—whether individual or "specific"—cannot fail to arouse the anxiety of the conscientious investigator.

12. *Ibid.*, pp. 151f.—TRANS.

In the second volume of his *Logische Untersuchungen* Husserl formulates the same idea in a calmer but no less powerful way: "We shall never admit that anything which is logically or geometrically absurd can be psychologically possible." We admit, he explains, that "logical concepts have a psychological origin, but we reject the conclusion which is drawn from this fact." What conclusion? And why do we reject it?—"For our discipline the psychological question of the origin of given abstract ideas is of no interest."

The original and unconventional character of Husserl's philosophic construction is here clearly evident. He fearlessly defends the validity of generic (or ideal) objects, as well as individual (or real) objects.

> This is the point [he writes] at which relativistic and empiricistic psychologism is to be distinguished from idealism, and it offers the only possibility of a self-consistent theory of knowledge.[13]

Husserl distinguishes between *truth* and an individual's act of *judging truly*. I assert the judgment that $2 \times 2 = 4$. This judgment is, of course, a purely psychological act and as such may be studied by the psychologist. But, no matter how much the psychologist may discover about the laws of actual thinking, he can never deduce from these laws a principle which will distinguish truth from falsehood. On the contrary, all of his reasoning presupposes that he is in possession of a criterion for distinguishing truth from falsehood. The philosopher is not in the least concerned with John's or Peter's judgment that $2 \times 2 = 4$. There are thousands of individual judgments about a given object, but there is only one truth.

> If a natural scientist draws conclusions from the laws of gravity, the lever, etc., concerning the functioning of a machine he, of course, experiences certain subjective acts. But corresponding to the subjective relations of thought there is an objective unit of meaning (i.e., one adequate to the evidently given objective reality), which is what

13. *Logische Untersuchungen*, II, i, 107.—TRANS.

it is, irrespective of whether anyone actualizes it in thought.

This same idea is even more clearly expressed in the first volume of the *Logische Untersuchungen:*

> If all gravitating bodies should disappear, the law of gravity would not be destroyed; it would simply remain without any possibility of actual application. For it says nothing about the existence of gravitating masses, but only of what is inherent in gravitating masses as such.

In these resolute words one feels the central nerve of phenomenology. This idea pervades all of Husserl's thinking. To dispel any doubt as to his intention, he offers the following example:

> The meaning of the statement "π is a transcendental number," what we understand by it when we read it, or mean by it when we say it, is not an individual, recurrent feature of our thinking experience. In each specific case this feature will be individually different, whereas the meaning [*Sinn*] of the statement must always be *identical*. . . . As opposed to the unlimited multiplicity of individual experiences, that which is expressed in them is everywhere identical: it is the *same* in the strictest sense of the term. The reference of the statement [*Satzbedeutung*] is not multiplied with the multiplicity of persons or acts; the judgment in the ideal, logical sense is one. . . . This not a mere hypothesis, to be justified by its explanatory fruitfulness. We take it as a directly graspable truth, and we rely in this upon self-evidence, the ultimate authority in all questions of knowledge.[14]

These are the words which Husserl hurled in the face of contemporary philosophy, a philosophy which was diffidently hiding its relativistic tendencies beneath the fuzzy theories of neo-Kantianism. Truth is one for men, for angels, and for gods. Truth rests upon self-evidence; before it mortals and immortals alike are powerless. Hence philosophy begins with what

14. *Ibid.,* pp. 99f.—TRANS.

Husserl calls the "phenomenological reduction." In order to break through to the sources, the principles, the roots of all that is, we must tear ourselves away from the real, from changing, transient phenomena and make an "*epoché*"—bracket the phenomena, so to speak. Outside the brackets there will be pure, ideal being, the truth which philosophy seeks, guaranteed against doubt by self-evidence itself. Husserl unhesitatingly declares:

> Self-evidence is not some index of consciousness which, appended to consciousness, speaks to us like a mystical voice from a better world, saying "here is the truth"—as though we, free-thinking men and women, would be ready to obey such a voice without requiring of it any proof of the validity of its assertions.

No contemporary philosopher has ventured to speak with such audacity and power of the autonomy and independence of truth. Husserl will not accept the compromises which lead a majority of thinkers astray. Either self-evidence is the ultimate court of appeal, at the bar of which the human spirit receives its full and definitive satisfaction, or else our knowledge is illusory and false, and sooner or later a realm of chaos and madness will appear on earth, and those who are not too lazy to stretch out their hands will begin to usurp the sovereign rights of reason, its scepter and crown. "Truth" will turn out to be very different from those firm and immutable laws which the exact sciences have hitherto sought and found. Seneca aptly formulated the basic proposition which inspired ancient philosophy: "*Ipse creator et conditor mundi semel jussit, semper paret.*" [15] The idea that anyone at any time established a command or decree is incompatible with the Greek conception of truth. They did not say this outright, but they were convinced that the idea of "*jubere*" [to command or decree] is indissolubly connected with the idea of arbitrariness, and that arbitrariness leads directly to those realms of "*Schwärmerei und Allerglauben*" of which Kant warned us. In essence, both Seneca and his teachers were deeply convinced that no one, not even the Creator and founder

15. "The creator and founder of the world decreed but once; he obeys forever." (*De Providentia*, V, 8.)—TRANS.

of the world, had ever laid down a decree. The Creator, as well as all rational and nonrational creatures, has always *obeyed*. And self-evidence, which is not a mystical voice from another world (such a voice would not impress free-thinking men and women), bears witness to this.

Self-evidence reveals the eternal structure of being, laid bare by the phenomenological reduction. Husserl refers to Leibniz's distinction between *"vérités de raison"* and *"vérités de fait."* For Leibniz the truths of reason enter God's consciousness without his consent. Kant, in his *Critique of Pure Reason*, which was intended to overthrow the dogmatism of Leibniz and Wolff, unhesitatingly declared that experience—which tells us only what exists, but does not tell us that what exists is necessarily what it is rather than something else—not only fails to satisfy but even irritates our reason. Reason thirsts for "compelling truth"; the free *"jubere"* must be driven out of philosophy once and for all, since philosophy is and wishes to be only a realm of eternal obedience (*parere*). Leibniz—and here he also anticipates Kant—sees in *"parere"* man's desired end. Eternal truths, in his view, not only compel, they also convince us. But neither Leibniz nor Kant was ready to place in the ikon-corner the ikon of the eternal truths to which they prayed. Husserl was the first to speak of self-evidence in a manner befitting the extraordinary philosophical significance of this idea. "What is true is absolutely true, is true in itself. Truth is identically one, whether it be apprehended in the judgments of men or of monsters, of angels or of gods."

III

In his striving to make philosophy a science of absolute truth, Husserl recognized no restraint. Not only did he apply his basic ideas to mathematics and the natural sciences ("the law of gravity would not be destroyed if all gravitating bodies should disappear," etc.); he also wanted to give directives to history. He wished through the phenomenological reduction to define all of the manifestations of the human spirit. With that noble and challenging resoluteness, that powerful intensity of his whole thinking self, which always was such a captivating trait of his character, Husserl rose to the defense of his cherished aims. Particularly instructive in this connection is Husserl's dispute with his distinguished contemporary Dilthey. Husserl esteemed Dilthey as only a scholar can esteem another scholar. Nevertheless, he consigned him, like Sigwart and Erdmann, to the madhouse—although in somewhat more moderate language. But a madhouse is still a madhouse, whatever you call it. Dilthey's central idea, which evoked such passionate resistance on Husserl's part, is expressed in these clear and simple words:

> Before a gaze which takes in the earth and its whole past, the absolute validity of any given form of life-organization, religion, or philosophy disappears. Thus, more decisively than any mere survey of the clash of systems, the development of the historical consciousness undermines belief in the universal validity of any of the many philosophies which have undertaken, through systems of concepts, to express the connectedness of the world in a compelling way.[16]

To this Husserl replies sharply:

> It is easy to see that historicism, when consistently carried through, passes over into extreme skeptical subjectivism. The ideas of truth, theory, science—like all ideas—would lose their absolute validity. Any idea would have validity so long as it was an actual product of *Geist*, held as such to be valid and defining thought by the mere fact of being such a product. In such a case, absolute validity, validity "as such"—the validity of an idea which is what it is even though no one is in a position to actualize it and no historical mankind might ever do so—simply would not exist. Hence no validity would attach to the principle of contradiction or to logic as a whole. . . . The final result might be that the principles of logical consistency would turn into their opposites. As a further consequence, all the propositions which we have now uttered, and even the possibilities which we have weighed and accepted as valid, would have

16. Wilhelm Dilthey, *Weltanschauung, Philosophie und Religion*, Berlin, 1911, quoted by Husserl in "Philosophie . . . ," p. 324.—TRANS.

no validity in themselves. There is no need to go further or
to repeat here what has already been discussed elsewhere.[17]

The "elsewhere," as Husserl himself makes clear, is Volume
I of the *Logische Untersuchungen*. As we know, he there con-
signs to the *madhouse* every defender of relativism—of "species"
relativism as well as "individual" relativism. He declares unhesitatingly:

History, the empirical *Geisteswissenschaft*, cannot decide
whether or not it is necessary to distinguish between religion as a form of culture and religion as an idea, i.e., valid
religion, between art as a form of culture and valid art,
between historical and valid law or right [*Recht*], and
finally between historical and valid philosophy. Nor can
history decide whether or not the two are related, to
speak with Plato, as Idea to its clouded phenomenal manifestation.[18] Philosophic understanding, and it alone, can and
must unveil for us the mysteries of life and the world.[19]

With these words Husserl's thought reaches its culmination.
The remarkable thing is that, although no philosopher has ever
ventured to speak with such candor and audacity of the
"*Schrankenlosigkeit der objektiven Vernunft*," [20] all philosophers
are *in fact* convinced that reason and reason alone has the power
to answer all the questions which trouble man's soul. Self-evidence is like a Medusa's head: everyone who looks at it is
rendered spiritually impotent, turned to stone, paralyzed in will,
and made to submit to every influence from without. But no one
is prepared to recognize that men are under the power of a
dark, enigmatic, and incomprehensible force, which compels
them to accept the judgments of reason even when those judgments encroach upon what is most precious to them, upon what
they consider sacred. Following Aristotle's advice, men keep to
the middle ranges of being, not risking an encounter with the
extremes; they have convinced themselves that they can infer the

17. "Philosophie . . . ," pp. 324f.—TRANS.
18. *Ibid.*, p. 325.—TRANS.
19. *Ibid.*, p. 336.—TRANS.
20. *Logische Untersuchungen*, II, ii, 90.—TRANS.

nature of the extremes from study of the mean. But the temperate zones of human and cosmic life are not in the least like the poles or the equator. To judge of the extremes of being one must first experience them.

The most fallacious of inferences is: Since reason has done so much, it can do everything. "Much" is not the same as "everything"; *much* and *everything* are distinct categories, neither of which can be reduced to the other. Even religion—as we have just heard from Husserl—takes on meaning and significance to the extent that it can draw support from self-evidence. Reason decides what kind of religion is valid—what kind of religion is valid in itself, and in general whether religion is valid at all; in which religion God's voice is heard; and, finally, in which religion a merely human voice sounds through the allegedly divine voice. And whatever reason declares must be the case: *Roma locuta.*

I say once more: Husserl's enormous contribution consists in his having had the audacity to formulate the question in this way. His *Einstellung*, as he calls it, is directed not only against contemporary philosophy but also against Kant, who, despite the radical character of his "critique of pure reason," could not resist introducing a contraband into his philosophy—the postulates concerning God, the immortality of the soul, and freedom. Husserl, faithful to the tasks which he set himself, remains closer to Plato. In the *Euthyphro* Plato asks: Is something holy because it is loved by the gods, or do the gods love it because it is holy? And, of course, he defends the second answer. The holy is above the gods, just as ideal truth is above the cosmos. The holy is not created, and whatever it declares to us, whatever it demands of us, we must accept and obey—not only we human beings, but also demons, angels, and gods. And the holy remains holy, just as ideal truths remain truths; it is utterly indifferent to them whether or not men need them, whether men (and even gods) are gladdened or saddened by them, filled with hope or with despair. For truth is truth in itself, taking no account of the "empirical phenomena" which are in its power.

It is just at this point that we find the most enigmatic and significant contribution of Husserl's philosophy. Here the question arises: Why did Husserl demand with such extraordinary insistence that I read Kierkegaard? For Kierkegaard, in contrast to Husserl, sought the truth not in reason but in the absurd. For him the law of contradiction—like an angel with a drawn sword, stationed by God at the entrance to Paradise—bears no witness to the truth and in no way defines the boundaries which separate the possible from the impossible. For Kierkegaard, philosophy (which he calls "existential") begins precisely at that point where reason sees, with the force of self-evidence, that all possibilities have already been exhausted, that everything is finished, that nothing remains but for man to look and grow cold. Kierkegaard here introduces into philosophy what he calls "faith," defined as "an insane struggle for the possible," that is, for the possibility of the impossible—clearly alluding to the words of Scripture: Man's wisdom is folly in the sight of the Lord.

Men fear folly and madness more than anything else in the world. Kierkegaard knows this; he repeatedly asserts that human frailty is afraid to look into the eyes of death and madness. To be sure, we read in the *Phaedo* that philosophy is "a preparation for death," that all men who have genuinely devoted themselves to philosophy, although "they may have concealed it from others, have done nothing else than prepare themselves for the act of dying and the fact of death." It seems likely that these extraordinary ideas were suggested to Plato by the death of Socrates. Plato did not return to them; he was wholly absorbed in the *Republic* and the *Laws*, even in his extreme old age— thus fulfilling, like ordinary mortals and gladiators, the age-old demand: "*Salve, Caesar, morituri te salutant.*" Even in the face of death men cannot tear themselves away from "Caesar," from what everyone accepts as "reality." And this is "natural"! For how are we to understand the "preparation for death"? Is it not a beginning of, and preparation for, the struggle against the demonstrative character of proof, against the law of contradiction, against reason's claim to unlimited rights, its seizure of the power of arbitrary definition of the point at which possibility ends and impossibility begins—the struggle against the angel who stands with drawn sword at the gate of Paradise? It seems to the inexperienced gaze that this measureless power rightfully belongs to reason, and that there is nothing dreadful or threatening in the fact that it does.

But the matter is really very different. The unconquerable and unendurable horrors of being spring precisely from the fact that the power of defining the limits of the possible is wholly and exclusively arrogated to reason. As Husserl put it: reason commands, man must obey. Not only must he obey, he must humble himself with joy and reverence. An example of this is Nietzsche's preaching of unrestrained cruelty, which so stunned everyone in his time. Husserl insisted that I should study Kierkegaard. He might just as well have insisted that I study Nietzsche, except for the fact that I had known Nietzsche long before I had even heard of Husserl. There is a profound inner kinship between Husserl's teaching on the one hand, and that of Nietzsche and Kierkegaard on the other. In absolutizing truth, Husserl was forced to relativize being, or more accurately human life. Nietzsche, too, was forced to do this. To the extent that he submitted to the power of reason, recognizing no other authority (which was often, though not always, the case with him), he had no choice but to exclaim: "Who can achieve anything great if he does not feel in himself the strength and capacity to bring about great sufferings? To suffer is a trifling matter; weak women and even slaves often achieve virtuosity in it. But not to perish from inward doubt and distress when one has to cause great suffering in others and to listen to their cries—this is greatness; in this greatness is manifest." [21]

What is the source of Nietzsche's certainty that the readiness to display inexorable cruelty is an evidence of greatness? And what greatness is this to which we are supposed to strive "with all our heart and with all our soul," just as Scripture demands with respect to man's love of God? As Nietzsche assures us, men, carrying out the demands of reason, have killed God. I regret that there is not room here to quote in its entirety the passage in which Nietzsche speaks, with a force and passion extraordinary even for him, of this "crime of crimes." But reason demanded it, and it was necessary to kill God, just as it is necessary to do whatever reason considers necessary and just. Reason

21. Nietzsche, *The Gay Science*, section 325.—TRANS.

is inexorable in its unlimited demands. "Must we not finally sacrifice," Nietzsche writes in another place, "all of the consoling, holy, healing things; all hopes, all faith in hidden harmony, in happiness and justice in the future? Must we not sacrifice God himself, and out of cruelty to ourselves deify the stone, stupidity, gravity, fate, nothingness? To sacrifice God for the sake of Nothingness—this paradoxical mystery of the ultimate cruelty has fallen to the lot of our generation. We all know something of this." [22]

Possibly—indeed, probably—these words of Nietzsche's are not wholly accurate. It is far from being the case that *all* men know that to carry out reason's demands we must *deify* the stone, stupidity, nothingness. Rather the contrary (and this is very important): Most men have not the least suspicion of this. With that unconcern of which Nietzsche himself has told us not a little, the most distinguished representatives of contemporary science and philosophy have wholly entrusted their fate and the fate of mankind to reason, without knowing or wishing to know the limits of its power and authority. Reason has made its demands and we have agreed unconditionally to deify the stone, stupidity, nothingness. No one has the courage to ask: what mysterious force compels us to renounce all of our hopes and aspirations, everything that we consider sacred and consoling, everything in which we see justice and happiness? Reason, which is not concerned about our hopes or our despair, sternly forbids us even to raise such a question. And to whom shall we address this question? To reason itself? But it has already given its answer. Reason recognizes no judge other than itself; such a recognition would amount to a renunciation of its sovereign rights.

IV

I have referred to certain of Nietzsche's ideas, although Husserl and I never had occasion to discuss Nietzsche. It is possible, even probable, that Husserl knew relatively little of Nietzsche. Nevertheless, he was close to Nietzsche as well as to Kierkegaard in demanding a direct approach to what they both considered

22. Nietzsche, *Beyond Good and Evil*, section 55.—TRANS.

the essence of philosophy—the principles, sources, and roots of all being. Both Husserl and Nietzsche placed boundless trust in reason, carrying out in their own way the principle: "*Roma locuta, causa finita.*" Nietzsche, for himself and all men, and thus for Husserl too, accepted reason's demands unmurmuringly and even reverently; he deified the stone, gravity, fate, as well as a heavy, stone-like, fateful morality.

It must be added that the cruelty which Nietzsche proclaimed and celebrated is not, as some people have thought, wholly unheard of in philosophy. Before Nietzsche no one had reveled in the idea of cruelty with such provocative trenchancy and almost superhuman inspiration. But this idea had been fully elaborated in ancient philosophy and, like a spark among the ashes, had lived unseen in the most exalted constructions of Hellenic genius. When Plato in the *Laws* solemnly declares, addressing himself to the individual. "You, poor mortal, are insignificant enough; but you have a certain significance in the general order [of being]. . . . You do not think of the fact that each individual creature comes into being for the sake of all [that exists], in order that it should lead a happy life; that nothing is done for your sake and that you yourself were created for the universe"—I say, when he asserts this he is already anticipating Nietzsche. The last great philosopher of Greece expressed this Platonic view in even more concrete and naked words: Your sons are killed, your daughters are violated, your homeland is laid waste; there is nothing dreadful or shocking about this. It is and must be, and therefore we must accept it calmly. This is the attitude which our reason takes toward "reality"; this is the way it judges reality. And one cannot quarrel with reason. It is true that Plotinus, in the last analysis, made a brilliant attempt to "soar above reason," to go beyond "knowledge and understanding." I cannot enter further into this question here; I have already said enough about it in other places.[23]

But insofar as he remained within the rut of ancient thought—bringing together the ideas of Plato, Aristotle, and the Stoics—

23. I had occasion to discuss Plotinus with Husserl only once. With characteristic and captivating honesty he admitted: "I have never studied Plotinus, and all I know of him is what I have read in your books."

Plotinus too, yielding to the self-evident, came to accept the horrors of human existence as something flowing inevitably from the principles and roots of being, hence definitive, right, and legitimate. Thus it continues to our own day. Everyone is convinced that our thinking should, as Seneca expressed it, submit joyfully and without a murmur to what reason reveals. The last word of both divine and human wisdom is: *fata volentem ducunt, nolentem trahunt.*[24] The idea of fate—a fate blind, deaf, and indifferent to all things—holds absolute sway over the thinking of all rational creatures. Nietzsche himself, who attacked slave morality so ferociously and glorified the morality of the rulers so exuberantly, submitted reverently to fate. To be a slave of fate, to carry out all of its commands not from fear but from conscience, seemed to him neither shameful nor dreadful. His preaching of submission to, and even love of, fate (*amor fati*)— fate with all of its inexorabilities and cruelties—was both candid and inspired. Reason and the knowledge which reason provides reveal truths to us which are unsurmountable not only for us but also for higher beings, for angels and gods. Every attempt to struggle with these truths is foredoomed to failure. Both Nietzsche and Husserl—each of them expressing this idea in his own way—felt that on this point they were invulnerable: here they stood defended by self-evidence.

But, I ask once more, why did Husserl refer me so insistently to Kierkegaard? Kierkegaard too had said a good deal about fate. With his characteristic penetration, anticipating both Husserl and Nietzsche, Kierkegaard declared that the more profound, significant, and endowed with genius a man is, the more absolutely is he dominated by the idea of fate. But, in contrast to Nietzsche and Husserl, he did not regard this as a sign of greatness. It is not easy, Kierkegaard declares, to admit this, but it must be said that the man of genius is a great *sinner*. Absolute trust in reason, not only when it assumes hegemony in the empirical world or the "temperate zones" of being, but also when the events of our life exalt us to the extremes of being, is a sin, a fall, the greatest fall imaginable—that of which we read in *Genesis*. Man, having tasted the fruits of the tree of

24. "The fates lead the willing; the unwilling they drag." (Seneca)—TRANS.

knowledge, was torn away from the source of life. To our understanding this is madness. Kierkegaard knows this very well, better than anyone else. But this "knowledge" does not restrain him. For him Job is not merely "an old man who suffers much." For him Job is a "thinker," a "private thinker," to be sure, but one from whom we can learn truths not revealed to the great representatives of contemporary philosophy (Hegel) nor to the brilliant symposiasts of antiquity: there are scales upon which human suffering weighs heavier than the sands of the sea. Kierkegaard knows very well the power of self-evident truth over human beings. He experienced this power in his own person as few men have. Nevertheless, inspired by the Scriptures, he made a grandiose effort to overcome the self-evident. In opposition to self-evidence he placed—as a fatal objection—man's great suffering and the horrors which fill our life. Of course, Kierkegaard was not alone in standing with open eyes before the horrors of being; others, both philosophers and non-philosophers, have done this. But he was confronted by a dreadful dilemma: whether to go on as before in the face of the horrors of being, to accept what reason offers as ultimate and final truth, or, following the Scriptures, to raise the question of the competence of reason and of the knowledge which reason provides. Human wisdom is folly before the Lord. Whether to oppose to the "considered judgments" of reason the "screams" of Job, the "lamentations" of Jeremiah, the thundering of the prophets and the Apocalypse? This, I say once more, is indubitable "madness." But then, are life's horrors—which reveal themselves to anyone who looks them straight in the face—not madness too? Does not Job's dreadful experience, Jeremiah lamenting the fate of his people, or even Plotinus recalling the slaughtered youths and violated maidens already stand at the limits of the rational?

We stand between two "madnesses"—between the madness of a reason for which the "truths" which it reveals about the horrors of real being are ultimate, definitive, eternal truths, obligatory for all, and the madness of Kierkegaard's "Absurd," which ventures to begin the struggle when, on the testimony of reason and self-evidence, struggle is impossible, is foredoomed to humiliating failure. With whom should we go—with the Hellenic symposiasts, or with Job and the prophets? Which madness is preferable? The book of Job, the lamentations of Jeremiah, the thundering of the prophets and of the Apocalypse leave no doubt that the horrors of human existence were not hidden from the "private thinkers" of the Bible, and that they had enough courage and fortitude to gaze squarely into the face of what is customarily called reality. Nevertheless—unlike the great representatives of *philosophia perennis*—they do not feel compelled by reality and its horrors to submit to the inevitable. At that point where speculative philosophy sees the end of all possibilities and submissively folds its hands, existential philosophy begins the great and final struggle. Existential philosophy is not *Besinnung*, "interrogating" reality and seeking truth in the immediate data of consciousness; it is a surmounting of what to our understanding seems insurmountable. "For God," Kierkegaard repeats unceasingly, "all things are possible," summing up in these few words what had hitherto reached men's ears from Scriptural sources. Possibilities are not determined by eternal truths inscribed by a dead or dying hand in the structure of the universe; possibilities are in the power of a living, all-perfect being who has created and blessed man. Whatever horrors being may reveal to us, and despite the assurances of reason, these horrors do not exhibit "truth" nor preclude the possibility of their own eradication.

The psalmist cries, "*De profundis ad te Domine, clamavi.*" Out of the depths of his dreadful, fallen, and despairing state man cries to the Lord. The prophets and apostles exclaim: "Death, where is thy sting? Hell, where is thy victory?" They bring us the tiding that God cares for each living human being, and that the ultimate victory lies not with the iniquities and inexorabilities of reality, but with a God who "numbers the hairs upon a man's head," a loving God, who promises that every tear shall be wiped away. It goes without saying that for reason this whole struggle, all of these promises, and the human hopes bound up with them, are an absurd illusion, a lie. This law of life is not given by the living God; the law of life is not love, but eternal, irreconcilable hostility. The great Hellenic philosopher "knew" that strife is the father and ruler of all things. One must deify not the Biblical Creator, but the stone, stupidity, nothingness. . . .

For a reason which worships self-evidence, interrogating reality in search of truth, the prophets' and apostles' preaching of love is childishness, mawkish sentimentality, which will be dissolved without trace by the events of history. The thundering of the prophets and apostles springs not from the clouds but from the dunghill. The Biblical legend of the fall of the first man is a naive and empty invention; not only do the fruits of the tree of knowledge not destroy the fruits of the tree of life; the former are the precondition and presupposition for the latter. As Husserl proclaimed: reason has spoken, wisdom must obey. The "Revelation of St. John" declares that God not only wipes away every tear, but gives men to eat of the fruits of the tree of life. But what enlightened man will agree to discuss seriously, let alone accept, such Scriptural assurances? Everyone wants to "know"; everyone is convinced that knowledge will bear away the ultimate and final truth—about what is and what is not, about what is possible and what is impossible. And no one ventures to dispute the truths which knowledge affords. How then did Kierkegaard, to whom Husserl referred me, dare to begin the struggle at that point where no one else ventured to dispute—at that point where everyone casts himself upon the mercy of the enemy? The answer to this question will also be an answer to the question which Max Scheler put to me.

V

For Husserl, as for Kierkegaard, moderate solutions were a turning away from philosophy. Both of them faced the gigantic problem of the "either-or" in its full dimensions. Husserl despaired at the thought that human knowledge is conditional, relative, transitory, that even an eternal, unshakable truth like "Socrates was poisoned" might totter, that indeed it has already tottered and does not exist for angels and gods, and that we have no ground for asserting that it will not someday cease to exist even for ordinary mortals. At this point, the reader will recall, Husserl formulated his own "either-or" with unprecedented power: *either* we are all insane, *or* "Socrates was poisoned" is an eternal truth, equally binding upon all conscious beings.

Kierkegaard's "either-or" has just as resolute and threatening a sound: *either* the "eternal" truths which reason discovers in the immediate data of consciousness are only transitory truths, and the horrors which Job suffered, the horrors which Jeremiah lamented, the horrors of which John thundered in his "revelation," will be turned into nothing, into an illusion, by the will of Him who created the universe and "all that dwell therein," just as the horrors of a nightmare which absolutely dominates the consciousness of the sleeping man turn into nothing when he awakens—*or* we live in a world of madness. . . .

Nor does the law of contradiction save self-evidence. In a dream, when a man is being pursued by a monster which threatens to destroy and reduce to ashes both the man himself and the whole world, while he himself feels paralyzed, incapable not only of defending himself but even of moving a limb, salvation comes with the contradictory consciousness that the nightmare is not real but only a temporary "obsessive" state. Consciousness is contradictory because it assumes that the sleeping person is aware that the state of consciousness of the dreamer is not true; it thus assumes a self-destroying truth. In order to escape from the nightmare, one must repudiate the "law" of contradiction upon which all the self-evident truths of waking consciousness are based. One must make an enormous effort—and wake up. This is why, as I said to Husserl, philosophy is not *Besinnung*, not a reflection or interpretation which deepens sleep to the point of no awakening—but a struggle. This is my basic objection to Husserl. And this is the meaning of the enigmatic legend in *Genesis* about the Fall of the first man: the death-bearing tree of knowledge is set in opposition to the tree of life. The truths provided by knowledge are vanquished by human suffering.

I know all too well the indignation felt by the enlightened thought of contemporary man at the possibility of such suppositions. Not only European thought, but also Hindu thought, cut off from the rest of the world by the impassable Himalayas, has moved in the same tracks. Brahmanism, and to an even greater degree Buddhism, which is regarded by European scholars as the highest achievement of Hindu thought, relies entirely upon knowledge based on self-evidence. One cannot overcome the eternal principle of the law-like causal connection of phenomena; one cannot put an end to metempsychosis or *karma;* one cannot change the eternal truth that everything which has a beginning must have an end. One must submit to all of these "cannots." To be sure, there is reason to believe that Western thought has modulated the Hindu world view into greater conformity with its own intellectual and cultural tradition. The idea of emancipation or redemption dominates Hindu thought, but perhaps it has a different meaning for Hindus from what it has for us. There is a legend that the Buddha himself, in the hour before his death, reiterated that everything which has a beginning must have an end. Yet he spoke no less passionately than Jeremiah or Saint John about human suffering: The sum of human tears, he said, would be greater than the four great oceans. Did not Buddha, like Job, compare the horrors of human existence to the sands of the sea? . . .

This is the substance of my answer to Max Scheler. At the same time it explains why I have such an extraordinarily high regard for Husserl's philosophic enterprise. Husserl dared, with rare courage and inspiration, to formulate the most essential, most difficult, and at the same time most painful of all questions—that of the "validity" of knowledge. To be valid, knowledge must be accepted as absolute, which means that we must accept whatever knowledge demands of us. We must deify stones, accept relentless cruelty, petrify ourselves, renounce everything that is most precious and essential to us—as Nietzsche, under the compulsion of truth, declared. Or else we must repudiate absolute knowledge, rebel against a truth which compels by we know not what right, and begin a struggle against those self-evident truths which arbitrarily convert the horror of empirical existence into eternal laws of being. In modern times the first path was chosen by Husserl, the second by Kierkegaard, to whom Husserl referred me. As I have already indicated, one must either absolutize truth and relativize life or else refuse to obey the compulsion of truth in order to save human life. The struggle with, and surmounting of, self-evidence is a translation into philosophical language of the testament or, if you will, the revelation of the Bible: man's wisdom is folly before the Lord. Husserl felt this with the full penetration of philosophic genius. That is why he directed me so insistently to Kierkegaard, in whom, to my great astonishment, I discovered a twin of Dostoevsky, the writer whose works had supported me in my struggle against Husserl. Who would expect to be sent by a philosopher to his most determined intellectual opponent? Who would think that a man who had penned a hymn to reason and its self-evident truths would value so highly a man who celebrated the absurd and waged relentless battle, a struggle to the death, against self-evidence? . . .

Is there ground for the hope that the provocative "either-or" of Husserl and Kierkegaard will reform contemporary thought, rousing it from its age-old torpor? I think not. A number of outstanding philosophers have already emerged from the phenomenological movement; but they have all repudiated the Husserl-Kierkegaard "either-or," even though they were acquainted with both Nietzsche and Kierkegaard from their early years. They preferred the old slogan: back to Kant—for whom Kierkegaard's absurd signifies the realm of *Schwärmerei und Allerglauben* which he found so distasteful and against which he was so careful to warn his readers. Kant deliberately softened the "critique of pure reason" with a "critique of practical reason." The postulates of the existence of God and the immortality of the soul were intended to calm man, shaken, as Kant himself was, by the news of the death of God which had come to him from the critique of pure reason. But surely these postulates are not acceptable to reason! Surely reason would consign them without hesitation to the realm of *Schwärmerei und Allerglauben*. There can be no doubt of it: it is the most fantastic superstition to admit the existence of God or to believe in the immortality of the soul, whether you call these truths axioms or postulates! It is not in man's power to unsettle self-evidence. Let us assume the alpha and omega of Scripture to be the story of the Fall, which is placed at the very beginning of the Old Testament, and the promise that God will give man to taste of the fruits of the tree of life, which is placed at the end of the New Testament. But surely it is obvious to everyone that both the Old and the

New Testaments are products of fantasy and superstition! An enlightened man will never seek truth in an ancient book written by an ignorant people, just as he will never consent to set the cries of Job, the lamentations of Jeremiah, the thundering of the Apocalypse, in opposition to the deliberate judgments of reason and its self-evidences. Philosophy will not renounce Kant.

Does this mean that the Kierkegaard-Husserl "either-or" will always be rejected?—That we are condemned to deify stones and preach relentless cruelty toward our neighbors, as Nietzsche proclaimed when he was possessed by reason?—That Kierkegaard's absurd will sooner or later be torn by the roots from human consciousness? I do not think so. In the general economy of man's spiritual life, the attempts to surmount self-evidence have their own enormous significance, even though this significance may be impossible to estimate. I consider myself infinitely indebted to Husserl for having forced me, by the power of his impetuous thought, to begin the struggle at that point where no one "considers" hope of victory at all possible. In order to struggle with self-evidence one must stop "considering." Husserl taught me this, and I rebelled against him, although I regarded him and continue to regard him as a great, a very great, philosopher of the modern period.

SIMON LYUDVIGOVICH FRANK

[1877–1950]

S. L. FRANK was born in Moscow, the son of a Russian Jewish doctor, in 1877. He studied law in the Faculty of Law of the University of Moscow, but his studies were interrupted by his arrest in 1899 for Marxist activities (he had been a member of a Marxist circle for several years). Forbidden to continue his university studies in Russia, he left for Berlin and Munich to study economics and philosophy. Between the years 1901 and 1906, he went back and forth between Moscow and Germany and in 1906 settled in Saint Petersburg, where the intellectual climate had momentarily become somewhat more liberal. It was during his stay in Germany that he became gradually disaffected with Marxism and turned first to Kantian idealism and then to Christianity (which he always interpreted in a highly idealistic manner) for his basic intellectual framework. In 1912 he joined the Russian Orthodox Church and became a lecturer in philosophy at the University of Saint Petersburg where, in 1915, he defended his master's thesis (*The Object of Knowledge*). His doctoral dissertation (*The Soul of Man*) was published in 1917, but he was unable to present it for defense at the University because of the Revolution. From 1917 to 1921 he held a chair at the University of Saratov and in 1921 was named to a chair at the University of Moscow.

But in 1922 he was among the hundred-odd "undesirable" intellectuals whom the Soviet government felt it expedient to exile from Russia forever. Upon his expulsion he went first to Berlin where he assisted Berdyaev and other émigré scholars in organizing the "Academy of Spiritual Culture." From 1930

278   PHILOSOPHERS IN EXILE

to 1937 he lectured on Russian thought and literature at the
University of Berlin. In 1937, driven out of Germany by Hitler's
persecution of the Jews, he moved to Paris and, after the war
(1945), to London where he died in 1950.

Frank's numerous philosophical writings exhibit two qualities
which are not frequently found together in philosophical prose:
they are remarkable both for their polished literary style and
for their stringently systematic character. In the whole history
of Russian philosophy there is no example of greater concern
over elaborating a *system* of philosophy.

The elements of Frank's system are not all original to his own
thought. He borrows heavily from the writings of Vladimir
Solovyov,[1] Nicholas Lossky, and, among the ancients, Plotinus
and Nicholas of Cusa especially. He takes up their doctrines,
develops them, speaks their language, and employs their vocabulary. Nevertheless, in his systematic presentation of a philosophy
of "Total-Unity," as he termed it, he goes beyond all his sources
and manages to present a significantly original and unified
approach to a Christian epistemology, anthropology, metaphysics,
and ethics. No recent Russian philosopher has been more highly
regarded by his colleagues and contemporaries for his achievements. Zenkovsky states forthrightly: "I consider Frank's the
most significant and profound system in the history of Russian
philosophy,"[2] and he calls Frank "the most outstanding among
Russian philosophers generally."[3]

The following selections from Frank's works give a fair introduction to the principal elements of his epistemological and
metaphysical doctrines, as well as a presentation of his philosophy
of history, religion, and culture. The first selection is taken from
Reality and Man, a book which Frank completed just before
his death in 1950 and which was published (in Russian) only
posthumously.[4] The second selection is taken from an article

1. Frank edited *A Solovyov Anthology*, translated by Natalie Duddington,
London, 1950.
2. Zenkovsky, *op. cit.*, p. 871.
3. *Ibid.*, p. 853.
4. This work, translated into English by Natalie Duddington, was published in London in 1966.

entitled "Of the Two Natures in Man," [5] which was completed at about the same time and, like *Reality and Man*, has never appeared in English before.

These selections have a special value in that they provide a final summary of some of Frank's major philosophical ideas. Among all the pages which he wrote—and Frank was known for his synthetic and concise style—these are some of the most compact and comprehensive. His critique of materialism and positivism is presented together with his own spiritualist philosophy in one continuous, architectonic argument.

In *Reality and Man*, Frank begins, typically, with a recapitulation of his epistemological position, the distinction between abstract cognition and the immediate intuition of the world of "absolute reality." From this he turns to an analysis of the *cogito*, the "spiritual reality of primary thinking" as he calls it, thanks to which there is a world of "absolute reality" (*realnost*). The *cogito* is established as a more fundamental kind of reality than the reality of the "world of fact" (*deystvitelnost*). On the basis of an enlarged conception of this "spiritual reality," Frank proceeds from epistemological questions concerning experience to the metaphysical question of the nature of the Absolute in its relations with man. The Absolute (Reality), which can be reached only through "inner (mystical) experience," is the "Total-Unity," the ground of all being, the Real *par excellence*.

However, this "Total-Unity" presents us with two aspects or faces, depending on whether we consider it *ad intra*, in itself, or *ad extra*, in its relations with man and the world. When Frank considers the Absolute *in itself*, he speaks the language of Plotinus and Nicholas of Cusa; when he considers the Absolute in its *relation* to man, he speaks the "sophiological" language of Solovyov. Apart from the fact that he gives this language his own accent and development, his originality lies in his ability to synthesize these viewpoints and to use them as the basis for a new Christian philosophy.

5. Also translated by Natalie Duddington, this article has not been previously published.

SELECTED BIBLIOGRAPHY

Works:

S. L. Frank, *God with Us,* trans. Natalie Duddington, London, 1946.

——————, *La connaissance et l'être,* Paris, 1937. This is an abridged translation of *Predmet znaniya* (The Object of Knowledge), St. Petersburg, 1915.

——————, *Dusha cheloveka* (The Soul of Man), Moscow, 1917.

——————, *Die russische Weltanschauung,* Charlottensburg, 1926.

——————, *Dukhovnyye osnovy obshchestva* (The Spiritual Foundations of Society), Paris, 1930.

——————, *Nepostizhimoye* (The Unfathomable), Paris, 1939.

——————, *Svet vo tme* (Light in Darkness), Paris, 1949.

——————, *Reality and Man,* trans. Natalie Duddington, London, 1966.

Secondary Sources:

Nicholas O. Lossky, *History of Russian Philosophy,* New York, 1951, pp. 266-292.

V. V. Zenkovsky, *A History of Russian Philosophy,* trans. George L. Kline, 2 vols., London and New York, 1953, pp. 852-872.

Nicolas Zernov, *The Russian Religious Renaissance of the Twentieth Century,* New York, 1963, pp. 158-164.

Reality and Man *

. . . Ideal elements are a species of being which transcends existence in space and time. The same kind of being is to be found, as it were, at the opposite pole of the cognitive field, through the consideration of "living knowledge" as opposed to knowledge of objects. People unfamiliar with the idea of living knowledge will ask in surprise, "But what more can there be for us to know except the totality of the objects of knowledge?" A simple and self-evident answer to this question at once suggests itself: beyond the confines of the world of objects there is at any rate *the actual mental gaze directed upon it.* That mental gaze stands for the mysterious and not easily definable reality of its source or bearer which is given us in a different way than all the objects of knowledge.

A characteristic instance of mental blindness which fails to observe this irrefutably obvious fact is to be found in Hume's famous denial of the reality of the self. "When I enter most intimately into what I call myself, I always stumble on some particular perception or other, of heat or cold, light or shade, pain or pleasure. I . . . can never observe anything but the perception." [1] In the present connection it is irrelevant to point out that Hume's assertion about our mental life consisting solely of perceptions has been finally disproved by closer psychological analysis. The real point of importance is this: the assertion that "I cannot find in myself any I"—for this is what Hume's words amount to—is self-contradictory. If there were no "I" at all, there would be no one to seek it. It is perfectly natural that I cannot find "myself" among objects, for I am the seeker—not an object, but a subject. I cannot meet my own self for the simple reason that my self is that which *meets* everything else.

* Translated by Natalie Duddington and printed here with her permission and that of Mrs. Tatiana Frank and Mr. Victor Frank. This selection has not been previously published in English.

1. David Hume, *Treatise on Human Nature*, Vol. I, Pt. 4, Section 6.

Thus an absent-minded man will sometimes look in the room for the spectacles which he is wearing: he does not see them because he is looking *through* them.

It will be remembered that in modern philosophy the credit for discovering the reality which transcends the world of objects belongs to Descartes. He expressed it in his formula *cogito ergo sum*. For Descartes himself, that idea signified primarily and almost exclusively the discovery of a perfectly secure basis for absolutely certain knowledge. I may doubt whether any content of objective knowledge actually exists or is only an idea in my mind, but I cannot doubt the reality of my own thought; it is a self-contradiction to doubt the reality of the doubt itself and therefore of my doubting thought. Descartes himself, however, did not fully grasp the significance of his discovery. Having found this starting point of knowledge he goes on to build a metaphysic of the objective type: he transforms the thinking self into a substance, which, alongside other kinds of substances, forms part of the world's structure. But the use which Descartes made of his discovery does not prevent us from recognizing that in truth he discovered a special kind of reality, different in principle from the world of objects—a reality which we generally fail to notice simply because it is too close to us and coincides with him who seeks it. Speaking approximately and in familiar terms, it may be said that the "I" which is conscious of itself in the very act of thinking is a reality in which subject and object coincide. In its primary nature, however, it is a reality in which there is neither object nor thought directed upon it: it is given us not as standing over against our cognizing thought but as an actual self-revealing and self-evident reality. In other words, that reality is revealed to us in the form of *living knowledge*.

It will be remembered that the same discovery was made twelve centuries before Descartes by Saint Augustine; but for him, in contradistinction to Descartes, it was a true revelation which revolutionized his life as well as his philosophy. . . . There is no doubt that his discovery of the self-evidence of the thinking ego revealed to him a new dimension of being, unnoticeable from our usual point of view—namely, the primary reality which lies beyond the confines both of infinite space and even of the human soul understood as a special component part of the world. This is hinted at in Plato's philosophy and more clearly indicated in Plotinus' mystical speculation which directly influenced Saint Augustine; but it was to Augustine that the self-evidence of the supra-mundane, trans-objective reality was for the first time clearly revealed in all its significance. This reality is not a dumb, passive conglomeration of facts standing over against our thought and revealing itself to it from without, but self-subsistent, immediate life revealing itself to itself; and as the primary essence of our own being, it is seen by us to be the primary essence of reality as such. In other words, it is a reality which transcends the supposedly all-embracing system of objective existence and lies at the basis of it. It does not confront us from without but is given to us from within as the ground in which we are rooted and out of which we grow.

Another man of genius, nearer to us in time, who made the same discovery, afresh, thereby giving rise to quite a new type of philosophical thought ("German Idealism") was Immanuel Kant. Starting like Descartes with the problem of trustworthiness of knowledge, Kant expressed his awareness of the difference between the ideal and the actual by showing the relativity of the world of objects. The unsophisticated consciousness takes that world to be an absolute, self-contained, and all-embracing reality, but Kant saw that it was only the correlate (or, in his interpretation, the "product") of the cognizing thought itself and therefore had only a limited and relative significance. The questionable details of Kant's system are not relevant in this connection; the important point is his demonstrating that complete and all-embracing insight into reality cannot be gained through any theory about the structure of the world of objects (or, as Kant calls it, through "dogmatic metaphysics"). The truly all-embracing whole is not the world of objects, which is merely a correlate of theoretical reason, but the realm of "consciousness" which transcends it. In moral life—in the striving of the will toward absolute duty, and in the religious attitude based upon this—that consciousness transcends the theoretical knowledge of the world of objects and quite independently of it, following its own paths and guided by other criteria of truth, discovers the true, transcendental reality ("thing in itself"). Further development of this line of thought (in Fichte and Hegel) finds this reality beyond the objective sphere in the deeper and more primary principle of "spirit." This conclusion naturally follows from the discovery that not the object standing over against our thought but the subject in his immediate givenness to himself is the revelation of the true nature of reality. There is a great deal that is vague, debatable, and untrue in the philosophical systems founded by Kant and his successors upon this primary intuition, but permanent value attaches to the general result of the change in consciousness—in Plato's language, of "the soul turning its gaze" from outside inward—in virtue of which reality is revealed to us not as a world of objects confronting us from without but as it actually is in the living depths of self-consciousness. . . .

It is one thing to experience from within the joys, the sufferings, and the deepest revelations of love, and quite another psychologically to study and observe from without "the psychological process of being in love." Were it not so, Faust, weighed down with science and scholarship, would not have complained that though he had gained objective knowledge of all things he had missed life itself, for he had never tasted and therefore never known its inmost mysterious essence.

While distinguishing the act of experiencing from the knowledge of it, i.e., from the thought directed upon it, we must not forget that such knowledge may take two entirely different forms. Thus a lover may not only enjoy his love, suffer from it, and experience all the emotions connected therewith, but may also think about it and try to understand what is happening to him. But such intellectual analysis of one's own experience from within is utterly different from indifferent observation of somebody else being in love, or from a scientifically psychological analysis of the process. Or, to take another example, it is one thing to know social and political life from within, to take part in it, have a living experience of it, and enter into it emotionally, and quite another to study it as a naturalist studies the life of an ant hill. In the first case the living experience in all its vitality, concreteness, and fullness directly reveals itself to the thought which apprehends it from within; such thought discovers a dimension of reality, inaccessible to the second type of thought which apprehends from without, as it were, only the external picture or the outer layer of the reality before it.

We must not be confused by the general consideration that all thought and knowledge consist in the subject's cognitive activity being directed upon an object. This is true in a general sense, but the object and the cognitive act directed upon it may be given us in two totally different ways. It is essential to distinguish between the object remote from us, confronting us from without (not in a spatial but in a purely epistemological sense) and the object immanent within our mental life and revealing itself from within. Just as ideal objects are a reality dwelling in the sphere of thought itself and having the same type of being as it, so the objects of which we are now speaking belong to the sphere of the inner *life:* both the knowing subject and the known object, though theoretically distinguishable, are immanent in the same realm of being. The German philosopher Dilthey, who devoted himself to problems of spiritual life, distinguished between these two types of knowing by using two different terms, *begreifen* and *verstehen.* It is precisely because living knowledge reveals to us the depths of reality inaccessible to objective knowledge that we cannot hope to apprehend reality completely and as a whole while remaining within the confines of objective existence and constructing systems of ontology.

It is to the credit of modern existentialism, in spite of all its defects and limitations as a general philosophical theory, that its founder, Kierkegaard, was the first (unless we count Pascal) to insist that *Existenz,* man's concrete and immediate being-for-himself, is deeper, more primary, and quite other than his mental life as the domain of objective psychological inquiry; it is a reality completely overlooked by philosophers who strive to understand the whole of being through an objective contemplation of it. That primary, immediate being-for-self is a reality in and through which man transcends the world of objective fact and discovers quite a new dimension of being; he finds the ultimate depths therein and has them directly in his own self.

Thus it becomes manifest that reality in its living concreteness is wider and deeper than "the world of objective fact." A philosophy adequate to the task of obtaining true knowledge of reality is therefore always based upon the living inner experience in some sense akin to the experience that is called "mystical."

But what, precisely, does that experience signify? In other words, what reality is revealed to us in it? . . .

That sphere includes, in the first instance, all that I experience and that appears to external, objective observation as my "psychological life," insofar as it is bound up with the indescribable depths, the absolute, primary, self-given reality which I call my "self." My sensuous, bodily sensations (e.g., physical pain or hunger) and images that appear before me (e.g., in dreams) are not as such felt to be a part of my inner life; they are merely given to me and invade me, so to speak, from without. They come from the periphery and not from the depths of my self. Sometimes the same character attaches to feelings and desires that are actually indistinguishable from sensations: sudden irritation, a sense of pleasure, a desire to take or do something "get hold of me" and possess me; they do not arise out of my own depths and are not experienced as rooted in them. But when experiences and emotions are felt, as it were, to live in me and to arise from within, from the depths of my "self," they are for me the contents of that unique, self-revealing, and self-conscious reality which I call my "self."

In other words, some of my experiences—those of the peripheral type—naturally transform themselves into an "objective" picture given to me and observed by me as something different from myself. Experiences of this kind are easily expressible in words—and that is the way in which we objectify and describe them to others. Thus, for instance, I describe to a doctor my bodily sensations, and in doing so I clearly distinguish them from that which forms the intimate content of my inner life and which I can only tell—and even then with great difficulty—to a close friend or to a priest at confession. It is this intimate content that I experience as the manifestation of my real self. That inner reality is often called "spiritual" as distinct from "psychological" life. My spiritual life is directly accessible to me alone, for it is the content of my self; it cannot be observed from without. As will be shown later, another person can only come to know it through quite a special act of knowing that has nothing in common with the cold observation of me as an object, or an element of the external reality. On the basis of such specific experience my spiritual life can in a derivative way become, like all else, an object of thought. . . .

In short, "spiritual life" is only another name for life experienced as actual self-revealing reality in contradistinction to the world of objects, whether physical or mental. It is remarkable that there are a number of people—at the present day they are probably the majority—to whom it never occurs, at any rate in the usual course of things, that the true basis of their being is to be found in that deeper level, manifesting itself as "spiritual life." They have self-consciousness, of course, since in the human being it is inseparable from consciousness, i.e., they are aware of their experiences. But since their whole attention is directed outward, upon the perception of external facts, their experiences are for them a kind of unsubstantial and unessential shadow that quietly and almost imperceptibly accompanies the outer course of their life; and insofar as they attend to those experiences and try to account for them, they regard them too as it were from outside, i.e., as events forming part of the world of objects. They may know their mental life as a complex of events and processes, but they have no true self-consciousness in the specific and significant sense of the term, i.e., their self as a unique primary *reality*, not comparable to anything else, eludes their attention. For those who know that reality, the awareness of it always comes as a sudden discovery—or, rather, a revelation, in connection with some particularly deep and stirring experience. It then suddenly appears that my habitual "I" is not simply an indifferent, colorless, and almost unnoticeable companion of my external life, but has concrete fullness and substantial depth in virtue of which it is a bearer of a certain self-subsistent, mysterious, and absolutely unique transcendent reality, hidden from the eyes of the world.

The usual type of mind bent upon the perception of the objective world, and as it were hypnotized by its specific characteristics, will be sure to protest against this. For the sake of clarity, the protest must be considered even at the risk of repeating what has already been said. Positivists, as well as metaphysicians concerned with the objective world of existence, will say that this vaunted transcendent reality revealed in the depths of the self can be reduced to the simple and well-known fact that every human being not only forms part of the objective world common to all but also has his own special little world of subjectivity. That little world consists simply of all kinds of illusions, fancies, dreams, visions, and subjective feelings and is the vague, shifting, and purely personal sphere in which everyone is shut and which, in contradistinction to objective being, is devoid of any universal significance. By insisting upon the primary nature and the unique value of that underlying reality, we simply encourage man, to his detriment, to sink into the personal, subjective sphere and cut himself off from the sober and firm common basis of human existence as belonging to the world of objective fact.

There are two arguments in this contention, both of them erroneous. One is easily answered by an additional explanation of what has been pointed out above. The other requires fuller discussion which may lead us further.

While adhering for the present to the general statement that the primary reality is the reality of the subject's inner life, we must do away once and for all with the obvious though highly prevalent ambiguity in the ordinary usage of the words "subjectivity" or "subjective being." They are generally taken to mean at the same time and without sufficient demarcation "the illusory," "the fictitious," "the apparent," as well as "everything that belongs to the subject's realm of being." But those two meanings are totally different, and it would be wiser to designate them by two different words—e.g., "subjective" and "subject's." When a psychological fact, such as a sense presentation, is wrongly taken to be a sign or evidence of some fact in the external objective world, we call it subjective in the sense of illusory. It is never the fact itself that is illusory, or mistaken—that would be simply meaningless. It is only the interpretation of a fact that may be mistaken—i.e., the judgment passed upon it. Ringing in one's ears may be mistaken for the ringing of the front door bell; a dream may be confused with an event in the external, coherent, and stable reality equally perceived by all; when we observe our error we call the fact that gave rise to it "merely subjective." That does not prevent it, however, from being as real as the external reality to which it is wrongly referred. The ringing in one's ears is different from a ring at the door, but in itself it is fully and indisputably real; if it is prolonged it is an illness that requires medical treatment. A dream is not a part of the external reality but it is a real event in human life, sometimes more important than certain external events in it; it is not for nothing that psychoanalysts investigate dreams. This implies that, as already pointed out, "the subjective" in the sense of belonging to the subject's inner life, insofar as it is made an object of observation and knowledge, itself forms part of the "objective world," and there can be no question of calling it illusory or apparent and ascribing to it a kind of pseudo-being.

This has a close bearing upon our "psychological life." Although its contents are experienced and recognized as taking place "in me"—in every separate individual—and therefore differing from the external material world common to us all, they somehow naturally and of themselves form part of the objective sphere and have the same kind of reality. The case is different, as we have seen already, with the peculiar reality of man's inmost self-consciousness, revealed in the "spiritual life." It is qualitatively or, more exactly, categorically distinct from all objective existence and yet it is not less, but rather more, real than it. It is therefore utterly inappropriate to designate that primary, most certain, and self-evident reality as "subjective," implying by that term a contemptuous rejection of it as fictitious, illusory, or unessential. Such an attitude merely confirms the fact, already pointed out, that we easily fail to observe the reality with which we coincide or in which we abide, simply because our

attention is wholly taken up with things that confront us from
without. The reality of the subject himself is not "subjective";
though not forming part of the world of objects, it is an actual
and in a sense self-subsistent, stable, and primary reality. That
reality is far more serious and significant than the world of
objects. I can to a certain extent "shut my eyes" to the world
of objects, draw away, detach myself and lose touch with it, but
I can never and in no way escape from the inner reality of my
own self: it is the very essence of my being and it remains in
me even when I do not notice it. It is precisely in this sense that
both religion and philosophy have always taught that a man's
"soul" or life is of more importance and value to him than all
the riches and kingdoms of the world. Everything external and
objective has significance for me only insofar as it is related to
this basic and immediate being of my own self. The external
world is a comparatively unimportant accompaniment of our
true being which reveals itself in the primary, unmediated reality of personal inner life.

Let us now consider the second implication of the positivists'
argument quoted above. There can be no doubt of the genuine-
ness and importance of the reality revealed to us in the inner
life, but it may be asked whether that reality is a self-contained
sphere, separate and distinct for every individual. In that case,
to be absorbed in it would mean to detach oneself from the
universal reality of our common world and, as it were, to desert
the general life, hiding in the solitary depths of purely individual
being as one does in dreams. All that has hitherto been said about
reality as "the sphere of inner life" seems to support this view.

The idea that the inner reality is self-enclosed and individually
isolated has its psychological source in the naive conception, due
to a kind of unconscious materialism, that the "soul" is situated
somewhere inside the body; through the sense organs it comes
into contact with the external material reality, but from within
it is enclosed in the impenetrable sheath of the body and is
therefore something like a small, self-contained sphere, separate
for every human being.

The crudeness of the mythology presupposed by this popular
idea will become apparent if we recall the old and indisputable

truth established by Descartes that the "soul" is not extended, i.e., no spatial determinations are directly applicable to it. The statement that the "soul" is within the body really implies only two things: first, our organic sensations and the general sense of physical well-being or discomfort to which they give rise are localized within the body; secondly, our outer perceptions, determined by the action of the external environment upon our body, depend upon the body's position in space: we see, hear, and touch different objects according to where our body happens to be. In other respects, however, my psychological life is independent of my body and is everywhere and nowhere: I can recall the past, can dream about the future, can mentally visit places far distant from my body; I have a number of other mental contents of which it is altogether impossible to say "where" they are. To speak in a general sense of my self or my inner life being localized within my body or to apply any spatial determinations to it is as absurd and meaningless as to say, e.g., that truth is situated within a triangle or that goodness dwells at such and such a degree of longitude. Sober and dispassionate consideration of psychological life compels us to admit that the "soul," being in one respect somehow connected with the individual body and therefore, through its mediation, indirectly localized, in another respect is by its very nature nonspatial or super-spatial. Accordingly, there are no grounds whatever for concluding that it is shut up within the body. And as to the inner primary reality which lies in an altogether different dimension of being than the world of objects, it would be a mere confusion of thought to place it somewhere in the material universe and conclude that it therefore is limited. When we apprehend that reality as it is in itself, i.e., apprehend it from within, it appears to us—insofar as pictorial images are symbolically and indirectly applicable to it—not as a small, self-contained sphere but rather as a peculiar kind of infinity, as something that recedes into immeasurable, fathomless depths. Thus we could picture the inner reality of our self as a kind of subterraneous cavern: there is a small entrance to it from outside, from the external layer of "objectivity," and inside it is a vast, complex, and potentially infinite world. In the words of Heraclitus, "one

cannot find the limits of the soul even after treading all its ways
—so deep are its foundations."

There are, however, more subtle ways of maintaining that man
is shut in and isolated in his inner life; at the present day this
is done, for instance by Heidegger. Just as modern physics, in
speaking of the curvature of space, maintains that the world is
finite though unbounded, so Heidegger, having discovered the
boundless fullness of the peculiar reality present within man's
inner being (his *Existenz*), affirms that, nevertheless, it is finite
and self-contained. From his point of view, although the "soul"
is an immeasurable universe, it is a universe shut in within itself
and forever immanent within its own boundaries; it is "cast into
the world" from outside—a world common to all—and in that
sense coexists with all other "souls," but from within, it exists
only in and for itself and remains as it were in lifelong solitary
confinement.

This conception, however, is essentially invalid. Psychologically
it is due to a kind of spiritual blindness—a special disease of our
time—that destroys the normal, healthy sense of life. In truth,
it is precisely at this point that clear insight, undeceived by
external appearances and popular theories, discovers the most
essential and fundamental feature of the realm of being which,
in contradistinction to the world of fact, I have called the primary reality. So far that reality has been identified with the
subject's being, with "my inner life." But although "my inner
life" revealed to me from within is, so to speak, the nearest and
most immediately given stratum of the primary reality, it is by
no means the whole of it. That stratum is from its very nature
unthinkable except in connection with something else that lies
beyond it. In dealing with the world of fact we are used to fix
upon separate objects, separate self-subsistent entities (physical
or psychic), "substances" as traditional philosophy calls them.
From the point of view of common sense, this separateness is an
irreducible primary characteristic of all individual existence. But
even a purely scientific analysis of the objective world compels us to modify this conception: the presence of temporal and
spatial relations, causal ties, interaction, functional dependence,
creative activity, etc., implies that existence is inwardly inter-

connected and has a common background; we have to think of the multiplicity of separate elements as lying within a certain unity that embraces and pervades it. And when the usual popular conception of the world of objects is applied to a totally different realm of primary self-revealing being, it will be seen, on closer inspection, to be utterly untenable. The point is that this primary reality is from its very nature perpetually transcending itself, going beyond its own limits. . . .

The essential meaning of transcendence is that I cannot have "my own being" except as a part of being in general, which transcends mine. To be conscious of a limit and to transcend it means in this case one and the same thing. This correlation was already noted by Descartes when he discovered the primary reality in the subject of thought. In and through being conscious of my self as finite, I know the infinite and have it in me. Descartes rightly pointed out that, although in language the term "limited" or "finite" comes first and has a positive meaning, while the term "unlimited" or "infinite" is derivative and is formed through negation of the first, in reality the very reverse is the case. It is precisely the infinite as "the fullness of all" that is primary and is positively given, while the conception of the finite is formed through the negation of that fullness. The finite is that which does not contain the fullness and is therefore only a part; the finite is that which has limits, and limit is a line of demarcation between "one" and "the other," i.e., it means division within an all-embracing whole.

The same correlation may be expressed in another way. In dealing with the world of fact we are accustomed to regard all negation and distinction implied by it not as a constituent part of the concrete objective content but as merely a formal instrument of our thought. When we say that a horse is not a ruminating animal or that a whale is not a fish, it seems self-evident that those negative definitions do not concern the actual, positive content of the objects themselves: the "not's" are obviously not something to be seen in the real horse or whale. From the practical point of view this is perfectly true, but that is only because objects are conditioned by an already made distinction; it is, so to speak, *behind* them and that is the only reason why it is not *in* them: for, clearly, apart from distinction and differentiation there could be no separate objects at all. On the other hand, the primary, self-revealing reality, not being an object of thought, *has everything within itself.* Its division into parts is its own immanent structure; but that means that it cannot reveal itself to us except as an all-embracing unity; each part of it manifests itself just as a part of a whole which includes it; hence, that which is external to it constitutes its being no less than that which belongs to it. This correlation has been expressed by Plotinus who interpreted with the insight of genius the primary reality intuitively apprehended through the depths of the spirit: "Here below (in the sensuous world) no one part could be begotten by any other, for each part has its own individual existence. On the contrary, in the intelligible world every part is born from the whole, and is simultaneously the whole and a part; wherever is a part, the whole reveals itself. . . . Every being contains within itself the entire intelligible world, and also beholds it entire in any particular being. All things there are located everywhere. Everything there is all, and all is each thing." [2]

Nothing, it seems, could be more "separate," more self-contained than my own being, that which I call my self. And in a sense this is unquestionably true: the being which I call "mine" is constituted by having its own special *center,* and any attempt to deny this (as for instance in the Indian philosophy) obviously contradicts a certain empirically given and therefore incontrovertible fact. And yet when I try to make clear what exactly I mean by my "self" I can only do so by dividing it off from "all other being." This means, I cannot have my own being, be conscious of it as "mine," unless I have—in a different sense, but in as primary a way—that "other" being. I have my being as a part of universal being, i.e., in immediate connection with other being which is not mine. The primary reality given from within by no means coincides with "my" being. Primary reality from its very nature is not limited or determinate in content; on the contrary, it is always given as something infinite and un-

2. Ennead, V 8, 4; III 2, 1, and many other passages. (Quoted from K. S. Guthrie's translation)

limited. It is only against the background of this infinite all-embracing being that my own being stands out, as its inalienable part. It is not a self-contained sphere but, as it were, a sprouting plant whose roots go deep into the general soil of reality. My inner being or "soul" is not enclosed from within, not isolated from all else; in the "inward" direction, the soul does not find any end or barrier that limits it. On the contrary, it expands, passing imperceptibly into that which is no longer itself and merging in it. Although it still remains conscious of the distinction between itself and that which lies beyond it and is other than it, the distinction becomes less clear and definite as the final depths are reached. Thus (to anticipate for a moment), in mystical experience the soul is aware of God as of a reality into which it flows or which flows into it and lives in it, and at the same time is conscious that this indissoluble unity is a union of two—of itself and of God who transcends it. . . .

The considerations put forward in the preceding chapter should have convinced the reader that in addition to the world of fact there is something which truly *is*—not less, but rather more truly than the world of fact—and which, in contradistinction to it, I call "reality." It immediately reveals itself to us in the first instance as our inner spiritual life; and at the same time it inevitably transcends the purely inner, personal world of the self uniting it from within to that which lies beyond it, and ultimately constitutes the all-embracing and all-pervading unity and basis of all that is.

But how are we to define more closely the meaning of "reality"? And is it possible to define it as we define any other idea?

At first sight this seems to be an unrealizable and pointless task. All description and definition, all logical analysis presuppose a certain multiplicity and consist in breaking it up, in discriminating one part from another and discovering the relations between them. Something that is absolutely primary, simple, and at the same time all-embracing may be experienced, but cannot possibly be described, expressed in words,. or defined; we may know *it*, but we cannot know anything *about it*—beyond the very fact that it is given us, is present, *is*. This appears to be the nature of that which has been designated by the term "real-

ity." Just as we know perfectly well what we mean by our
own existence—know it incomparably better and more intimately
than anything else—and yet are unable to express it in words
or to describe the content of it, so, having attained in our
inner experience insight into "reality" in its general, all-embracing sense, we know what this basis and background of our
own being is, and yet are unable to express or define this knowledge or to analyze its content. From the nature of the case it
would appear to be a kind of mute, inexpressible knowledge.
Insofar as to understand, to fathom, means to express by means
of concepts, i.e., to establish differences and interconnections
between things, to explain one thing by reference to its relation
to something else—"reality" essentially coincides with "the
unfathomable." [3] It is clear from what has just been said that
"the unfathomable" does not mean "the unknown," "the hidden,"
"the unfamiliar." On the contrary, it is perfectly manifest and
is only mysterious insofar as it is inexplicable, irreducible to
anything else, and inaccessible to logical analysis. It is what
Goethe called "an open mystery" (*offenes Geheimnis*). The field
of consciousness or experience is wider than that of thought;
thought helps us to disentangle its multifarious contents but
does not extend to that ultimate datum which is both the primary
basis and the general essence of all that we experience. . . .

"Negative theology," dating back to the unknown Christian
mystic designated by the name of Dionysius the Areopagite,
asserts that we reach an understanding of God or approach Him
only through *denying* to Him all qualities known to us from
our experience of the created world. And since all our ideas are
derived from that experience, we can have no positive definitions of the nature of God. We do not know and cannot say
what God is; we only know what He is not. We only know
that He is absolutely heterogenous to all that we know from
our experience of created being. We have no right to apply
to God any spatial or sensuously given ideas, or, indeed, even
such spiritual and abstract categories as "mercy" or "being,"
etc., for all these concepts as generally used are burdened with

3. See my book *Nepostizhimoye* (The Unfathomable), Paris, 1939.

implications applicable to earthly, created existence and are therefore inadequate to express God's transcendent nature:

But what, exactly, is meant by saying that we only know what God is not, and do not know what He is? In our ordinary knowledge, which is logical in form, negation signifies distinction (in addition to its didactically psychological significance of rejecting false opinions). We know or define something by distinguishing it from something else. Affirmative and negative judgments are merely different logical forms, correlative aspects of knowledge as determination, i.e., as awareness of something definite. Hence it follows that negation in its ordinary logical sense of distinction is only possible with respect to separate, particular contents, for it implies selection between them. In that case, what can be the meaning of the negative theology's demand to deny *all* known or thinkable characteristics with regard to God? If negation be taken in its ordinary logical sense, it must be said that to deny to some object all possible and conceivable characteristics is to deprive it of all content: to deny *all* simply means to assert nothing. On such an interpretation, negative theology would be tantamount to absolute agnosticism with regard to God—it would be simply reduced to the assertion that we cannot know anything whatever about Him.

Of course, in fact negative theology has something utterly different in view. Its adherents are not dry pedants who "define" the nature of God through the logical function of negation, and they are anything but agnostics. They have a special, inexpressible, *positive* vision of God, and in maintaining that God is different from all else they are solely concerned with the inexpressibility of their vision. If, however, we attempt to express its positive content in abstract logical form, we shall have to say that to deny with reference to God all positive characteristics simply means to deny them as particular and derivative determinations. God is neither *this* nor *that* in the sense that He is everything at once or is the primary source of all. But that means that the logical form in and through which we know everything particular, singular, derivative is as such inapplicable to God. Negative theology is guided by the intuition that the nature of God as the first source and primary basis of being is supra-logical and supra-rational, and for that very reason eludes all logical determinations which have meaning only with reference to particular and derivative forms of being. All positive characteristics are denied in order to convey the *categorical* difference between God and all that we meet in earthly experience.

The most obvious and historically the most important result of this view is the apprehension of the Divine reality as absolutely transcendent and removed from the world we know. The mind is plunged into some completely new, unknown dimension of being and recedes into dark depths which lead infinitely far from the familiar "earthly" reality. There is no need to consider here the usual practical consequence of this religious attitude—the boundless and immeasurable spiritual detachment, somewhat reminiscent of the Hindu religion; it is only its general logical aspect that is of moment to us.

It is perfectly obvious that there is a certain amount of truth in refusing to apply to God the logical form in which we think of all other contents of being. But the precise meaning of such refusal must be made clear if we are to avoid a contradiction which may be formulated as follows: Negation in general conditions the logical form of knowledge (since negation is a means of determining one particular content in contradistinction to all others). If we apply negation to the logical form itself we are involved in the contradiction of using that form in the very act of denying it.

Insofar as we attempt to know the nature of God solely through its *negative* relation to all earthly experience and to its logical form, we inevitably subordinate it to that form, making it into something limited, exclusive, and particular. For negation as such, whatever it may be applied to, is precisely the form of rational "earthly" knowledge.

Accordingly, in order to apprehend the truly transcendent and absolutely unique nature of God, simple negation in its customary logical sense is useless: the categories of earthly existence must be overcome in a special, *supra-logical* way. This can only be done by going beyond the law of contradiction, i.e., the incompatibility of affirmative and negative judgments. Only thus can we really rise above everything particular, "earthly," and subordinate; only by embracing and including it can we reach the sphere that lies above it.

The founder of negative theology understood this very well. The true import of his "mystical theology" was not mere negation of earthly conceptions as applied to God but a certain unity or combination of affirmation and negation, transcending the ordinary logical form of thought. Although no positive determinations in their usual sense are applicable to God, they are applicable to Him in a different, metaphorical sense. It cannot be said, for instance, that God is "good" in the sense of possessing this quality as something that determines His nature, but at the same time it can and must be said that, being the source of goodness, He is "surpassing good"; He cannot be called existent in the usual, "creaturely" sense of existence, but as the source of all existence He must be recognized as "surpassing existent." "It should not be thought that here negation contradicts affirmation, for the first cause, rising above all limitations, transcends all affirmations and all negations." [4]

Let us now apply this consideration to the general problem of reality. In what exact sense must we pronounce it to be "unfathomable," and what follows from this definition if rightly understood?

Reality is unknowable insofar as we mean by knowledge immediate apprehension of the nature of the object in a *conceptual* form. For reality is essentially different from any particular content apprehended through concepts; its nature lies precisely in its complete, self-contained, and self-sufficient concreteness, as opposed to any abstract content in which the object of thought is determined as something particular by distinguishing it from all else and discriminating its relation to that "else." But in saying that reality is other than the content of a concept we must guard against taking the idea of otherness in its usual logical sense, or we would fall into the contradiction already

4. *Mystic. Theologia*, I, 2.

mentioned and transform reality into a specific concept, i.e., into
an abstract particular content (which is to be found wherever
one thing is logically distinguished from another).

But how is it possible to have something in mind except as
a definite particular content, i.e., as an abstract concept? The
argument of the preceding chapter started with the admission
that our experience is wider than our thought. This of course
is indisputable and in virtue of it we can come into touch with
that which eludes the conceptual form. But must such experience
remain dumb and inexpressible and therefore unconscious, and
utterly inaccessible to thought? There is at least one actual testimony to the contrary—namely, art, and in particular poetry as
the art of the word. Poetry is a mysterious way of expressing
things that cannot be put in an abstract logical form. It expresses
a certain concrete reality without breaking it up into a system of
abstract concepts, but taking it as it actually is, in all its concreteness. This is possible because the purpose of words is not
limited to their function of designating concepts: words are also
the means of spiritually mastering and imparting meaning to
experience in its actual, supra-logical nature. The existence of
poetry shows that experience is not doomed to remain dumb
and incomprehensible, but has a specific form of expression, i.e.,
of being "understood" just on that side of it on which it transcends abstract thought.

This would seem to imply that to express reality in its concreteness, i.e., as distinct from concepts, must be the work of
poetry alone and that philosophy, being purely intellectual, must
give up the task as obviously beyond its powers. A closer consideration of the problem leads, however, to quite a different
conclusion. If poetry is the highest and most perfect way of
using the supra-rational, immediately expressive function of
words, this means—as linguists have observed long ago—that all
speech to a certain extent partakes, or can partake, of the nature
of poetry and that the difference between poetry and prose is
not absolute, but relative. All that we call "expressiveness" in
speech is the poetical element in it. True, poetry in the narrow
and specific sense of the term utilizes the expressive power of
the purely irrational aspect of words—of the involuntary asso-

ciations of ideas, images, emotions connected with the nuances of meaning and even with the actual auditory texture of words, so to speak with their "aura." But poetry also includes another aspect of expressiveness, accessible to prose as well: thoughts and concepts expressed by words are in poetry so combined that their purely rational, abstract meaning is transcended and they convey concrete reality precisely insofar as it rises above concepts and differs from them in principle. This is the meaning of what may be called the *description* of concrete reality in contradistinction to the logical analysis of it. Accordingly, such description is possible for philosophy as well.

In addition to the general method of describing the supra-logical nature of reality by such a combination of words and ideas as gives a tacit, conceptually inexpressible knowledge of it, philosophy has its own special way of transcending the limitations and inadequacy of abstract knowledge. By directing our thought upon its logical form, i.e., by considering the form, extent, and conditions of logical rational knowledge as a whole, we can learn its limitations. In doing so we use the power of abstract logical knowledge as it were *against* it, i.e., against its tendency to impoverish and distort reality; we use it as an antidote against itself, on the homeopathic principle *similia similibus curantur*. Observing the limited nature of abstract knowledge, we indirectly apprehend, by contrast with it, the unique character of that which lies beyond its confines—namely of reality itself. Thus—to take an example that goes to the root of the matter—in giving an abstract explanation of the principle of definition through logical distinction and contraposition, we transcend that principle in and through understanding its conditions—that is, we go beyond the confines of abstract knowledge and in doing so indirectly apprehend the concrete reality that lies beyond it. (This is the positive significance of applying the principle of negation to the logical form of knowledge itself.) But the perceived contrast between reality and the sphere of rational knowledge will then no longer be a *logical* relation, i.e., will not be negation in the logical sense constitutive of the world of concepts only. The contrast will be supra-logical. We will thus obtain indirect knowledge by means of *ignorance*, that is, by means of contrasting reality with the domain of the logically knowable. This is the form of knowledge described by Nicolas of Cusa, the main representative of this line of thought, as *docta ignorantia*—learned ignorance.

Thus concrete experience of reality is not doomed to remain "dumb" and inexpressible. It is intellectually attained through description or a combination of concepts which, taken together, suggest what reality is; and it can be indirectly expressed through a form of thought which may be described as "transcendental thinking." In it, thought is directed upon itself and recognizes the general formal nature of the domain of particular, logically definable contents; in doing so, it transcends that domain and gains insight into the actual essence of reality which lies beyond it.

True philosophy, i.e., intellectual apprehension of the whole as such, is, in the first instance, rational knowledge, i.e., it finds expression in concepts like all other knowledge. But insofar as it aims at describing reality and recognizes the limitations of the logical aspect of knowledge, it can transcend abstract thought and intuitively apprehend and express the supra-rational. In contradistinction to all particular knowledge directed upon abstractly-differentiated particular elements of being, *philosophy is the rational transcendence of the limitations of rational thought.* It is intellectual life nurtured by the living intuition of supra-rational reality and conscious of its directly inapprehensible nature.

This indirect knowledge, or knowledge through ignorance, is not confined to the mere general awareness of the supra-rational nature of reality. By contrast with the multiplicity of elements that enter into rational knowledge, we can grasp and indirectly determine the multiplicity in the structure of reality itself; and the concrete manifestations of that multiplicity can be elucidated by the already referred to concrete intellectual description.

. . . Starting with the meaning which the word "God" has for most religious minds, and not as yet defining it more closely, we must say in the first place that God has a direct and immediate relation to reality, and is but indirectly related through it to the world of objects; He certainly does not form part of that world. In a sense this is taken for granted in the usual conception of God. He is conceived as that which is, apart from the objective world of fact, as a supra-mundane, transcendent Being. This is why pantheism—at any rate insofar as it is supposed to identify God and the world—is always regarded as "atheism," i.e., as a denial of God's existence.

In another respect, however, the prevalent type of religious thought tends to conceive God as a reality existing outside us, as an *object* the existence of which has to be intellectually established. In the judgment of faith, "God exists," the word "existence" is used much in the same sense in which it is applied to objects or to the world as a whole. In that case objective reality is conceived as falling into two distinct halves: the world and the supra-mundane God. Ancient and medieval thought definitely localized God "above the heavens," i.e., beyond the utmost boundary of the fixed stars. The Copernican revolution, and especially modern physics which makes a concrete picture of the universe altogether impossible, rule out this naive conception; and yet in some other and more subtle sense, the prevalent type of religious thought still takes God to exist as objectively and so to speak in the same kind of way or on the same plane of being as the world, though externally to it. The dispute between religion and atheism takes the form of arguing whether there are grounds for admitting "the existence" of God, i.e., of including Him among objects of our knowledge proved to exist outside and independently of us. Thus the classical theological "proofs of the existence of God," e.g., most of those used by Thomas Aquinas, are inferences from the world's structure; they are intended to show that in studying nature we are compelled to admit the existence of God as the "first mover" or "the first cause," or the source of the world's purposive character. God is conceived as, so to speak, the foundation of the world-structure and in that sense as possessing categorically the same character of objective being as the world—just as the foundation and the building upon which it rests are equally subject to the general laws of physics.

In opposition to this prevalent type of religious thought it must

be urged that God belongs to the sphere of reality as distinct
in principle from the world of fact and therefore cannot form
part of that world, even if it be taken to include the supra-
mundane realm. If to exist means to form part of the world of
fact, faith and unbelief—paradoxically enough—must agree in
denying this predicate to God. True, they will understand such
a denial in different ways and draw totally different conclusions
from it. Unbelief identifies the world of fact with reality, or,
in other words, takes it to be all-inclusive; accordingly, to
exclude God from it is the same as to say that He is a human
invention, a fiction—just as to deny the existence of winged
serpents is identical with saying that they are imaginary. From
the point of view of faith, on the contrary, it will simply mean
that the word "existence," which implies belonging to the world
of fact, is inapplicable to God, because it gives a wrong idea
of Him; the negative judgment does not in the least affect the
value or the truth of the idea of God.

This argument is not an idle refinement of logical thought
or an indulgence in pedantic subtlety. It is of decisive significance for interpreting the very essence of religious faith. It
takes the sting out of the atheists' main contention. The whole
point of atheism is that in our direct experience of objective
reality we do not encounter any such object as God and that
all we know about the world gives us no sufficient grounds, to
say the least of it, for inferring the existence of God, which is
therefore an unjustified hypothesis. The first part of the argument is unquestionably true, and with regard to it, faith really
agrees with unbelief. The possibility spoken of by the mystics,
of coming into direct contact with God in and through experience, is in any case something utterly different from a sober
recognition of His presence in the familiar, everyday world
of fact equally valid for all. But however incontestable the
assertion that God does not form part of the world of objects
may be, from the religious standpoint it is as irrelevant as the
notorious remark of a Soviet airman that in his flights into the
stratosphere he never met God. . . .

But what does it all mean? It means one thing only: God
cannot be found—cannot even be sought—on the paths of

external experience and rational thought which lead us to dispassionate recognition or, as it were, a cold and sober registration of "objects": God may and must be sought only on paths that lead to actual living meeting with *reality*. Since reality is not a dumb and passive object of our cognitive efforts, but something that reveals itself to us through its own activity, we can repeat the old and generally recognized religious truth that God is not an "object" directly accessible to knowledge, but becomes accessible only through *revelation* in the general and literal sense of that term.

Hence it follows that if and insofar as the idea of God can be substantiated at all, we can reach it, in the first instance at any rate, only by means of inner experience. For it is only in inner experience that we come into direct contact with reality and that it is revealed to us. In moral experience and in the experience of communion (the "I-Thou" relation) we meet reality or come upon it, as it were, from without; but our awareness of this is only possible on the basis of a previous inner experience of reality, or else already contains such experience. This is why the experience of meeting God as a reality has the character of primary self-evidence and, as such, is completely independent of any other knowledge, of all that we think or know about the nature and structure of the objective world, and indeed of the whole domain of thought and reason.

Of the Two Natures in Man *

The whole of so-called "modern" history (and especially the last two hundred years, beginning with the age of enlightenment) is spiritually conditioned by the view which may be described as non-religious humanism. It consists in *deifying man*. Having lost faith in God, man came to believe in himself. In other words, having lost the sense of his transcendental, supramundane spiritual basis, he replaced the bi-unity "without division or confusion" which constitutes his being by a vague and contradictory mixture of the two principles, trying to find room for it in the purely natural aspect of himself and imagining that he detects its presence there. Admitting only "this" world and recognizing himself as entirely a part and a member of it, he at the same time believes in his own all-goodness and omnipotence. Hence the comfortably optimistic blind faith—one might say absurd faith, for it contradicts the whole experience of history—in uninterrupted moral and intellectual progress and in an easy realization of the kingdom of reason, goodness, and righteousness (what believers used to call the Kingdom of God) on earth.

The driving power of that blind faith has been so great that even Darwin's theory of evolution, proving that man is simply a descendant of some ape-like animal, failed to undermine it. Indeed that theory has actually been regarded as the best confirmation of the belief in progress. With devastating irony Vladimir Solovyov summed up the absurdity and inconsistency of optimistic, non-religious humanism in a concise formula, "man is an ape and *therefore* is called to realize the kingdom of goodness upon earth."

This, so to speak, classical form of non-religious humanistic faith is still widely prevalent in the semi-educated strata of

* Translated by Natalie Duddington and printed here with her permission and that of Mrs. Tatiana Frank and Mr. Victor Frank. This selection has not been previously published in English.

society, but it is no longer gaining ground. The world-wide troubles which have followed the apparently peaceful well-being and progress of the nineteenth century have been a convincing argument against it. They have shown that by nature man is not wise and good but stupid and wicked, and, as such, is incapable of realizing goodness and reason in the world and arranging his life justly and reasonably. Experience has shown that man is a plaything of dark, blind forces raging in his breast and dragging him to ruin. Two centuries of deification of man and faith in progress are ending in the horrible prospect that this wicked and stupid animal in a fit of fury and madness, perfectly natural to him, may at any moment put a sudden end to human culture with the atomic bomb and revert to his original brutish state.

But even before its tragic downfall, non-religious humanism underwent a significant evolution, which is the history of its inner distintegration; and the results of that disintegration are the sources of the present world-wide confusion. The breakdown of faith in the goodness and rationality of man as a natural being had begun before the fallacy of it was demonstrated by historical events; but in order fully to recognize the fallacy, human thought had to follow it out to the bitter end. In thinking out the initial assumptions of non-religious humanism, it was inevitable to discover the inconsistency of amiable optimism based upon the false idealization of man. It was not hard to see that faith in man's goodness and reasonableness was nothing other than the old religious faith in man as the image and likeness of God, unlawfully inherited by atheism and essentially incompatible with the conception of man as a merely natural being, in principle not different from animals. The ideals of liberty, equality, and fraternity that man feels called upon to realize and that are so unsuitable and unnatural to a purely earthly creature could only have arisen from faith in man's divine parentage. Thus, both in deifying himself and in serving moral principles, man, while intellectually rejecting faith in God, was in fact building his life upon the heritage of that faith. It was natural to counter such inconsistency by conclusions that really followed from atheism, namely, to reject morality as an illegitimate residue of religion and recognize that man must organize his life in accordance with his true, purely earthly, nature. In the nineteenth century two formidable thinkers of genius worked out, each in his own way, that fateful culmination (and disintegration) of non-religious humanism—Marx and Nietzsche.

Both thinkers were full of contempt—in a certain sense perfectly justifiable—for the actual condition of man as expressing his natural, i.e., his animal being. Both recognized dark, evil passions as the only active realities in human life. Both rejected religion and morality as an idolatry that paralyzes the human will; both wanted to use the elemental passions as a creative and regenerative power, thus transforming non-religious humanism into a titanic struggle against God. But at that point their paths diverged. Marx regarded greed and economic envy as the core of human nature and dreamed of turning those passions into class hatred and furious rebellion of the enslaved masses in order to *socialize* life and thus end the chaos and suffering rooted in the individual existence of man as a spiteful animal. By replacing personal existence by well-regulated collective life, man might utilize the elemental forces of his own being, just as in machinery he utilizes the forces of nature.

Nietzsche's dream, more noble in its original form, is still bolder and even more insane. "Man is something that must be surpassed"—this alarming formula sums up the crisis of non-religious humanism. Since Nietzsche definitely rejected all transcendental reality, the only solution left him was that man, contemptible and insignificant in his present state, should ennoble himself by his own resources, sublimate his dark passions into creative self-will, transfigure himself into a man-god, and produce the "overman." Inspired by a vague idea of the divine principle in man—an idea similar to Meister Eckhardt's teaching about the "spark" of divinity in the depths of the human spirit and the Christian mystics' conception of *theosis*—Nietzsche distorted it into the proud scheme that man, the representative of the highest biological race, should make himself God. But, as Nietzsche himself admitted, on that view the only precursors of the man-god were to be found in such "overmen" as the shameless monster Caesar Borgia or the Teutonic "blond beast."

Marx avoids the false humanistic idealization of man at the cost of turning man into an ant in a human ant hill or into a soulless cogwheel in the social machine. Nietzsche's way of transcending humanism leads in the last resort to the affirmation of *bestialism*. The deadly consequences of both theories, akin in their initial conception, though in nothing else, have been empirically proved by two momentous social movements which arose out of them and of course inevitably vulgarized them. Evil cannot be made into a creative principle: it always destroys or paralyzes life. A pure anthropocracy that denies the Holy cannot provide a stable foundation for life whether by merging human beings into one impersonal mass or subjecting them to the power of an overman or of a predatory race: either path means the extinction of life. That result is an instructive confirmation of the fact that the bi-unity of the human being noted above is indestructible. The bond between *purely* human nature and its transcendental basis is so close and inviolable that when man tries to break away from it and to affirm himself as self-sufficient, he finds that instead of exercising autocratic self-will, as was his aim, he falls under the sway of demonic powers which are also supramundane and superhuman. Simply to forget his transcendental basis and to remain detached and indifferent proves to be impossible for man: the only choice open to him is between a free dependence upon God or subjection to the powers of evil. But even captivity to anti-divine forces is merely a painful and destructively negative form of the soul's real dependence upon God.

The degeneration of non-religious humanism into a struggle against God involves a profoundly pessimistic view of the world, as opposed to the naive optimism of the early forms of humanism. Its weakness, obvious to all sound thought, lies in the fact that it combines awareness of the tragic aspect of life and of the power of evil in the world with an insanely optimistic faith— truly a diabolical delusion—in the realization of a lofty, ideal aim by means of evil. But even in this unnatural form it contains the recognition that life is a stern and merciless struggle with the fatal imperfection of reality. In that sense it is an expression of the movement that had been gathering strength throughout the nineteenth century and is now completely victorious—namely, of the gradual change from an optimistic to a profoundly pessimistic view of life. At first man lived by the illusion that he could simply and easily organize life by his own devices, without any connection with the transcendental divine basis of his being; but he is gradually learning to understand that his position is desperate. Having torn himself away from God, man comes to recognize his subjection to the dark, elemental forces of cosmic being. Not Christianity, as Nietzsche thought, but the godless design of saving the world by purely human means is "the revolt of the slaves"—an outburst born of despair and foredoomed to failure. It was natural that the more keen and honest thinkers should have come openly to recognize the hopeless tragedy of human existence; but such an attitude cannot, from the nature of the case, inspire any social movement, for genuine, unadulterated pessimism is bound to be sterile. Nevertheless, it is one of the most prevalent expressions of the modern spirit.

The crudest form of it is mere cynical "unbelief." Life's evil and suffering outweigh goodness and joy; there is no deliverance to hope for; faith in goodness and holiness is absurd; therefore "let us drink and be merry, for tomorrow we die." *Carpe diem!* Man has succumbed to that spiritual condition at all times, but it is particularly characteristic of the epochs of disillusionment in the Utopian ideals of non-religious humanism. When the would-be saviours of humanity become convinced that life cannot be regenerated by purely human ways of reorganizing it, that evil is unconquerable and all is vanity, they easily turn into mere cynics. A state of moral disintegration often comes after a revolution. At bottom it is simply an expression of stark despair, a form of moral suicide, and as such it obviously cannot be man's permanent standpoint.

But there is another kind of unbelief, deeper and more significant—"sorrowful" unbelief. It is widespread and is one of the most instructive and characteristic signs of the time. In contradistinction to cynical unbelievers, "sorrowful" unbelievers do not reject the Holy; they are keenly conscious of the difference between good and evil, between the higher principle that ennobles life and gives it meaning, and the hideous senselessness of the dark elemental forces in man and nature. But while believing that the higher principle is significant and binding upon man, they do not believe in its objective force and reality; they regard it as merely a property of the human spirit, unstable, impotent, and heterogenous to the rest of existence. For them, man's task in life is a heroic defense—foredoomed to defeat— of the higher spiritual principles against a "hostile universe" (to use Bertrand Russell's expression). Their standpoint recalls the pessimistic varieties of latter-day Stoicism: *victrix causa diis placuit, sed victa Catoni.* In our own time it has found a philosophical expression in the doctrines of existentialism. As a philosophical system existentialism is not worth mentioning, for it is obvious that it starts with an artificially impoverished conception of the world and that its assumptions are inconsistent with the fundamental traditions of *philosophia perennis.* But it is characteristic and significant as the expression of the mental attitude which I call "sorrowful unbelief." Its essence is an intense awareness of the insoluble opposition between the higher spiritual principles and aspirations that struggle helplessly within the narrow confines of the human heart, and the whole structure of objective reality. That leads to a would-be, rigorously sober vision of the tragic doom that hangs over the destiny of man. All that could mitigate it and bring comfort is regarded as a pitiful illusion, due to cowardice and lack of intellectual integrity—to a kind of "ostrich policy" on man's part.

. . . It is not difficult to see that the source of the narrowness and therefore the falsity of this standpoint is naturalism, i.e., the confusion of reality as such with natural objective reality. Hence the spirit is regarded as a purely subjective aspect of the limited and self-contained human mind; it seems to be a fragile and insignificant element in the context of nature. But to admit the ideal supremacy of the Holy, and man's duty to defend it against the dark and irrational forces of the natural world, means to recognize a certain higher, supra-mundane principle of being—

and that contradicts the original assumption of naturalism. When thought out to the end, sorrowful unbelief proves to be a kind of religious faith, impoverished by its dualism—and somewhat similar to the ancient Gnostic faith in an all-merciful but distant God, alien to the world and powerless in it. Indeed, we may go further and say that since the ideal supremacy and the morally binding character of the Holy is, in truth, a token of its supra-mundane, supra-physical reality, it is also a token of its real and effective—though also supra-physical—power in the world. In moral and spiritual heroism, the subject experiences from within the action upon the world and in the world of the transcendent reality of the Deity. At any rate, one point in the realm of exist-ence—the human heart, with its noble sense of "you ought and therefore you can," in the words of Kant's formula—presents a breach through which the power and reality of the Holy pours like a mighty stream into the world. It then becomes clear that man in his spiritual essence is a stranger and a helpless exile in this world precisely because his true birthplace is in another and a higher dimension of reality.

Thus sorrowful unbelief, when some of its tacit assumptions are thought out to the end, turns out—contrary to its ostensible creed—to be a peculiar form of potentially positive faith. For the true dividing line between faith and unbelief, in the funda-mental sense that determines man's path in life, lies not in the intellectual admission or denial of "the existence of God," but in the presence or absence (or rejection) of heartfelt reverence before the Holy and of service to it—in the difference, explained in the Gospel parable, between true and merely verbal obedi-ence. One of the main sources of the present-day spiritual con-fusion in which man does not know his friends from his foes would disappear if it were clearly recognized that sorrowful unbelief (like all non-religious humanism) is secretly akin to religious faith, and radically different from real unbelief, whether in the form of merely cynical godlessness or of defiant struggle against God.

Of course, this attenuated and unconscious faith is a long way from spontaneous, childlike, and wholehearted faith in the abso-lute supremacy and real omnipotence of all-merciful Providence.

Such faith gives man a feeling of perfect security and is, in a sense, the final and most adequate expression of truly religious consciousness. And yet, the fact that modern man's faith is lacking in harmonious simplicity and beset by tormenting doubts testifies not merely to the weakness of it but also to the peculiar intensity of his religious life.

. . . Pantheism and atheism; faith in man's goodness and rationality carried to the point of man-worship; proud schemes to rearrange the world at the will of its master—man; the view that the world is a meaningless chaos of blind forces; and, finally, the feeling of the loneliness of the human spirit in the universe and therefore of its tragic doom—all that is a direct challenge to the Christian tradition. This new spiritual attitude means deliberate rejection of the Christian revelation, but just because it is a hostile reaction against it, it is itself determined by it. At any rate those forms of it which preserve faith in the good and the holy may be regarded as typically Christian heresies, though far more radical and therefore dangerous than the heresies of the early centuries. At the same time they may be said to be expressions—distorted expressions—of strivings which the Christian revelation has created in the human mind.

There was a moment in the spiritual history of Europe when human thought seemed to be successfully combining new intellectual vistas and new spiritual impulses with a fuller and deeper understanding of the Christian faith. This was the movement of so-called Christian humanism in the fifteenth and the sixteenth centuries, at the end of the Middle Ages and on the threshold of modern times. It found its most significant expression in the religious and philosophical system of Cardinal Nicolas of Cusa, one of the greatest, though as yet underestimated, European thinkers of genius. Had that movement been historically successful, there would have been no break between Christian faith and non-religious humanism, and the whole spiritual history of the Western nations might have taken a different and a healthier course. That was not to be. But having harvested all the bitter fruits of error, we are confronted with the same problem once more. The main point of it is the adequate apprehension of the nature of man in his relation to God and the world.

. . . Man's greatest and most fatal error lies in identifying the personal character of his being with his existence as an individual, i.e., in being aware of himself as a self-contained element of reality, as a separate, self-sufficient entity. That leads on the one hand to the pride of self-deification and on the other to a tragic sense of loneliness, of being different from all else, of being forsaken in a hostile, alien world. But in truth that which we call our self is not an isolated point; it might, rather, be compared to a root that goes into the very depths of the common soil of reality and is nurtured by its creative life-giving forces. The image of the soil and of being rooted in it is a suitable symbol for expressing the supra-rational relation between God and man. It suggests that not only the original source but also the ground and, so to speak, the center of the human self and of its existence lie not within but beyond man himself, in another, deeper, and more primary reality than he—and that the conceptions of "beyond" and "within" in this case coincide. That which is deepest and most intimately-inward in man is nurtured, as it were, by a living substance penetrating into him from without. The same idea is suggested by the Gospel parable of the vine and its branches. Another symbol of this supra-rational relation to which mystic experience bears witness is love as the union or mergence of two into one. The lover finds the center of his existence not in himself but in another—in the beloved; he affirms his own being and enriches himself both through self-surrender to the beloved and through the incoming flow of responsive love, inseparable from such self-surrender. Thus, the very essence of personal, inward, intimate "being-for-itself"—of that which we call our "ego," contrasting it as a special primary reality with the rest of the world—proves to be not lonely and barren self-sufficiency, but an indissoluble bond or connectedness with a principle that is above and beyond us. It is life with God and in God—nay, more, it is God's life, or the presence of the divine principle in ourselves.

NICHOLAS ONUFRIYEVICH LOSSKY

[1870-1965]

Nicholas lossky is one of the few Russian philosophers already well known in the English-speaking world. In 1946, he took up residence in the United States for a long period, and his widely read *History of Russian Philosophy* (1951) was published in English during his stay in this country. Long before coming to this country, however, Lossky gained an audience in the English-speaking world through the efforts of Natalie Dudington, who began to serve as his interpreter to the West half a century ago. Mrs. Duddington read her translation of Lossky's representative article, "Intuitivism," to the Aristotelian Society in England in 1914. Her translation in 1919 of his book, *The Intuitive Basis of Knowledge* (1906), was the first English translation of a technical philosophical work by any Russian philosopher.

Born in 1870 in the province of Vitebsk west of Moscow, Lossky was educated both in Russia and abroad, studying under Windelband and Wundt in Germany. From the first years of the present century, when he took his advanced degrees at the University of Saint Petersburg and subsequently became Professor of Philosophy there, his long and active life was wholly devoted to the teaching and writing of philosophy—despite numerous changes of scene. In 1921 he was compelled to leave the University because of his religious views. After his expulsion from the Soviet Union in 1922, he settled in Prague and lived there until 1942, when he was made Professor of Philosophy at the University of Bratislava. In 1945 he emigrated to France and in 1946 to the United States, where for many years he was Professor of Philosophy at the Russian Orthodox Seminary in New York. He died in Paris early in 1965.

Throughout his professional life Lossky wrote voluminously, on questions of philosophical psychology, ethics, epistemology, metaphysics, and religion. One of the few strictly professional Russian philosophers, he generally avoided the dimensions of social criticism and cultural history which have had so compelling an attraction for most Russian thinkers. Like the other Russian émigré philosophers he has a strong religious interest connected specifically with his Russian Orthodox faith, but even in his religious writings, as he himself points out, he is "less concerned with theology than with the task of working out a system of metaphysics necessary for a Christian interpretation of the world." [1]

The metaphysical system developed by Lossky can best be described as an imaginative variation of Leibniz's monadology which owes much to the thought of the first major Russian Leibnizian, Alexis Kozlov [2]—the only Russian philosopher who had a direct and extensive influence on Lossky. Best presented in *The World as an Organic Whole* (1915), Lossky's view envisages reality as a plurality of supertemporal, superspatial beings created by a "Supracosmic principle" or God. Like Kozlov, Lossky emphasizes the activity of these monads, calling them "substantival agents," and he sees this activity as radically free and creative. The substantival agents receive no determinate character from their Creator; from the moment they come into being they freely forge their own destiny. Some choose the path of Divine righteousness and remain supertemporal, superspatial spirits, forming the Kingdom of Heaven; others, asserting their egoistic selfhood, do not enter this Kingdom but fall into struggle with one another. The material world as we know it is a product of this struggle; time and space are "modes of activity of substantival agents." [3] Thus the material world is inherently imperfect and "fallen." But even in this fallen world substantival agents exist on different levels of complexity and

1. Lossky, *History of Russian Philosophy*, p. 266.
2. See pp. 4-6 above.
3. Zenkovsky, *op. cit.*, pp. 667.

value, leading Lossky to call his view "hierarchical personalism": the substantival agent, initially incarnated, perhaps, as a lowly atom, through its "self-creative" activity raises itself to higher stages of being—molecule, unicellular organism, ultimately a human self—through a series of reincarnations or Leibnizian "metamorphoses."

The cosmic order thus envisaged by Lossky is not, however, a system of isolated entities pursuing independent careers. Lossky, again like Kozlov, denies that the monads or substantival agents are closed or "windowless"; rather he sees them as interacting in an organic unity. Lossky recounts the moment in his life at which he suddenly realized, he says, that "everything is immanent in everything," and he asserts that "from that time on, the idea of an all-pervading universal unity became my guiding idea." [4] It is in these terms that Lossky constructs the epistemological "intuitivism" for which he is best known.

Intuitivism, as Lossky understands it, is the answer to the impasse created by what he calls the epistemological "individualism" of Descartes, Locke, and most modern philosophers. Their view, which takes subjective states to be the sole content of consciousness, cuts off the knowing subject from the object of knowledge and regards the two as being related only causally— the object merely causes the subjective state. The resulting conception that the object of knowledge always transcends the knowing mind is the source of problems and contradictions which can be avoided, according to Lossky, only by accepting the immanent interpenetration of subject and object and the consequent "coordinate," rather than causal, relation between them that lies at the foundation of "intuitivism." In a passage summarizing his own view in the third person, Lossky defines "intuitivism" as

the doctrine that the cognized object, even if it forms part of the external world, enters the knowing subject's consciousness directly, so to speak in person, and is therefore apprehended as it exists independently of the act of knowing. Such contemplation of other entities as they are

4. Quoted in *ibid.*, p. 661.

in themselves is possible because the world is an organic whole, and the knowing subject, the individual human self, is a supertemporal and superspatial being, intimately connected with the whole world. The subject's relation to all other entities in the world that renders intuition possible is called by Lossky *epistemological coordination*. That relation as such is not knowledge. In order that the subject should be not merely connected with the self but also cognized by it, the subject must direct upon it a series of intentional mental acts—of awareness, attention, differentiation, etc.[5]

These, then, are the epistemological themes developed in detail in Lossky's first major philosophical work, *The Intuitive Basis of Knowledge* (1906), and succinctly presented in the essay, "Intuitivism," which follows. In the essay Lossky presents his basic epistemology in the form of a theory of judgment in which he distinguishes between the object, the content, and the act of cognition. While the *act* is subjective, he argues, the content and the object are objective, and we are mistaken if we transfer the subjective characteristics of the act to the other elements. This theory of judgment is significant not only as a vehicle of Lossky's views but for its application to issues which occupy the forefront of contemporary philosophical discussion: for example, Lossky attacks the division of judgments into synthetic and analytic, arguing that *all* judgments are *both* analytic and synthetic—analytic from the subjective side and synthetic from the objective.

In this essay Lossky also suggests the distinction between "real being" (that which has temporal existence) and "ideal being" (non-temporal entities, conceived by Lossky in explicitly Platonic terms). This distinction was later developed in his last major epistemological work, *Sensory, Intellectual, and Mystical Intuition* (1938).[6] Real being, Lossky maintains, takes on "systematic

5. Lossky, *op. cit.*, p. 252.

6. According to Lossky (*ibid.*, p. 251), the first part of this book appeared in English translation in five booklets published in Prague by the *Université libre Russe* in the years 1934-1938.

character" only on the basis of ideal being; thus Lossky came to call his world view "ideal realism." [7] Each of these types of being is the subject of a specific type of intuition—sensory and intellectual intuition, respectively. Mystical intuition is the appropriate cognitive approach to still a third type of being later defined by Lossky—what he calls "metalogical being" or "being which transcends the laws of identity, contradiction, and excluded middle, for instance, God." [8]

Lossky's works abound in bold philosophical and religious doctrines on many subjects more or less closely connected with the epistemological and metaphysical views outlined above, and fortunately Lossky himself has provided a clear guide to his ideas on all these subjects in the chapter discussing his own views in his *History of Russian Philosophy*.[9] In a number of works he addressed himself to problems of ethics, for example, taking his departure from his conception of the human person as a radically free moral agent. In philosophy of religion he shows that he is indebted to Vladimir Solovyov by accepting, along with so many other Russian religious philosophers influenced by Solovyov, a concept of Sophia. In Lossky's system, however, Sophia occupies a subordinate status as a created being who is the chief member of the Kingdom of Heaven mentioned above, standing "next to Christ as His closest co-worker." [10] In this as in all other aspects of his philosophy, Lossky's independence is evident even in his use of concepts originally suggested by other thinkers.

7. *Ibid.*, p. 253.
8. *Loc. cit.*
9. *Ibid.*, pp. 251-266.
10. *Ibid.*, p. 266.

SELECTED BIBLIOGRAPHY

Works:
Nicholas O. Lossky, *The Intuitive Basis of Knowledge*, trans. Natalie Duddington, London, 1919.
——————, *The World as an Organic Whole*, trans. Natalie Duddington, London, 1928.
——————, *Freedom of Will*, trans. Natalie Duddington, London, 1932.
——————, *Value and Existence*, trans. S. S. Vinokooroff, London, 1935.
——————, *History of Russian Philosophy*, New York, 1951.

Secondary Sources:
Festschrift N. O. Losskij zum 60. Geburtstag, Bonn, 1932.
A. S. Kohanski, *Lossky's Theory of Knowledge*, Nashville, 1936.
V. V. Zenkovsky, *A History of Russian Philosophy*, trans. George L. Kline, 2 vols., London and New York, 1953, pp. 657-675.

[NICHOLAS LOSSKY]

Intuitivism *

A theory of knowledge must be free from any assumptions with regard to the relation between the knowing mind and the external world. It must begin simply by an examination of consciousness and an exact description of the elements and relations which may be contained in it. Kant set himself the task of following this plan. But he did not carry it out, for, under the influence of the traditions established by his predecessors, he started with the assumption that the contents of consciousness must necessarily be mental states of the individual.

Let us then discard all preconceived ideas about the world, the human soul, body, etc., and confine attention to such manifestations of consciousness as are expressed by the phrases "I am glad," "I want to listen to the music," "I see stars in the heavens," "I touch something hard," "I know that $2 \times 2 = 4$." That of which I am conscious—the joy, the wish to hear the music, the seen stars, etc.—is very different in the several examples; but in all cases it is something which stands in a certain specific relation to the self. This relation cannot be described or defined by analyzing it into its elements, for it is simple and unique. The nature of the relation may be hinted at by means of a figurative expression which should not be understood literally; everything that the self "has" enters the domain of consciousness.

That which the self "has" may be called a content of consciousness. A mental state can then be analyzed as follows: The fact of being conscious must involve at least three elements: (1) the self, (2) a content (a "something"), (3) a relation of "having" between the self and the content. On the ground of this relation it may be said that the self is that which is conscious and the content is that which it is conscious of. Any "something," such as the fall of a star or the hardness of iron,

* Translated by Natalie Duddington and reprinted by permission from *Proceedings of the Aristotelian Society*, N.S., XIV (1913-1914), 126-151.

will be a content of my consciousness when I become aware of it. In order that there should be consciousness there must be this relation of awareness. But the particular nature of the content to which the self stands in the relation in question is not essential. No rational grounds can be adduced to prove that that of which we are aware, i.e., the contents of consciousness, must needs be mental states of the conscious individual. So far as one can see there is nothing but tradition and prejudice to prevent us from admitting that a physical fact forming part of the external world may, while I concentrate my attention upon it, enter the domain of my consciousness. For instance, the movement of the pendulum is a fact in the external world and not a psychical event. But there is no difficulty in conceiving that at the moment of perception it becomes apprehended by me.

I have somewhat anticipated in order to make clearer the distinction between my view of the structure of consciousness and the traditional theory. I have yet really no right to call some contents psychical and others physical, some subjective and others objective. All that has so far been pointed out is the indisputable fact that contents of consciousness may be infinitely various, as different from one another as for example "my joy" and "the movement of the pendulum" observed by me. I must now define what I mean by the "psychical" and "non-psychical" elements of the world, as well as by the "inner" or the "subjective" and the "external" world. This can only be done by making use of the differences between the contents that the analysis of consciousness has brought to light.

To begin with, the following circumstance should be noted: As has been said above, consciousness is the totality of all the contents to which the self stands in the peculiar relation figuratively described as that of "having." This "having" is of two kinds which are totally distinct. Some contents are immediately experienced as manifestations of myself (joy, wish, etc.) while others (the observed "blue" of the sky, the "hardness" of iron, the "swinging of the pendulum," etc.) are immediately experienced as something foreign to myself. They enter the sphere of my consciousness only as something "given to me," only insofar as I direct my attention upon them and "bear them in mind."

Contents of the first category are always unanimously recognized as psychical and as belonging to the inner life of the conscious subject. Those of the second category are, on the contrary, regarded on the evidence of immediate experience as belonging to the external world. Only under the influence of theories based upon physics, physiology, psychology, and metaphysics do we begin to assert that these contents are also psychical (like joy and wish) and form part of the inner life of the subject. It will then follow that the external world is not "given to me" in consciousness for one single instant, that it remains forever transcendent in relation to the knowing mind. This conclusion occasions insoluble difficulties and contradictions in epistemology. The difficulties and contradictions are not due, however, to the real nature of the facts, but to an interpretation which does violence to the facts. At the basis of this interpretation lies the mistaken view that the self and the external world can only communicate by means of causal interaction—for example, by means of impressions or impacts. As soon as this prejudice is discarded it will be seen that there are no sufficient grounds for suppressing the instinctive tendency of the human mind to take the second group of the contents of consciousness for the actual features of the external world.

In accordance with the dictates of immediate experience, the first group of contents may then be described as "my" states of consciousness, and the second as "the given" states of consciousness. Let us refer to the sphere of the inner psychical world only the states immediately experienced by me as "mine," and regard all other states as actual portions of the external world.[1]

It should be noted that "my" states (joy, wish) may also become objects of my attention. In that case they will stand in a twofold relation to me. They will be "mine" (in the sense of being a state of myself) and they will be "given" to "me" for observation.

It is the second kind of "having" something in consciousness that is of particular importance to epistemology. Here the relation between the self and some content arises through atten-

1. This question is worked out in detail in my book *The Intuitive Basis of Knowledge.*

tion being directed upon this content, whether it be psychical or physical, whether it form part of the external world or of the mental life of the individual. The peculiar relation which is thus established through attention and which results in some part of the world being "given to me," may be described as contemplation, immediate apprehension, or intuition. Or, in order to avoid misconception that might arise owing to historical associations connected with these terms, it might be designated by the words "epistemological coordination" between subject and object. A theory of knowledge founded upon such a conception of the relation between the knowing subject and the known object may be called Intuitivism or Universalistic Empiricism (in contradistinction to the Individualistic Empiricism of Locke and Hume).

The epistemological coordination of subject and object, i.e., the relation between them which consists in the subject's contemplating the object, clearly has no causal character. It does not consist in the action of the world upon the self or *vice versa*. This is the reason why the scientist, accustomed to dealing with relations that obtain in physics, chemistry, physiology, and especially with the relations essential to a purely mechanical and materialistic conception of the world, viz., the relations of push and pressure between particles of matter, does not perceive the relation indicated above which lies at the basis of all processes of knowing. Indeed, he finds it hard to understand the Intuitive theory of the structure of consciousness.

It is convenient to describe the relation in question by the term "coordination," because we can thus emphasize the absence of subordination between subject and object. Such subordination is assumed both in the empiricism of Locke and in the critical philosophy of Kant. For Locke the object is the cause of sensation in the mind of the subject. For Kant, on the contrary, the object is due to the thinking activity of the subject.

No theory of knowledge can altogether avoid admitting the relation of coordination between subject and object, but as a rule the admission is not clearly expressed. Thus, for example, both Locke and Descartes deny the existence of such a relation so long as they are dealing with our knowledge of the external world. But as soon as they begin to consider the data of inner experience they think it perfectly clear and self-evident that the mind observes its own states as they actually occur (that, for example, the mind is aware of actually experienced joy and not of a symbol or copy of that emotion). In other words, they admit, without stating it explicitly, that there exists a relation of coordination between the knowing mind and the known object (the joy); they maintain that the self contemplates or immediately perceives its own states. According to them not only my knowledge of my own joy but also my knowledge of the color "red"—insofar as I am concerned with my own sensation and not with the external world—belongs to the sphere of inner experience and takes the form of immediate contemplation or intuition.

It seems to me that even the critical theory cannot avoid admitting that some knowledge is obtained through contemplation. Speaking of the inner sense, Kant, it is true, affirms that we know ourselves, as well as the external world, only as phenomenal. But if the question be asked how is knowledge itself known, how, for instance, do we know the forms of knowledge, the Categories described in the *Critique of Pure Reason*, the follower of Kant will have to admit that in that case at least the mind contemplates the object of its study, apprehends it immediately, and describes it just as it is found in the process of knowledge.

Intuitivism makes a much wider use of the doctrine of immediate perception than is made, for instance, by the empiricism of Locke. According to the Intuitive theory, there is no difference between knowledge of the inner and of the outer world. The knowledge of both is founded upon immediate apprehension (contemplation or intuition).

Now since the mind becomes aware of a "given" part of the world by means of contemplation, without any causal interaction between the subject and the object, there is no ground for supposing that contents of knowledge must needs be sensuous in character. Space, time, motion, etc., can be regarded as non-sensuous and yet "contemplated" elements of the objective world. They need not in any sense be derived from the tactual, motor, and visual sensations, though they are apprehended together with them. What is more important, this view of knowledge does away with the reasons which led both the empiricists and Kant to deny that relations such as causality may be given in experience. To put it briefly, according to the Intuitive theory that which transcends sense does not transcend experience.

The view that "given" contents are a part of the external world may seem very doubtful. Colors, sounds, etc., in contradistinction to the activity of attention directed upon them, are felt to be "given to me" and not to be "my" states. It follows that for Intuitivism, colors, sounds, and other so-called sensible qualities of things are not mental states of the knowing subject, but form part of the external world. Does it mean then that Intuitivism leaves out of account facts established by physiology which prove the dependence of sensations upon the structure and condition of the sense organs and of the nervous system of the knowing subject—the facts which apparently prove fatal to naive realism?

The answer is that Intuitivism admits the facts established by physiology but puts upon them an interpretation different from the one usually accepted. . . .

Take, for instance, the case when different stimuli, x, y, z (electric current, ray of light, mechanical pressure) act upon the sense organ, and the subject is aware of one and the same sensation a. This fact in no way proves that a is a process within the body, and still less that a is a mental state of the knowing subject. The external stimuli, x, y, z (electric current, ray of light, mechanical pressure) are complex. It may well be that they each contain an element a which is exactly alike in all of them ($x = abc$, $y = ade$, $z = afg$) and is apprehended in the different cases.

The opposite case, when the same stimulus x is applied to different sense organs and, as a result, the subject becomes aware of different sense qualities, a, b, c, may perhaps be explained as follows: the external stimulus x is complex, it consists of a, b, c, and in the several cases the knowing subject apprehends its different aspects. The brain and the nervous system do not in any way create the images of the things apprehended, and the physiology of the future must build an entirely new hypothesis to explain the part played in the process of apprehension by the nervous centers and the sense organs.[2] Such a hypothesis will have to show that an external A is apprehended by means of the brain and the sense organs but is not produced by a physiological process in the sense organs or the nervous centers. It may be said, then, that even the so-called sensuous apprehension has a non-sensuous character. The sense organs merely direct the knowing mind to apprehend A, a feature in the external world; they do not create that A.

It must of course be remembered that in the case of the so-called sensuous apprehension, there is causal interaction between the human body and the external thing. As a result of it, processes arise within the body which may to some extent be apprehended together with the external object.

It often happens too that side by side with the non-causal coordination of the subject and the object (side by side with "contemplation") there is also causal interaction between them. Owing to such interaction the subject will experience some subjective affection—e.g., a feeling of satisfaction—and his apprehension of the object will be colored by his awareness of that affection.

The state of apprehending, especially of apprehending the so-called sensuous things, may be very complex. It may contain (1) elements belonging to the objective world outside the body, (2) elements belonging to the objective world within the body, and (3) subjective elements.

The critics of such a theory may say that it is a re-statement of naive realism. There is some truth in this remark; Schuppe in his article *"Die Bestätigung des naiven Realismus"* admits it. He is in favor of returning to naive realism, and in speaking of modern theories which tend in that direction, he observes that they re-introduce the realism but discard its naive character. They do not ascribe external reality to objects uncritically;

2. Bergson strongly insists that the brain does not produce the images of the things apprehended. In *Matière et mémoire* he formulates an interesting hypothesis about the part played by the brain in the process of apprehension.

they are driven to it by an elaborate analysis of knowledge. Such a return to naive realism is a widespread movement in modern philosophy. (In my forthcoming work, *Modern Theories of Knowledge*, I shall attempt to describe the different forms it takes.)

When the object is "given" to the knowing subject, knowledge of it involves more than the three elements enumerated above—the self, the content of consciousness, and the coordination between them. As I have already said, there is also the activity of attention on the part of the self. Moreover, the epistemological coordination which results from the activity of attention is a necessary, but not a sufficient, condition of knowledge. Simply to "have" something in consciousness, to be simply aware of something, is not knowledge.[3] I may be conscious of something (e.g., I may feel envy or be "bathed" in the blue of the sky as I lie on my back on the grass) and not know *that* I am conscious and especially not know *what* is the something I am conscious of. A content of consciousness may be unknown, either completely or at least insofar as I am not able to describe it. For instance, I may be aware that I experience some feeling, but be unable to decide whether it is envy or righteous anger. In order to *know* the content of his consciousness, the knowing subject must not only attend to it, but also mentally place the "given" content by the side of other contents, so as to compare it with them. Comparison gives rise to the perception of sameness and of difference which enables me to account for the content I "have" before my consciousness.

In my book *The Intuitive Basis of Knowledge* this process is described as follows: "The object of knowledge is immanent in the process of cognition, it is reality itself, life itself present in and experienced through the act of knowing. But reality as such is not knowledge; it only becomes knowledge when the process of comparison is brought to bear upon it. Therefore knowledge is an experience compared with other experiences. Until reality is subject to comparison it flows before me as something dark, shapeless, unconscious (i.e., uncognized). If on a hot summer afternoon I walk on a riverbank which is covered with luxurious

3. See my *Voluntarismus*, Chapter II.

vegetation and do not think of anything, do not wish for anything, seem to lose my personality and to become one with nature —nothing distinct exists for me, all things are merged in one confused, powerful stream of life. But now something splashes over the water, attracts my attention, and the intellectual process of discriminating begins. The mirror-like surface of the water, the green banks, the reeds near the shore begin to grow distinct from one another. And there is no end to this process of differentiation so long as I feel inclined to look into reality and to seek greater depths in it.

"The growth near the banks had appeared to me like a confused uniform mass and now the dark green of the reeds stands out against the lighter green of the sweet sedge, and even in the dark mass of the reeds their stems, leaves, and dark brown brushes can be distinguished from one another by their color, shape, and position. As I go on discriminating, everything grows more distinct; the formless acquires form, the vague becomes definite.

"Knowledge then is a process of differentiation of the real by means of comparison. By means of this process reality, without losing its real character, becomes a known reality, a presentation or an idea."

To avoid misunderstanding, it should be noted that the differentiation of the object is a result of discriminating and comparing, and this implies that the characteristics of the object are not created by me, but exist in the object and become distinctions for me when I recognize them. Suppose there are three things before me—SAP, SAD, SMN. So long as I have not distinguished them from one another and from other things, I have no knowledge of them, they lie shrouded in the darkness of the unknown. If I distinguish S, the first stage of knowledge is attained; my knowledge, however, would be not of three things but only of one, S, common to them. The other features, though they exist in reality, would not be discriminated by my consciousness and would still remain dark for me. At the second stage of knowledge I would distinguish also A and M and would therefore have an idea of SA, SA, SM, and so on.

If as a result of this process we obtain the actual image of the object, our purpose is reached—we have the truth. By "image" I do not mean a copy of the object but the object itself, with all its characteristics discriminated. In other words, we have truth only when the differentiated image consists entirely of elements present in the object and nothing foreign is introduced into it. In this sense it can be said that truth is an objective image of a thing, and falsity a subjective image of it.

It follows that it would be impossible to distinguish truth from falsity if it were not for certain marks which enable us to determine which elements form part of the object and which are added to it by the knowing subject. In other words, every act of knowledge must contain aspects colored by a feeling of subjectivity as well as aspects that have an objective character. One example is sufficient to prove that this really is the case. Suppose I am making up a story and relating, for instance, that there are four huge oak trees by the monument of Peter the Great in Petersburg. There is no doubt that the image of the monument stands before my consciousness as something which I do not in any way regard as a product of my own activities. Oak trees which I have seen somewhere before may also have the same objective character attaching to them. But the *conjunction* of the monument and the oaks is certainly felt to be an act of synthesis produced by myself and not to be contained in the object. On the contrary, when I say that the mounted figure of Peter stands on a granite rock I am conscious that this conjunction emanates from the object itself.

It should be noted that objectivity is not identical with externality. My own activity may become an object of my knowledge, e.g., I may recall my story about the monument and the oaks and it will stand over against me as something that I cannot undo. It will compel me to admit its presence and will bind me in an objective fashion in the act of judgment. Anything then which is "given to me" for contemplation can be described as objective, but the term "external" should be applied only to those "given" contents which are not experienced by me as the contemplated activities of my own self. The truth that results from the process of discriminating is always expressed in the form of a judgment, or in a form equivalent to a judgment in its meaning. Indeed the process of differentiating an object by means of comparison must inevitably pursue the following course: Until comparison is brought to bear upon it, reality appears to us dark and chaotic. The first act of discriminating separates out of it some aspect A. Reality as a whole still remains for us dark and confused, but now one aspect of it is clearly and definitely characterized as A. This stage of knowledge is still preserved in language in the form of such expressions as "it rains," "it is dusk," etc. Through further acts of discriminating, something vague but already defined on one side as A is now defined as B, something defined as AB is now described as C, and so on. For instance, as I walk along a wood path I notice that something small darts across my way; that the "something small that darts across the way" squeaks, etc. Every such act of discriminating contains all the three elements considered necessary for a judgment—the subject, the predicate, and the relation of the predicate to the subject. Indeed, in every act of discriminating and comparing there must be a starting point— a confused reality, unknown as yet and therefore not described by any word. In more complex acts of knowledge the starting point is a reality some aspects of which have already become distinct; the act of discriminating separates out of this reality some fresh aspect, of which we are aware precisely as of an aspect of or an element in the part of reality under investigation. In this way there is preserved a living and intimate connection— closer than mere temporal sequence—between the point from which the discrimination started and the result obtained. It is clear then that since the process of knowledge is a process of discriminating and comparing, it must inevitably assume the form of judgment.

From the above description of the process of knowledge it is clear that if several successive acts of knowing are directed on one and the same object they will result in the formation of a concept as well as of judgments. Suppose that by means of the first act we learn that something is S; through the second we learn that S is P, through the third that SP is M, and so on. Features discriminated in the preceding judgments will be thought of as one complex mass of elements S, SP, SPM, on

the background of a reality still undifferentiated. Every such
complex arises out of a coming together of judgments, so to
speak, and may again be broken up into judgments. But of
course explicit acts of judgment do not necessarily precede the
formation of such a complex. Sometimes the discriminated elements form a complex idea immediately, without passing through
the explicit form of judgment. It may therefore be said that
such ideas when they have an objective character (as, for
instance, the images of perception or memory) are the abbre-
viated, i.e., the undeveloped, or the overdeveloped, complexes of
judgments. Thus in the judgment "this tall thin man resembles my
brother," the idea "this tall thin man" is a complex of undeveloped or of overdeveloped judgments—"this is a man," "this man
is tall," etc.

I must now return to the question of the subject of judgment
in order to prevent a dangerous misunderstanding. It appears at
first sight as if the subject of a developed judgment were an
idea or a concept with a limited, strictly defined meaning. As
a matter of fact this is not the case. The subject of every judgment is the dark, inexhaustible, unknown reality, but in a highly
developed judgment it is referred to by means of some idea which
designates the previously discriminated aspects of this reality. It
therefore might easily seem as if this idea as such were the
subject of the judgment.

According to the Intuitive theory, then, the subject of judgment is that about which we are seeking to obtain information.
Following the accepted use of the terms, it is natural to describe
that which our knowledge is about as the object of knowledge.
Our theory then can be expressed thus: "The object of knowledge is the subject of judgment." The information obtained in
any given judgment about the object of knowledge is expressed
by the predicate and may be called the content of knowledge.

The theory that cognition is a process of discriminating and
comparing features of the real easily settles the complicated
question about analytic and synthetic judgments. According to
the Intuitive theory, all judgments are in one respect analytic,
and in another synthetic. In relation to the still unknown part
of the subject, or, speaking generally, in relation to the still

unknown portion of reality, every judgment has an analytic character. Thus, for instance, the judgment "this tall thin man is remarkably pale" is undoubtedly formed by a further differentiation—i.e., analysis—of the subject which was at first described as "this" (S), "man" (M), "tall" (N), "thin" (R). But on the other hand, if we look at the formula of this judgment—SMNR-P—and confine attention to the already known part of the subject, characterized as SMNR, we shall see that the judgment was formed synthetically, viz., by adding P to SMNR which do not in the least resemble P and could not by any analysis be made to yield P.

Every judgment is an analysis made by the individual of a hitherto unknown reality. But in relation to the already known aspects of an object, every judgment is a synthesis. The analysis is the work of the knowing mind, but the synthetic connection between the known part of the subject and the predicate is "given" for contemplation by reality itself. Knowledge then consists in the mind's analyzing reality and thus being able to trace synthetic connections that obtain in the real.

Analysis is the subjective side of knowledge, it is the mental activity of the knowing individual. The objective side of knowledge (the "given" in a judgment) is always a synthesis.

If the subjective and the objective sides of knowledge are not distinguished, hopeless difficulties and contradictions are bound to ensue. Let us dwell a little further on this point in order to show how important the distinction is.

We have seen that the process of judging contains the following three elements—the object of knowledge, the content of knowledge, and the act of knowledge. The meaning of the object and the content of knowledge have already been defined. By the act of knowledge are to be understood the activities of the knowing subject, attention and comparison, necessary for obtaining knowledge. There is a fundamental difference between the act of knowledge on the one hand and the object and content of knowledge on the other. The act of knowledge is the subjective, the mental and individual side of knowledge—the object and the content are the objective or logical side of knowledge.

The act of knowing is only a means to attain our end, viz., to get at the objective side of knowledge which contains the truth about the object.

The act of knowledge (attention and comparison) is always a state of the knowing subject. The object and the content of knowledge may form part of the external world. The act of knowledge is always a mental state; the content and object of knowledge need not be mental. They may, for instance, be material processes (swinging of the pendulum) or ideas (idea of harmony).

The objective side of knowledge cannot be realized in human consciousness except by means of the subjective side (i.e., an act of knowledge). These two sides are always present together and on this account it is difficult to separate them in thought in spite of the great difference between them. We imagine that they form an inseparable whole, and we tend to transfer the characteristics of the act of knowledge to the object and content or, in other words, to transfer the characteristics of the subjective side of knowledge to its objective side. This tendency, together with the erroneous view that there can be no empirical knowledge without causal interaction between subject and object, lies at the root of theories which affirm that knowledge consists exclusively of mental processes (Descartes, Leibniz, Locke, Berkeley, Hume, Kant), that the object of knowledge must be mental (Berkeley), and that the knowing subject can know only his own mental states (Hume's solipsism).

To transfer the characteristics of the subjective side of knowledge to its objective side is an error extremely dangerous to epistemology. In order to avoid it, it is necessary to consider various examples of it. I will point out, for instance, what results from transferring the spatial and temporal characteristics of the act to the content of knowledge.

The act of apprehension, i.e., the activity of attending and comparing, is not spatial in character. But the object on which attention is directed may well be extended. It would be absurd to say that the act of apprehending a mountain must itself be the size of a mountain. But it would be equally erroneous to assert that a mountain as the content of a presentation is unextended. The doctrine that our ideas of extended things are unextended caused the philosophers of the eighteenth century a great deal of trouble over the insoluble question as to how the unextended mental states of the knowing subject can give him knowledge of extended things. But this difficulty is the result of a misunderstanding. It is due to transferring the characteristics of the act of knowledge (attending and comparing) to the content and object of knowledge.

Still more dangerous are the errors that arise from transferring the temporal characteristics of the act of knowledge to the objective side of knowledge. An act of knowledge is an event taking place in time, at the moment of perceiving, judging, etc. Hence we are led to imagine that the object and content of knowledge must also be an event taking place at the moment of perception, and that things come into existence and disappear contemporaneously with the acts of perceiving. According to Hume we have no immediate experience which could prove that things exist when they are not perceived. To assert that they do so exist would be equivalent to saying that "the senses continue to operate even after they have ceased all manner of operation"[4], that the eye continues to see a thing when it sees it no longer. Hume maintains that the discontinuity of perception prevents us from having any experience of a continuous existence and that reason has no material for making inferences about such an existence.

Hume's argument is an example of transferring the characteristics of the subjective side of knowledge to its objective side. If the two sides are distinguished there will obviously be no foundation for denying that the object of my attention at the present moment may be an event which takes place at some other moment, in the past or in the future. An act of knowledge may last a second, but its object may be a process lasting a minute, an hour, a year, several centuries. We are continually making use of the power to contemplate that which at the given moment no longer exists—without it we could not, for instance, perceive movement. Without it not a single datum of memory

4. *Treatise*, Part IV, Section 2.

would be of value for knowledge. This last consideration is usually overlooked, but the validity of knowledge cannot be established without reference to the importance of memory.

The difference between the object and the act of knowledge may be greater still. The object may be altogether devoid of temporal character. It may belong to the sphere of being and not to that of becoming and stand outside the stream of change as something timeless. Nevertheless, the attention of the knowing subject may be concentrated upon it. There is no reason why eternal (timeless) being should not be an object of contemplation. The act of contemplation may last one second, but that which is contemplated may be eternal.

Intuitivism comes back to the doctrine of the contemplation of ideas which dates from Plato. If the temporal be called "real being" and the non-temporal "ideal being," it may be said that according to the Intuitive theory both may be objects of knowledge.

One case of confusion between the objective and subjective sides of knowledge should now be considered; it is of special importance to Logic. The subjective side of knowledge contains comparison, which results in identification and distinction, i.e., in analysis. To carry out this mental process we must have something with which the content of consciousness is compared and from which it is distinguished. A thinker who does not draw a distinction between the act and the object of knowledge will be convinced that the meaning of a judgment lies simply in discovering identity or contradiction between the compared contents. It will further appear to him that the whole of what has been compared must enter into the judgment, and that the subject and predicate are the two contents compared. Judgment will then consist in observing identity or contradiction between subject and predicate. According to one form of this doctrine, the subject of the judgment "this rose is red" is my perception of a red rose, and the predicate is added to the subject through partial identification of my idea of red color with my perception of "this red rose."

Logicians and epistemologists who take this view of judgment hold that inference is also based on the discovery of identity (or contradiction) between the premises and the conclusion or between parts of the premises. Now, this view implies the rationalistic doctrine that the connection between ground and consequent should be called logical only when it is analytically necessary. Some of the thinkers in question expressly uphold this doctrine, while most of them are even unaware of holding it. At the same time they tend to lay stress on the analytical laws of thought, viz., the laws of Identity, of Contradiction, and of the Excluded Middle. They either disregard the principle of Sufficient Reason or transform it simply into a complex of analytic laws, treating it as a law which declares that there is a sufficient reason only for the judgments that follow from their grounds with analytic necessity. But we have already seen that analytic necessity which is of value for knowledge is always based upon synthetic necessity. At the basis of analysis which gives us truth there always lies a synthesis which contains truth. An interpretation of judgment and inference which reduces them to an analytical formula, "wherever there is SP, there is P," has an artificial character. As a matter of fact, all judgments are synthetic and can be expressed by the formula "where there is S, there is P."

An act of knowledge is, then, contemplation accompanied by comparison, i.e., by analysis, but judgment is synthetic in character and is not confined to the discovery of identity and difference between subject and predicate. How is this possible? To understand it we must distinguish the subjective and the objective side of judgment. The first, i.e., the process of comparing, distinguishing, analyzing, is only a psychological scaffolding necessary in order that I might become aware of the differences and the connections between elements of the world. It enables me to separate the object that interests me out of its environment and to find out what its characteristics are—to learn, e.g., that P is necessarily present wherever the object S is found. That *from which* I distinguish the part of the world "S is P" does not form part of the judgment; it is merely a background against which the "S is P" that is of interest to me stands out in relief. Thus, in answering (to myself or to others) the question as to the color of "this rose" I distinguish this rose (S) by its color from other roses or from its surroundings, and say that it is red. By comparing this rose with other roses I discriminate a fresh quality in it, redness (P), and discover that the redness belongs to "this" rose and not to some other part of the reality before me; the relation between this rose and redness is singled out from all other relations before me. The judgment contains S, P, and their connection, but not the elements with which they were compared.

Judgment then is an analysis which brings out for contemplation the synthetic necessity of sequence between parts of reality. The relation between the subject and the predicate is not identity or contradiction but a synthetic necessity of sequence. In order to emphasize this fact it is advisable to express judgment by means of the formula "wherever there is S, there must be P." The relation expressed by this formula is found under many forms, for instance under the form of causal connection, of mathematical functional dependence (e.g., between the size of a side of the square and its surface), of the connection between a motive and an action, etc. The term "functional dependence" might be selected as a genus term for all the species of the relation which consists in a certain x being necessarily connected with y. Such a relation subsists between the subject and predicate of a judgment and between the premises and the conclusion of an inference. As an element in judgment and inference it may be called a logical relation or the relation of ground and consequent which has a synthetic and not an analytic character.[5]

To avoid misunderstanding it should be noted that from the point of view of Intuitivism there is no essential difference between the logical and the ontological functional relation. Suppose that between the real elements S and P there is a causal relation; insofar as it enters into a judgment it is a logical relation or the relation of ground and consequent. Generally speaking the word "logical" is applied by Intuitivism to the objective content of judgment insofar as it furnishes the ground for the general elementary methods of establishing the validity of judgment. But since the objective content of judgment is according

5. The view that the relation of subject and predicate is the relation of ground and consequent is worked out in a masterly way in Lipps, *Foundations of Logic*, Section 82.

to Intuitivism reality itself, ontology and logic come very near together. A fact (e.g., functional relation) considered apart from the mental activities of the knowing subject is ontologically real. The same fact insofar as it becomes the content of judgment forms its logical side.

At first sight it seems as if all judgments could not be expressed by the synthetic formula, and that the relation of subject and predicate was not always that of ground and consequent. Thus it may seem that in the case of judgments of identity the relation between the subject and predicate is that of identity. But as a matter of fact this is not the case. The meaning of the judgment "the magnitudes A and B are identical" is that, "given the magnitudes A and B, there is also given the relation of identity between them." In such judgments identity is the predicate and not the relation between the subject and the predicate. The symbolic language of mathematics strengthens our tendency to misinterpret judgments of identity. The formula $A = B$ makes us imagine that B is the predicate and that the equation sign expresses the logical relation between the subject and the predicate. In truth the subject of such judgments is "the relation, unknown to me until I discover the predicate, between the magnitudes A and B," and the predicate is "the relation of identity." The logical relation between the two is the synthetic necessity of dependence, i.e., the relation of ground and consequent.

It is important to note that judgments of perception stating some single fact ("this rose is red") contain the necessary connection of ground and consequent just as much as do the apodictic judgments of mathematics. To understand how this is possible and to see what the characteristic peculiarities of such judgments are, we must note the following circumstance: The relations of synthetic necessity of dependence form in the world an endless chain consisting of an innumerable number of links: S—M—N—P—R. . . . Even if we take two links that do not lie side by side, for instance S and R, the relation between them will still be the necessary relation of ground and consequent. But when we express this fact we do so blindly, submitting to a necessity we do not understand, for we are not aware of all the intermediate links. Judgments of perception (the object of which is real, not ideal being) generally have such a character. If after I have had a look at the garden I come back and say "the rose bush in the round bed is withered," this judgment will be no less necessary than the judgment, "the sum of the angles of this isosceles triangle equals two right angles." If the subjects of these two judgments are given to me I cannot but add to them their predicates—and this means that in both cases the subject contains the ground of the predicate. In each case the subject is an infinitely rich and complex part of reality, and is known, or differentiated in the consciousness of the knowing individual, only to a certain extent. The difference between the two judgments is solely in the elements of the subjects that have been discriminated. The only features discriminated in the subject of the first judgment are that it is "a rose bush" and that it grows "in the round bed." Let us take these two features and consider them in abstraction from all the richness and fullness of the living subject "this bush." It will at once be apparent that they contain nothing which compels us to add to them the predicate "is withered." The known aspects of the subject do not fully contain the ground of the predicate. This ground then is hidden in the uncognized depths of the subject. It must be hidden there, for otherwise we should not feel compelled to ascribe the predicate to "this bush." If we could trace the structure of all the tissues of this bush and all the physiological processes in them, the ground of the predicate would come into the light of knowledge.

The second judgment has a different character. In it the ground of the predicate is contained in the differentiated aspect of the subject. Indeed the subject is differentiated more than is necessary. The triangle need not be isosceles nor "this" triangle. If there is a surface and three straight lines on it that cross at any angle and enclose the surface, the sum of the angles must equal two right angles.

There are then two kinds of judgment. In some the predicate follows from the unknown aspects of the subject and only a vague awareness of the connection as a whole warrants the belief that the predicate really has its ground in the subject. If the discriminated aspect of the subject is abstracted from the rest and attention is confined to it alone, we shall clearly see that it does not compel us to add the predicate to it. This is true of most judgments of perception. In other judgments the predicate follows from the known aspect of the subject and therefore even if that aspect is considered in abstraction, the predicate is seen to follow from it of necessity. This is the case with the judgments of highly developed sciences—mathematics, for instance.

Minds inclined to attend chiefly to the known aspects of things look down upon judgments of perception and even distrust them. This is natural, since the known side of the subject in such judgments does not contain the ground of the predicate. On the other hand, a mind sensitive to living concrete reality in all its fullness—the mind of the artist, for instance—is more apt to see the necessity of judgments of perception than of abstract scientific statements. As a matter of fact, however, both kinds of judgment are equally necessary and the difference between them is simply in the degree in which the subject has been differentiated. But since the ideal of knowledge is that all aspects of reality should be known, it must be said that judgments of the first kind, though containing some truth, fall short of the ideal—they are undeveloped. In a fully developed true judgment the predicate should follow from the known aspects of the subject.

According to this view of the connection between subject and predicate, in a true judgment the subject contains a full, i.e., a sufficient, reason for the predicate. This statement is simply the law of sufficient reason understood as a synthetic logical law. This law governs the relation between the subject and predicate of judgment as well as the relation between judgments. If a judgment is deduced from other judgments there is a sufficient reason for it in their objective content.

The sign whereby we can discover the presence of a sufficient reason is that the predicate (or the conclusion) follows from the objective content of the subject (or of the premises) without any intervention on the part of the knowing mind. All that is left for the individual is passively to follow what the content of the subject compels him to admit. The whole content of such a judgment is in the true sense objective, that is to say, it springs from the nature of the object known. The criterion of truth, then, is the presence in knowledge of the reality we are striving to know.

It is undoubtedly present whenever the content of knowledge is "given" to me and not produced by an activity felt to be my subjective effort. It is present whenever the content develops independently of me and I merely follow it, concentrating my attention upon it, and differentiate it by means of comparison.

It follows that thought (i.e., contemplation accompanied by analysis and comparison) can lead to nothing but truth. It never results in error, for the content of the subject of judgment can never "require" anything that is not functionally dependent upon it. Error arises when the knowing subject, instead of following an objective synthesis, creates a synthesis of his own. In that case, however, we have to deal not with thinking, but with some other subjective activity—imagining and the like. The assertion does not deserve to be called a judgment, for its elements are connected by "my" subjective efforts, and not by the objective connection of ground and consequent. Error, then, is always a result of unconsciously substituting imagination or some other activity for thinking.

The above description of the structure of judgment easily explains the most important properties of truth—its universality (i.e., independence of the knowing subject), identity, and eternity. The objective contents of judgment are elements of reality itself, and not its copies or symbols. Hence, whenever different people (or the same person at different times) form a judgment about any object A (e.g., "Peter the Great died in 1725") the objective content of their judgment is identical, it is one and the same A. The subjective side of knowledge, i.e., the mental act of judging, may be very different and changeable, but the object of the knowledge is the same. The objective side of knowledge, i.e., the truth expressed in it, is therefore universal, identical, and eternal.

Book Nine

MARXISTS AND COMMUNISTS

THE FUNDAMENTALS of the Marxist outlook are too well known to need recounting here. On the other hand, the growth and development of Marxism in Russia are not always familiar. Both the thought and the works of Marx became known to Russian intellectuals remarkably early.[1] This is no doubt due in part to the fact that Marx lived in London at the same time as Herzen, and that Bakunin, although personally and intellectually in disagreement with Marx, could not avoid publicizing Marx's views, if only by attacking them.[2] The first volume of *Capital* was published in 1867. By 1870, Mikhailovsky, although generally opposed to Marx's outlook, was finding support in *Capital* for his own views on the dangers of the division of labor.[3] In 1871, N. Ziber (1844-1888), Professor of Economics at the University of Kiev, in his book, *Ricardo's Theory of Value and of Capital in Relation to Subsequent Elucidations and Enlargements*, wrote a detailed discussion of Marxist economic theory. In 1872, N. F. Danielson (1844-1918) completed G. A. Lopatin's (1845-1918) translation of the first volume of *Capital* into Russian—the first translation of *Capital* into any foreign language. The censor who read it let it pass on the assumption that it was much too dull to be politically dangerous!

Marx had a prejudice against Russians. But many Russians found Marx's philosophy enormously to their taste. They fol-

1. According to Thomas G. Masaryk, *The Spirit of Russia*, trans. E. and C. Paul, New York, 1955, II, 289, toward the end of the 1840's.

2. It was Bakunin who made the first Russian translation of the *Communist Manifesto* (1862).

3. See Masaryk, *op. cit.*, pp. 139, 145.

lowed Marx about and showered him with letters—to Marx's surprise and embarrassment. Their main concern was about being left out: did Marx's theory of history hold for Russia, i.e., must Russia go through the capitalist stage to reach communism or could that stage be skipped? It may be observed that Marx's reply was evasive, although he suggested that his theory of economic development was meant for Western Europe and did not necessarily hold for Russia.[4]

Although Marxism was known to intellectuals in the seventies and eighties and was popular with them, and although Marx corresponded with a number of them, no active Marxist faction existed in Russia until the last decade of the nineteenth century. By 1883, GEORGE PLEKHANOV (1856-1918), an exile in Switzerland, had spent three years studying Marx in theory and practice. The former leader of the temperate faction of the Populist Land and Liberty movement was, by the early 1880's, convinced that the ideals of Populism were not the solution for Russia. Marxism, on the other hand, seemed to offer the theory, the method, and the end he was looking for. Accordingly, in the year of Marx's death (1883), Plekhanov, together with his fellow exiles P. B. Axelrod (1850-1928) and V. Zasulich (1849-1919), founded the group for the Liberation of Labor. This was the first Russian Marxist party, later to become known as the Russian Social Democratic Workers' party. Through it, Plekhanov spread Marxism among Russian exiles and eventually in Russia. By the mid-1890's, there were Marxist groups in every major Russian city. A labor movement was well enough organized to lead a serious strike of textile workers in Saint Petersburg in 1896. Marxist pamphlets, particularly concerned to correct the misguided views of the Populists, were published abroad and handed about at home. Marxist newspapers, the *Novoye Slovo* (New Word) and *Nachalo* (The Beginning), were also published abroad. In 1901, the political journal *Iskra* (The Spark) made its appearance. Marxism in Russia was enjoying its first youthful awakening.

In 1903, the Second Congress of the Russian Social Democratic Workers' party met in Brussels and then London. (The First

4. Letter to Vera Zasulich, March 8, 1881, and "Preface" to her translation of the *Communist Manifesto*, printed in Geneva in 1882.

Congress in Minsk in 1898, which formally established the party, was hardly a success: although a manifesto was written, a central committee appointed, and a declaration made to the effect that the party was the party of the proletariat, every delegate to it was arrested within hours of the adjournment.) At the Second Congress, the party was split into two major factions, those who argued in terms of slow development and a loosely knit, large membership, and those who favored immediate revolution to be effected by a small, highly disciplined group. The second faction, the group of VLADIMIR LENIN (1870-1924), won the majority of the votes,[5] and with it, the party newspaper, *Iskra*.

Thus the Russian Social Democratic Workers' party divided in two: the theories behind the divisions implied two interpretations of Marxism. But variety in interpretation was not a new event even in Russia. Marx is open to varied interpretation; Marx himself offers several interpretations of Marxism. In addition, there was revisionism, that is, the "improving" of Marx where he was found deficient. Such a method was suggested by the German Eduard Bernstein, and Russians were not slow in taking up the suggestion, even before the turn of the century: wherever Marx's world view did not seem complete enough in itself, it was supplemented by that of another philosopher. Thus, ALEXANDER BOGDANOV (Malinovsky) (1873-1928), who questioned Marx's theory of knowledge, supplemented it with the views of Ernst Mach. Berdyaev, who sought an objective moral standard, supplemented the relativistic ethics of Marxism with Kant. Even the "orthodox" Plekhanov supplemented Marx's determinism with Spinoza's interpretation of freedom. Further, in attempting to defend Marxism against revision, Marxists frequently found themselves revising in the opposite direction: to refute Bogdanov, Plekhanov suggested an epistemology which is clearly based on Kant. The main revisions may be classified as follows: [6]

    1. Kantian in ethics and epistemology;

5. And hence acquired the name, *Bolshevik* (the majority party).
6. This classification is that of George L. Kline, suggested in his article, "Philosophic Revisions of Marxism," *Proceedings of the Thirteenth International Congress of Philosophy*, Mexico City, 1965.

2. Nietzschean in ethics and positivist (Machian or "empiriocritical") in epistemology;
3. "Spinozist" in ethics and "quasi-Kantian" in epistemology (Plekhanov's theory of hieroglyphics).

With time, extreme revisionists, such as Berdyaev and Serge Bulgakov, disassociated themselves from the Marxist world view. Others overlooked their disagreements for the sake of the common cause. Philosophical revisionism, after the beginning of World War I, did not become an issue again until the regime set up by the Bolshevik Revolution had become relatively stabilized. Then, in the late 1920's, when the official political viewpoint found itself fighting "a war on two fronts" against rightist and leftist Bolshevik deviations, the philosophical controversy was revived. Following the principle of the union of theory and practice, the government argued that each political deviation was linked with a deviation in philosophy. The right wing was represented in philosophy by Mechanism, the left by Deborinism, or "Menshevizing Idealism."

Mechanism, taking its cue from passages in Engels' *Anti-Dühring*, asserted that philosophy had no field of its own, that it consisted merely "in the latest and most general findings of modern science." [7] Science *is* philosophy; there is no ground for saying that dialectic is present in reality. The earliest proponent of this positivistic view was O. Minin. It was elaborated—and altered—by Nicholas Ivanovich Bukharin (1888-1937).

In developing his position, Bukharin was strongly influenced by the Empiriomonism of Bogdanov. According to Bukharin, the origin of motion lies, indeed, in the union and struggle of opposites, but Bukharin sees this struggle and union as external rather than internal: although he admits a "dialectic," it is not *in* things, but *among* them. Motion is thus in fact conceived mechanically, and not really dialectically, and every process is seen as consisting of an equilibrium and its disturbance. Although Bukharin uses the vocabulary of dialectical materialism, from what he says reality consists not of self-moving matter, but of matter on the

7. I. I. Stepanov, *Historical Materialism and Modern Natural Science*, 1927, p. 57, quoted in Gustav A. Wetter, *Dialectical Materialism: A Historical and Systematic Survey of Philosophy in the Soviet Union*, trans. from the 4th German edition by Peter Heath, London and New York, 1958, p. 138.

one hand and of motion on the other. With Bukharin, materialism is in fact no longer dialectical at all.

The most famous exponent of "Menshevizing Idealism," the
philosophy associated with the leftist deviation and which gave
very high importance to the dialectic, was Abram Moiseyevich
Deborin (real name, Yoffe) (1881-1964). Deborin concentrated on
Engels' *Dialectics of Nature* rather than on the *Anti-Dühring*.
In this later work (first published in 1925) Engels' earlier positivist suggestions are no longer apparent; rather, the author
argues that the sciences cannot do without philosophy.[8] Accordingly, Deborin says that "dialectical materialism exists as an independent discipline alongside the other positive sciences, more
especially as the *methodology and theory of scientific knowledge.*"[9] The publication of Lenin's *Philosophical Notebooks* in
1929 gave further support to Deborin and his group, for in the
Notebooks dialectic is Lenin's main concern. According to
Deborin, dialectic is the method of the sciences, and is so because
it lies in the very nature of things. Change is an instance of the
Law of the Transformation of Quantity into Quality and thus
has its force inside the things themselves and consists both of
gradual development and of leaps.

The Mechanists as well as the official philosophers objected
to Deborin's views, arguing that he was employing the dialectic
in an abstract and a priori fashion, that his interpretation of it
was Hegelian and idealist rather than Marxist and concrete. This
point of view led the Deborinists, it was said, to ignore the social
roots of philosophical systems and thus, in general, to divorce
theory from practice. That Deborin and his followers had a
high regard for Plekhanov did not add at this time to their
acceptability.

Both the right and left revisions of the first decade of the
Bolshevik regime were finally silenced in 1931 when the Central
Committee of the Bolshevik party condemned both and called
for new philosophical leadership: "In the field of philosophy the
journal *Pod Znamenem Marksizma* (Under the Banner of Marxism) must wage a relentless struggle on two fronts: against the

8. *Dialectics of Nature*, Moscow-London, 1953-1954, p. 279.
9. *Dialectics and Natural Science*, Moscow-Leningrad, 1930, p. 11, quoted
in Wetter, *op. cit.*, pp. 160-161.

Mechanist revision of Marxism, as the chief danger at the present time, and also against the idealist distortion of Marxism on the part of comrades Deborin, Karev, Sten, and others." [10]

The new leadership was the view presented by M. B. Mitin (b. 1901),[11] V. V. Adoratsky (1878-1945), P. F. Yudin (b. 1899), et al. In fact, this "middle" path was much closer to Deborinism than to Mechanism, and differs from the former primarily in its attempts to unite theory to practice and to inject more partisanship into the theory. Thus, its authorities included not only the classics—Marx, Engels, and Lenin—but also Stalin. Once established, this philosophy suffered little change and encountered no important revisions until 1950. The official view is expressed in the *History of the Communist Party of the Soviet Union (Bolshevik) Short Course*, published in 1938 and generally attributed to Stalin. The significant change from earlier Marxism to be found in the *Short Course* is the omission of the Law of the Negation of Negation, according to which each transformation of quantity into quality necessitates the negation of the previous quality but also implies a new process of development which will culminate in a further negation, that of the new quality. In each negation, the significant element of the old quality is retained but "transcended" into a higher synthesis. This process had, it would seem, reached its last stage in the Stalin regime and no further negation of that regime was to be expected. The Law of the Negation of Negation reappeared in expositions of dialectical materialism shortly after the death of Stalin.

In 1950, however, Stalin himself opened the door to a new possibility of revision in his *Letters on Linguistics*.[12] In these

10. *Pravda,* January 26, 1931.

11. Now an Academician and the editor-in-chief of *Voprosy Filosofii* (Problems of Philosophy), the major official Soviet philosophical journal.

12. Collected under the title *Comrade Stalin's Articles on the Problems of Linguistics and the Tasks in the Fields of History and Philosophical Science, Bulletin* of the Academy of Sciences of the U.S.S.R., History and Philosophy Series, VII, 4. The English translation is available under the titles *The Soviet Linguistic Controversy*, trans. John V. Murra, Robert M. Hankin, and Fred Holling, New York, 1951, and Joseph Stalin, *Marxism and Linguistics*, New York, 1951.

letters Stalin's thesis was that language as a social phenomenon is a part neither of superstructure nor of base. This implies a class of social phenomena which does not fall under the authority of the dialectic and which, therefore, is free from the requirement of partisanship. The letters also argue for *gradual* development from quantity to quality, "gradual leaps," rather than violent ones. This notion is useful in explaining the "peaceful" transition from socialism to communism.

It is difficult to generalize and assess the developments in Marxist philosophy since the death of Stalin in 1953. The present official view (1960) is expressed in the final selection in this volume. As has been noted, the Law of the Negation of Negation has been reinstituted. The "declassification" of linguistics has led to further declassification and the possibility of non-partisan discussion in such fields as formal logic and relativity theory in physics.[13] Indeed, it has led to original and valuable work in mathematical logic, information theory, and mathematical linguistics. Thus, the door opened for officially permitted revisions was used and revisionism as a deviation was avoided. Although there was a wave of philosophical revisionism in the late fifties—encouraged by the short-lived "thaw"—most of this had time to develop only in Eastern European countries such as Poland and Yugoslavia, and not in the U.S.S.R. itself. As for the mutual accusations of revisionism being made by China and Russia today, they are, from the philosophical point of view, easily countered by charges of dogmatism on the one hand and by arguments based on the "creative development of Marxism" on the other. The revisions of Marxism can be said to have been started by Marx. Almost a century after his death, the issue cannot be one of faithful adherence to the teachings of the Philosopher, but rather one of what views are acceptable to official Marxism-Leninism.

13. See Joseph M. Bochenski, "Three Components of Communist Ideology," *Studies in Soviet Thought*, Vol. II, No. 1 (March 1962), pp. 7-11, and George L. Kline, "Philosophy, Ideology, and Policy in the Soviet Union," *The Review of Politics*, Vol. 26, No. 2 (April 1964), pp. 174-190.

GEORGE VALENTINOVICH PLEKHANOV

[1856–1918]

"IT IS *impossible*," Lenin wrote in 1921, "to become an intelligent, *real* communist without studying . . . all that Plekhanov wrote on philosophy, because that is the best there is in the whole international literature on Marxism." [1] Whatever Lenin's reasons for making this statement, there is no question but that it embarrassed his followers for close to four decades. George Plekhanov was a Marxist; he is often called "the philosopher of Marxism," but he was not in agreement with Lenin, nor can he be fully classified in any one category of the revisionists of Marxism. Although it is an exaggeration to call him without qualification an independent thinker, within the framework of Marxist philosophy he can justly be so described.

Plekhanov was born in 1856 in Tambov province, the son of a conservative member of the landed gentry, of Tatar origin, whose financial situation declined steadily after the Emancipation of the Serfs. His mother, a distant relative of Belinsky, taught school in order to support her twelve children and stepchildren after her husband's death. George Plekhanov was graduated from the Voronezh Military Academy and entered the Institute of Mines in Saint Petersburg. During the two years that he attended the Institute (1874-1876) he became seriously involved in the revolutionary activities of the Populist movement. In 1876 he aided in the organization of the Land and Liberty movement and achieved prominence as the speaker at a demonstration in front of Kazan Cathedral—a meeting protesting the government's

1. *Once More the Trade Unions.*

arrest of many revolutionaries months before and its delay in bringing them to trial. Plekhanov escaped to Europe where he took the opportunity to observe revolutionary groups in the West. He returned with "borrowed' papers in 1877. In 1879, the Land and Liberty group dissolved—a major dispute concerned terrorism and the desirability of assassinating Alexander II. Land and Liberty was reorganized into two groups, the terroristic People's Will (*Narodnaya Volya*) and the more moderate, agrarian, Black Repartition (*Chyorny Peredel*). Plekhanov assumed leadership of the latter, but police raids confiscated the faction's printing press and arrested almost all its members within a matter of months. Plekhanov was able to escape to Europe in 1880.

Settling in Geneva, he took time to consider the situation and to study the works of Marx and Engels. Populism—at least as Plekhanov saw it—was doomed. On the other hand, the Populism which Plekhanov adopted had always been at least partially Marxist in form—insofar as it came from Bakunin, and Bakunin himself held a dialectical and materialist view of history. Moreover, life in the West made it evident to Plekhanov that agrarian socialism would not fit even Russia in the near future. Thus, it is not really surprising that in 1883 Plekhanov founded the first Russian Marxist (émigré) group, the group for the Liberation of Labor. It is primarily because of this that Plekhanov can be called the founder of Russian Marxism.

From then on Plekhanov's work, published under his own name or the pseudonym "Beltov," was that of a crusader: to convert socialists to his view and to attack the die-hard remnant of the Populists as well as the revisionists of Marxism who were cropping up both in Russia and in the West. It is this crusading and militant spirit, as well as Plekhanov's own independence of thought and creative ability, which led him to views that do not accord with official Soviet Marxist-Leninist philosophy. His writings during the 1890's are, in general, accepted, although the heresies he has been accused of can easily be found in them. However, shortly after the famous 1903 Congress of the Social Democratic party—at which he sided with

Lenin, with whom he had been closely associated, especially as co-editor of *Iskra*—Plekhanov found that he could not wholly agree with the political views of the leader of the Bolshevik faction. He did not think Russia was ready for revolution, he continued to oppose terrorism, he advocated parliamentary methods and attacked Lenin's Machiavellian tactics. He disagreed with Lenin on the revolutionary role of the peasant. During World War I, he favored the Allied cause and denounced Germany's violation of the neutrality of Belgium. In 1917, after thirty-seven years of exile, he returned to Russia and supported the Provisional Government. He did not approve the October Revolution, considering it premature, but he felt partly responsible for it: "Did we not begin the propaganda of Marxism too early in backward, semi-Asiatic Russia?" [2]

Plekhanov died in Finland in 1918. Although he had opposed many of the now dominant views, his role as the theoretician of Marxism and the respect he commanded were too great for the sons to turn against the father of the Revolution. He was buried in Petrograd, beside Belinsky, the kinsman he had always admired.

Plekhanov's political views have a philosophical grounding in his interpretation of Marxism. Unlike Lenin, who accepted Marx's "scientific socialism" but who also accepted the Utopian side of Marx and the methods of the People's Will, Plekhanov clung to Marx's historical determinism, the philosophy underlying Marx's mature work. With this in mind, it was only reasonable for Plekhanov to oppose attempts to hurry history or to interfere in its course. This has led to the accusation from official Marxist-Leninists that his approach was, especially in later years, mechanistic rather than dialectical. He has been said to interpret Marxism as an expansion of Darwinism and to overemphasize the geographical factor in history. There is basis for these criticisms in *Fundamental Problems of Marxism* (1908), but also in *The Development of the Monist View of History* (1895), two selections below.

In attacking revisions of Marxism, Plekhanov was particularly

2. Quoted in Samuel H. Baron, *Plekhanov, the Father of Russian Marxism,* Stanford, 1963, p. 358.

anxious to oppose the Empiriomonism of Bogdanov—a view which denies any distinction between appearance and reality and reduces everything, "material" or "mental," to experience. To combat this, Plekhanov developed the "theory of hieroglyphics"— the idea is different from the object of which it is the idea, but corresponds to it, as the shadow of a cube cast on a cylinder is different in shape from the shape of the cube but corresponds to it. Thus the distinction between appearance and reality is maintained, error is possible, the independent, objective existence of the world remains, yet the idealism of Kant's theory of the unknown thing-in-itself is avoided. The theory of hieroglyphics was developed as early as 1892, in Plekhanov's "Notes" to his translation of Engels' book on *Feuerbach*. He revised his wording but maintained the theory in the edition of 1905 and in the essays entitled *Materialism or Kantianism* found below. Lenin, equally opposed to Bogdanov, took exception to Plekhanov's view, considering it a form of idealism according to which knowledge is in fact limited to appearance and is never of reality as such. Plekhanov's theory is, accordingly, a deviation from the "naive realism" of Lenin.

Other official objections to Plekhanov have included lack of concern with modern discoveries in physics and their implications for materialism, dealing with idealism too abstractly rather than seeking its roots in the bourgeois background of the philosophers who favor it,[3] and overemphasizing the influence of Feuerbach on Marx to the detriment of Marx's originality.

On the other hand, Soviet critics have been at pains to praise Plekhanov's discussions of the role of the individual in history (in the essay by that name) and his treatment of the relation of freedom and necessity which he discusses both in the essay on *The Role of the Individual in History* and in *The Development of the Monist View of History*. So far as the former is concerned, Plekhanov, arguing against the Populists, holds that historical change results from objective factors—geography and the state of the forces of production—and that, although there are great men in history, these men are great not because their personal qualities shape historical events, but because these quali-

3. But see below, "Notes to Engels' *Ludwig Feuerbach*," pp. 380-381.

ties make them the most capable of serving the social needs of
a particular time. Outstanding historical figures are thus the product of their historical environment; no one is indispensable.[4]

In reply to Populist criticisms that Marxist determinism
destroys freedom and therefore moral responsibility, Plekhanov
turns to Spinoza and Hegel and argues that freedom in fact
exists: it is the recognition of necessity.

> When my consciousness of the unfreedom of my will
> appears to me in the form of the complete subjective and
> objective impossibility of acting differently from the way I
> am acting, and when, at the same time, my actions are to
> me the most desirable of all possible actions, then, in my
> consciousness, necessity is identified with freedom and free-
> dom with necessity.[5]

The origin of Plekhanov's later Kantian leanings in ethics
may, like his semi-Kantian epistemology, lie here. The recognition of the necessity of an action and of its being the most
desirable can, with proper interpretation, become the recognition of the moral law and the willing of it for its own sake.
Plekhanov, like Mill, suggests that through education "those acts
which are useful to society [can be made] an instinctive requirement." [6] Thus, for the new social man that Marxist communism
promises, freedom and necessity can be one.

The current Soviet attitude toward Plekhanov is far more
favorable than it was for many years. The *Filosofsky Slovar*
(Philosophical Dictionary), published in 1963, although it points
out some of the old "errors," such as Plekhanov's "concession to
the theory of hieroglyphics," and a new one of underrating the
role of the subjective factor in historical development, concludes:

> In the total system of the philosophical views of Plekhanov,
> who all his life fought for dialectical and historical material-
> ism, his particular errors seem like an alien element. The
> richness and cogency of Plekhanov's philosophical works,

4. *The Role of the Individual in History.* See below, p. 368.
5. *Ibid.,* p. 16.
6. *Sochineniya,* Moscow, 1924, V, 219.

and the popularity and attractiveness of their exposition make them even today valuable aids to the study of Marxist philosophy.

SELECTED BIBLIOGRAPHY

Works:

George V. Plekhanov, *Selected Philosophical Works in Five Volumes,* trans. R. Dixon, A. Fineberg, and A. Rothstein, Moscow, Vol. I, 1961.

—————, *Essays in Historical Materialism,* New York, 1940.

—————, *Essays in the History of Materialism,* trans. Ralph Fox, New York, 1967.

—————, *The Development of the Monist View of History* [also included in the *Selected Philosophical Works,* Vol. I], trans. A. Rothstein, Moscow, 1956.

—————, *Fundamental Problems of Marxism,* trans. E. and C. Paul, New York, 1928.

Secondary Sources:

S. H. Baron, *Plekhanov, the Father of Russian Marxism,* Stanford, 1963.

Gustav A. Wetter, *Dialectical Materialism,* trans. Peter Heath, London and New York, 1958, pp. 100-109.

[GEORGE PLEKHANOV]

The Development of the Monist View of History*

What is "materialism in the general philosophical sense"?

Materialism is the direct opposite of *idealism*. Idealism strives to explain all the phenomena of nature, all the qualities of matter, by these or those qualities of the *spirit*. Materialism acts in the exactly opposite way. It tries to explain psychic phenomena by these or those qualities of *matter*, by this or that organization of the human, or, in more general terms, of the animal *body*. All those philosophers in the eyes of whom the prime factor is *matter* belong to the camp of the *materialists;* and all those who consider such a factor to be the *spirit* are *idealists*. . . .

Materialism and idealism exhaust the most important tendencies of philosophical thought. True, by their side there have almost always existed *dualist* systems of one kind or another, which recognize *spirit* and *matter* as separate and independent *substances*. *Dualism* was never able to reply satisfactorily to the inevitable question: how could these two separate substances, which have nothing in common between them, influence each other? Therefore the most consistent and most profound thinkers were always inclined to *monism*, i.e., to explaining phenomena with the help of *some one main principle*. . . . Every consistent *idealist* is a monist to the same extent as every consistent *materialist*. In *this* respect there is no difference, for example, between Berkeley and Holbach. One was a consistent *idealist*, the other a no less consistent *materialist*, but both were equally *monistic;* both one and the other equally well understood the worthlessness of the *dualist outlook on the world*, which up to this day is still, perhaps, the most widespread. . . .

Hegel called *metaphysical* the point of view of those thinkers

* From *The Development of the Monist View of History*, trans. Andrew Rothstein, Moscow, 1956, pp. 13-14, 92-100, 108-109, 271-275, slightly revised. With one exception, footnotes have been omitted.

—irrespective of whether they were idealists or materialists—who, failing to understand the process of development of phenomena, willy-nilly represent them to themselves and others as petrified, disconnected, incapable of passing one into another. To this point of view he opposed *dialectics*, which studies phenomena precisely in their development and, consequently, in their interconnection.

According to Hegel, dialectics is *the principle of all life*. Frequently one meets people who, having expressed some abstract proposition, willingly recognize that perhaps they are mistaken, and that perhaps the exactly opposite point of view is correct. These are well-bred people, saturated to their finger tips with *"tolerance"*: live and let live, they say to their intellect. Dialectics has nothing in common with the skeptical tolerance of men of the world, but it too knows how to reconcile directly opposite abstract propositions. Man is mortal, we say, regarding death as something rooted in external circumstances and quite alien to the nature of living man. It follows that a man has two qualities: first of being alive, and secondly of also being mortal. But upon closer investigation it turns out that *life* itself bears in itself the germ of *death*, and that in general any phenomenon is *contradictory*, in the sense that it develops out of itself the elements which, sooner or later, will put an end to its existence and will transform it into its own opposite. Everything flows, everything changes; and there is no force capable of holding back this constant flux, or arresting this eternal movement. There is no force capable of resisting the dialectics of phenomena. . . .

Every phenomenon, by the action of those same forces which condition its existence, sooner or later, but inevitably, is transformed into its own opposite.

We have said that the idealist German philosophy regarded all phenomena from the point of view of their evolution, and that this is what is meant by regarding them *dialectically*. It must be remarked that the *metaphysicians* know how to distort the very doctrine of evolution itself. They affirm that neither in nature nor in history are there any leaps. When they speak of the *origin* of some phenomenon or social institution, they represent matters as though this phenomenon or institution was once upon a time very tiny, quite unnoticeable, and then gradually grew up. When it is a question of *destroying* this or that phenomenon and institution, they presuppose, on the contrary, its gradual diminution, continuing up to the point when the phenomenon becomes quite unnoticeable on account of its microscopic dimensions. Evolution conceived of in this way explains absolutely nothing; it presupposes the existence of the phenomena which it has to explain, and reckons only with the *quantitative changes* which take place in them. The supremacy of metaphysical thought was once so powerful in natural science that many naturalists could not imagine evolution otherwise than just in the form of such a gradual increase or diminution of the magnitude of the phenomenon being investigated. Although from the time of Harvey it was already recognized that *"everything living develops out of the egg,"* no exact conception was linked, evidently, with such development from the egg, and the discovery of spermatozoa immediately served as the occasion for the appearance of a theory according to which in the seminal cell there already existed a ready-made, completely developed but microscopic little animal, so that all its *"development"* amounted to *growth*. Some wise sages, including many famous European evolutionary sociologists, still regard the "evolution," say, of political institutions, precisely in this way: history makes no leaps: *va piano* [go softly]. . . .

German idealist philosophy decisively revolted against such a misshapen conception of evolution. Hegel bitingly ridiculed it and demonstrated irrefutably that both in nature and in human society *leaps* constituted just as essential a stage of evolution as gradual quantitative changes. "Changes in being," he says, "consist not only in the fact that one quantity passes into another quantity, but also that quality passes into quantity, and vice versa. Each transition of the latter kind represents an *interruption in gradualness (ein Abbrechen des Allmählichen)*, and gives the phenomenon a new aspect, qualitatively distinct from the previous one. Thus, water when it is cooled grows hard, not gradually . . . but all at once.". . .

Now we have learned the principal distinguishing features of dialectical thought, but the reader feels himself unsatisfied. But where is the famous triad, he asks, the triad which is, as is well known, the whole essence of Hegelian dialectics? Your pardon, reader, we do not mention the triad for the simple reason that it *does not at all play in Hegel's work the part which is attributed to it* by people who have not the least idea of the philosophy of that thinker, and who have studied it, for example, from the "*textbook of criminal law*" of Mr. Spasovich. Filled with sacred simplicity, these lighthearted people are convinced that the whole argumentation of the German idealists was reduced to references to the triad; that whatever theoretical difficulties the old man came up against, he left others to rack their poor "unenlightened" brains over them while he, with a tranquil smile, immediately built up a syllogism: all phenomena occur according to a triad, I am faced with a phenomenon, consequently I shall turn to the triad. This is simply *lunatic nonsense*, as one of the characters of Karonin puts it, or *unnaturally idle talk*, if you prefer the expression of Shchedrin. Not once in the eighteen volumes of Hegel's works does the "*triad*" play the part of an *argument*, and anyone in the least familiar with his philosophical doctrine understands that it *could not play such a part*. With Hegel the triad has the same significance as it had previously with Fichte, whose philosophy is essentially different from the Hegelian. Obviously, only gross ignorance can consider the principal distinguishing feature of one philosophical system to be that which applies to *at least* two quite different systems. . . .

When you apply the dialectical method to the study of phenomena, you need to remember that *forms change eternally in consequence of the "higher development of their content."* You will have to trace this process of rejection of forms in all its fullness, if you wish to exhaust the subject. But whether the new form is the opposite of the old you will find from experience, and it is not at all important to know this beforehand. True, it is just on the basis of the historical experience of mankind that every lawyer knowing his business will tell you that every legal institution sooner or later is transformed into its own opposite. Today it promotes the satisfaction of certain social needs; today it is valuable and necessary precisely in view of these needs. Then it begins to satisfy those needs worse and

worse. Finally it is transformed into an *obstacle* to their satisfaction. From something *necessary* it becomes something *harmful*—and then it is destroyed. Take whatever you like—the history of literature or the history of species—wherever there is
development, you will see similar dialectics. But nevertheless, if
someone wanted to penetrate the essence of the dialectical process
and were to begin, of all things, with testing the idea of the
oppositeness of the phenomena which constitute a series in each
particular process of development, he would be approaching the
problem from the wrong end.

In selecting the viewpoint for such a test, there would always
turn out to be very much that was *arbitrary*. The question must
be regarded from its objective side, or, in other words, one must
make clear to oneself what is the inevitable change of forms
involved in the development of the particular content? This is
the same idea, only expressed in other words. But in testing it
in practice there is no place for arbitrary choice, because the
point of view of the investigator is determined by *the very
character of the forms and content themselves*. . . .

Let us compare with this indistinct muttering of the tomtit [1]
the courageous, astonishingly coherent, historical philosophy
of Marx.

Our anthropoid ancestors, like all other animals, were in complete subjection to *nature*. All their development was that completely unconscious development which was conditioned by
adaptation to their environment, by means of natural selection
in the struggle for existence. This was the dark kingdom of
physical necessity. At that time even the *dawn of consciousness*,
and therefore of *freedom*, was not breaking. But physical necessity brought man to a stage of development at which he began,
little by little, to separate himself from the remaining animal
world. He became a *tool-making animal*. The tool is an organ
with the help of which man acts on nature to achieve his ends.
It is an organ which subjects *necessity* to the human *consciousness*, although at first only to a very weak degree, by fits and
starts, if one can put it that way. *The degree of development*

1. Mikhailovsky—ED.

of the productive forces determines the measure of man's power over nature.

The development of the productive forces is itself determined by the qualities of the geographical environment surrounding man. In this way nature itself gives man the means for its own subjection.

But man is not struggling with nature individually: the struggle with her is carried on, in the expression of Marx, by social man (*der Gesellschaftsmensch*), i.e., a more or less considerable social union. The characteristics of *social* man are determined at every given time by the degree of development of the productive forces, because on the degree of the development of those forces depends the entire structure of the social union. Thus, this structure is determined in the long run by the characteristics of the geographical environment, which affords men a greater or lesser possibility of developing their productive forces. But once definite social relations have arisen, their further development takes place according to *its own inner laws*, the operation of which accelerates or retards the development of the productive forces which conditions the historical progress of man. The dependence of man on his geographical environment is transformed from *direct* to *indirect*. The *geographical* environment influences man through the *social* environment. But *thanks to this*, the relationship of man with his geographical environment becomes extremely changeable. At every new stage of development of the productive forces it proves to be different from what it was before. The geographical environment influenced the Britons of Caesar's time quite otherwise than it influences the present inhabitants of Great Britain. That is how modern *dialectical materialism* resolves the contradictions with which the writers of the Enlightenment of the eighteenth century could not cope.

The development of the social environment is subjected to its own laws. This means that its characteristics depend just as little on the will and consciousness of men as the characteristics of the geographical environment. The productive action of man on nature gives rise to a new form of dependence of man, a new variety of his slavery: *economic necessity*. And the greater grows man's dominion over nature, the more his productive forces develop, the more stable becomes this new slavery: *with the development of the productive forces the mutual relations of men in the social process of production become more complex;* the course of that process completely slips from under their control, *the producer proves to be the slave of his own creation* (as an example, the capitalist anarchy of production).

But just as the nature surrounding man itself gave him the first opportunity to develop his productive forces and, consequently, gradually to emancipate himself from nature's yoke— so the relations of production, social relations, by the very logic of their development bring man to realization of the causes of his enslavement by *economic* necessity. This provides the opportunity for a new and final triumph of *consciousness* over *necessity*, of *reason* over blind *law*.

Having realized that the cause of his enslavement by his own creation lies in the anarchy of production, the producer ("social man") organizes that production and thereby subjects it to his will. Then terminates the kingdom of *necessity*, and there begins the reign of *freedom*, which itself proves to be *necessity*. The prologue of human history has been played out, history begins.[2]

---

2. After all that has been said it will be clear, we hope, what is the relation between the teaching of Marx and the teaching of Darwin. Darwin succeeded in solving the problem of how there originate plant and animal species in the struggle for existence. Marx succeeded in solving the problem of how there arise different types of social organization in the struggle of men for their existence. Logically, the investigation of Marx begins precisely where the investigation of Darwin ends. Animals and plants are under the influence of their *physical* environment. The physical environment acts on social man through those social relations which arise on the basis of the productive forces, which at first develop more or less quickly according to the characteristics of the physical environment. Darwin explains the origin of species not by an allegedly *innate* tendency to develop in the animal organism, as Lamarck did, but by the adaptation of the organism to the conditions existing outside it: not by the *nature of the organism* but by the influence of *external nature*. Marx explains the historical development of man not by the *nature of man*, but by the characteristics of those social *relations* between men which arise when social man is acting on *external nature*. The spirit of their research is absolutely the same in

Thus dialectical materialism not only does not strive, as its opponents attribute to it, to convince man that it is absurd to revolt against economic necessity, but it is the first to point out *how to overcome* the latter. Thus is eliminated the *inevitably fatalist* character inherent in *metaphysical materialism*. And in exactly the same way is eliminated every foundation for that pessimism to which, as we saw, consistent *idealist* thinking leads of necessity. The individual personality is only foam on the crest of the wave, men are subjected to an iron law which can only be discovered, but which cannot be subjected to the human will, said Georg Büchner. No, replies Marx: once we have *discovered* that iron law, it depends on us to overthrow its yoke, it depends on us to make *necessity* the obedient slave of *reason*.

I am a worm, says the idealist. I am a worm while I am ignorant, retorts the dialectical materialist: but I am a god when I *know*. *Tantum possumus, quantum scimus* [we can do as much as we know]!

---

both thinkers. That is why one can say that Marxism is Darwinism in its application to social science (we know that *chronologically* this is not so, but that is unimportant). And that is its only *scientific* application; because the conclusions which were drawn from Darwinism by some bourgeois writers were not its scientific application to the study of the development of social man, but a mere bourgeois Utopia, a moral sermon with a very ugly content, just as subjectivists engage in sermons with a beautiful content. The bourgeois writers, when referring to Darwin, were in reality recommending to their readers *not the scientific method of Darwin, but only the bestial instincts* of those animals about whom Darwin wrote. Marx resembles *Darwin*: the bourgeois writers resemble *the beasts and cattle which Darwin studied*.

For the Sixtieth Anniversary of Hegel's Death *

Modern dialectical materialism has made clear to itself incomparably better than idealism the truth that people make history unconsciously: from its standpoint the course of history is determined in the final account not by man's will, but by the development of the material productive forces. Materialism also knows *when* the "owl of Minerva" starts its flight, but it sees nothing mysterious in the flight of this bird, any more than in anything else. It has succeeded in applying to history the relation between freedom and necessity discovered by idealism. People made and had to make their history *unconsciously* as long as the motive forces of historical development worked behind their backs, independently of their consciousness. Once those forces have been discovered, once the laws by which they work have been studied, people will be able to take them in their own hands and submit them to their own reason. The service rendered by Marx consists in having discovered those laws and made a rigorous scientific study of their working. Modern dialectical materialism, which, in the opinion of Philistines, must turn man into an automaton, in actual fact opens for the first time in history the road to the kingdom of freedom and conscious activity. But it is possible to enter that kingdom only by means of a radical change in the present social activity. The Philistines realize or at least have a foreboding of this. That is why the materialist explanation of history causes them such vexation and grief; and for that reason too not a single Philistine is able or willing to understand or grasp Marx's theory in all its fullness. Hegel saw the proletariat as a *mob*. For Marx and the Marxists

* From "For the Sixtieth Anniversary of Hegel's Death," trans. R. Dixon, *Selected Philosophical Works in Five Volumes*, Moscow, 1961-, I, 478-479. The original text is in German.

the proletariat is a majestic force, the bearer of the future. Only the proletariat is capable of mastering the teaching of Marx (we are not speaking of exceptions), and we see how it is in fact becoming more and more permeated with its content.

[GEORGE PLEKHANOV]

On the Role of the Individual in History *

Owing to the specific qualities of their minds and characters, influential individuals can change the *individual features of events and some of their particular consequences*, but they cannot change their general *trend*, which is determined by other forces. . . .

Furthermore, we must also note the following: In discussing the role great men play in history, we nearly always fall victims to a sort of optical illusion, to which it will be useful to draw the reader's attention. . . .

When a given state of society sets certain problems before its intellectual representatives, the attention of prominent minds is concentrated upon them until these problems are solved. As soon as they have succeeded in solving them, their attention is transferred to another object. By solving a problem, a given talent A diverts the attention of talent B from the problem already solved to another problem. And when we are asked: What would have happened if A had died before he had solved problem X?—we imagine that the thread of development of the human intellect would have been broken. We forget that had A died, B, or C, or D might have tackled the problem, and the thread of intellectual development would have remained intact in spite of A's premature demise.

In order that a man who possesses a particular kind of talent may, by means of it, greatly influence the course of events, two conditions are needed: First, this talent must make him more comfortable to the social needs of the given epoch than anyone else. If Napoleon had possessed the musical gifts of Beethoven instead of his own military genius he would not, of course, have become an emperor. Second, the existing social order must not bar the road to the person possessing the talent which is needed and useful precisely at the given time. This very

* From *The Role of the Individual in History*, New York, 1940, pp. 48-50, 52, 58-61. Informational footnotes have been omitted.

Napoleon would have died as the barely known General, or Colonel, *Bonaparte* had the older order in France existed another seventy-five years. . . .

It has long been observed that great talents appear everywhere, whenever the social conditions favorable to their development exist. This means that every man of talent who *actually appears*, every man of talent who becomes a *social force*, is the product of *social relations*. Since this is the case, it is clear why talented people can, as we have said, change only individual features of events, but not their general trend; *they are themselves the product of this trend; were it not for that trend they would never have crossed the threshold that divides the potential from the real.* . . .

At the present time, human nature can no longer be regarded as the final and most general cause of historical progress: if it is constant, then it cannot explain the extremely changeable course of history; if it is changeable, then obviously its changes are themselves determined by historical progress. At the present time we must regard the development of productive forces as the final and most general cause of the historical progress of mankind, and it is these productive forces that determine the consecutive changes in the social relations of men. Parallel with this *general* cause there are *particular* causes, i.e., *the historical situation* in which the development of the productive forces of a given nation [*narod*] proceeds and which, in the last analysis, is itself created by the development of these forces among other nations, i.e., the same general cause.

Finally, the influence of the *particular* causes is supplemented by the operation of *individual* causes, i.e., the personal qualities of public men and other "accidents," thanks to which events finally assume their *individual features*. Individual causes cannot bring about fundamental changes in the operation of *general and particular* causes which, moreover, determine the trend and limits of the influence of individual causes. Nevertheless, there is no doubt that history would have had different features had the individual causes which had influenced it been replaced by other causes of the same order. . . .

But let us return to our subject. A great man is great not

because his personal qualities give individual features to great historical events, but because he possesses qualities which make him most capable of serving the great social needs of his time, needs which arose as a result of general and particular causes. Carlyle, in his well-known book on heroes and hero worship, calls great men *beginners*. This is a very apt description. A great man is precisely a beginner because he sees *further* than others, and desires things *more strongly* than others. He solves the scientific problems brought up by the preceding process of intellectual development of society; he points to the new social needs created by the preceding development of social relationships; he takes the initiative in satisfying these needs. He is a hero. But he is not a hero in the sense that he can stop, or change, the natural course of things, but in the sense that his activities are the conscious and free expression of this inevitable and unconscious course. Herein lies all his significance; herein lies his whole power. But this significance is colossal, and the power is terrible. . . .

Bismarck said that we cannot make history and must wait while it is being made. But who makes history? It is made by the *social man*, who is its *sole "factor."* The social man creates his own, social, relationships. But if in a given period he creates given relationships and not others, there must be some cause for it, of course; it is determined by the state of his productive forces. No great man can foist on society relations which *no longer* conform to the state of these forces, or which *do not yet* conform to them. In this sense, indeed, he cannot make history, and in this sense he would advance the hands of his clock in vain: he would not [by so doing] hasten the passage of time, nor turn it back. . . .

But if I know in what direction social relations are changing owing to given changes in the social-economic process of production, I also know in what direction social psychology is changing; consequently I am able to influence it. Influencing social psychology means influencing historical events. Hence, in a certain sense, *I can make history*, and there is no need for me to wait while "it is being made."

Notes to Engels' *Ludwig Feuerbach* *

In 1902 the editorial board of the *Mouvement socialiste* under-took a wide *enquête* on the attitude of the socialist parties in different countries to *clericalism*. This question now has obvious *practical* importance. But in order to solve it correctly we must first of all make clear to ourselves another mainly *theoretical* ques-tion: the attitude of *scientific socialism toward religion*. This last question is hardly analyzed at all in the international socialist literature of our time. And this is a great deficiency, which is explained precisely by the *"practicalness"* of the majority of present-day socialists. They say: religion is a personal matter. That is true, but only in a definite, limited sense. It goes without saying that the socialist party in each individual country would act very *improvidently* if it refused to accept in its ranks a man who recognizes its program and is ready to work for its fulfillment but at the same time still entertains certain religious prejudices. Yet it would be still more improvident of any party to renounce the theory underlying its program. And the theory —modern *scientific socialism*—rejects religion as the product of an erroneous view of nature and society and condemns it as an obstacle to the all-round development of the proletariat. We *have not the right* to close the doors of our organization to a man who is infected with religious belief; but we *are obliged* to do all that depends on us in order to destroy that faith in him or at least to prevent—with spiritual weapons, of course—our religious-minded comrade from spreading his preju-dices among the workers. A consistent socialist outlook is in absolute disagreement with religion. It is therefore not surprising that the founders of scientific socialism had a sharply negative attitude toward it. Engels wrote: "We wish to remove from our path all that appears to us under the banner of the super-

* From "Plekhanov's Notes to Engels' Book *Ludwig Feuerbach* . . . ," trans. R. Dixon, *Selected Philosophical Works in Five Volumes*, Moscow, 1961-, I, 505, 512-516, 518-522, 524-525, 527-529, 536, slightly revised. Footnotes have been omitted.

human and the supernatural. . . . That is why we declare war once and for all on religion and religious conceptions." Marx in turn called religion the opium with which the higher classes try to put to sleep the consciousness of the people. . . .

If the phenomenon is caused by the action upon us of the thing-in-itself, the action of this thing is the *cause of the phenomenon*. And yet, according to Kant's doctrine, *the category of causality is applicable only within the limits of the world of phenomena but is inapplicable to the thing-in-itself*. There are only two ways out of this obvious contradiction which has already been pointed out in German philosophy of the end of the eighteenth century: *either* we continue to maintain that the category of causality is inapplicable to things-in-themselves and consequently reject the thought that the phenomenon is brought forth by the *action upon us* of the thing-in-itself; *or* we continue to consider this thought as correct and then admit that the category of causality is applicable to things-in-themselves. In the first case we are taking the direct road to *subjective idealism*, because, if the thing in itself does *not* act upon us, we know nothing of its existence and the very idea of it must be declared unnecessary, that is, superfluous in our philosophy; in the second case we enter upon the *path of materialism*, for the materialists have never asserted that we know what things-in-themselves are like—i.e., what things are independently of their effects upon us—but have only asserted that things are known to us precisely because they act upon our sense organs, and in just the degree to which they so act. "We do not know the true nature of matter," says Holbach, "although we may judge of certain of its properties by its effect upon us. . . . For us, matter is that which acts, in one way or another, upon our senses." If Lange wrote in his *History of Materialism* (Vol. I, p. 349 of the Russian translation, where he deals precisely with Holbach) that ". . . materialism obstinately considers the world of sensuous appearance as the world of real things," this is explained only by the fact that he "obstinately" *refused to understand materialism*. But however this may be, the question of the unknowableness of the external world in both the cases I have mentioned is settled *positively*. Indeed, if we go on to the standpoint of subjective idealism it will be clear to us that our *ego* is capable of knowing the *non-ego* which it itself creates. And if we prefer to be materialists, with a little reflection we must come to the conviction that if we know *certain properties* of things-in-themselves as a result of their action upon us, then, despite Holbach, their *nature* is *known* to us *to some degree:* for the *nature* of the thing is revealed precisely in its *properties.* The current counterposition of nature to properties is completely unfounded and it is precisely this counterposition that has led the theory of knowledge into the scholastic labyrinth in which Kant got lost and in which the present opponents of materialism continue to wander helplessly. . . .

Hegel revealed with extraordinary clarity the logical, or, if you prefer, the *epistemological,* error which underlies all arguments that things-in-themselves are inaccessible to our knowledge. It is, indeed, impossible for us to answer the question what a thing-in-itself is. And the reason for this is very simple: the question *"what is?"* presupposes that the thing in question has properties which must be pointed out; this question still has sense *only with this presumption.* But "philosophical people" who indulge in talk about the unknowableness of things-in-themselves *preliminarily make abstraction of all properties of the thing* and by this abstraction make *the question absurd* and therefore *the answer impossible.* Kant's transcendental idealism, Hegel says, "transports into consciousness all the properties of things, in relation to both form and content. It is understandable that from this standpoint it depends only on me, on the subject, that the leaf of the tree appears to me green, not black; that sugar is sweet, not bitter; and that when the clock strikes two, I perceive its strokes successively, not simultaneously and that I do not consider the first stroke as either the cause or the effect of the second," etc. (*Wissenschaft der Logik,* I., Band, I. Abth., S. 55; II. Abth., S. 150. . . .)

But pardon, the reader may object,[1] is not light or sound

1. At this point the first edition includes the following passage: "Our sensations are hieroglyphics of a special kind, which make us aware of what is happening in reality. Hieroglyphics do not resemble the events which they convey, but they are capable of conveying *with complete accuracy* both the events themselves and—what is of prime importance—the relations which exist between them."—TRANS.

something quite subjective? Is the perception of sound or color similar to that kind of movement by which it is caused, according to the teaching of modern natural science? Of course, it is not. But if *iron* at different *temperatures* has different *colors*, there is an *objective cause* of this which does not depend on the qualities of my "spiritual" organization. Our famous physiologist Sechenov was perfectly right when he wrote that "every vibration or transition of sound according to intensity, pitch, or duration that we feel, corresponds to a perfectly definite change in the sound movement in reality. Sound and light as sensations are products of the organization of man; but the roots of the forms and movements which we see, just as the modulations of sound which we hear, lie outside us in reality" ("Objective Thought and Reality" in the collection *Help for the Hungry*, ed. of *Russkiye Vedomosti*, p. 188). Sechenov adds: "*Whatever objects may be in themselves, independently of consciousness— even if our impressions of them are only conventional signs— in any case there is a real similarity and difference which corresponds to the sensed similarity and difference of the signs.*" In other words, "*the similarities and differences which we find among sense objects are real similarities and differences*" (*ibid.*, p. 207). This is true. We need only add that Sechenov does not express himself with complete precision. When he assumes that our impressions are only conventional signs of things-in-themselves, he seems to admit that things-in-themselves have a "form" or "appearance" [*vid*], which is unknown to us, inaccessible to our consciousness. But such an "*appearance*" is precisely the result of the action of things-in-themselves upon us; *apart from this action they have no "appearance" at all.* Therefore to oppose their "appearance" as it exists in our consciousness to their real "appearance" would indicate a failure to grasp the nature of the concept which is connected with the word "appearance." Such an imprecision of expression underlies, as we said above, all the "epistemological" scholasticism of Kantianism. I know that Mr. Sechenov is not inclined to such scholasticism; I have already said that *his* theory of knowledge is perfectly correct, but we must not make to our opponents in philosophy concessions in terminology which prevent us from expressing our own thoughts with complete precision. Another reason why I make this reservation is because in my notes to the first edition of my translation of this pamphlet by Engels I still expressed myself in a way that was not wholly precise; only later did I come to feel all of the disadvantages of such imprecision.

And so, things-in-themselves have no "appearance" at all. Their "appearance" exists only in the consciousness of those subjects on whom they act. The question is now, who are those subjects? People? No, not only people, but all organisms which, thanks to certain peculiarities of their structure, have the possibility to "*see*" the external world in one way or another. But the structure of these organisms is not identical; for that reason the external world has not for them an identical "appearance"; I do not know how the snail "sees" things, but I am sure that it does not "see" things the same as people do. From this, however, it does not follow that the properties of the external world have only subjective significance. By no means! If a man and a snail move from point A to point B, the straight line will be the shortest distance between those two points for both the man and the snail; if both these organisms went along a broken line *they would have to expend a greater amount of labor for their advance*. Consequently, *the properties of space* have *also objective significance*, although they are "seen" differently by different organisms at different stages of evolutionary development.

Nor is that all. What is a snail for *me?* A part of the external world which acts upon me in a definite manner determined by my organism. So that if I admit that a snail "sees" the external world in one way or another, I am forced to admit that the "form" or "aspect" [*vid*] in which the external world appears to the snail is itself conditioned by the properties of this real world. Thus, the relation of object to subject, of being to thought, this, Engels says, basic question of modern philosophy presents itself to us in a completely new light. The counterposition of the subject to the object disappears: the *subject* becomes *object* too; *matter* (remember Holbach's definition: "for us matter is what acts in one way or another upon our senses") turns out under definite conditions to be endowed with *consciousness*. This is the purest materialism; but it is the only at all satisfactory answer not contradicting science to the question of the relation of subject to object. . . .

I must admit either one or the other: *either* other people exist *only in my imagination*, and in that case they did not exist before me and will not exist after my death; *or* they exist *outside me* and independently of my consciousness, in which case the idea of their existence before and after me naturally does not contain any contradiction; but now is the time when new and insuperable difficulties arise for Kant's philosophy. If people exist *outside me*, that *"outside me"* is apparently what, thanks to the structure of my brain, appears to me as *space*. So that space is not only a subjective form of [sensory] intuition; to it corresponds also a certain objective *"an sich"* ("in itself"). If people lived *before me* and will live *after me*, then again to this *"before me"* and to this *"after me"* apparently corresponds some *"an sich"* which does not depend on my consciousness and is only reflected in that consciousness in the form of time. So that *time is not only subjective either*. Finally, if people exist outside me they are among those things-in-themselves on the possibility of knowing which we materialists are arguing with the Kantians. And if *their* actions are in any way capable of determining *my* actions, and mine are capable of influencing theirs —which he must necessarily admit who acknowledges that human society and the development of its culture do not exist only in his consciousness—then it is clear that the category of causality is applicable to the really existing external world, i.e., to the world of noumena, to things-in-themselves. In a word, there is no other way out: *either subjective idealism*, leading logically to *solipsism* (i.e., the acknowledgment that other people exist only in my imagination) *or* the renunciation of Kant's premises, a renunciation whose logical consummation must be the transition to the standpoint of *materialism*, as I already proved in my argument with Konrad Schmidt.

Let us go further. Let us transport ourselves in thought to the time when only very remote ancestors of man existed upon the earth, for example in the Secondary Period. The question is: how did the matter of space, time, and causality stand *then?* *Whose* subjective forms were they then? Subjective forms of the ichthyosaurus? And *whose understanding* dictated its laws to nature *then?* The understanding of the archaeopteryx? Kant's philosophy *cannot give any answer* to this question. And it must be rejected as disagreeing with modern science.

Idealism says: *without a subject there is no object.* The history of the earth shows that *the object existed long before the subject appeared,* i.e., long before any organism appeared which had any perceptible degree of consciousness. The idealist says: *understanding dictates its laws to nature.* The history of the organic world shows that "understanding" appears only on a high rung of the ladder of development. And as this development can be explained only by the laws of nature, it follows that nature dictated its laws to understanding. The theory of evolutionary development *reveals the truth of materialism.*

The history of mankind is a particular case of *development in general.* That is why what has been said includes the answer to the question whether Kant's teaching can be united with the materialist explanation of history. Of course, the eclectic can unite everything in his mind. With the help of eclectic thinking one can unite Marx not only with Kant, but even with the "realists" of the Middle Ages. But for people who think logically, the illicit cohabitation of Marx with the philosophy of Kant must appear as something monstrous in the fullest sense of the word. . . .

The "critics of Marx," including the above-mentioned *armer* Konrad, have shouted much and loud that Engels showed utter misunderstanding of Kant when he said that the teaching of the unknowableness of the external world was refuted best of all by experiment and industry. In actual fact Engels was absolutely right. Every experiment and every productive activity of man represents an *active* relation on his part to the external world, a deliberate calling forth of definite phenomena. And as a phenomenon is the fruit of the action of a thing-in-itself upon me (Kant says: the *affecting* of me by that thing), in carrying out an experiment or engaging in production of this or that product, I force the thing-in-itself to "affect" my "ego" in a definite manner determined beforehand by me. Consequently, I know at least some of its properties, namely those through whose intermediary I force it to act. But that is not all. By forcing this thing to act upon me in a certain way, I enter into a relation of *cause* toward it. But Kant says that the category of cause has no relation whatsoever to "things-in-themselves"; consequently, experience here refutes him better than he refuted himself when he said that the category of cause is related only to *phenomena* (not to things-in-themselves) and at the same time maintained that the thing "in itself" acts upon our "*ego*," in other words, that it is the *cause* of phenomena. From this again it follows that Kant was seriously mistaken when he said that the "forms of our thought" (categories, or "basic concepts of the understanding," e.g., causality, interaction, existence, necessity) are only "*a priori forms*," i.e., that things-in-themselves are not subjected to causal relations, interaction, etc. In reality the basic forms of our thought not only correspond completely to the relations existing between things-in-themselves, they *cannot fail to correspond* to them, because otherwise our existence in general, and consequently, the existence of our "forms of thought," would be made impossible. . . .

Well, granted that Kant is wrong, granted that his dualism cannot withstand criticism. But the very existence of external objects is all the same still not proved. How will you prove that Hume is not right, that the subjective idealists—for example, Berkeley—whose views you set forth at the beginning of this note, are not right? . . .

Man must act, reason, and believe in the existence of the external world, said Hume. It remains for us materialists to add that such "belief" is the necessary preliminary condition for thought, *critical* thought in the best sense of the word, that it is the inevitable *salto vitale* of philosophy. The basic question in philosophy is not solved by opposing "*ego*" to "*non-ego*," i.e., to the external world; such a counterposition can only lead us into the blind alley of the absurd. The solution of this particular question requires one to go beyond the limits of the "*ego*" and consider how "*it*" (an organism endowed with consciousness) stands in regard to the *external world* surrounding it. But as soon as the question assumes this—the only rational—form, it becomes obvious that the "subject" in general, and consequently my "ego" too, far from dictating laws to the objective world, represents only a component part of that world, *considered from another aspect,* from that of thought, not of extension, as Spinoza would say, he being an indisputable materialist, although historians of philosophy refuse to recognize him as such.

This decisive step of thought cuts the Gordian knot of Hume's skepticism. It goes without saying that as long as I doubt the existence of external objects, the question of the causal connection *between them* necessarily remains before me in the same form that it assumed with Hume: I am entitled to talk only of the succession of my own impressions, the source of which is unknown. But when the work of my thought convinces me that doubt in the existence of the external world leads my mind to absurdity, and when *I, no longer "dogmatically," but "critically,"* declare the existence of the external world indubitable, I then, by the very fact, admit that my impressions are the result of the action upon me of external objects, i.e., I attribute an objective significance to causality. . . .

Our "legal" Narodniks strove with complete sincerity toward their "ideals." But see what came of their sincere attitude to those ideals. Their social ideal was a free "people," developing independently, without any hindrances from the government and the higher estates. Both the government and the higher estates were completely deleted, if not completely annihilated in the Narodist ideal. But what did the Narodniks do to fulfill their ideals? Sometimes they simply moaned over the disintegration of the "foundations" ("they wept over figures," as G. I. Uspensky put it). Sometimes they advised the government to increase the peasants' allotments and to lighten the burden of taxation. Sometimes—these were the most consistent and irreconcilable—they "settled on the land." But all this did not bring Russian reality any closer to the Narodist ideal. That is why the Narodniks wept not only over figures, but over themselves too. They were conscious of the complete impotence of their ideals. But what was the cause of this impotence? It is clear: there was *no organic connection between their ideals and reality.* Reality went in one direction and their ideals in another, or, to put it better, they remained stationary, continuing *"settled on the land"* with

Messrs. the liberal Narodniks, so that the distance between ideals and reality kept increasing, as a result of which their ideals became more and more powerless day by day. Engels would have laughed at *such* ideals, of course, as Hegel indeed did. However, the mockery would be directed not against the loftiness of the ideals, but against their very *impotence*, their severance from the general course of the Russian movement. Engels dedicated his entire life to an extremely lofty aim: the emancipation of the proletariat. He also had his "ideal," but he was not severed forever from reality. His ideal was reality itself, but *the reality of tomorrow*, a reality which will be fulfilled, not because Engels was a man of an ideal, but because the properties of the present reality are such that out of it, by its own interior laws, there must develop that reality of tomorrow which we may call Engels' ideal. Uneducated people may ask us: if the whole point consists in the properties of the real, then what has Engels to do with it, why does he intervene with his ideals in the inevitable historical process? Cannot the matter do without him? *From the objective standpoint* the position of Engels appears as follows: in the process of the transition from one form to another, reality seized on him as on one of the necessary instruments of the impending revolution. *From the subjective standpoint* it turns out that it was pleasant for Engels to partake in that historical movement, that he considered it his duty and the great task of his life. The laws of social development can no more be fulfilled without the intermediary of people than the laws of nature without the intermediary of matter. But this does not in any sense mean that the "*individual person*" can ignore the laws of social development. In the best of cases he will be punished for this by being reduced to the position of a ridiculous Don Quixote. . . .

Hegel says that with Kant each definite law of morality is an empty statement, a meaningless tautology like the formula $A = A$, chattels entrusted for safekeeping are chattels entrusted for safekeeping, property is property. That is . . . correct and quite comprehensible. For Kant there simply existed no such questions as those which Hegel counterposes to his "empty statements": Where is the harm if things are not entrusted for safekeeping? Why is property needed? etc. *Kant's ideal*, his "kingdom of ends" (*Reich der Zwecke*, cf. *Grundlegung*, p. 58) *was an abstract ideal of bourgeois society, whose standards seemed to Kant to be unquestionable commands of* "practical reason." Kant's morality is bourgeois morality, translated into the language of his philosophy, whose main defect, as we have seen, was the complete inability to cope with the questions of *development.* . . .

What could be more utilitarian? Besides, I wish to draw the reader's attention to the circumstance that while objecting to utilitarians, Kant always has in mind the principle of *"personal happiness"* which he correctly calls the *principle of self-love*. And that is precisely why he cannot cope with the basic questions of morality. Indeed, morality is founded on the striving not for *personal happiness*, but for the *happiness of the whole:* the clan, the people, the class, humanity. *This* striving has nothing in common with *egoism*. On the contrary, it *always presupposes* a greater or lesser degree of *self-sacrifice*. And as social feelings can be transmitted from generation to generation and strengthened by natural selection (cf. Darwin's most apt remarks on this point in his book on the origin of man), self-sacrifice can take a form as if it were a matter of "autonomous will," without any admixture of "the faculty of desire." But this indisputable circumstance does not in the least preclude the *utilitarian principle* of this lofty faculty. If self-sacrifice were not useful for the particular society, class, or, finally, the particular animal species in its struggle for existence (remember that social feelings are *not* characteristic of man alone), then it would be alien to the individuals belonging to this society, class, or species. That is all. A particular individual is born with an *a priori* "ability for self-sacrifice" just as it is born—according to the remark by Reinke . . . —with an *"a priori"* ability to breathe and digest; but there is nothing mysterious in this *"a priori*-ness": it was formed gradually in the long, long process of development.

Materialism or Kantianism *

The development from Kantianism to idealism, although it does away with the contradiction which is the basis of the Kantian system, leads to the most obvious and ludicrous absurdities.

On the other hand, let us see to what the development from Kantianism to materialism leads us. But first let us agree on our terms. What kind of materialism are we talking about? . . .

My most esteemed opponent [1] belongs to the number of those who set out to refute materialism without giving themselves the trouble of studying and understanding it properly. He says, for instance, "materialism must maintain that this essence [i.e., the essence which corresponds to appearances—G.P.] is identical with the appearances.". . .

According to Holbach, i.e., to the authors of the book, *Système de la Nature,* which Holbach did not write alone, there are things outside us and independent of us, things which have an actual and not merely a "mental" existence. These things, *whose nature is unknown to us,* act upon us and produce impressions on our senses and, *in accordance with the impressions which are provoked in us by their action,* we attribute one or another set of properties to the things. *These impressions represent the sole knowledge* (a superficial and very limited knowledge) *which we can have of things-in-themselves.* "We do not know the essence of a single thing if by the term 'essence' is understood that which constitutes the nature of the thing. We know matter only according to the impressions, representations [*predstavleniya*], and ideas it provokes in us. And we make a true

---

* Translated for this volume by Mary-Barbara Zeldin, from "Materializm ili Kantianizm" and "Yeshchyo raz Materializm," pp. 163, 165, 167-169, 175-176, 177-179 of *Protiv filosofskovo revizionizma,* Moscow, 1935. "Materializm ili Kantianizm" first appeared in *Neue Zeit,* No. 19 and 20, Vol. I for 1898-1899; "Yeshchyo raz Materializm" was written for *Vorwärts* in German, but was not published by that journal; it first appeared in Russian in the collection, *Kritika nashikh kritikov,* 1906. Footnotes have been omitted.

1. Konrad Schmidt.—TRANS.

or mistaken judgment about it according to the nature of our organs."

Is that to maintain that the essence of things and their appearance [*yavleniye*] are "*identical*"? Obviously not. . . .

The materialist calls nature the totality of the things which constitute the objects of our sense perception. Nature is the sensory world in all its extension. The French materialists of the eighteenth century also talked about this sensory world. They constantly contrasted this concept of nature with a "phantom," i.e., imaginary supernatural being. . . . Human reason is lost in the dark as soon as it goes beyond the bounds of the world of sensation or, what is the same thing, beyond experience. In this connection the materialists understand experience somewhat differently from the author of the *Critique of Pure Reason*.

According to Kant, nature is the "immediate being" (*Dasein*) of things insofar as it is defined by universal laws. These universal laws (or pure laws of nature) are the laws of our understanding. "Understanding does not receive its laws (*a priori*) from nature, but, on the contrary, dictates to nature its own laws," Kant tells us. Consequently, these laws do not have objective significance. In other words, they are applicable only to phenomena, not to things-in-themselves. But insofar as phenomena exist *only in us* it is evident that in the last analysis the Kantian theory of experience takes on a wholly subjective character and is in no way distinguished from the idealistic theory of Fichte. We have already seen into what a labyrinth of absurdities anyone is inevitably led who takes this theory seriously and who is not afraid to follow its implications to their ultimate conclusions. Now let us look a little more closely at the *materialist* theory of experience.

According to this theory, nature is first of all the totality of phenomena. But since things-in-themselves constitute the necessary condition of phenomena, in other words, since phenomena are evoked by the action of an object on a subject, we are compelled to admit that the laws of nature have not only *subjective*, but also *objective* significance, i.e., that the mutual relation of ideas in the *subject* corresponds—when a man is not *in error*—to the mutual relation of things *outside him*. Konrad

Schmidt will say, of course, that this is a "philosophy of identity" and that it takes "the elements of phenomena as things-in-themselves." He will be mistaken. In order to keep him from making a mistake I shall ask my opponent to remember the geometrical figure by means of which Spencer tried to help his readers understand "transformed realism." Let us imagine a cylinder and a cube. The cylinder is the subject; the cube is the object. The shadow which the cube casts upon the cylinder is an image or representation. This shadow does not resemble the cube: in it the cube's straight edges are bent, its plane surfaces are warped. Nevertheless, each change in the cube will be accompanied by a corresponding change in the shadow. We can imagine that something similar takes place in the process of forming images. The sensations which are called forth in the subject by the action of the object do not resemble the object any more than they resemble the subject: nevertheless, *each change in the object will be accompanied by a corresponding change in its action upon the subject.* This is by no means the crude and vulgar philosophy of identity which Konrad Schmidt imputes to us. This theory of experience, which takes nature as its point of departure, permits us to escape from the inconsistency of Kantianism as well as from the absurdity of subjective idealism. . . .

Once More Materialism

Marx says that "the ideal is nothing other than the material when it has been reflected and translated in the human head." . . . If I translate (*übersetze*) anything, for instance, from Russian into French, does my action mean that the language of Voltaire can be explained only by the language of Pushkin, and that in general the language of Pushkin is *"more real"* than the language of Voltaire? Absolutely not! It means that there exist *two languages,* each of which has its own particular construction, and that if I disregard French grammar I shall not have a translation but nonsense pure and simple which no one will be able either to understand or to read. If, according to Marx's expression, "the ideal is a translation and transposition of the material inside the human head," then it is evident that, according to this view, the "material" is not *identical* with the "ideal," because, if it were, there would be no need to transpose and translate it. That is why that absurd *identity* which Schmidt tries to impute to Marx is completely senseless.

But if a given French sentence is unlike that Russian sentence of which it is supposed to be the translation, it still does not follow that the sense of the first sentence must diverge from that of the second. On the contrary, if the translation is good, then regardless of the dissimilarity of the sentences *the sense will be one and the same in both.*

Similarly, although the "ideal" existing in my head is unlike that "material" from which it is "translated," still it possesses the very same sense, so long as the translation is correct. And the criterion of correct translation is experience. If the sense of the "ideal" existing in my head did not correspond to the actual character of the "material," i.e., to the things existing outside my head and independently of it, then I would receive a more or less harsh lesson from those things on my first encounter with them—a lesson thanks to which the discrepancy between the ideal and the material would be more or less quickly removed, provided I have not already perished as a victim of this discrepancy, of course. In this sense (and only in this sense) one can and must speak of the *identity* (*Identität*) of the ideal and the material. But against this kind of identity the weapons of Schmidtian "criticism" are completely powerless. . . .

In opposition to "mind," "matter" is the name of that which acts upon our sense organs, evoking specific sensations in us. But what, precisely, acts upon our sense organs? To this question I answer with Kant: things-in-themselves. Thus, *matter is nothing more than the aggregate of things-in-themselves insofar as the latter are the source of our sensations.*

Since I am entirely "serious" in recognizing the existence outside of me and independent of my consciousness of Herr Doktor Schmidt, I am compelled to count him among the number of those things-in-themselves which constitute the external world around me. A thing-in-itself called Dr. Schmidt can act on my external senses: it is *material,* but it is capable also of writing a bad article on philosophy. *This is sensing and thinking matter.* In this way consciousness (to a greater or lesser degree) is an attribute of that substance which acts on my external senses and which I call *matter*. That this substance "in itself" is unlike my *representation* of matter was already known to Thomas Hobbes, but one cannot refute materialism on these grounds. On the contrary, it would be very strange if a sensation and the representation arising from it *resembled* that thing which provoked it and which itself was, of course, *neither sensation nor representation*. Who does not know that being-in-itself is neither being-for-itself nor being-for-others?

Mr. Schmidt says also that if I "seriously" admit the action of things-in-themselves upon me, I must also admit that time and space are conditions (or perhaps he meant determinations?) applying not with less but with greater validity to things-in-themselves.

He could say that if I "seriously" admit the existence of things-in-themselves, I must recognize that they *exist in space and time*. . . . That space and time are forms of consciousness, and that therefore their first distinctive property is *subjectivity*, was already known to Thomas Hobbes and not a single materialist today would deny it. The whole question is this: whether certain forms or relations of *things* correspond to these forms of consciousness. Materialists, of course, must give an affirmative answer to this question. This naturally does not mean that they admit that bad (or more correctly absurd) identity which the Kantians and among them Mr. Schmidt attribute to them with obliging naiveté. No, the forms and relations of things-in-themselves cannot be such as they *seem* to us to be, i.e., such as they appear when "transposed" into our heads. Our images or representations of the forms and relations of things are only *hieroglyphics*. But these *hieroglyphics* designate the forms and relations of things with precision, and this permits us to study the action upon us of things-in-themselves and in turn to act upon them. I repeat, if the correspondence between objective relations and their subjective reflections ("translations") in our heads were incorrect, *our very existence would be impossible*. The recognition of the correctness of these considerations is unavoidable to anyone who has not surrendered to the absurdities of subjective idealism. . . .

Fundamental Problems of Marxism *

Hegel, in his *Philosophy of History*, had already drawn attention
to the importance of the "geographical basis of universal history." But since, in his view, the ultimate cause of all evolution
was the idea, and since he referred only in passing and reluc-
tantly, as concerns matters of secondary importance, to the
materialist explanation of phenomena, it was impossible that
the thoroughly sound idea he entertained as to the great significance of geographical environment should bear fruit. The
supremely important conclusions of this theory could only be
drawn by the materialist Marx. The properties of the geographical environment determine the character, not only of the natural
products with which man satisfies his wants, but also of the
objects which man himself produces in order to satisfy these
wants. Where there were no metals, aboriginal tribes could not,
unaided, get beyond the limits of what is termed the Stone
Age. In like manner, if primitive fishers and primitive hunters
were to pass on to the stage of cattle-breeding and that of agriculture, suitable geographical conditions were requisite, a suitable fauna and flora. Lewis Morgan has shown that the remarkable difference between the social evolution of the New World
and that of the Old is to be explained by the lack in the New
World of animals capable of being domesticated, and by the
differences between the flora of the New World and the Old.[1]
. . .

Nor is this all. Already in the lowest stages of social evolution,
tribes enter into relation one with another, mutually exchanging
some of their products. The result is an enlargement of the
boundaries of their geographical environment, and that in its
turn has an effect upon the evolution of the productive forces
in each of the tribes, quickening this evolution. It will readily

* From *Fundamental Problems of Marxism*, trans. E. and C. Paul, New
York, 1928, pp. 32-34, 72-73.
1. See *Ancient Society*.

be understood that the ease with which such relations become established and developed depends also upon the characteristics of the geographical environment. Hegel said that seas and rivers bring men closer together, whereas mountains keep them apart. Though this is true, the seas only bring men closer together when the development of the forces of production has already attained a tolerably high level. As long as that level is low, the sea (as Ratzel rightly points out) is a great hindrance to intercourse between the races which it separates.[2] However this may be, it is certain that the more variable the properties of the geographical environment, the more favorable they are to the development of the forces of production. Marx writes: "It is not the absolute fertility of the soil but the multifariousness of its natural products which constitutes the natural foundation of the social division of labor, and, by changing the natural conditions of his environment, spurs man on to multiply his own needs, capacities, means of labor, and methods of labor." [3] Using almost the same terms as Marx, Ratzel says: "The most important thing is, not that there is a greater facility in procuring food, but that certain inclinations, certain habits, and, finally, certain wants are awakened in man."[4]

Thus the peculiarities of the geographical environment determine the evolution of the forces of production, and this, in its turn, determines the development of economic forces and, therefore, the development of all the other social relations. . . .

If we wish to summarize the views of Marx and Engels on the relation between the famous "foundation" and the no less famous "superstructure," we shall get something like this:

1. The state of the forces of production;
2. Economic relations conditioned by these forces;
3. The socio-political regime erected upon a given economic foundation;
4. The psychology of man in society, determined in part directly by economic conditions, and in part by the

2. *Anthropogeographie,* Stuttgart, 1882, p. 92.
3. *Capital,* new translation, 1928, I, 557.
4. *Völkerkunde,* Leipzig, 1887, I, 56.

whole socio-political regime erected upon the economic foundation;

5. Various ideologies reflecting this psychology.

The formula is sufficiently comprehensive to embrace all the forms of historical development. At the same time it is utterly alien to the eclecticism which cannot get beyond the idea of a reciprocal action between the various social forces and does not realize that such reciprocal action between forces cannot solve the problem of their origin. Our formula is a monistic formula, and this monistic formula is impregnated with materialism. In his *Philosophy of Spirit* Hegel said: "Spirit [Mind] is the only motive principle of history." We cannot take any other view if we accept that idealist standpoint according to which being is determined by thought. Marxian materialism shows how the history of thought is determined by the history of being. But idealism did not prevent Hegel from recognizing that economic conditions were causes "mediated by the development of spirit." In the same way, materialism did not prevent Marx from recognizing that in history "spirit" acted as a force whose direction, at any given moment, was determined by the development of economic conditions.

ALEXANDER ALEXANDROVICH
BOGDANOV (Malinovsky)
[1873–1928]

A. A. BOGDANOV was the leading figure of the revisionist group known as Machians or Empiriocritics. It was as an attempt to refute Bogdanov that Plekhanov developed his epistemological views, and the philosophical attack and counterattack that ensued continued for over a decade. This article is one of Bogdanov's replies.

Bogdanov's mature philosophy can be divided into two phases, that of what he called "Empiriomonism" and that of "Tectology." In his Empiriomonism, Bogdanov took as a metaphysical basis the views of Ernst Mach, but altered them to avoid the dualism he detected in them. According to Bogdanov, reality is experience. Physical objects are part of socially organized experience, while mental objects are experience individually organized: "The objective character of the physical world consists in the fact that it exists, not only for me personally, but for everybody. . . . The 'subjective' element in experience, on the other hand, is that which has no universality, having meaning only for one or more individuals." [1] Physical experience is the highest level of experience since it is collective. In this way, as Wetter points out,[2] Bogdanov hopes "to preserve that primacy of the physical over the mental which is incumbent on any form of materialism."

Bogdanov, however, diverges from Lenin's view of Marxism in that he must and does deny the objectivity of space, time,

1. *Empiriomonizm: stati po filosofii*, 3rd ed., Moscow, 1908, I, 23, quoted in Wetter, *op. cit.*, p. 93.
2. Wetter, *op. cit.*, p. 94.

causality, and truth. Truth cannot consist in the correspondence of ideas with objects, since the only objects are our experience. Truth, therefore, becomes a *method* for organizing experience, and the aim of knowledge is the construction of a coherent system.

In his system of Tectology (1922), Bogdanov follows the road taken by Bakunin and suggested by Marx: the point is not to interpret the world, but to change it. Tectology is a science concerned with organization as such: all knowledge, all activity is organizing activity. The fundamental principle which governs this process is *equilibrium*, which is achieved by whatever is organized and to the extent to which it is organized. Such equilibrium can be and is disturbed and then re-established, thus accounting for change. This is how Bogdanov envisages the dialectic. It is not surprising that Empiriomonism was accused of idealism, and that Tectology was seen as a mechanization of the dialectic.

Bogdanov does not, on the whole, attack the orthodoxy of Plekhanov's theory of knowledge—as Lenin does in his book, *Materialism and Empirio-Criticism* [3]—but rather its logical cogency within the framework of Marxism and of Plekhanov's own arguments. And Bogdanov's criticism—including its politically judicious and intellectually sarcastic confrontation of Plekhanov with Plekhanov's pseudonym—cannot be overlooked. In the end, Plekhanov, according to Bogdanov, is reasserting a world of things-in-themselves which Bogdanov condemns in the fashion of Aristotle and William of Occam—at best it explains the known by the unknown and uselessly multiplies entities. Bogdanov's final criticism is one that has become familiar to students of Soviet Marxism-Leninism: that Plekhanov's Marxism is orthodox only according to the letter and not according to the spirit.

3. See below, p. 422.

SELECTED BIBLIOGRAPHY

S. V. Utechin, "Philosophy and Society: Alexander Bogdanov," in *Revisionism: Essays on the History of Marxist Ideas*, ed. L. Labedz, New York, 1962, pp. 117-125.

Gustav A. Wetter, *Dialectical Materialism*, trans. Peter Heath, London and New York, 1958, pp. 92-100.

[ALEXANDER BOGDANOV]

Matter as Thing-in-Itself *

The School of Plekhanov calls itself materialistic and builds its
whole picture of the world on a foundation of "matter." But if
the reader thinks that theirs is the ordinary matter studied by
physics and chemistry, the matter whose laws of motion were
investigated by Newton, the matter which Lavoisier declared
eternal, the matter whose eternity [i.e., indestructibility] the
contemporary theory of electricity is about to deny—that matter
which is reducible to inertia, impenetrability, light, temperature,
and similar "sensory qualities"—if the reader assumes that the
philosophic edifice of our "materialists" rests upon *this*, then
he is cruelly mistaken. No, *this* matter is not permanent or
solid enough for them. It lies entirely within the realm of
experience; and what is experience? Experience is merely "our
own sensations and the images of things which are based upon
them," [1] as Plekhanov says, or "the aggregate of subjective sensations," [2] as Ortodoks expresses it. Again, it is "the whole sum
of my individual experiences and cognitive acts, and their results
as imprinted upon my consciousness"—in a word, "the inner
world" of the separate psyche, as N. Rakh-ov puts it.[3]

In brief, the unanimous verdict of the whole school is that
"experience" is *only* subjective, *only* individual, *only* psychic.
But such are the "phenomena" with which science is directly
concerned—whether they be called physical, material, or something else again. Understandably, in their philosophy, our materialists are not concerned with phenomena, that is, with vulgar,
empirical "matter."

---

* Translated for this volume by George L. Kline from *Priklyucheniya
odnoy filosofskoy shkoly*, St. Petersburg, 1908, pp. 6-18, 21, 64-66.

1. Plekhanov, Notes to the Russian translation of Engels' *Ludwig Feuerbach*, 1905, p. 97.

2. *Filosofskiye ocherki* (Philosophical Essays), p. 84. ["Ortodoks" was
the pseudonym of L. I. Akselrod, a woman philosopher. Bogdanov refers
to her only as "Ortodoks," using the masculine pronoun.—TRANS.]

3. *K filosofii marksizma* (On the Philosophy of Marxism), 1908, pp. 16-17.

"But what kind of matter *are* they concerned with?" the reader will ask.

"Matter as *thing-in-itself*."

If experience is nothing more than "subjective impressions," still it requires, on the one hand, a *subject* which receives these "impressions," and, on the other hand, something *from which* they are received. The subject is the "I"—what Marx ironically called "the owner of experiences"—to whom all the "impressions" and "sensations" which make up "experience" belong. . . . And what produces impressions in the "subject" is an "object" or "thing-in-itself" or "matter."

Naturally the reader will be interested in learning something in detail about this peculiar "matter" which does not belong to experience but lies hidden beneath it as its "objective" foundation. I was very much interested in this question myself. I shall attempt to place before the reader in a conscientious way everything that I have been able to gather on this point from the writings of the School.

> In opposition to *"mind"* or *"spirit"* [*dukh*], Beltov declares —*"matter"* is the name of that which *acts upon our sense organs, evoking specific sensations in us*. But what precisely acts upon our sense organs? To this question I answer with Kant: things-in-themselves. Thus, *matter is nothing more than the aggregate of things-in-themselves, insofar as the latter are the source of our sensations.*[4]

The "sense organs" figure rather strangely in the definition of "matter" as here formulated. I permit myself to raise the question as to just what these "sense organs" may be—are they "matter" or are they "experience"? Rakh-ov has kindly explained in his brochure that "for the materialist they represent in any given case either a *thing-in-itself* or a *phenomenon*, depending on how we approach them." He adds that "in the epistemological problem which interests us the sense organs as such play no role

---

4. *Kritika nashikh kritikov*, p. 233. Italics in original. [Here, as elsewhere, Bogdanov—perhaps for the benefit of Tsarist censors or security agents— gives no hint of what he surely knew: that Beltov and Plekhanov were the same person.—TRANS.]

at all; they are, if we may so express it, only an instrument of transmission." [5] Thus, of the above-quoted definition only one point remains: "matter" is the cause of sensations.

This doesn't seem like very much; one would like to know more. But in attempting to discover something more one is met with very discouraging statements. Thus Plekhanov informs us:

> . . . materialists have never asserted that we know what things-in-themselves are like—i.e., what things are independently of their effects upon us—but have only asserted that things are known to us precisely because they act upon our sense organs, and in just the degree to which they so act. "We do not know the true nature of matter," says Holbach, "although we may judge of certain of its properties by its effect upon us. . . . For us, matter is that which acts, in one way or another, upon our senses." [6]

Further on, to be sure, Plekhanov offers what at first glance seems to be a more encouraging account: ". . . if," he says, "we know *certain properties* of things-in-themselves as a result of their action upon us, then, despite Holbach, their *nature* is *known* to us *to some degree:* for the *nature* of the thing is revealed precisely in its *properties.*" [7] But this *"to some degree,"* obviously adds nothing to Holbach's position; for he spoke of the "nature" of matter *in itself*, and not of the "nature" of its reflection by the senses. If *only* the latter is known, then nothing is known of the former, and we have no encouragement at all.

Compare the following account: ". . . if I admit that a snail 'sees' the external world in one way or another, I am forced to admit that the 'form' or 'aspect' [*vid*] in which the external world appears to the snail is itself conditioned by the properties of this real world. . . ." [8] These "properties," *by which* the impressions of both snail and man are conditioned, are precisely what is interesting, since they represent the "true nature" of

5. Rakh-ov, *op. cit.,* p. 75.
6. Plekhanov, Notes to Engels' *Ludwig Feuerbach*, p. 100.
7. *Ibid.,* p. 101. Italics in original.
8. *Ibid.,* p. 104.

matter in itself. But all we know about them is, (1) that they exist, and (2) that . . . , that they are unknown.

Ortodoks actually says what Plekhanov had stopped short of saying. On the question of the nature of matter, he asserts:

> . . . such a question is wholly without scientific meaning or rational content. Matter is matter; it is the primordial fact, the point of departure both for external and internal experience, because "no action is possible except upon matter and through matter" [Claude Bernard's expression.— A.B.]. But if matter is the primordial fact, it naturally cannot be defined through some *other cause* that is external to it. From this it follows that we know matter through its action upon us.[9]

"We know matter through its action upon us" means that we know only its effects but do not know matter itself, and in fact are forbidden to ask what it is in itself. Does it make things any easier to say that the x which concerns us is a "primordial fact"? Wouldn't it be even more interesting to know something about it? But one must not venture to ask. The very question is a heresy—in the religious and not just the philosophic sense of the term:

> "Of course, it is impossible to give an absolute and finished definition of matter," explains Deborin, "because such a definition presupposes a knowledge of the totality of things and properties [Good heavens! Who would ask for such a horror as an *absolute* and *finished* definition?—A.B.]. To define matter, the *first principle* [*pervoosnova*] of all that is, through a cause, is as absurd as to ask the theologian for an explanation of the cause of his deity." [10]

I have long insisted that such an indefinite and undefined concept cannot be the foundation of any philosophical world-view. This is how Rakh-ov answers me:

Matter is precisely that which underlies the historical and

9. Ortodoks, *op. cit.*, p. 74.
10. *Sovremennaya zhizn* (Contemporary Life), No. 2 (1907), pp. 205-206.

intellectual development of human beings [and is intellectual development not historical?—A.B.]. That is all. Philosophy cannot give a more precise answer; in order to obtain one we must turn to other sciences, above all to *natural science,* but also to *history.* . . .[11]

So, let us turn to natural science; here we will find a clear and precise answer. Scientific language is necessarily clear and precise.

"What is matter?" we ask. Natural science begins to answer: "This name is used to designate a specific class of phenomena. . . ."

"Just a minute," we interrupt, "that's not what we're asking about. Aren't you talking about phenomena, i.e., experience?"

"Yes, of course," natural science answers in some astonishment. "What else?"

"We want to know about that matter which is *beyond* experience; Rakh-ov assures us that you will define *it* 'more precisely,' since, you see, philosophy cannot do it. Instead of a definition it only repeats the same words."

"I don't know what you're talking about," natural science answers coldly, "My concern is with experience; what is beyond it doesn't concern me. Evidently they have sent you to the wrong place. And I'm afraid I don't know your Mr. Rakh-ov; I don't know him at all."

Let us leave the question of a direct definition of "matter"— the School clearly finds it unanswerable—and look for at least indirect indications of what this matter consists of.

First of all, if "matter" is the cause of sensation, then the *law of causality* must be applicable to it. Plekhanov sees the principal advantage of his "thing-in-itself" over the unknowable Kantian thing-in-itself precisely in this: since the law of causality is not applicable to Kant's thing-in-itself, it cannot—despite Kant—be the "cause" of phenomena.

But now we may ask from what Plekhanov's "thing-in-itself" derives this advantage.

The law of causality *arose* out of *experience.* This is beyond doubt; even our materialists do not deny it. But the "thing-in-

11. Rakh-ov, *op. cit.,* p. 76.

itself" lies *beyond* experience—*c'est son métier*, as Heine would have said—for this is all we have succeeded in learning about it. But how can the law of causality extend *beyond the limits* of experience? Is this not a blatant violation of these limits, an illicit penetration into an alien realm on the part of the law of *phenomena*—a real "exceeding of its authority"? It undoubtedly is. The result is an abnormal situation, from which there can be only two ways of escape:

[1] Either we hold to the assertion that "the true nature of matter is unknown to us," and then we refuse to apply our rules in what we know is somebody else's monastery—to extend an empirical law to the transempirical world,

[2] Or we seriously acknowledge the law of causality to be applicable to "things-in-themselves," and give up the unhappy thought that their "true nature,"—except for the property of producing sensations—is "unknown" to us, saying straight out that their nature is the same as the "nature" of experience.

The first way of escape leads to Kantianism, the second to empiriomonism. The first tempts almost none of us [Marxists] and there is no need to discuss it in detail. I shall explain the second briefly.

The world of experience, both physical and psychic, is entirely composed of *elements*—spatial, tactile, acoustical, thermal, etc. Combinations of these elements make up different "phenomena," both "psychic" and "physical." If the law of causality, inferred for all of these phenomena—i.e., for the world of *elements connected by various relations*—is applicable to "things-in-themselves," serving as an *immediate link* between "phenomena" and "things," it is clear that "phenomena" and "things-in-themselves" are of the *same nature*. "Things-in-themselves" would then represent a direct continuation of the world of *empirical elements*, and in fact would be only *combinations of elements*—elements which we now experience and perhaps others which at present are unknown to us but in any case are not essentially different from the empirical elements. Then we are faced with the problem of determining what kinds of combinations of such elements form "things-in-themselves." This problem may be difficult, but in principle it is solvable. Empiriomonism provides a *method* for solving it. . . .

Wishing to illustrate the relation of "thing-in-itself" to "phe-nomenon," [Beltov] makes use of an analogy borrowed from Spencer:

> Let us imagine a cylinder and a cube. The cylinder is the subject; the cube is the object. The shadow which the cube casts upon the cylinder is an image or representation [*predstavleniye*]. This shadow does not resemble the cube: in it the cube's straight edges are bent, its plane surfaces are warped. Nevertheless, each change in the cube will be accompanied by a corresponding change in the shadow. We can imagine that something similar takes place in the process of forming images. The sensations which are called forth in the subject by the action of the object do not resemble the object any more than they resemble the subject: never-theless, *each change in the object will be accompanied by a corresponding change in its action upon the subject. . . .*[12]

Let us look more closely at this example. How is the action of the object-cube upon the subject-cylinder possible at all? It is possible because they both belong to the same world of ele-ments, that of geometric forms. Their elements are of the same type—spatial elements and light elements—though, of course, arranged in different combinations. If their "true nature" were not the same—if, for example, the object were a cube and the subject a melody—there would be no action of "object" upon "subject," nor would there be any "shadow." And what is this image-shadow in the Spencer-Beltov example? Once again, it is a combination of the same spatial and light elements which make up the object-cube and the subject-cylinder, excluding others, such as thermal elements.[13] It turns out that the "image" or "representation"—which for Beltov means the same thing as "experience"—must be no more than a new combination of

12. *Kritika* . . . , p. 199.
13. Of course, a certain *wooden* cube, let us say, might act upon a vibrating string, thus changing its sound; but this is possible only because the wooden cube and the vibrating string belong to the same order of complexes—that of concrete physical experience—containing a *mass* of ele-ments of the same order: in both cases there are spatial elements, elements of light, hardness, etc.

the same kinds of elements which make up "things-in-themselves." Thus the "nature" of these "things" is in principle fully established: *they are different combinations of elements which are the same as the elements of experience.* . . .

Let us turn to the question of space and time. What are they? They are "subjective forms of [sensory] intuition [*sozertsaniye*]" answer Plekhanov and Beltov, following Kant. But they are not *just* subjective forms. ". . . The whole question is whether certain forms or relations of things do not correspond to these forms of consciousness. Materialists, of course, must give an affirmative answer to this question. . . ." And Beltov goes on to explain:

> . . . the forms and relations of things-in-themselves cannot be such as they seem to us to be, i.e., such as they appear when "transposed" into our heads. Our images or representations of the forms and relations of things are only hieroglyphics; but these hieroglyphics designate the forms and relations of things with precision, and this permits us to study the action upon us of things-in-themselves, and in turn to act upon them. . . .[14]

This talk about hieroglyphics is all very well. But a serious misunderstanding rather unexpectedly arises between Beltov and Plekhanov. Beltov has no doubt that "things-in-themselves" have definite "forms"; but he admits that these forms are unknown to us, so that we have to make do with "hieroglyphics" of them. Plekhanov says something quite different. He quotes the following words of Sechenov:

> . . . Whatever objects may be in themselves, independently of consciousness—even if our impressions of them are only conventional signs—in any case there is a real similarity and difference which corresponds to the sensed similarity and difference of the signs. In other words, the similarities and differences which we find among sense objects are real similarities and differences.

With respect to this passage Plekhanov remarks:

14. *Kritika* . . . , p. 234.

This is true. We need only add that Sechenov does not express himself with complete precision. When he assumes that our impressions are only conventional signs of things-in-themselves, he seems to admit that things in themselves have a "form" or "appearance" [*vid*], which is unknown to us, inaccessible to our consciousness. But such an *"appearance"* is precisely the result of the action of things-in-themselves upon us; *apart from this action they have no "appearance" at all.* Therefore to oppose their "appearance" as it exists in our consciousness to their real "appearance" would indicate a failure to grasp the nature of the concept which is connected with the word "appearance." [15]

Clearly, in the passage just quoted the word "appearance" is used not in the narrow optical sense, but in the much broader sense of "form" or even "property." If there were any doubt about this it would be enough to call attention to the quotation from Sechenov. The word "appearance" does not appear in it at all; Sechenov speaks only of "similarities" and "differences"— expressions which apply to *all kinds of* "properties." Nevertheless, Plekhanov criticizes this formulation as giving rise to the inference that things-in-themselves have their own kind of "appearance."

It thus appears that "in itself" the thing has no *properties* at all; all its properties are the sensory "results of its action upon us." Consequently, these sense properties are not "hieroglyphics" of the forms and relations of things as they are in themselves, because "forms" and "relations" are properties too; rather, the thing has no properties, hence there is nothing for the "hieroglyphics" to refer to except themselves.

Plekhanov himself vouches for the accuracy of our interpretation of his views. The first edition [16] of the same brochure includes the following passage:

Our sensations are hieroglyphics of a special kind, which make us aware of what is happening in reality. Hieroglyphics do not resemble the events which they convey, but they are capable of conveying *with complete accuracy*

15. Plekhanov, . . . *Feuerbach* . . . , 1905, p. 103.
16. Plekhanov, . . . *Feuerbach* . . . , 1892.

both the events themselves and—what is of prime importance—the relations which exist between them.[17]

In the second edition (1905) Plekhanov deletes this passage,
revising this whole section of his commentary, and adding:
". . . in my notes to the first edition . . . I still expressed myself
in a way that was not wholly precise; only later did I come to
feel all of the disadvantages of such imprecision." [18]
Beltov, however, as we have seen, refers in 1906 to "hieroglyphics which express the forms and relations of things as they are
in themselves," i.e., he admits an "appearance" or set of properties in "things-in-themselves"—precisely what Plekhanov had admitted in 1892 but denied in 1905. From Beltov's point of view,
for example, there are "certain forms or relations of *things*" which
correspond to the spatial relations that we experience. But from
Plekhanov's point of view, things as they are "in themselves"
cannot have a spatial character, because such a character would
indicate a certain "form" or "appearance."
I have not dwelt upon this question in order to show how
little essential agreement there is among the chief representatives of this School, despite their external solidarity. That is comparatively unimportant. We are concerned with the *fundamental*
philosophical concept of this School: and we see how unclarified
and indefinite, even obscure, it is. What can such a concept
explain? In particular, how can it explain experience as a whole?
The role of "matter" in the philosophy of Plekhanov-Beltov
is truly an unhappy one. Empirical phenomena are taken, and
investigated, as phenomena; but a footnote is added to each
of them: "The cause of this phenomenon, as of all others, is
matter, which acts upon our senses; but the properties of matter
as it is in itself are unknown. It may not have any—beyond
the property of producing the given phenomenon." But *no inference* or *working hypothesis* is drawn from this footnote; it
bears the same relationship to each phenomenon, and to each
it equally adds—nothing. A useless and tiresome exercise!

17. *Ibid.*, 1892, p. 99.
18. *Ibid.*, 1905, p. 103.

We do know empirical phenomena—some better, some worse—and we know something about them. Yet to "explain" them we are offered a "matter" whose "true nature" we cannot know, the "forms" and "relations" of which are inaccessible in themselves. What precisely is this matter?

We may find an answer in Rakh-ov, one of the junior members of the School:

> What is characteristic of metaphysics? The fact that it attempts to explain the known by the *unknown*, what is accessible by what is *unexperienced* and *inexperienceable*.[19]

This is absolutely true and it is a condemnation. . . .

The historian of the future will note with perplexity that, in the twentieth century, among *Marxists*, there existed—and even made a claim to influence Marxist thought—a world view as childishly naive from the viewpoint of the science and philosophy of this century as this one. . . .

The School of Plekhanov-Ortodoks makes a loud and insistent claim to represent Marxism in philosophy; this, in essence, is its chief argument against its opponents. Many comrades, accepting this argument on faith, transfer their unbounded confidence in the authority of Marx to this School and become sincerely indignant at the "heretics" who lay siege to the "philosophy of Marxism" from within. . . .

A careful study of the philosophical legacy of Marx and Engels—a legacy which, unfortunately, is neither complete nor adequate—would lead these credulous comrades, even without my guidance, into great perplexity. First of all, they would look in vain for anything like the juxtaposition of "matter" and "experience" which serves as the point of departure for our Russian School of Marxism. They would find nothing like the ascetically dismal reduction of the empirical world to a world of "subjective" individual experiencings, offering no true reality but only "hieroglyphics" of something . . . or other. They would find nothing like the piously solemn assertion that "matter" is the first cause and, as such, exempt from definition and explana-

19. Rakh-ov, *op. cit.*, p. 34.

tion—like the god [20] of the theologians. On the contrary, they would find a straightforward definition of the "objective world" as a world of the "sensuously actual" (*sinnlich wirkliche*).[21] Finally, they would find nothing like Beltov's eternal "objective truth," but rather a definitely changing criterion of truth— human practice. All of this, of course, is only the *foundation* for a philosophical world-view. . . .

In any case, the philosophy of the proletariat needs further elaboration, not only because Marx and Engels did not succeed in formulating it fully enough, but also because of the accumulation of new scientific material which philosophy must take into account. Can the great scientific and technological revolution which is going on before our eyes remain without influence upon philosophy? It is the spirit, not the letter, of the Marx-Engels tradition which should be precious to us. . . .

20. It is worth noting that in this work, published in Saint Petersburg in 1908, the word "god" (*bog*) is regularly written with a small letter— an anticipation of the orthographic atheism which became mandatory after 1917.—TRANS.

21. Marx and Engels, *Nachlass*, II, 304.

VLADIMIR ILYICH LENIN (Ulyanov)
[1870–1924]

LENIN'S LIFE and political opinions are familiar, and his position within the framework of Marxism is well known. But his more strictly philosophical views are less available to the general reader, especially in the West. The selections in this volume are intended to familiarize the reader with these views and to clarify Lenin's interpretation of Marx. They are, accordingly, taken from Lenin's two chief philosophical works, *Materialism and Empirio-Criticism* (1909), and the *Philosophical Notebooks* (1914-1916).

Lenin was born Vladimir Ilyich Ulyanov in Simbirsk (now Ulyanovsk) in 1870. His father was a school inspector, his mother the daughter of a doctor—both belonged to the petty bourgeoisie. In 1887, the same year that his brother, Alexander, was executed for complicity in an attempt to assassinate Alexander III, Lenin entered the Faculty of Law of the University of Kazan. Within three months he was expelled for attending a student protest meeting. He studied on his own, however, and passed the University of Saint Petersburg law examinations in 1891, placing first among the candidates for the diploma.

For the next three years Lenin studied socialism, and particularly the views of Marx. He moved to Saint Petersburg in 1894 and immediately joined Marxist circles. The same year he published his first polemical work, *What the "Friends of the People" Are*, a violent attack on the Populists. He obtained permission to go abroad, met Plekhanov, returned to Russia to make contacts for Plekhanov's Liberation of Labor party, and, in December, 1895, was arrested for his illegal activities. After a year in prison, spent in study and writing, he was exiled to Siberia. He returned to European Russia in 1900 and again received permission to go abroad. This time he was to remain in Western Europe (except for two years after the 1905 Revolution) for seventeen years, to form his own version of the Social Democratic party, gain ascendency in it, and finally return to Petrograd in triumph after the February Revolution of 1917. A few months later he was to lead the Bolshevik *coup* that brought to birth the U.S.S.R.

His activities and his political views during this period are a matter of history. But preparation for revolution and fighting political deviations were not enough to use all the energy or all the available time of the leader of the Bolshevik faction of the Social Democratic party. Lenin's character did not permit him to ignore intellectual pursuits. Moreover, for the first decade after Lenin left Siberia the theory of Marxism was being threatened by "revisions" as much as its practical and political application was by "deviations." Plekhanov was aware of this and combated it, but Lenin did not find Plekhanov's criticism sufficiently telling or even always suitably "orthodox." It was for these reasons that, in 1909, Lenin published *Materialism and Empirio-Criticism*, his main philosophical work, intended primarily as a crushing attack on Bogdanov and the Machians.[1]

The book covers much more, however. Taking Marx's and Engels' views as premises, Lenin proceeds to elaborate them in order to defend Marxism against all "revisions" which seem to threaten their purity and against all obstacles which seem to refute their validity. In *Materialism and Empirio-Criticism*, therefore, Lenin first defines matter: "Matter is a philosophical category denoting the objective reality which is given to man by his sensations." He asserts its ontological primacy, a position which, he is careful to point out in reply to the Machians, is "in full agreement with natural science." Lenin goes on to discuss the relation of consciousness to the external world: "Thought, consciousness, sensation are products of a very high development [of matter]." "Things exist outside us. Our perceptions and ideas are their images." "Sensation is indeed the direct connection between consciousness and the external world; it is the

1. See above, pp. 390-404.

transformation of the energy of external excitation into the fact of consciousness." With this in mind, he criticizes Plekhanov's and Helmholtz's epistemology, calling it "agnosticism." Objective truth, i.e., "truth not dependent on man," is possible, he tells us, and is asserted by the materialist point of view. Consequently, so is absolute truth, which "is compounded of a sum-total of relative truths." The criterion of truth is practice. Thus, by its recognition of objective truth, materialism recognizes necessity in nature. Furthermore, as modes of the motion of matter, space and time are also objectively real.

Since dialectical materialism is in full agreement with natural science, it obviously assimilates the new discoveries in science: Lenin is at pains to make this clear to his Machian opponents. "Matter disappears" merely means "that the limit within which we have hitherto known matter is vanishing and that our knowledge is penetrating deeper." That knowledge can so penetrate comes as no surprise to the dialectical materialist who insists on the relative character of scientific theory and the lack of boundaries in nature.

Finally, having pointed out all the fallacies of Machism, its idealism, agnosticism, and disagreement with science, Lenin studies the historical and social sources of this school—a study which, he remarks, Plekhanov failed to make.

Lenin's other major philosophical work was not written in book form. It consists of notebooks in which he commented on philosophical texts which he was reading. These notebooks were written chiefly during World War I, while Lenin was in Switzerland. They were collected and published as Volumes 11 and 12 of the *Leninskiye sborniki* (1929 and 1930) and, in 1933, published separately under the title *Philosophical Notebooks*. Lenin's main philosophical concern during this period was with the nature of the dialectic, which he considered the essential element of Marxism. The *Notebooks* accordingly comment primarily on works of Hegel, and find illustrations of contradictions in the actual events of the period through which Lenin was then living.

In his interpretation of Hegel, Lenin tells us, "I am in general trying to read Hegel materialistically." Dialectic, he says, is

"the study of the contradiction in the very essence of objects."
As one reads Lenin's comments, however, one begins to question
whose influence is the stronger: is Lenin materializing Hegel or
is Hegel dematerializing Lenin's materialism—as physics had already partially succeeded in dematerializing matter for Lenin
in 1909?

Lenin was primarily a revolutionary.[2] In revolutionary theory
his interpretation of Marx was based far more on Marx's
"Utopian" side than on the deterministic, scientific side of
Marxism which Plekhanov favored. In method Lenin took over
many of the views of his Populist rivals. Lenin's favoring of a
small, strongly centralized elite revolutionary group was taken
from such Populist theoreticians of revolution as Lavrov and
P. N. Tkachyov (1844-1885). His pragmatism and opportunism
are reminiscent of Bakunin's early views and of those attributed
to Nechaev. Lenin's primary concern is not with economics
or with the state of the forces of production, it is not with matter
as such, but at best with the *motion* of matter, the nature of
change through internal and external opposition. If, with this
in mind, one also remembers that the *Notebooks* were written
during a period of world war and when Lenin was in the last
stages of preparing for revolution, Lenin's concern with the
nature of dialectic as such to the detriment of materialism is not
so surprising. Dialectic, not matter, is the revolutionary element
in dialectical materialism, both as a theory of knowledge and as a
world view.

Lenin's philosophy is narrow—he never questions his premises,
never studies a philosophy for itself but always in its relation to
dialectical materialism and his interpretation of it. Pragmatic as a
revolutionary leader, he is such in his approach to philosophy:
whatever supports dialectical materialism is acceptable, whatever
weakens it is to be opposed. Thus his views are remarkably
unsophisticated: "Naive realism" in epistemology; thoroughgoing
but ill-defined materialism; dialectic as a theory of change by
leaps. But one of his main principles is the Marxist principle of
the union of theory and practice. He had to bring about a
revolution and for this he needed the theory of dialectical mate-

2. Although he described himself as a journalist.

rialism. Dialectical materialism provided the theory of the inevitability of the revolution, of its inevitable success, of its justification as the nature of natural and historical change. Properly interpreted, Marxism was the most efficient intellectual tool of the revolution, and, by its own criterion, it was validated in the success of the coup of October, 1917. The narrowness of Lenin's philosophy and the content of it are justified by his own practice as a revolutionary leader.

SELECTED BIBLIOGRAPHY

Works:

V. I. Lenin, *Collected Works*, Moscow, 1960— (a translation of the 4th Russian edition of the collected works in 40 volumes).
——————, *Selected Works*, 3 vols., Moscow, 1963-1964.

Secondary Sources:

J. M. Bochenski, *Soviet Russian Dialectical Materialism*, trans. N. Sollohub, Dordrecht, 1963, pp. 27-31.
A. Pastore, *La filosofia di Lenin*, Milan, 1946.
Gustav A. Wetter, *Dialectical Materialism*, trans. Peter Heath, London and New York, 1958, pp. 110-127.

[V. I. LENIN]

Materialism and Empirio-Criticism*

Materialism, in full agreement with natural science, takes matter as primary and regards consciousness, thought, sensation as secondary, because in its well-defined form sensation is associated only with the higher forms of matter (organic matter), while "in the foundation of the structure of matter" one can only surmise the existence of a faculty akin to sensation. . . .

For every scientist who has not been led astray by professorial philosophy, as well as for every materialist, sensation is indeed the direct connection between consciousness and the external world; it is the transformation of the energy of external excitation into a state of consciousness. This transformation has been, and is, observed by each of us a million times on every hand. The sophism of idealist philosophy consists in the fact that it regards sensation as being not the connection between consciousness and the external world, but as a fence, a wall, separating consciousness from the external world—not an image of the external phenomenon corresponding to the sensation, but as the "sole entity." . . .

The "naive realism" of any healthy person who has not been an inmate of a lunatic asylum or a pupil of the idealist philosophers consists in the view that things, the environment, the world, exist *independently* of our sensation, of our consciousness, of our *Self* and of man in general. The same *experience* (not in the Machist sense, but in the human sense of the term) that has produced in us the firm conviction that *independently* of us there exist other people, and not mere complexes of my sensations of high, short, yellow, hard, etc.—this same *experience* produces in us the conviction that things, the world, the environment

* From V. I. Lenin, *Collected Works*, Vol. 14, trans. Abraham Fineberg, ed. Clemens Dutt, Moscow, 1962, pp. 46, 51, 69-70, 75, 102-104, 110, 127-130, 133, 135-137, 139-140, 142-143, 145-147, 155, 166, 175, 184-185, 235, 250-252, 260-262, 302-304, 306, 308-313, 322-326, 329-330, 348, 357-358. Informational footnotes have been omitted.

exist independently of us. Our sensation, our consciousness is only *an image* of the external world, and it is obvious that an image cannot exist without the thing imaged, and that the latter exists independently of that which images it. Materialism *deliberately* makes the "naive" belief of mankind the foundation of its theory of knowledge. . . .

Natural science positively asserts that the earth once existed in such a state that no man or any other creature existed or could have existed on it. Organic matter is a later phenomenon, the fruit of a long evolution. It follows that there was no sentient matter, no "complexes of sensations," no *self* that was supposedly "indissolubly" connected with the environment in accordance with Avenarius' doctrine. Matter is primary, and thought, consciousness, sensation are products of a very high development. Such is the materialist theory of knowledge, to which natural science instinctively subscribes. . . .

Engels clearly and explicitly states that he is contesting both Hume and Kant. . . .

What is the kernel of Engels' objections? Yesterday we did not know that coal tar contained alizarin. Today we learned that it does. The question is, did coal tar contain alizarin yesterday?

Of course it did. To doubt it would be to make a mockery of modern science.

And if that is so, three important epistemological conclusions follow:

(1) Things exist independently of our consciousness, independently of our perceptions, outside of us, for it is beyond doubt that alizarin existed in coal tar yesterday and it is equally beyond doubt that yesterday we knew nothing of the existence of this alizarin and received no sensations from it.

(2) There is definitely no difference in principle between the phenomenon and the thing-in-itself, and there cannot be any such difference. The only difference is between what is known and what is not yet known. And philosophical inventions of specific boundaries between the one and the other, inventions to the effect that the thing-in-itself is "beyond" phenomena (Kant), or that we can and must fence ourselves off by some philosophical partition from the problem of a world which in

one part or another is still unknown but which exists outside us (Hume)—all this is the sheerest nonsense, *Schrulle*, crotchet, fantasy.

(3) In the theory of knowledge, as in every other sphere of science, we must think dialectically, that is, we must not regard our knowledge as ready-made and unalterable, but must determine how *knowledge* emerges from *ignorance*, how incomplete, inexact knowledge becomes more complete and more exact.

Once we accept the point of view that human knowledge develops from ignorance, we shall find millions of examples of it just as simple as the discovery of alizarin in coal tar, millions of observations not only in the history of science and technology but in the everyday life of each and every one of us that illustrate the transformation of "things-in-themselves" into "things-for-us," the appearance of "phenomena" when our sense organs experience an impact from external objects, the disappearance of "phenomena" when some obstacle prevents the action upon our sense organs of an object which we know to exist. The sole and unavoidable deduction to be made from this—a deduction which all of us make in everyday practice and which materialism deliberately places at the foundation of its epistemology—is that outside us, and independently of us, there exist objects, things, bodies, and that our perceptions are images of the external world. Mach's converse theory (that bodies are complexes of sensations) is pitiful idealist nonsense. . . .

Thus, the materialist theory, the theory of the reflection of objects by our mind, is here presented with absolute clarity: things exist outside us. Our perceptions and ideas are their images. Verification of these images, differentiation between true and false images, is given by practice. . . .

All knowledge comes from experience, from sensation, from perception. That is true. But the question arises, does *objective reality* "belong to perception," i.e., is it the source of perception? If you answer yes, you are a materialist. If you answer no, you are inconsistent and will inevitably arrive at subjectivism, or agnosticism, irrespective of whether you deny the knowability of the thing-in-itself, or the objectivity of time, space, and causality (with Kant), or whether you do not even permit the thought of a thing-in-itself (with Hume). The inconsistency of your empiricism, of your philosophy of experience, will in that case lie in the fact that you deny the objective content of experience, the objective truth of experimental knowledge.

Those who hold to the line of Kant and Hume (Mach and Avenarius are among the latter, insofar as they are not pure Berkeleians) call us, the materialists, "metaphysicians" because we recognize objective reality which is given us in experience, because we recognize an objective source of our sensations independent of man. We materialists follow Engels in calling the Kantians and Humeans *agnostics*, because they deny objective reality as the source of our sensations. Agnostic is a Greek word: *a* in Greek means "no," *gnosis* "knowledge." The agnostic says: *I do not know* if there is an objective reality which is reflected, imaged by our sensations; I declare there is no way of knowing this. . . . Hence the denial of objective truth by the agnostic, and the tolerance—the Philistine, cowardly tolerance—of the dogmas regarding sprites, hobgoblins, Catholic saints, and the like. Mach and Avenarius, pretentiously advancing a "new" terminology, a supposedly "new" point of view, repeat, in fact, although in a confused and muddled way, the reply of the agnostic: on the one hand, bodies are complexes of sensations (pure subjectivism, pure Berkeleianism); on the other hand, if we rechristen our sensations "elements," we may think of them as existing independently of our sense organs!

The Machists love to declaim that they are philosophers who completely trust the evidence of our sense organs, who regard the world as actually being what it seems to us to be, full of sounds, colors, etc., whereas to the materialists, they say, the world is dead, devoid of sound and color, and in its reality different from what it seems to be, and so forth. Such declamations are indulged in by J. Petzoldt, both in his *Introduction to the Philosophy of Pure Experience* and in his *World Problem from the Positivist Standpoint (Weltproblem von positivistischen Standpunkte aus)*, 1906. Petzoldt is parroted by Mr. Victor Chernov,[1] who waxes enthusiastic over the "new" idea. But, in fact,

1. Victor M. Chernov (1876-1952), a revisionist Marxist and leader of the Socialist Revolutionary party.—TRANS.

the Machists are subjectivists and agnostics, for they *do not suf-ficiently* trust the evidence of our sense organs and are inconsistent in their sensationalism. They do not recognize objective reality, independent of man, as the source of our sensations. They do not regard sensations as a true copy of this objective reality, thereby directly conflicting with natural science and throwing the door open for fideism. On the contrary, for the materialist the world is richer, livelier, more varied than it seems, for with each step in the development of science new aspects are discovered. For the materialist, our sensations are images of the sole and ultimate objective reality, ultimate not in the sense that it has already been cognized to the end, but in the sense that there is not and cannot be any other. This view irrevocably closes the door not only to every species of fideism, but also to that professorial scholasticism which, while not recognizing an objective reality as the source of our sensations, "deduces" the concept of the objective by means of such artificial verbal constructions as universal significance, socially-organized, and so on and so forth, and which is unable, and frequently unwilling, to separate objective truth from belief in sprites and hobgoblins.

The Machists contemptuously shrug their shoulders at the "antiquated" views of the "dogmatists," the materialists, who still cling to the concept *matter*, which supposedly has been refuted by "recent science" and "recent positivism." We shall speak separately of the new theories of physics on the structure of matter. But it is absolutely unpardonable to confuse, as the Machists do, any particular theory of the structure of matter with the epistemological category, to confuse the problem of the new properties of new aspects of matter (electrons, for example) with the old problem of the theory of knowledge, with the problem of the sources of our knowledge, the existence of objective truth, etc. Mach "discovered the world-elements": red, green, hard, soft, loud, long, etc. We ask, is a man given objective reality when he sees something red or feels something hard, etc., or not? This hoary philosophical query is confused by Mach. If you hold that it is not given, you, together with Mach, inevitably sink to subjectivism and agnosticism and deservedly fall into the embrace of the immanentists, i.e., the philosophical Menshikovs.[2] If you hold that it is given, a philosophical concept is needed for this objective reality, and this concept has been worked out long, long ago. This concept is *matter*. Matter is a philosophical category denoting the objective reality which is given to man by his sensations, and which is copied, photographed, and reflected by our sensations, while existing independently of them. Therefore, to say that such a concept can become "antiquated" is *childish talk*, a senseless repetition of the arguments of fashionable *reactionary* philosophy. Could the struggle between materialism and idealism, the struggle between the tendencies or lines of Plato and Democritus in philosophy, the struggle between religion and science, the denial of objective truth and its assertion, the struggle between the adherents of supersensible knowledge and its adversaries, have become antiquated during the two thousand years of the development of philosophy?

Acceptance or rejection of the concept matter is a question of the confidence man places in the evidence of his sense organs, a question of the source of our knowledge, a question which has been asked and debated from the very inception of philosophy, which may be disguised in a thousand different garbs by professorial clowns, but which can no more become antiquated than the question whether the source of human cognition is sight and touch, hearing and smell. To regard our sensations as images of the external world, to recognize objective truth, to hold the materialist theory of knowledge—these are all one and the same thing. . . .

To be a materialist is to acknowledge objective truth, which is revealed to us by our sense organs. To acknowledge objective truth, i.e., truth not dependent upon man and mankind, is, in one way or another, to recognize absolute truth. . . .

Human thought, then, by its nature, is capable of giving, and does give, absolute truth, which is compounded of a sum-total of relative truths. Each step in the development of science adds

2. Michael O. Menshikov (1859-1918)—a conservative political commentator executed by the Bolsheviks.—TRANS.

new grains to the sum of absolute truth, but the limits of the truth of each scientific proposition are relative, now expanding, now shrinking with the growth of knowledge. . . .

For dialectical materialism there is no impassable boundary between relative and absolute truth. Bogdanov entirely failed to grasp this if he could write: "It [the world outlook of the old materialism] sets itself up as the absolute *objective knowledge of the essence of things* [Bogdanov's italics] and is incompatible with the historically conditional nature of all ideologies" (*Empirio-Monism*, Bk. III, p. iv). From the standpoint of modern materialism, i.e., Marxism, the *limits* of approximation of our knowledge to objective, absolute truth are historically conditional, but the existence of such truth is *unconditional*, and the fact that we are approaching nearer to it is also unconditional. The contours of the picture are historically conditional, but the fact that this picture depicts an objectively existing model is unconditional. When and under what circumstances we reached, in our knowledge of the essential nature of things, the discovery of alizarin in coal tar or the discovery of electrons in the atom is historically conditional; but that every such discovery is an advance of "absolutely objective knowledge" is unconditional. In a word, every ideology is historically conditional, but it is unconditionally true that to every scientific ideology (as distinct, for instance, from religious ideology), there corresponds an objective truth, absolute nature. You will say that this distinction between relative and absolute truth is indefinite. And I shall reply: it is sufficiently "indefinite" to prevent science from becoming a dogma in the bad sense of the term, from becoming something dead, frozen, ossified; but it is at the same time sufficiently "definite" to enable us to dissociate ourselves in the most emphatic and irrevocable manner from fideism and agnosticism, from philosophical idealism and the sophistry of the followers of Hume and Kant. Here is a boundary which you have not noticed, and not having noticed it, you have fallen into the swamp of reactionary philosophy. It is the boundary between dialectical materialism and relativism. . . .

To make relativism the basis of the theory of knowledge is inevitably to condemn oneself either to absolute skepticism, agnosticism, and sophistry, or to subjectivism. Relativism as a basis of the theory of knowledge is not only the recognition of the relativity of our knowledge, but also a denial of any objective measure or model existing independently of mankind to which our relative knowledge approximates. From the standpoint of naked relativism, one can justify any sophistry; one may regard as "conditional" whether Napoleon died on May 5, 1821, or not; one may declare the admission, alongside of scientific ideology ("convenient" in one respect), of religious ideology (very "convenient" in another respect) to be a mere "convenience" for man or mankind, and so forth.

Dialectics—as Hegel in his time explained—*contains* an element of relativism, of negation, of skepticism, but *is not reducible* to relativism. The materialist dialectics of Marx and Engels certainly does contain relativism, but is not reducible to relativism, that is, it recognizes the relativity of all our knowledge, not in the sense of denying objective truth, but in the sense that the limits of the approximation of our knowledge of this truth are historically conditional.

Bogdanov writes in italics: *"Consistent Marxism does not admit such dogmatism and such static concepts"* as eternal truths. (*Empirio-Monism*, Bk. III, p. ix.) This is a muddle. If the world is eternally moving and developing matter (as the Marxists think), reflected by the developing human consciousness, what is there "static" here? The point at issue is not the immutable essence of things, or an immutable consciousness, but the *correspondence* between the consciousness which reflects nature and the nature which is reflected by consciousness. . . .

And a twisted professorial idealism it is, indeed, when the criterion of practice, which for every one of us distinguishes illusion from reality, is removed by Mach from the realm of science, from the realm of the theory of knowledge. Human practice proves the correctness of the materialist theory of knowledge, said Marx and Engels, who dubbed attempts to solve the fundamental question of epistemology without the aid of practice "scholastic" and "philosophical crotchets." But for Mach practice is one thing and the theory of knowledge something quite different. . . . For the materialist the "success" of human prac-

tice proves the correspondence between our ideas and the objective nature of the things we perceive. For the solipsist "success"
is everything needed *by me in practice*, which can be regarded
separately from the theory of knowledge. If we include the
criterion of practice in the foundation of the theory of knowledge we inevitably arrive at materialism, says the Marxist. . . .

Of course, we must not forget that the criterion of practice
can never, in the nature of things, either confirm or refute any
human idea *completely*. This criterion also is sufficiently "indefinite" not to allow human knowledge to become "absolute," but
at the same time it is sufficiently definite to wage a ruthless
fight on all varieties of idealism and agnosticism. If what our practice confirms is the sole, ultimate, and objective truth, then from
this must follow the recognition that the only path to this
truth is the path of science, which holds the materialist point
of view. For instance, Bogdanov is prepared to recognize Marx's
theory of the circulation of money as an objective truth only for
"our time," and calls it "dogmatism" to attribute to this theory
a "super-historically objective" truth (*Empirio-Monism*, Bk. III,
p. vii). This is again a muddle. The correspondence of this theory
to practice cannot be altered by any future circumstances, for
the same simple reason that makes it an *eternal* truth that Napoleon died on May 5, 1821. But inasmuch as the criterion of practice, i.e., the course of development of *all* capitalist countries
in the last few decades, proves only the objective truth of Marx's
whole social and economic theory in general, and not merely of
one or other of its parts, formulations, etc., it is clear that to
talk of the "dogmatism" of the Marxists is to make an unpardonable concession to bourgeois economics. The sole conclusion to
be drawn from the opinion held by Marxists that Marx's theory
is an objective truth is that by following the *path* of Marxian
theory we shall draw closer and closer to objective truth (without ever exhausting it); but by following *any other path* we
shall arrive at nothing but confusion and lies. . . .

On the other hand, the recognition of the philosophical line
denied by the idealists and agnostics is expressed in the definitions:
matter is that which, acting upon our sense organs, produces

sensation; matter is the objective reality given to us in sensation, and so forth.

Bogdanov, pretending to argue only against Beltov and cravenly ignoring Engels, is indignant at such definitions, which, don't you see, "prove to be simple repetitions" (*Empirio-Monism*, Bk. III, p. xvi) of the "formula" (*of Engels*, our "Marxist" forgets to add) that for one trend in philosophy matter is primary and spirit secondary, while for the other trend the reverse is the case. All the Russian Machists exultantly echo Bogdanov's "refutation"! But the slightest reflection could have shown these people that it is impossible, in the very nature of the case, to give any definition of these two ultimate concepts of epistemology, except an indication which of them is taken as primary. What is meant by giving a "definition"? It means essentially to bring a given concept within a more comprehensive concept. For example, when I give the definition "an ass is an animal," I am bringing the concept "ass" within a more comprehensive concept. The question then is, are there more comprehensive concepts with which the theory of knowledge could operate than those of being and thinking, matter and sensation, physical and mental? No. These are the ultimate, most comprehensive concepts, which epistemology has in point of fact so far not surpassed (apart from changes in *nomenclature*, which are *always* possible). One must be a charlatan or an utter blockhead to demand a "definition" of these two "series" of concepts of ultimate comprehensiveness which would not be a "mere repetition": one or the other must be taken as the primary. Take the three aforementioned arguments on matter. What do they all amount to? To this, that these philosophers proceed from the mental, or the *self*, to the physical, or environment, as from the central term to the counter-term—or from sensation to matter, or from sense perception to matter. Could Avenarius, Mach, and Pearson in fact have given any other "definition" of these fundamental concepts, save by indicating the *trend* of their philosophical line? Could they have defined in any other way, in any specific way, what the *self* is, what sensation is, what sense perception is? One has only to formulate the question clearly to realize what sheer nonsense the Machists talk when they demand that the materialists give a definition of matter which would not amount to a repetition of the proposition that matter, nature, being, the physical—is primary, and spirit, consciousness, sensation, the psychical—is secondary.

One expression of the genius of Marx and Engels was that they despised pedantic playing with new words, erudite terms, and subtle "isms," and said simply and plainly: there is a materialist line and an idealist line in philosophy, and between them there are various shades of agnosticism. The vain attempts to find a "new" point of view in philosophy betrays the same poverty of spirit that is revealed in the similar efforts to create a "new" theory of value, or a "new" theory of rent, and so forth. . . .

Of course, even the antithesis of matter and mind has absolute significance only within the bounds of a very limited field—in this case exclusively within the bounds of the fundamental epistemological problem of what is to be regarded as primary and what as secondary. Beyond these bounds the relative character of this antithesis is indubitable. . . .

The subjectivist line on the question of causality is philosophical idealism (varieties of which are the theories of causality of both Hume and Kant), i.e., fideism more or less weakened and diluted. The recognition of objective law in nature and the recognition that this law is reflected with approximate fidelity in the mind of man is materialism. . . .

The recognition of necessity in nature and the derivation from it of necessity in thought is materialism. The derivation of necessity, causality, law, etc., from thought is idealism. . . .

Recognizing the existence of objective reality, i.e., matter in motion independently of our mind, materialism must also inevitably recognize the objective reality of time and space, in contrast above all to Kantianism, which in this question sides with idealism and regards time and space not as objective realities but as forms of human understanding. The basic difference between the two fundamental philosophical lines on this question too is quite clearly recognized by writers of the most diverse trends who are at all consistent thinkers. Let us begin with the materialists.

"Space and time," says Feuerbach, "are not mere forms of phenomena but essential conditions (*Wesensbedingungen*) . . . of being" (*Werke*, II, S. 332). Regarding the sensible world we know through sensations as objective reality, Feuerbach naturally also rejects the phenomenalist (as Mach would call his own conception) or the agnostic (as Engels calls it) conception of space and time. Just as things or bodies are not mere phenomena, not complexes of sensations, but objective realities acting on our senses, so space and time are not mere forms of phenomena, but objectively real forms of being. There is nothing in the world but matter in motion, and matter in motion cannot move otherwise than in space and time. Human conceptions of space and time are relative, but these relative conceptions go to compound absolute truth. These relative conceptions, in their development, move toward absolute truth and approach nearer and nearer to it. The mutability of human conceptions of space and time no more refutes the objective reality of space and time than the mutability of scientific knowledge of the structure and forms of matter in motion refutes the objective reality of the external world. . . .

"Many of Engels' particular views," V. Bazarov, for instance, writes, in the *Studies* (p. 67), "as, for example, his conception of 'pure' space and time, are now obsolete."

Indeed! The views of the materialist Engels are now obsolete, but the views of the idealist Pearson and the muddled idealist Mach are very modern! The most curious thing of all is that Bazarov does not even doubt that the views of space and time, viz., the recognition or denial of their objective reality, can be classed among *"particular views,"* in contradistinction to the *"starting point of the world outlook"* spoken of by this author in his next sentence. Here you have a glaring example of that "eclectic pauper's broth" of which Engels used to speak in reference to German philosophy of the eighties. For to contrast the "starting point" of Marx's and Engels' materialist world outlook with their "particular view" of the objective reality of time and space is as utterly nonsensical as if you were to contrast the "starting point" of Marx's economic theory with his "particular view" of surplus-value. To sever Engels' doctrine of the objective reality of time and space from his doctrine of the transformation of "things-in-themselves" into "things-for-us," from his recognition of objective and absolute truth: the objective reality given us in our sensations, and from his recognition of objective law, causality, and necessity in nature—is to reduce an integral philosophy to a hodgepodge. Like all the Machists, Bazarov erred in confusing the mutability of human conceptions of time and space, their exclusively relative character, with the immutability of the fact that man and nature exist only in time and space, and that beings outside time and space, as invented by the priests and maintained by the imagination of the ignorant and downtrodden mass of humanity, are disordered fantasies, the artifices of philosophical idealism, rotten products of a rotten social system. The teachings of science on the structure of matter, on the chemical composition of food, on the atom and the electron, may and constantly do become obsolete, but the truth that man is unable to subsist on ideas and to beget children by Platonic love alone never becomes obsolete. And a philosophy that denies the objective reality of time and space is as absurd, as intrinsically rotten and false as is the denial of these latter truths. The artifices of the idealists and the agnostics are, taken as a whole, as hypocritical as the Pharisees' sermons on Platonic love! . . .

The theory of symbols cannot be reconciled with such a view (which, as we have seen, is wholly materialist), for it implies a certain distrust of perception, a distrust of the evidence of our sense organs. It is beyond doubt that an image can never wholly compare with the model, but an image is one thing; a symbol, a *conventional sign*, another. The image inevitably and of necessity implies the objective reality of that which it "images." "Conventional sign," symbol, hieroglyphic are concepts which introduce an entirely unnecessary element of agnosticism. . . .

A year ago, in *Die Neue Zeit* (1907, No. 52), there appeared an article by Joseph Diner-Dénes entitled "Marxism and the Recent Revolution in the Natural Sciences.". . . Joseph Diner-Dénes, like the present writer, holds the view of the "rank-and-file Marxist," of whom our Machists speak with such haughty contempt. . . . And now this rank-and-file Marxist, in the person of J. Diner-Dénes, has *directly* compared the recent discoveries in science, and especially in physics (X-rays, Becquerel rays, radium, etc.), with Engels' *Anti-Dühring*. To what conclusion has this comparison led him? "In the most varied fields of natural science," writes Diner-Dénes, "new knowledge has been acquired, all of which tends toward that single point which Engels desired to make clear, namely, that in nature 'there are no irreconcilable contradictions, no forcibly fixed boundary lines and distinctions,' and that if contradictions and distinctions are met with in nature, it is because we alone have introduced their rigidity and absoluteness into nature." It was discovered, for instance, that light and electricity are only manifestations of one and the same force of nature. Each day it becomes more probable that chemical affinity may be reduced to electrical processes. The indestructible and non-disintegrable elements of chemistry, whose number continues to grow as though in derision of the unity of the world, now prove to be destructible and disintegrable. The element radium has been converted into the element helium. "Just as all the forces of nature have been reduced to one force, so, with this knowledge, all substances in nature have been reduced to *one substance*" (Diner-Dénes' italics). Quoting the opinion of one of the writers who regard the atom as only a condensation of the ether, the author exclaims: "How brilliantly does this confirm the statement made by Engels thirty years ago that motion is the mode of existence of matter." "All phenomena of nature are motion, and the differences between them lie only in the fact that we human beings perceive this motion in different forms. . . . It is as Engels said. Nature, like history, is subject to the dialectical law of motion."

On the other hand, you cannot take up any of the writings of the Machists or about Machism without encountering pretentious references to the new physics, which is said to have refuted materialism, and so on and so forth. Whether these assertions are well founded is another question, but the connection between the new physics, or rather a definite school of the new physics, and Machism and other varieties of modern idealist philosophy is beyond doubt. To analyze Machism and at the same time to ignore this connection—as Plekhanov does—is to scoff at the spirit of dialectical materialism, i.e., to sacrifice the method of Engels to the letter of Engels. Engels says explicitly that "with each epoch-making discovery even in the sphere of natural science [not to speak of the history of mankind], materialism has to change its form" (*Ludwig Feuerbach*, German edition, p. 19). Hence, a revision of the "form" of Engels' materialism, a revision of his natural-philosophical propositions is not only not "revisionism," in the accepted meaning of the term, but, on the contrary, is an essential element of Marxism. We criticize the Machists not for making such a revision, but for their *purely revisionist* trick of betraying the *essence* of materialism under the guise of criticizing its *form* and of adopting the fundamental propositions of reactionary bourgeois philosophy without making the slightest attempt to deal directly, frankly, and definitely with assertions of Engels' which are unquestionably of extreme importance for the given question, as, for example, his assertion that ". . . motion without matter is unthinkable" (*Anti-Dühring*, p. 50).

It goes without saying that in examining the connection between one of the schools of modern physicists and the rebirth of philosophical idealism, it is far from being our intention to deal with specific physical theories. What interests us exclusively are the epistemological conclusions that follow from certain definite propositions and generally known discoveries. These epistemological conclusions are of themselves so insistent that many physicists are already reaching for them. What is more, there are already various trends among the physicists, and definite schools are beginning to be formed on this basis. Our object, therefore, will be confined to explaining clearly the essence of the difference between these various trends and the relation in which they stand to the fundamental lines of philosophy. . . .

"Matter disappears" means that the limit within which we have hitherto known matter is vanishing and that our knowledge is penetrating deeper; properties of matter are likewise disappearing which formerly seemed absolute, immutable, and primary (impenetrability, inertia, mass, etc.) and which are now revealed to be relative and characteristic only of certain states of matter. For the *sole* "property" of matter with whose recognition philosophical materialism is bound up is the property of *being an objective reality*, of existing outside our mind.

The error of Machism in general, as of the Machist new physics, is that it ignores this basis of philosophical materialism and the distinction between metaphysical materialism and dialectical materialism. The recognition of immutable elements, "of the immutable substance of things," and so forth, is not materialism, but *metaphysical*, i.e., anti-dialectical, materialism. That is why J. Dietzgen emphasized that the "subject matter of science is endless," that not only the infinite, but the "smallest atom" is immeasurable, unknowable to the end, *inexhaustible*, "for nature in all her parts has no beginning and no end" (*Kleinere philosophische Schriften*, S. 229-230). That is why Engels gave the example of the discovery of alizarin in coal tar and criticized *mechanical* materialism. In order to present the question in the only correct way, that is, from the dialectical materialist standpoint, we must ask: Do electrons, ether, *and so on* exist as objective realities outside the human mind or not? The scientists will also have to answer this question unhesitatingly; and they do invariably answer it in the *affirmative*, just as they unhesitatingly recognize that nature existed prior to man and prior to organic matter. Thus the question is decided in favor of materialism, for the concept matter, as we already stated, epistemologically implies *nothing but* objective reality existing independently of the human mind and reflected by it.

But dialectical materialism insists on the approximate, relative character of every scientific theory of the structure of matter and its properties; it insists on the absence of absolute boundaries in nature, on the transformation of moving matter from one state into another, that from our point of view is apparently irreconcilable with it, and so forth. However bizarre from the standpoint of "common sense" the transformation of imponderable ether into ponderable matter and vice versa may appear, however "strange" may seem the absence of any other kind of mass in the electron save electromagnetic mass, however extraordinary may be the fact that the mechanical laws of motion are confined only to a single sphere of natural phenomena and are subordinated to the more profound laws of electromagnetic phenomena, and so forth—all this is but another *corroboration* of dialectical materialism. It is mainly because the physicists did not know dialectics that the new physics strayed into idealism. They combated metaphysical (in Engels', and not the positivist, i.e., Humean, sense of the word) materialism and its one-sided "mechanism," and in so doing threw the baby out with the bath water. Denying the immutability of the elements and the properties of matter known hitherto, they ended in denying matter, i.e., the objective reality of the physical world. Denying the absolute character of some of the most important and basic laws, they ended by denying all objective law in nature and by declaring that a law of nature is a mere convention, "a limitation of expectation," "a logical necessity," and so forth. Insisting on the approximate and relative character of our knowledge, they ended in denying the object independent of the mind, reflected approximately-correctly and relatively-truthfully by the mind. And so on, and so forth, without end.

The opinions expressed by Bogdanov in 1899 regarding "the immutable essence of things," the opinions of Valentinov and Yushkevich regarding "substance," and so forth—are similar fruits of ignorance of dialectics. From Engels' point of view, the only immutability is the reflection by the human mind (when there is a human mind) of an external world existing and developing independently of the mind. No other "immutability," no other "essence," no other "absolute substance," in the sense in which these concepts were depicted by the empty professorial philosophy, exist for Marx and Engels. The "essence" of things, or "substance," is *also* relative; it expresses only the degree of profundity of man's knowledge of objects; and while yesterday the profundity of this knowledge did not go beyond the atom, and today does not go beyond the electron and ether, dialectical materialism insists on the temporary, relative, approximate character of all these *milestones* in the knowledge of nature gained by the progressing science of man. The electron is as *inexhaustible* as the atom, nature is infinite, but it infinitely *exists*. And it is this sole categorical, this sole unconditional recognition of nature's *existence* outside the mind and perceptions of man that distinguishes dialectical materialism from relativist agnosticism and idealism. . . .

Sensation is an image of matter in motion. Save through sensations, we can know nothing either of the forms of matter or of the forms of motion; sensations are evoked by the action of matter in motion upon our sense organs. That is how science views it. The sensation of red reflects ether vibrations of a frequency of approximately 450 trillions per second. The sensation of blue reflects ether vibrations of a frequency of approximately 620 trillions per second. The vibrations of the ether exist independently of our sensations of light. Our sensations of light depend on the action of the vibrations of the ether on the human organ of vision. Our sensations reflect objective reality, i.e., something that exists independently of humanity and of human sensations. That is how science views it. . . .

We have seen that the question of the epistemological deductions that can be drawn from the new physics has been raised and is being discussed from the most varied points of view in English, German, and French literature. There can be no doubt that we have before us a certain international ideological current, which is not dependent upon any one philosophical system, but which is the result of certain general causes lying outside the sphere of philosophy. The foregoing review of the facts undoubtedly shows that Machism is "connected" with the new physics, but at the same time reveals that the idea of this connection spread by our Machists is *fundamentally incorrect*. As in philosophy, so in physics, our Machists slavishly follow the *fashion*, and are unable from their own, Marxist, standpoint to give a general survey of particular currents and to judge the place they occupy.

A double falsity pervades all the talk about Mach's philosophy being "the philosophy of twentieth-century natural science," "the recent philosophy of the sciences," "recent natural-scientific positivism," and so forth. (Bogdanov, in the Introduction to *Analysis of Sensations*, pp. iv, xii; cf. also Yushkevich, Valentinov, and Co.) Firstly, Machism is ideologically connected with only *one* school in *one* branch of modern natural science. Secondly, and *this is the main point,* what in Machism is connected with this school *is not what distinguishes it from all other trends and systems of idealist philosophy, but what it has in common with philosophical idealism in general.* It suffices to cast a glance at the entire ideological current in question *as a whole* in order to leave no shadow of doubt as to the truth of this statement. . . .

The fundamental idea of the school of the new physics under discussion is the denial that objective reality is given us in our sensation and reflected in our theories, doubt as to the existence of such a reality. Here this school departs from *materialism* (inaccurately called realism, neo-mechanism, hylo-kinetism, and not in any appreciable degree consciously developed by the physicists themselves) which by *general acknowledgment* prevails among the physicists—and departs from it as a school of "physical" idealism. . . .

The basic materialist spirit of physics, as of all modern science, will overcome all crises, but only by the indispensable replacement of metaphysical materialism by dialectical materialism. . . .

Reactionary attempts are engendered by the very progress of science. The great successes achieved by natural science, the approach to elements of matter so homogeneous and simple that their laws of motion can be treated mathematically, caused the mathematicians to overlook matter. "Matter disappears," only equations remain. At a new stage of development and apparently in a new manner, we get the old Kantian idea: reason prescribes laws to nature. Hermann Cohen, who, as we have seen, rejoices over the idealist spirit of the new physics, goes so far as to advocate the introduction of higher mathematics in the schools in order to imbue high school students with the spirit of idealism, which is being driven out by our materialistic age (F. A. Lange, *Geschichte des Materialismus,* 5. Auflage, 1896, Bd. II, S. xlix). This, of course, is the ridiculous dream of a reactionary and, in fact, there is and can be nothing here but a temporary infatuation with idealism on the part of a small number of specialists. But what is highly characteristic is the way the drowning man clutches at a straw, the subtle means whereby representatives of the educated bourgeoisie artificially attempt to preserve, or to find a place for, the fideism which is engendered among the masses of the people by their ignorance and their downtrodden condition, and by the senseless barbarity of capitalist contradictions.

The other cause which gave rise to "physical" idealism is the principle of *relativism*, the relativity of our knowledge, a principle which, in a period of abrupt breakdown of the old theories, is taking a firm hold upon the physicists, and which, *if the latter are ignorant of dialectics*, inevitably leads to idealism.

This question of the relation between relativism and dialectics plays perhaps the most important part in explaining the theoretical misadventures of Machism. Take Rey, for instance, who like all European positivists has no conception whatever of Marxian dialectics. He employs the word dialectics exclusively in the sense of idealist philosophical speculation. As a result, although he feels that the new physics has gone astray on the question of relativism, he nevertheless flounders helplessly and attempts to differentiate between moderate and immoderate relativism. Of course, "immoderate relativism logically, if not in practice, borders on actual skepticism" ([*La théorie de la physique chez les physiciens contemporains*, Paris, 1907] p. 215), but there is none of this "immoderate" relativism, you see, in Poincaré. Just fancy—one can, like an apothecary, weigh out a little more or a little less relativism and thus save Machism!

As a matter of fact, the only theoretically correct formulation of the question of relativism is given in the dialectical materialism of Marx and Engels, and ignorance of it is *bound* to lead from relativism to philosophical idealism. Incidentally, the failure to understand this fact is enough to render Mr. Berman's absurd book, *Dialectics in the Light of the Modern Theory of Knowledge*, utterly valueless. Mr. Berman repeats the old, old nonsense about dialectics, which he has entirely failed to understand. We have already seen that in the theory of knowledge *all* the Machists, *at every step*, reveal a similar lack of understanding.

All the old truths of physics, including those which were regarded as firmly established and incontestable, prove to be relative truths—*hence*, there can be no objective truth independent of mankind. Such is the argument not only of the Machists, but of the "physical" idealists in general: that absolute truth results from the sum-total of relative truths in the course of their development; that relative truths represent relatively faithful reflections of an object existing independently of mankind; that these reflections become more and more faithful; that every scientific truth, notwithstanding its relative nature, contains an element of absolute truth—all these propositions, which are obvious to anyone who has thought over Engels' *Anti-Dühring*, are for the "modern" theory of knowledge a book with seven seals. . . .

Engels reproached the earlier materialists for their failure to appreciate the relativity of all scientific theories, for their ignorance of dialectics, and for their exaggeration of the mechanical point of view. But Engels . . . was able to discard Hegelian idealism and *to grasp* the great and true kernel of Hegelian dialectics. Engels rejected the old metaphysical materialism for *dialectical* materialism, and not for relativism that sinks into subjectivism. . . .

The trouble with Duhem, Stallo, Mach, and Poincaré [is] that they do not perceive the door opened by dialectical materialism. Being unable to give a correct formulation of relativism, they slide from the latter into idealism. "A law of physics, properly speaking, is neither true nor false, but approximate"— writes Duhem.[3] And this "but" contains the beginning of the falsity, the beginning of the obliteration of the boundary between a scientific theory that approximately *reflects the object*, i.e., approaches objective truth, and an arbitrary, fantastic, and purely conventional theory, such as, for example, a religious theory or the theory of the game of chess.

Duhem carries this falsity to the point of declaring that the question whether "material reality" corresponds to perceptual phenomena is *metaphysics* (p. 10). Away with the question of reality! Our concepts and hypotheses are mere signs (p. 26), "arbitrary" (p. 27) constructions, and so forth. There is only one step from this to idealism, to the "physics of the believer," which M. Pierre Duhem preaches in the Kantian spirit (Rey, p. 162; cf. p. 160). But the good Adler (Fritz)—also a Machist would-be Marxist!—could find nothing cleverer to do than to

3. *La théorie physique, son objet et sa structure*, Paris, 1906, p. 274.

"correct" Duhem as follows: Duhem, he claims, eliminates the "realities concealed behind phenomena only as objects of theory, but not as *objects of reality*." [4] This is the familiar criticism of Kantianism from the standpoint of Hume and Berkeley. . . .

In short, the "physical" idealism of today, exactly like the "physiological" idealism of yesterday, merely signifies that one school of natural scientists in one branch of natural science has slid into a reactionary philosophy, being unable to rise directly and at once from metaphysical materialism to dialectical materialism. This step is being made, and will be made, by modern physics; but it is advancing toward the only true method and the only true philosophy of natural science not directly but by zigzags, not consciously but instinctively, not clearly perceiving its "final goal" but drawing closer to it gropingly, unsteadily, and sometimes even with its back turned to it. Modern physics is in travail; it is giving birth to dialectical materialism. The process of childbirth is painful. And in addition to a living healthy being, there are bound to be produced certain dead products, refuse fit only for the garbage heap. And the entire school of physical idealism, the entire empirio-critical philosophy, together with empirio-symbolism, empirio-monism, and so on, and so forth, must be regarded as such refuse! . . .

Having quoted Marx's words, Bogdanov declares that the "old formulation of historical monism, without ceasing to be basically true, no longer fully satisfies us" (*[The Psychology of Society,* 1902] p. 37). The author wishes, therefore, to correct the theory, or to develop it, *starting from the basis of the theory itself.* The author's chief conclusion is as follows:

"We have shown that social forms belong to the comprehensive *genus*—biological adaptations. But we have not thereby defined the province of social forms; for a definition, not only the *genus,* but also the *species* must be established. . . . In their struggle for existence men can unite only with the help of *consciousness:* without consciousness there can be no intercourse. Hence, *social life in all its manifestations is a consciously psychical life.*

4. Translator's note to the German translation of Duhem, Leipzig, 1903, J. Barth.

. . . Society is inseparable from consciousness. *Social being and social consciousness are, in the exact meaning of these terms, identical"* (pp. 50, 51, Bogdanov's italics).

That this conclusion has nothing in common with Marxism has been pointed out by Ortodoks (*Philosophical Essays*, Saint Petersburg, 1906, p. 183 and preceding). . . . Social being and social consciousness are not identical, just as being in general and consciousness in general are not identical. From the fact that in their intercourse men act as conscious beings, it *does not follow* at all that social consciousness is identical with social being. In all social formations of any complexity—and in the capitalist social formation in particular—people in their inter-course are *not conscious* of what kind of social relations are being formed, in accordance with what laws they develop, etc. For instance, a peasant when he sells his grain enters into "inter-course" with the world producers of grain in the world market, but he is not conscious of it; nor is he conscious of the kind of social relations that are formed on the basis of exchange. Social consciousness *reflects* social being—that is Marx's teaching. A reflection may be an approximately true copy of the reflected, but to speak of identity is absurd. Consciousness in general *reflects* being—that is a general principle of *all* materialism. It is impossible not to see its direct and *inseparable* connection with the thesis of historical materialism: social consciousness *reflects* social being.

Bogdanov's attempt imperceptibly to correct and develop Marx in the "spirit of his principles" is an obvious distortion of these *materialist* principles in the spirit of *idealism*. It would be ludicrous to deny it. Let us recall Bazarov's exposition of empirio-criticism (not empirio-monism, oh no!—there is such a wide, wide dif-ference between these "systems"!): "sense-perception *is* the real-ity existing outside us." This is plain idealism, a plain theory of the identity of consciousness and being. . . .

Let Bogdanov, accepting in the best sense and with the best of intentions *all the conclusions* of Marx, preach the "iden-tity" of social being and social consciousness; we shall say: Bog-danov *minus* "empirio-monism" (or rather, *minus* Machism) is a Marxist. For this theory of the identity of social being and social consciousness is *sheer nonsense* and an *absolutely reactionary* theory. If certain people reconcile it with Marxism, with Marxist behavior, we must admit that these people are better than their theory, but we cannot justify outrageous theoretical distortions of Marxism.

Bogdanov reconciles his theory with Marx's conclusions, and sacrifices elementary consistency for the sake of these conclusions. Every individual producer in the world economic system realizes that he is introducing this or that change into the technique of production; every owner realizes that he exchanges certain products for others; but these producers and these owners do not realize that in doing so they are thereby changing *social being*. The sum-total of these changes in all their ramifications in the capitalist world economy could not be grasped even by seventy Marxes. The most important thing is that the *laws* of these changes have been discovered, that the *objective* logic of these changes and of their historical development has in its chief and basic features been disclosed—objective, not in the sense that a society of conscious beings, of people, could exist and develop independently of the existence of conscious beings (and it is only such trifles that Bogdanov *stresses* by his "theory"), but in the sense that social being is *independent* of *the social consciousness* of people. The fact that you live and conduct your business, beget children, produce products and exchange them, gives rise to an objectively necessary chain of events, a chain of development, which is independent of your *social* consciousness, and is never grasped by the latter completely. The highest task of humanity is to comprehend the objective logic of economic evolution (the evolution of social life) in its general and fundamental features, so that it may be possible to adapt *to it* one's social consciousness and the consciousness of the advanced classes of all capitalist countries in as definite, clear, and critical a fashion as possible.

Bogdanov admits all this. And what does this mean? It means *in effect* that he throws overboard his theory of the "identity of social being and social consciousness," that it remains an empty scholastic appendage, as empty, dead, and useless as the "theory of general substitution" or the doctrine of "elements," "introjection," and the rest of the Machist nonsense. But the "dead lay hold of the living"; the dead scholastic appendage, *against the will of and independently of the consciousness* of Bogdanov, converts his philosophy into a *serviceable tool* of the Schubert-Solderns and other reactionaries, who in a thousand different keys, from a hundred professorial chairs, disseminate *this* dead thing as a living thing, direct it against the living thing, for the purpose of stifling the latter. Bogdanov personally is a sworn enemy of reaction in general and of bourgeois reaction in particular. Bogdanov's "substitution" and theory of the "identity of social being and social consciousness" *serve* this reaction. It is sad, but true.

Materialism in general recognizes objectively real being (matter) as independent of the consciousness, sensation, experience, etc., of humanity. Historical materialism recognizes social being as independent of the social consciousness of humanity. In both cases consciousness is only the reflection of being, at best an approximately true (adequate, perfectly exact) reflection of it. From this Marxist philosophy, which is cast from a single piece of steel, you cannot eliminate one basic premise, one essential part, without departing from objective truth, without falling a prey to a bourgeois-reactionary falsehood. . . .

Marx and Engels, as they grew out of Feuerbach and matured in the fight against the scribblers, naturally paid most attention to crowning the structure of philosophical materialism, that is, not to the materialist epistemology but to the materialist conception of history. That is why Marx and Engels laid the emphasis in their works rather on *dialectical* materialism than on dialectical *materialism*, and insisted on *historical* materialism rather than on historical *materialism*. Our would-be Marxist Machists approached Marxism in an entirely different historical period, at a time when bourgeois philosophy was particularly specializing in epistemology, and, having assimilated in a one-sided and mutilated form certain of the component parts of dialectics (relativism, for instance), was directing its attention chiefly to a defense or restoration of idealism below and not of idealism above. At any rate, positivism in general, and Machism in particular, have been much more occupied in subtly falsifying epistemology—simulating materialism and concealing their idealism under a pseudo-materialist terminology—and have paid comparatively little attention to the philosophy of history. Our Machists did not understand Marxism because they happened to approach it *from the other side*, so to speak, and they have assimilated——and at times not so much assimilated as learned by rote—Marx's economic and historical theory, without clearly apprehending its foundation, viz., philosophical materialism. . . .

The philosophy of the scientist Mach is to science what the kiss of the Christian Judas was to Christ. Mach likewise betrays science into the hands of fideism by virtually deserting to the camp of philosophical idealism. Mach's renunciation of natural-scientific materialism is a reactionary phenomenon in every respect. We saw this quite clearly when we spoke of the struggle of the "physical idealists" against the *majority* of natural scientists, who continue to maintain the standpoint of the old philosophy. . . .

There are four standpoints from which a Marxist must proceed to form a judgment of empirio-criticism.

First and foremost, the theoretical foundations of this philosophy must be compared with those of dialectical materialism. Such a comparison . . . reveals, *along the whole line* of epistemological problems, the *thoroughly reactionary* character of empirio-criticism, which uses new artifices, terms, and subtleties to disguise the old errors of *idealism and agnosticism*. Only sheer ignorance of the nature of philosophical materialism generally and of the nature of Marx's and Engels' dialectical method can lead one to speak of "combining" empirio-criticism and Marxism.

Secondly, the place of empirio-criticism, as one very small school of specialists in philosophy, in relation to the other modern schools of philosophy must be determined. Both Mach and Avenarius started with Kant and, leaving him, proceeded not toward materialism, but in the opposite direction, toward Hume and Berkeley. Imagining that he was "purifying experience" generally, Avenarius was in fact only purifying the agnosticism of Kantianism. The whole school of Mach and

Avenarius is moving more and more definitely toward idealism, hand in hand with one of the most reactionary of the idealist schools, viz., the so-called immanentists.

Thirdly, the indubitable connection between Machism and one school in one branch of modern science must be borne in mind. The vast majority of scientists, both generally and in the special branch of science in question, viz., physics, are invariably on the side of materialism. A minority of new physicists, however, influenced by the breakdown of old theories brought about by the great discoveries of recent years, influenced by the crisis in the new physics, which has very clearly revealed the relativity of our knowledge, have, owing to their ignorance of dialectics, slipped into idealism by way of relativism. The physical idealism in vogue today is as reactionary and transitory an infatuation as the fashionable physiological idealism of the recent past.

Fourthly, behind the epistemological scholasticism of empirio-criticism one must not fail to see the struggle of parties in philosophy, a struggle which in the last analysis reflects the tendencies and ideology of the antagonistic classes in modern society. Recent philosophy is as partisan as was philosophy two thousand years ago. The contending parties are essentially—although this is concealed by a pseudo-erudite quackery of new terms or by a weak-minded non-partisanship—materialism and idealism. The latter is merely a subtle, refined form of fideism, which stands fully armed, commands vast organizations, and steadily continues to exercise influence on the masses, turning the slightest vacillation in philosophical thought to its own advantage. The objective, class role played by empirio-criticism consists entirely in rendering faithful service to the fideists in their struggle against materialism in general and historical materialism in particular.

[V. I. LENIN]

Philosophical Notebooks *

Conspectus of Hegel's Book, The Science of Logic

1.

p. 18: Logic is the science not of external forms of thought, but of the laws of development "of all material, natural, and spiritual things," i.e., of the development of the entire concrete content of the world and of its cognition, i.e., the sum-total, the conclusion of the *History* of knowledge of the world.

2.

p. 18: Man is confronted with a *web* of natural phenomena. Instinctive man, the savage, does not distinguish himself from nature. Conscious man does distinguish, categories are stages of distinguishing, i.e., of cognizing the world, focal points in the web, which assist in cognizing and mastering it.

3.

Nonsense about the absolute (68-69). I am in general trying to read Hegel materialistically: Hegel is materialism which has been stood on its head (according to Engels)—that is to say, I cast aside for the most part god [*bozhenka*], the absolute, the Pure Idea, etc.

* From V. I. Lenin, *Collected Works*, Vol. 38, "Philosophical Notebooks," trans. Clemens Dutt, ed. Stewart Smith, Moscow, 1961, pp. 92-93, 104, 109, 110, 134, 143, 146-147, 160, 162, 171, 178-179, 180, 182, 183, 190, 195, 196-197, 201, 208, 217, 221-223, 226, 234, 253-254, 255-256, 276, 278, 283-284, 303, 359-363. Revised. Except in cases where foreign expressions are translated, the Russian editor's notes have been omitted. Page references in the margin of the text are Lenin's. They are to the following editions: for Selections #1-6: Hegel, *Werke*, Bd. III, Berlin, 1833; #7-11: *ibid.*, Bd. IV, Berlin, 1834; #12-15: *ibid.*, Bd. V, Berlin, 1834; #16-17: *ibid.*, Bd. VI, Berlin, 1840; #18-19: *ibid.*, Bd. V; #20-21: *ibid.*, Bd. VI; #22: *ibid.*, Bd. V; #23: *ibid.*, Bd. VI; #24-27: *ibid.*, Bd. V; #28-29: *ibid.*, Bd. XIII, Berlin, 1833; #30-32: *ibid.*, Bd. XIV, Berlin, 1833; #33: *ibid.*, Bd. XV, Berlin, 1836. The numbering of the passages here is the editor's.

4.

p. 127   . . . Consequently, the thing-in-itself is "nothing but an abstraction, void of truth and content." . . .

N.B.   This is very profound: the thing-in-itself and its conversion into a thing-for-others (cf. Engels). The thing-in-itself is *altogether* an empty, lifeless abstraction. In life, in movement, each thing and everything exists both "in itself" and "for others" in relation to an other, being transformed from one state to the other.

5.

p. 129:   *Dialectics* is the teaching which shows how *opposites* can be and how they happen to be (how they become) *identical*,—under what conditions they are identical, becoming transformed into one another,—why the human mind should grasp these opposites not as dead, rigid, but as living, conditional, mobile, becoming transformed into one another. *En lisant Hegel.*[1]

6.

Thoughts on dialectics en lisant *Hegel:*

p. 137:   Shrewd and clever! Hegel analyzes concepts that usually appear to be dead and shows that there *is* movement in them. Finite? That means *moving* to an end! Something?— means *not that* which is other. Being in general?—means such indeterminateness that Being = non-Being. All-sided, universal flexibility of concepts, a flexibility reaching to the identity of opposites—that is the essence of the matter. This flexibility, applied subjectively = eclecticism and sophistry. Flexibility, applied *objectively*, i.e., reflecting the all-sidedness of the material process and its unity, is dialectics, is the correct reflection of the eternal development of the world.

N.B.

1. In reading Hegel—ED.

7.

p. 21:   Thus here, too, Hegel charges Kant with *subjectivism*. This N.B. Hegel defends the "objective validity" (*sit venia verbo* [2]) of appearance, "of that which is immediately given." . . . The more petty philosophers dispute whether essence *or* that which is immediately given should be taken as basis (Kant, Hume, all the Machists). Instead of *or*, Hegel puts *and*, explaining the concrete content of this "and."

8.

pp. 70-71:   (1) Ordinary imagination grasps difference and contradiction, but not the *transition* from the one to the other, *this however is the most important*.

(2) Intelligence and understanding. Intelligence grasps contradiction, *enunciates* it, brings things into relation with one another, allows the "concept to show through the contradiction," but does not *express* the concept of things and their relations.

N.B.

(3) Thinking reason (understanding) sharpens the blunt difference of variety, the mere manifold of imagination, into *essential* difference, into *opposition*. Only when raised to the peak of contradiction do the manifold entities become active (*regsam*) and lively in relation to one another,—they receive [3] acquire that negativity which is the *inherent pulsation of self-movement and vitality*.

9.

p. 97:   If I am not mistaken, there is much mysticism and *leeres* [4] pedantry in these conclusions of Hegel, but the basic idea is one of genius: that of the universal, all-sided, *vital* connection of everything with everything and the reflection of this connection—*materialistisch auf den Kopf gestellter*

2. If it may be called that—ED.
3. The word "receive" is crossed out in the MS.—ED.
4. Empty—ED.

Hegel [5]—in human concepts, which must also be rough-hewn, treated, flexible, mobile, relative, mutually connected, united in opposites, in order to embrace the world. Continuation of the work of Hegel and Marx must consist in the *dialectical* elaboration of the history of human thought, science, and technology.

10.

p. 230:   This "inner spirit"—cf. Plekhanov—is an idealistic, *mystical*, but a very profound indication of the historical causes of events. Hegel subsumes history *completely* under causality and understands causality a thousand times more profoundly and richly than the multitude of "*savants*" nowadays.

11.

pp. 241-242:   When one reads Hegel on causality, it appears strange at first glance that he dwells so relatively lightly on this theme, beloved of the Kantians. Why? Because, indeed, for him causality is only *one* of the determinations of universal connection, which he had already covered earlier, in his *entire* exposition, much more deeply and all-sidedly; *always* and from the very outset emphasizing this connection, the reciprocal transitions, etc., etc. It would be very instructive to compare the "*birth pangs*" of neo-empiricism (that is, "physical idealism") with the solutions, or rather with the dialectical method, of Hegel.

12.

pp. 19-20:   *Essentially*, Hegel is completely right as opposed to Kant. Thought proceeding from the concrete to the abstract —provided it is *correct* (N.B.) (and Kant, like all philosophers, speaks of correct thought)—does not get away *from* the truth but comes closer to it. The abstraction of *matter*, of a *law* of nature, the abstraction of *value*, etc., in short *all* scientific (correct, serious, not absurd) abstractions reflect nature more deeply, truly, and *completely*. From living perception to abstract thought, *and from this to practice,*—such is the dialectical path of the cognition of *truth,* of the cognition of

5. Hegel materialistically stood on his head—ED.

objective reality. Kant disparages knowledge in order to make way for faith: Hegel exalts knowledge, asserting that knowledge is knowledge of god. The materialist exalts the knowledge of matter, of nature, consigning god, and the philosophical rabble that defends god, to the rubbish heap.

13.

Concerning the question of the true significance of Hegel's Logic:

pp. 128-129:   The formation of (abstract) concepts and operations with them *already* includes idea, conviction, *consciousness* of the law-governed character of the objective connection of the world. To distinguish causality from this connection is stupid. To deny the objectivity of concepts, the objectivity of the universal in the individual and in the particular, is impossible. Consequently, Hegel is much more profound than Kant, and others, in tracing the reflection of the movement of the objective world in the movement of concepts. Just as the simple form of value, the individual act of exchange of one given commodity for another, already includes in an undeveloped form *all* the main contradictions of capitalism,—so the simplest *generalization*, the first and simplest formation of *concepts* (judgments, syllogisms, etc.) already denotes man's ever deeper cognition of the *objective* connection of the world. Here is where one should look for the true meaning, significance, and role of Hegel's *Logic*. This N.B.

14.

p. 154:   *Aphorism:* It is impossible completely to understand Marx's *Capital*, and especially its first chapter, without having thoroughly studied and understood the *whole* of Hegel's *Logic*. Consequently, half a century later none of the Marxists understood Marx!!

15.

p. 154:   The *transition* from inference by analogy (about analogy) to the inference of necessity, and from inference by induction to inference by analogy,—inference from the universal to the particular—inference from the particular to the universal,—the exposition of *connection* and *transitions* [connection *is* transition], that is Hegel's task. Hegel actually *proved* that logical forms and laws are not an empty shell, but the *reflection* of the objective world. More correctly, he did not prove, but *made a brilliant guess*.

16.

pp. 353-354:   "Nature, this immediate totality, unfolds itself in the Logical Idea and Mind." Logic is the science of cognition. It is the theory of knowledge. Knowledge is the reflection of nature by man. But this is not a simple, not an immediate, not a complete reflection, but the process of a series of abstractions, the formation and development of concepts, laws, etc., and these concepts, laws, etc. (thought, science = "the logical Idea") *embrace* conditionally, approximately, the universal law-governed character of eternally moving and developing nature. Here are *actually*, objectively, *three* members: (1) nature, (2) human cognition = the human *brain* (as the highest product of this same nature), and (3) the form of reflection of nature in human cognition, and this form consists precisely of concepts, laws, categories, etc. Man cannot comprehend = reflect = mirror nature *as a whole*, in its completeness, its "immediate totality," he can only *eternally* come closer to this, creating abstractions, concepts, laws, a scientific picture of the world, etc., etc.

N.B.: Hegel *"only"* deifies this "logical idea," obedience to law, universality.

17.

p. 360:   Very profound and clever! The laws of logic are the reflections of the objective in the subjective consciousness of man.

18.

The Categories of Logic and Human Practice:

p. 227: When Hegel endeavors—sometimes even huffs and
puffs—to bring man's purposive activity under the categories

N.B. of logic, saying that this activity is the "syllogism" (*Schluss*),
that the subject (man) plays the role of a "member" in the
logical "figure" of the "syllogism," and so on,—THEN THAT IS
NOT MERELY STRETCHING A POINT, A MERE GAME. THIS HAS A
VERY PROFOUND, PURELY MATERIALISTIC CONTENT. It has to be
inverted: the practical activity of man had to lead his con-

N.B. sciousness to the repetition of the various logical figures
thousands of million of times *in order that* these figures *could*
obtain the significance of *axioms*. This *nota bene*.

19.

p. 242: Cognition is the eternal, endless approximation of
thought to the object. The *reflection* of nature in man's
thought must be understood not "lifelessly," not "abstractly,"
not devoid of movement, not without contradictions, but in the

N.B. eternal *process* of movement, the arising of contradictions
and their solution.

20.

p. 385: The *totality of all* sides of the phenomenon, of reality and their (reciprocal) *relations*—that is what
truth is composed of. The relations (= transitions = Hegel brilliantly
contradictions) of concepts = the main content of *divined* the
logic, *by which* these concepts (and their relations, dialectics of thing
transitions, contradictions) are shown as reflections (phenomena, the
of the objective world. The dialectics of *things* pro- world, *nature*) in
duces the dialectics of *ideas*, and not vice versa. the dialectics of
concepts#

\# This aphorism should be expressed more popularly, *without*
the word dialectics: approximately as follows: In
the alternation, reciprocal dependence of *all* concepts, indeed *divined*,
in the *identity of their opposites*, in the *transitions* not more
of one concept into another, in the eternal change, movement of
concepts, Hegel brilliantly *divined* PRECISELY THIS RELATION OF
THINGS, OF NATURE.

	$=$	
what consti- tutes dialec- tics?	mutual dependence of concepts " " *all* " without exception transitions of concepts from one into another	$=$ N.B. Every concept oc- curs in a certain *relation,* in a certain connection with *all* the others
	transition of all concepts without exception. the relativity of opposition between concepts . . . the identity of opposites between concepts.	‖

21.

The idea is "truth" (p. 385, §213). The idea, i.e., *truth* as a process—for truth is a *process*—passes in its *development* (*Entwicklung*) through three stages: (1) life; (2) the process of knowledge, which includes human *practice* and *technology* (see above); (3) the stage of the absolute idea (i.e., of complete truth).

Life gives rise to the brain. Nature is reflected in the human brain. By checking and applying the correctness of these reflections in his practice and technology, man arrives at objective truth.

Truth is a process. From the subjective idea, man advances toward objective truth *through* "practice" (and technology).

22.

p. 280:   Logical concepts are subjective so long as they remain "abstract," in their abstract form, but at the same time they express also the things-in-themselves. Nature is *both* concrete *and* abstract, *both* phenomenon *and* essence, *both* moment *and* relation. Human concepts are subjective in their abstractness, separateness, but objective as a whole, in the process, in the sum-total, in the tendency, in the source.

23.

Very good is §225 of the *Encylopaedia* where "*cognition*" ("theoretical") and "will," "practical activity," are depicted as two sides, two methods, two means of abolishing the "one-sidedness" both of subjectivity and of objectivity.

24.

p. 324:   The "syllogism of action" . . . For Hegel *action*, practice, is a *logical* "*syllogism*," a figure of logic. And that is true! Not, of course, in the sense that the figure of logic has its other being in the practice of man (=absolute idealism), but vice versa: man's practice, repeating itself a thousand million times, becomes consolidated in man's consciousness as figures of logic. Precisely (and only) on account of this thousand-million-fold repetition, these figures have the stability of a prejudice, an axiomatic character.

First premise: The *good end* (subjective end) versus *actuality* ("external actuality").

Second premise: The objective external *means* (instrument).

Third premise or conclusion: The coincidence of subjective and objective, the test of subjective ideas, the criterion of objective truth.

25.

Elements of Dialectics

p. 336:   (1) the *objectivity* of consideration (not examples, not digressions, but the thing-in-itself).

X

(2) the entire totality of the manifold *relations* of this thing to others.

(3) the *development* of this thing (phenomenon, respectively), its own movement, its own life.

(4) the internally contradictory *tendencies* (*and* aspects) in this thing.

(5) the thing (phenomenon, etc.) as the sum *and unity of opposites.*

(6) the *struggle*, or unfolding, of these opposites, contradictory strivings, etc.

(7) the union of analysis and synthesis—the breakdown of the separate parts and the totality, the summation of these parts.

(8) the relations of each thing (phenomenon, etc.) are not only manifold, but general, universal. Each thing (phenomenon, process, etc.) is connected with *every other*.

(9) not only the unity of opposites but the *transitions* of *every* determination, quality, feature, aspect, property into *every* other [into its opposite?].

(10) the endless process of the discovery of *new* aspects, relations, etc.

(11) the endless process of the deepening of man's knowledge of the thing, of phenomena, processes, etc., from appearance to essence and from less profound to more profound essence.

(12) from co-existence to causality and from one form of connection and reciprocal dependence to another, deeper, more general form.

(13) the repetition at a higher stage of certain features, properties, etc., of the lower and

(14) the apparent return to the old (negation of the negation).

(15) the struggle of content with form and conversely. The throwing off of the form, the transformation of the content.

(16) the transition of quantity into quality and *vice versa*. ((15 and 16 are *examples* of 9))

In brief, dialectics can be defined as the doctrine of the unity of opposites. This embodies the essence of dialectics, but it requires explanations and development.

26.

p. 340:   Not empty negation, not futile negation, *not skeptical* negation, vacillation and doubt is characteristic and essential in dialectics,—which undoubtedly contains the element of negation and indeed as its most important element—no, but negation as a moment of connection, as a moment of development, retaining the positive, i.e., without any vacillations, without any eclecticism.

27.

[Comment at the end of Hegel's *Logic*]

It is noteworthy that the whole chapter on the "Absolute Idea" scarcely says a word about god (hardly ever has a "divine" "concept" slipped out accidentally) and apart from that— *this N.B.*—it contains almost nothing that is specifically *idealism*, but has for its main subject the *dialectical method*. The sum-total, the last word and essence of Hegel's logic is the *dialectical method*—this is extremely noteworthy. And one thing more: in this *most idealistic* of Hegel's works there is the *least* idealism and the *most materialism*. "Contradictory," but a fact!

N.B.

Conspectus of Hegel's Book,
Lectures on the History of Philosophy

28.

p. 280:   Here are essentially two determinations (*Bestimmungen, keine Definitionen* [6]) of dialectics:
  (a) "the pure movement of thought in Concepts";
  (b) "in the (very) essence of objects (to elucidate) (to reveal) the contradiction which it (this essence) has in itself (*dialectics proper*)."

In other words, this "fragment" of Hegel's should be reproduced as follows:

Dialectics in general is "the pure movement of thought in Concepts" (i.e., putting it without the mysticism of idealism:

6. Determinations, not definitions—ED.

human concepts are not fixed but are eternally in movement, they pass into one another, they flow into one another, otherwise they do not reflect living life. The analysis of concepts, the study of them, the "art of operating with them" (Engels) always demands study of the *movement* of concepts, of their interconnection, of their mutual transitions).

In particular, dialectics is the study of the opposition of the thing-in-itself (*Ansich*), of the essence, substratum, substance —from the appearance, from "Being-for-Others." (Here, too, we see a transition, a flow from the one to the other: the essence appears. The appearance is essential.) Human thought goes endlessly deeper from appearance to essence, from essence of the first order, as it were, to essence of the second order, and so on *without end*.

Dialectics in the proper sense is the study of contradiction *in the very essence of objects:* not only are appearances transitory, mobile, fluid, demarcated only by conventional boundaries, but the *essence* of things is so as well.

29.

Regarding the question of *dialectics*
and its objective significance . . .

p. 311:   With the "principle of development" in the twentieth century (indeed, at the end of the nineteenth century also) "all are agreed." Yes, but this superficial, not thought out, accidental, Philistine "agreement" is an agreement of *such a kind* as stifles and vulgarizes the truth. —If everything develops, then everything passes from one into another, for development as is well known is not a simple, universal, and eternal *growth*, *enlargement* (or diminution), etc. —If that is so, then, in the first place, evolution has to be understood *more exactly*, as the arising and passing away of everything, as mutual transitions. —And, in the second place, if *everything* develops, does not that apply also to the most general *concepts* and *categories* of thought? If not, it means that thinking is not connected with being. If it does, it means that there is a dialectics of concepts and a dialectics of cognition which has objective significance.†

N.B.	I. The principle of development . . . II. The principle of unity . . .	† In addition, the universal principle of development must be combined, linked, made to correspond with the universal principle of the *unity of the world*, nature, motion, matter, etc.

30.

pp. 74-75: Intelligent idealism is closer to intelligent materialism than stupid materialism.

Dialectical idealism instead of intelligent; metaphysical, undeveloped, dead, crude, rigid instead of stupid.

31.

p. 144: Hegel seriously "believed," thought, that materialism as a philosophy was impossible, for philosophy is the science of thinking, of the *universal*, but the universal is a thought. Here he repeated the error of the same subjective idealism that he always called "bad" idealism. Objective (and still more, absolute) idealism came *very close* to materialism by a zigzag (and a somersault), even partially *became transformed into it.*

32.

p. 328: Hegel, the supporter of dialectics, could not understand the *dialectical* transition *from* matter *to* motion, *from* matter *to* consciousness—especially the second. Marx corrected the error (or weakness?) of the mystic.

N.B.

N.B. Not only is the transition from matter to consciousness dialectical, but also that from sensation to thought, etc.

What distinguishes the dialectical transition from the undialectical transition? The leap. The contradiction. The interruption of gradualness. The unity (identity) of Being and non-Being.

33.

. . . "The return to god. . . ." (5) "self-consciousness is absolute Essence" . . . (7) "the world-spirit" . . . (7) . . . "Christian religion.". . . (8) And *a mass of thin porridge* ladled out about god. . . . (8-18)

But this philosophical idealism, openly, "seriously" leading to god, is more honest than modern agnosticism with its hypocrisy and cowardice.

On the Question of Dialectics

The splitting of a single whole and the cognition of its contradictory parts (see the quotation from Philo on Heraclitus at the beginning of Section III, "On Cognition," in Lassalle's book on Heraclitus) is the *essence* (one of the "essentials," one of the principal, if not the principal, characteristics or features) of dialectics. That is precisely how Hegel, too, puts the matter (Aristotle in his *Metaphysics* continually *grapples* with it and *combats* Heraclitus and Heraclitean ideas).

The correctness of this aspect of the content of dialectics must be tested by the history of science. This aspect of dialectics (e.g., in Plekhanov) usually receives inadequate attention: the identity of opposites is taken as the sum-total of *examples* ["for example, a seed," "for example, primitive communism." The same is true of Engels. But it is "in the interests of popularization . . ."] and not as a *law of cognition* (*and* as a law of the objective world).

In mathematics: + and —. Differential and integral.

In mechanics: action and reaction.

In physics: positive and negative electricity.

In chemistry: the combination and dissociation of atoms.

In social science: the class struggle.

=====

The identity of opposites (it would be more correct, perhaps, to say their "unity,"—although the difference between the terms identity and unity is not particularly important here. In a certain sense both are correct) is the recognition (discovery) of the contradictory, *mutually exclusive*, opposite tendencies in *all* phenomena and processes of nature (*including* mind and society).

The condition for the knowledge of all processes of the world in their "*self-movement*," in their spontaneous development, in their real life, is the knowledge of them as a unity of opposites. Development is the "struggle" of opposites. The two basic (or two possible? or two historically observable?) conceptions of development (evolution) are: development as decrease and increase, as repetition, *and* development as a unity of opposites (the division of a unity into mutually exclusive opposites and their reciprocal relation).

In the first conception of motion, *self*-movement, its *driving* force, its source, its motive, remains in the shade (or this source is made *external*—god, subject, etc.). In the second conception the chief attention is directed precisely to knowledge of the *source* of "*self*"-movement.

The first conception is lifeless, pale, and dry. The second is living. The second *alone* furnishes the key to the "self-movement" of everything existing; it alone furnishes the key to the "leaps," to the "break in continuity," to the "transformation into the opposite," to the destruction of the old and the emergence of the new.

The unity (coincidence, identity, equal action) of opposites is conditional, temporary, transitory, relative. The struggle of mutually exclusive opposites is absolute, just as development and motion are absolute.

N.B.: The distinction between subjectivism (skepticism, sophistry, etc.) and dialectics, incidentally, is that in (objective) dialectics the difference between the relative and the absolute is itself relative. For objective dialectics there *is* an absolute *within* the relative. For subjectivism and sophistry the relative is only relative and excludes the absolute.

In his *Capital*, Marx first analyzes the simplest, most ordinary and fundamental, most common and everyday *relation* of bourgeois (commodity) society, a relation encountered billions of times, viz., the exchange of commodities. In this very simple phenomenon (in this "cell" of bourgeois society) analysis reveals *all* the contradictions (or the germs of *all* the contradictions) of modern society. The subsequent exposition shows us the development (*both* growth *and* movement) of these contradictions and of this society in the Σ [7] of its individual parts, from its beginning to its end.

Such must also be the method of exposition (or study) of dialectics in general (for with Marx the dialectics of bourgeois society is only a particular case of dialectics). To begin with what is the simplest, most ordinary, common, etc., with *any proposition:* the leaves of a tree are green; John is a man; Fido is a dog, etc. Here already we have *dialectics* (as Hegel's genius recognized): the *individual* is the *universal* (cf. Aristotle, *Metaphysik*, translation by Schwegler, Bd. II, S. 40, 3. Buch, 4. Kapitel, 8-9: *"denn natürlich kann man nicht der Meinung sein, dass es ein Haus* (a house in general) *gebe auser den sichtbaren Häusern,"* "οὐ γάρ ἂν θείημεν εἶναί τινα οἰκίαν παρὰ τὰς τινὰς οἰκίας").[8] Consequently, the opposites (the individual is opposed to the universal) are identical: the individual exists only in the connection that leads to the universal. The universal exists only in the individual and through the individual. Every individual is (in one way or another) a universal. Every universal is (a fragment, or an aspect, or the essence of) an individual. Every universal only approximately embraces all the individual objects. Every individual enters incompletely into the universal, etc., etc. Every individual is connected by thousands of transitions with other *kinds* of individuals (things, phenomena, processes), etc. *Here already* we have the elements, the germs, the concepts of *necessity*, of objective connection in nature, etc. Here already we have the contingent and the necessary, the phenomenon and the essence; for when we say: John is a man, Fido is a dog, *this* is a leaf of a tree, etc., we *disregard* a number of attributes as *contingent;* we separate the essence from the appearance, and counterpose the one to the other.

Thus in *any* proposition we can (and must) disclose as in a "nucleus" ("cell") the germs of *all* the elements of dialectics, and thereby show that dialectics is a property of all human knowledge

7. Summation—ED.

8. "For, of course, one cannot hold the opinion that there can be a house (in general) apart from visible houses." —ED.

in general. And natural science shows us (and here again it must be demonstrated in *any* simple instance) objective nature with the same qualities, the transformation of the individual into the universal, of the contingent into the necessary, transitions, modulations, and the reciprocal connection of opposites. Dialectics *is* the theory of knowledge of (Hegel and) Marxism. This is the "aspect" of the matter (it is not "an aspect" but the *essence* of the matter) to which Plekhanov, not to speak of other Marxists, paid no attention.

*　　*　　*

Knowledge is represented in the form of a series of circles both by Hegel (see *Logic*) and by the modern "epistemologist" of natural science, the eclectic and foe of Hegelianism (which he did not understand!), Paul Volkmann (see his *Erkenntnistheoretische Grundzüge*;[9] S.)

"Circles" in philosophy: [is a chronology of *persons* essential? No!]
Ancient: from Democritus to Plato and the dialectics of Heraclitus.
Renaissance: Descartes versus Gassendi (Spinoza?)
Modern: Holbach-Hegel (via Berkeley, Hume, Kant).
Hegel—Feuerbach—Marx.

Dialectics as *living*, many-sided knowledge (with the number of sides eternally increasing), with an infinite number of shades of every approach and approximation to reality (with a philosophical system growing into a whole out of each shade)—here we have an immeasurably rich content as compared with "metaphysical" materialism, the fundamental *misfortune* of which is its inability to apply dialectics to the *Bildertheorie*,[10] to the process and development of knowledge.

Philosophical idealism is *only* nonsense from the standpoint of crude, simple, metaphysical materialism. From the standpoint

9. P. Volkmann, *Erkenntnistheoretische Grundzüge der Naturwissenschaften*, Leipzig-Berlin, 1910, p. 35.—ED.

10. Picture theory.—ED.

of *dialectical* materialism, on the other hand, philosophical idealism is a *one-sided*, exaggerated, *überschwengliches* (Dietzgen)
development (inflation, distention) of one of the features, aspects,
facets of knowledge into an absolute, *divorced* from matter, from
nature, apotheosized. Idealism is clerical obscurantism. || N.B.
True. But philosophical idealism is (*"more correctly"* || this
and *"in addition"*) a *road* to clerical obscurantism || aphor-
|| ism
through one of the shades of the infinitely complex (dialectical)
knowledge of man.

Human knowledge is not (or does not follow) a straight line,
but a curve, which endlessly approximates a series of circles, a
spiral. Any fragment, segment, section of this curve can be
transformed (transformed one-sidedly) into an independent, complete, straight line, which then (if one does not see the wood
for the trees) leads into the quagmire, into clerical obscurantism
(where it is *anchored* by the class interests of the ruling classes).
Rectilinearity and one-sidedness, woodenness and petrification,
subjectivism and subjective blindness—*voilà* the epistemological
roots of idealism. And clerical obscurantism (= philosophical
idealism), of course, has *epistemological* roots, it is not groundless; it is a *sterile flower* undoubtedly, but a sterile flower that
grows on the living tree of living, fertile, genuine, powerful,
omnipotent, objective, absolute human knowledge.

LYUBOV ISAAKOVNA AKSELROD
(Ortodoks)
[1868–1946]

L<small>YUBOV</small> A<small>KSELROD</small>, who wrote under the pen name of Ortodoks, and whose review of Lenin's *Materialism and Empirio-Criticism* follows, is not only the most famous of Russian women philosophers, but also is among the most prominent of the first generation of Russian Marxists regardless of sex. Ortodoks aligned herself with the followers of Marx against the Kantian and Machian revisionists—hence her pen name. She emigrated to Western Europe in 1887, received her doctorate in philosophy at the University of Berne (1900), and, about 1890, joined the Social Democratic party. Having sided with the Menshevik faction in 1903, she returned to Russia in 1906 and stayed in Russia after the Bolshevik Revolution, although she remained outside the party.

In her early work, with which we are here primarily concerned, Ortodoks sided with Plekhanov in epistemology and defended the correctness of the theory of hieroglyphics, both against Bogdanov's Empiriomonism and against Lenin's "naive realism." In the Mechanist-Deborinist controversy, on the other hand, she agreed with the Mechanists. Her later work, however, holds to an orthodox Marxist-Leninist dialectical materialism.

The review of Lenin's *Materialism and Empirio-Criticism*, aside from criticizing the form of Lenin's book—its over-use of quotations and its polemical tone—is primarily a defense of Plekhanov's epistemology. In the theory of hieroglyphics, Ortodoks argues, subject and object are not divorced: the "sensation [is] a product of the interaction between two objects, of which one is at the same time also a subject." [1] This is a monistic view in full accord with "contemporary science," which agrees that sensations are not like the objective processes that evoke them. Lenin's copy theory, on the other hand, is an inverted Platonism which re-creates the abyss between subject and object. Furthermore, Lenin is wrong in identifying naive realism with materialism: naive realism is in agreement neither with materialism nor with science; it is, in fact, the point of view of the very philosophy Lenin is trying to attack, Empiriomonism. Here Ortodoks, although her argument is forceful, does not make it clear whether she has fallen into the error of post-Marxian Marxists of confusing ontology and epistemology: is she saying that naive realism is not materialism, or that it is not a suitable theory of knowledge for materialism?

In her acceptance of the theory of hieroglyphics, Ortodoks seems unaware of its Kantian elements. This is not the only Kantian element in her thought, however. Elsewhere,[2] denying the need for a priori principles to enable man to infer universally valid propositions, she adds that "a law inferred *a posteriori* serves . . . as an *a priori* guiding principle, so long as it is not confuted by practical reality." Either, in this case, it *is* an a priori principle, knowledge of which has been occasioned by experience, in perfect agreement with Kant, or it is a Kantian "regulative principle." In either case, she has not divorced herself from Kant in epistemology.

SELECTED BIBLIOGRAPHY

Gustav A. Wetter, *Dialectical Materialism*, trans. Peter Heath, London and New York, 1958, pp. 149-153.

1. See below, p. 460.
2. *Filosofskiye ocherki*, St. Petersburg, 1906, p. 83, quoted in Wetter, *op. cit.*, p. 151.

Review of Lenin's Materialism and Empiriocriticism *

(*Sovremenny Mir*, July, 1909. No. 7)

V. I. Ilyin.[1] *Materialism and Empiriocriticism, Critical Notes on a Reactionary Philosophy. "Zveno" Edition. Moscow. 1909. 438 pages. Price, 2 Rubles, 60 Kopeks.*

The basic philosophical content of this book may be stated very briefly. It is as follows:

Empiriocriticism is essentially a revival of the philosophy of Berkeley and Hume. Although it claims to be a scientific philosophy, in harmony with the methods and tasks of contemporary natural science, empiriocritical epistemology—which is really a subjective idealism—plainly contradicts the actual foundations of positive science. The empiriocritics, in their feigned struggle against metaphysics and the Kantian thing-in-itself, have moved not forward but backward. Kant's thing-in-itself has been subjected to criticism from two sides, from the right and from the left. Right-wing thinkers, having banished the Kantian thing-in-itself from the realm of experience, have returned to the philosophy of Berkeley and Hume. The materialist thinkers of the left wing rebelled against the Kantian thing-in-itself from a different standpoint.[2]

The materialists agree with Kant in admitting an external real-

---

* Translated for this volume by John Liesveld, Jr., and George L. Kline, from the Russian text in V. I. Lenin, *Sochineniya*, 2nd ed., Moscow, 1928, Vol. 13, pp. 329-333.

1. "Ilyin" was Lenin's most widely used pseudonym in the period before 1917.—TRANS.

2. We may note, in passing, that this rough-and-ready classification of the critics of the Kantian thing-in-itself does not entirely correspond to the truth. Hegel, for example, was neither a subjective idealist nor a materialist, but he *vigorously* criticized the thing-in-itself.

ity, but they reject the thing-in-itself. Kant's thing-in-itself differs from the reality recognized by the materialists in that the former, being completely divorced from the phenomenon, remains beyond it, forming the intelligible world—while the latter, connected with the phenomenon, is manifested in it, thus comprising the actual source of experience. Furthermore, the *essence* and foundation of materialism consists precisely in the fact that it recognizes an external, objective reality which exists independently of the subject and is the cause of our sensations. All the problems touched upon by philosophy and by scientific thought in general are defined, from the point of view of the materialist theory, by this cardinal initial proposition.

Such are the main propositions of the book before us.

The thoughtful, alert, and attentive reader who has followed the philosophic polemics between various kinds of eclectic Marxists and the orthodox Marxists will notice immediately that *in essence* Ilyin has said nothing which has not been said by other orthodox Marxists. The trouble, however, is not the lack of new ideas in Ilyin's book; the elaboration of a well-known, already-formulated view can be extremely interesting and original, if only it is marked by serious, thoughtful, and subtle argumentation. Unfortunately, Ilyin's book does not possess these qualities. The author's argument exhibits neither flexibility of philosophic thought, exactness of philosophic definition, nor profound understanding of philosophic problems. The book consists largely of an enormous number of quotations from the works of writers on philosophy, together with a number of details of chronology. Such an eclectic mode of exposition, besides making the book extremely dull, is scarcely designed to stimulate the development of the reader's philosophic thought. Abundant quotations usually attract writers who paste books together out of them and, also, perhaps, writers who copy them down from just such a work.

As for the reader, he will seriously penetrate the meaning of the given quotation only when the author has succeeded, through his own analysis, in making it sufficiently interesting. Otherwise the reader will quickly glance through the quotations, in a hurry to learn the author's thoughts, since at any given moment these naturally are of greatest interest to him.

Let us now turn to the substance of the book.

Since we share its general theses, we shall try, within the limits of this review, to point out what we regard as the author's chief mistakes.

Attacking Plekhanov's theory of symbols [hieroglyphics], Ilyin writes: "Plekhanov was guilty of an obvious mistake in his exposition of materialism" (p. 282). For, "if sensations are not images of things, but only signs or symbols which do 'not resemble'" them, then "the existence of external objects becomes subject to doubt, for signs or symbols may quite possibly indicate imaginary objects, and everybody is familiar with instances of *such* [author's emphasis] signs or symbols" (p. 277).[3] This is forcefully put; but, despite the vigorous form of the argument, it is mistaken from beginning to end.

The theory according to which sensations are symbols of things no more calls into question the existence of external objects than the mathematical formula, 2d, which expresses the sum of the angles of a triangle, calls into question the existence of triangles. By reasoning in this way, Ilyin, all unawares, borrows arguments against the theory of symbols from Berkeley's philosophy. "It is quite possible," our author declares, "for signs and symbols to refer to imaginary objects." Of course it is possible. But surely hallucinations, dreams, illusions, and delusions are not forms or copies of objects.

Rejecting the theory of symbols and regarding sensations as images or "inexact" copies of things, Plekhanov's critic takes his stand on a dualistic ground, preaching an inverted Platonism rather than materialism, since the latter rests on a single principle. If sensations were images or copies of things, then why in the devil would we need the things themselves? In such a case they would turn out to be things-in-themselves in the absolute sense of the word. To admit that sensations are images or copies of objects is to create anew the unbridgeable dualistic gulf between object and subject.

The theory of symbols, *asserting the existence of both subject and object, unites both factors, regarding the subject as a special*

3. This argument is adduced against Helmholz, but it is a principal argument against Plekhanov as well.

kind of object, and its sensation as a product of the interaction between two objects, of which one is at the same time also a subject. Contemporary science accepts just this *objective* and *monistic* point of view.

As evidence of the groundlessness of the theory of symbols, Ilyin points to the dualistic conclusions which Helmholz drew from this theory.

A shaky proof. The fact that Helmholz, having entangled himself in Kantianism, drew false conclusions from the theory of symbols proves only the philosophic inconsistency of the famous natural scientist, not the erroneousness of the theory.

There is no philosophic truth of such a nature that one could not arrive at its exact opposite by developing it in a one-sided way. The theory of symbols is no exception to this rule.

Our author's groundless attacks on the theory of symbols have as their source his complete incomprehension of the essence of naive realism. Judging by his scattered and fragmentary remarks, Ilyin identifies naive realism with materialism, reproaching empiriocritics for not being true naive realists. For a materialist, this is an inexcusable error. What is naive realism? Naive realism is the point of view of the man who is unacquainted with the scientific explanation of natural phenomena. Such a naive person considers sound, color, smell, heat, cold, etc., as objective elements. Empiriocritics defend just this point of view, giving it a subtle metaphysical form. Thus they are true naive realists. It goes without saying that there is a vast difference between the "natural" naive realist and the naive realist who is a theorist of knowledge; but the basis of naive realism, which amounts to the complete identification of the mental and physical, remains the same for both.

Materialism adopts the point of view that sensations, evoked by the action of different forms of moving matter, are not like the objective processes which generate them.

The theory of symbols is thus related to the materialistic explanation of nature in the closest and most indissoluble way. Hence it follows that Ilyin, and not Plekhanov, "was guilty of an obvious mistake in his exposition of materialism."

Ilyin's second attack against Plekhanov is no more successful.

Ilyin quotes the following lines from Plekhanov's preface to Engels' *Ludwig Feuerbach:* "One German writer has remarked that for empiriocriticism *experience* is only an object of investigation, and not a means of knowledge. If that is so, then the distinction between empiriocriticism and materialism loses all meaning, and the discussion of the question whether or not empiriocriticism is destined to replace materialism is absolutely shallow and idle." Ilyin devotes a short chapter, under the imposing title: "Plekhanov's Error Concerning the Conception of 'Experience,'" to a criticism of this passage. In this chapter, Ilyin, following his usual practice, quotes copiously, compares quotations, offers explanations, and eventually concludes: "According to Plekhanov, the opposition between the views of Carstanjen, Avenarius, Petzoldt, and materialism is meaningless!" (p. 170). No, this is not at all what Plekhanov said; Ilyin has completely missed the point. Plekhanov does not identify the empiriocritics' conception of experience with that of the materialists, as Ilyin would have it, but rather speaks hypothetically: *if* it is true that empiriocritics view experience as an object of analysis, *then* empiriocriticism is occupied not with the *theory of experience*, but with *psychology;* hence the opposition between materialism and empiriocriticism amounts to an opposition of part to whole. This is all that Plekhanov said; but, we repeat, Ilyin didn't understand or didn't want to understand his meaning.

Let us go further.

The chapters of this book devoted to the analysis of the law of causality and of the mutual relation of freedom and necessity don't stand up under even the slightest criticism. "The question of causality," the author declares, "is particularly important in determining the philosophical line of any new 'ism' [such jargon!], and we must therefore dwell on it in some detail" (p. 173).

Ilyin, as you see, understands the serious significance of this question and actually dwells on it in some detail; but, unfortunately, quality does not keep pace with quantity. In a long chapter the author not only says nothing that is really to the point; he also exhibits his lack of understanding of this complex problem. Although he knows Wundt's critique of empiriocriticism, Ilyin

does not even make use of the Leipzig thinker's pointed charge—
that empiriocriticism confuses the conception of *causa* with that
of *ratio*, causation in natural processes with logical dependence.[4]

No less weak is the chapter on "Freedom and Necessity." To
characterize the contents of this chapter we need single out
only the following passage: "Engels," Ilyin writes, "does not
attempt to contrive 'definitions' of freedom and necessity, the
kind of scholastic definitions with which the reactionary professors (like Avenarius) and their disciples (like Bogdanov) are
most concerned. Engels takes the knowledge and will of man,
on the one hand, and the necessity of nature,[5] on the other, and
instead of giving definitions, simply says that the necessity of
nature is primary, and human will and consciousness secondary.
The latter must necessarily and inevitably adapt themselves to
the former. Engels regards this as so obvious that he does not
waste words explaining his view" (p. 218). It is a good thing
that Engels' views are sufficiently well known to the Russian
reading public; otherwise such a version of them as Ilyin offers
might compromise the thinker. Engels, as even Ilyin knows,
sided with Hegel on this question, but Hegel did not answer the
question of the relation between freedom and necessity as simple-
mindedly as Ilyin would have us think.

It is quite impossible to pass over the author's polemical method
in silence.

Ilyin's polemics, notable for a certain energy and insistence,
have also been marked by an extreme coarseness which offends
the reader's aesthetic sense. When such coarseness appears in
militant articles on current topics, there is some justification for
it: on the field of battle one has neither the time nor the tran-
quility for considering the beauty of one's weapons. But when
extreme, impermissible coarseness appears in voluminous works

4. *Philosophische Studien*, Bd. 13 (1897), p. 325. Wundt charges Avenarius
with this confusion, but he rightly sees the latter's doctrine as true empirio-
criticism.

5. We should note, by the way, that Engels' expression "*Naturnotwendig-
keiten*" means "necessities *in* nature." Ilyin translates it incorrectly as "necessities *of* nature," which gives Engels' thought a metaphysical, a priori
coloring.

concerned with philosophical problems, then such coarseness is absolutely intolerable.

Ilyin's epithets for thinkers of the positivist camp are wide of the mark as well as coarse and revolting. Avenarius is a "poseur" (p. 94), the "immanentists" are "philosophical Menshikovs" [6] (p. 142), Cornelius is a "police sergeant in the professorial chair" (p. 256), "in the Nozdryov [7]-Petzoldt sense of the term" (p. 262). Consider this pearl: "Hegelian dialectics—that pearl which those farmyard cocks, the Büchners, the Dührings, and Co. (as well as Leclair, Mach, Avenarius, and so forth) could not pick out from the dungheap of absolute idealism" (p. 287). It is beyond human comprehension how anyone could write such things; or, having written them, could fail to cross them out; or, having failed to cross them out, could fail to seize the proof-sheets impatiently in order to delete all such absurd and coarse comparisons!

Of Russian Machists, Ilyin is hardest on P. Yushkevich. He treats Bogdanov, Lunacharsky, and Bazarov somewhat more politely. Presumably, this is because, in the field of politics, Ilyin, like the Machian-Bolsheviks, takes his sensations and images as reality.

In conclusion, a word or two about the positive aspects of Ilyin's *Materialism and Empiriocriticism*. The fact that the author warmly and passionately defends the truth is a positive and important feature of this book. Secondly, the book is not without isolated remarks that are both witty and to the point. Thirdly, one feels in the book a lively, fresh, cheerful, and revolutionary tone. These qualities are quite enough to recommend the book to readers, for there are many books in the world which lack these qualities and yet enjoy great success.

6. Michael O. Menshikov.—TRANS.
7. Nozdryov—an engaging liar and cheat in Gogol's *Dead Souls*.—TRANS.

CONTEMPORARY SOVIET
PHILOSOPHY

(A. G. Spirkin)

THE FINAL SELECTION for this volume is a translation of
the main parts of the article on "Dialectical Materialism" written
by A. G. Spirkin for the current Soviet *Encyclopedia of Philosophy*.[1] The selection is the most recent succinct, authoritative
statement of the Marxist-Leninist position on this topic. Spirkin
has also written articles on concept formation, the nature of
consciousness and its relation to matter, and linguistics—the
latter published in the official Soviet philosophical journal, *Voprosy Filosofii* (Problems of Philosophy), in April, 1950, less
than a month before the beginning of the famous "linguistics
controversy."[2] More recently, he has published a textbook on
dialectical materialism (1963).

Although Spirkin's views in the article on linguistics did not
coincide with the final conclusion of the debate, what he says
in the present selection deviates in no way from the official view
—it presents the philosophy of dialectical materialism systemati-
cally, in its accepted Marxist-Leninist form. In this Spirkin is
typical of philosophers in the Soviet Union today: there are
very few famous names in Soviet philosophy, and those few—
M. B. Mitin (b. 1901), F. V. Konstantinov (b. 1901), P. N. Fedo-

1. Volume I, Moscow, 1960.
2. The article, "Scientific Session Devoted to Marr Anniversary" (*Voprosy
Filosofii*, No. 3, 1949, published in April, 1950), is available in English
translation in the *Current Digest of the Soviet Press* and in *The Soviet
Linguistic Controversy*, trans. John V. Murra, Robert M. Hankin, and Fred
Holling, New York, 1951.

seyev (b. 1908), among others—are the names of people who hold important administrative posts or who have achieved fame by taking the correct stand in a historical philosophical controversy. So far as philosophy as such is concerned, however, in the Soviet Union it is, like other activities, a collective effort and to that extent anonymous. Thus, A. G. Spirkin represents a school of philosophy, not an individual view. And collective work and "scientific objectivity"—at least to the extent that personality does not intrude—are both characteristics and principles of that school.

We are told that dialectical materialism is "the philosophy of Marxism," as elaborated by Marx's successors, particularly in Russia. Its historical founder is Marx. Its first manifestation was in Marx's scientific socialism—in contrast to the "Utopian" socialism of such authors as Saint-Simon and Fourier, and to the "true" socialism of Moses Hess and Karl Grün. Its present content is the content of all the sciences. All philosophy, according to dialectical materialists, is a generalization of science, and dialectical materialism is the correct generalization. Moreover, philosophy and the specialized sciences are mutually dependent: scientific research produces material for philosophy, philosophy develops it; the new development in philosophy then serves to develop scientific method, and thus to further research: "Dialectical materialism [as a philosophy of science] serves as a universal methodology of knowledge and as a basis for the knowledge of nature and the social sciences." [3] Thus philosophy has a place distinct from the specialized sciences—in opposition to the views of the early Mechanists—but this distinct place is such that it is wholly dependent on the sciences for subject matter.

In addition to having this position, in accordance with which it is a theory of knowledge, dialectical materialism is also a theory of reality—of the nature and process of the world. The world consists of moving matter, and the motion of matter is due to "contradictions" within matter. All aspects of reality—including consciousness, knowledge, and the theory of knowledge—

3. M. B. Mitin, "Dialectical Materialism and Philosophy of Science," paper read at the meeting of the Society for the Philosophical Study of Dialectical Materialism in Washington, D.C., December 27, 1963.

are, in fact, stages in the self-development of matter. Hence, a correct, scientifically based theory of knowledge will both be true of reality and develop as all reality develops. The laws of the objective world and the laws of consciousness are thus the same. This being the case, there is fundamentally no gap between knowing subject and known object, although there is, of course, a qualitative difference between crude matter and consciousness as a product of its highly organized form.

Consequently, philosophy can serve as a method to change the social relations from which it first arises. A social situation produces a philosophical development which can in turn serve for social development: in this sense dialectical materialism is a tool for the rising party of the proletariat.[4]

Dialectical materialism, then, is a world view. It is a world view which *includes* transformation of the world as well as knowledge of it. This inclusiveness is expressed in its principle of the Union of Theory and Practice. In accordance with this fundamental principle, Spirkin's article studies the social and historical roots of Marxism in the early sections (which have been omitted here) and concludes with the present-day application of dialectical materialism and its future practical effects: "The Communist and workers' parties lead their peoples with confidence of the radiant future of communism, basing their practical and ideological work on the teachings of Marxist-Leninist philosophy, the foundation of which is dialectical materialism." [5]

Spirkin finds the roots of Marxism in the social situation of the 1840's, "when the proletariat entered the historical scene as a new political force," [6] and in all the prior developments of science and philosophy. Marxism's more recent sources were the materialist philosophy of Feuerbach, the idealist dialectic of Hegel, and the historical experience of the revolutions of 1848. In addition, the achievements of science in the late eighteenth

4. See K. Marx and F. Engels, *Selected Essays*, trans. H. J. Stenning, London, 1926, p. 38 f., quoted in Wetter, *op. cit.*, pp. 258-259, and below, p. 495.

5. See below, p. 507.

6. A. G. Spirkin, "Dialectical Materialism," *Encyclopaedia of Philosophy*, Moscow, 1960, I, 480.

and early nineteenth centuries were such that the dominant philosophy of idealism could no longer cope with them. The contradiction of materialist science and idealist philosophy was resolved in the qualitatively new theory of dialectical materialism of Marx and Engels. Thus the development of Marxism is itself an example of the dialectical materialist course of history.

Dialectical materialism is, then, a completely unified philosophy. The world is one, its "*arche*" is one, knowing subject and known object are of one nature, theory and practice are united. In its unity and all-inclusiveness, dialectical materialism attains the goal sought by the Russian religious philosophers of the late nineteenth and early twentieth centuries. The ideals of truth-justice, of brotherhood, of total-unity are realized in the principle of the Union of Theory and Practice, in the collective life, in the thoroughgoing pervasiveness of self-moving matter. But, just as the Hegelian dialectic was turned upside down and materialized, so these ideals have been brought to earth and secularized by the Russian followers of Karl Marx.

SELECTED BIBLIOGRAPHY

Nicholas Berdyaev, *The Origin of Russian Communism*, Ann Arbor, 1960.
J. M. Bochenski, *The Dogmatic Principles of Soviet Philosophy* [*as of 1958*]: *Synopsis of the "Osnovy Marksistskoy Filosofii*," trans. T. J. Blakeley, Dordrecht, 1963.
—————, *Soviet Russian Dialectical Materialism*, trans. N. Sollohub, Dordrecht, 1963.
Richard T. De George, *Patterns of Soviet Thought: The Origins and Development of Dialectical and Historical Materialism*, Ann Arbor, 1966.
Ervin Laszlo, ed., *Philosophy in the Soviet Union: A Survey of the Mid-Sixties*, New York, 1967.
Herbert Marcuse, *Soviet Marxism: A Critical Analysis*, New York, 1958.
Joseph Stalin, *Dialectical and Historical Materialism*, New York, 1940.
Gustav A. Wetter, *Dialectical Materialism*, trans. Peter Heath, London and New York, 1958.

[A. G. SPIRKIN]

Dialectical Materialism *

I. *Subject Matter of Dialectical Materialism*

Dialectical materialism, i.e., the philosophy of Marxism, is the world outlook of the working class. Dialectical materialism— being the genuinely scientific and only true philosophy—is the advanced world outlook of all progressive mankind in contemporary times. Dialectical materialism is a science which studies the relation of consciousness to the objective material world; the most general laws of the movement and development of nature, society, and consciousness. Marxist philosophy is called dialectical materialism because it represents the organic unity of *materialism* and *dialectic*. It is called *materialistic* because it originates in the recognition that matter is the only basis of the world, considering consciousness as an attribute of highly organized matter, a function of the brain, a reflection of the objective world; it is called *dialectical* because it recognizes the general *interrelation* of the objects and phenomena of the world and the *motion and development* of the world as resulting from the action of internal *contradictions* in the world itself. . . .

IV. *Matter and Consciousness*

Dialectical materialism originates in the recognition of the primacy of matter and the derivativeness of consciousness, and considers that the world consists of moving matter. The existence of matter has an absolute character. Matter is uncreatable and indestructible, it is eternal and infinite. Such general modes of the existence of matter as *motion, space,* and *time* remain constant in the infinite changes of the relative properties and forms

* Translated for this volume by Vladimir D. Pastuhov and Mary-Barbara Zeldin, from "Dialekticheski Materializm," *Filosofskaya Entsiklopediya,* Moscow, 1960-, I, 479, 483-495. References to the works of Marx, Engels, and Lenin are to Russian editions. In cases where a standard translation into English exists, a reference to such a translation is also given, after the Russian reference, in brackets. In the case of quotations a standard translation was used whenever possible.

of existing matter. The world consists of the infinitely *various forms of the motion of matter* in space and time.

The world presents a picture of inexhaustible variety: inorganic and organic nature, mechanical, physical, and chemical phenomena, the life of plants and animals, the life of society, of man and his consciousness. But in spite of all the infinity of the qualitative variety of objects and processes which constitute the world, the world is *one* insofar as all that enters into its composition consists only of various forms, aspects, and varieties of moving matter. There is nothing and there can be nothing in the world except various states of matter, its various properties, manifestations, and relations. Matter, indeed, represents the unity of the whole picture of the world.

The findings of modern science show that the mechanical, physical, chemical, biological, and social processes which take place in the world are not each self-enclosed and isolated. They can all be interconverted, because among them there is a general connection, interdependence, and interaction.

The material unity of the world is expressed by the fact that all the objects and processes in the world are subject to general laws which appear as endless threads binding all into a single whole. The unity of the world would be impossible if any objects or phenomena escaped the action of general laws. . . .

The material world has a historical development in the course of which, for instance, in the limits of the planet Earth, a transition took place from inorganic to organic matter (as the plant and animal world) and finally to man and society. Matter existed before the appearance of consciousness, possessing in its "foundation" only a property similar to sensation, a property of reflection; at the level of living organization it possesses the faculty of *irritability*, of sensation, perception, and of the elementary intellect of the higher animals. The social mode of the motion of matter appears with the coming into being of human society, the bearer of which is *man*, who possesses consciousness and self-consciousness. The world, having reached a high degree of organization, keeps its material unity because consciousness, thinking, is inseparable from matter, which thinks.

The problem of the relation of consciousness to matter is the *basic problem of philosophy*, i.e., the initial point in the solution of all the other problems of philosophy in general and of dialectical materialism in particular. This problem was always and is today in the center of philosophical thought. All previously existing and all present philosophical trends are divided into two irreconcilable camps depending on how they solve this basic philosophical problem: *materialism* and *idealism*.

According to dialectical materialism, consciousness is a function of the brain, a reflection of the objective world. I. M. Sechenov and I. P. Pavlov have scientifically proved that consciousness is a psychological process, a reflex in terms of its physiological basis and type of action. This means that consciousness is determined by the natural reality existing outside of, and operating on, the brain. . . .

The ontological characteristics of consciousness, however, become understandable in the light of the clarification of its epistemological nature. Objects, their properties and relations, being reflections in the brain, exist in it in the form of images, i.e., ideally. The brain is not the *source* but the *organ* of consciousness, i.e., a part of the human body in which the object acting on it is transformed and receives its ideal form of being. This ideal is not a special substance or a side-companion of material processes which take place in the cortex, but the product of the activity of the brain, the subjective reflection of the objective world.

The question of the relation of consciousness to matter presupposes not only the solution of the question as to which of them precedes the other, but also the clarification of the possibility of man's knowledge of the objective world. Some philosophers express doubts regarding the trustworthiness of human knowledge or, taking the position of *agnosticism*, completely deny the possibility of the knowledge of the world. Materialism proceeds from the thesis that the world is knowable and that science actualizes knowledge, developing itself in the direction of a deeper penetration into the laws of being. On the premise of the endlessness of the process of knowledge, the possibility of the knowledge of the world is limitless.

V. *The Dialectic of the Process of Knowledge*

Dialectical materialism proceeds from the position that knowledge is a reflection of the world in human consciousness, inseparable from the change of the object of knowledge in the course of social practice. The premises of the *theory of knowledge* of dialectical materialism are the materialistic solution of the question of the relation of thinking to being and the recognition of social practice as the basis of the process of knowledge. Social practice consists in the interaction of man and the surrounding world by means of the relations of men to one another in the concrete historical conditions of social life. The basic aspect of practice is the productive activity of men as directed to the reproduction of the material process of their lives. . . . Practice is the basis of the formation and development of knowledge at all its stages, the source of knowledge, the basic stimulus and aim of knowledge, the sphere of application of knowledge, the criterion of the truth of the results of the process of knowledge, and the "determinant of the link of the object with what is needed by man." (V. I. Lenin, *Works*, 4th edition, Vol. 32, p. 72 [*Once More the Trade Unions*, "Dialectic and Eclecticism"].) . . .

The initial stage of knowledge is sensory knowledge. Whatever enters into the sphere of theoretical thinking is merely the transformed data of sensory knowledge. Sensory knowledge organically linked with logical thought is a product of history. In the course of the development of ever more complex modes of social production, the development of relations of production, and the inclusion of ever new objects in the process of the production and creation of things, man has discovered more and more new things, properties, and relations between them, as well as new kinds of relations between men and society. The object as well as the subject of perception change qualitatively in the course of the historical development of man. "The eye has become a *human* eye when its *object* has become a *human*, social object, created by man and destined for him. The *senses* have therefore become directly *theoreticians* in practice." (K. Marx and F. Engels, *From the Early Works*, Moscow, 1956, p. 592; ["Private Property and Communism," *Economic and Philosophical*

Manuscripts, trans. T. B. Bottomore; in Erich Fromm, *Marx's Concept of Man*, New York, 1961, p. 132].)

The process of knowledge begins with sensations and perceptions, i.e., with the sensory stage, and rises to the level of abstract, logical thought which originates in the senses and, after leaving their boundaries, never loses touch with them. The transition from sensory knowledge to logical thought is a leap from the knowledge of the singular, accidental, and external to the generalized knowledge of the essential, the regular, from the concrete forms of reflection to such forms as lack "sensory instantiation." The transformation of contemplation and representation into concepts takes place in thought; it is precisely in thought that the essential properties and regular relations of things, hidden to the sensory levels of knowledge, are disclosed to consciousness. Sensory reflection and thought, being qualitatively different levels of the knowledge of the world, are inseparably united and form successively ascending links of a single knowing process. An absolute line cannot be drawn between sensory reflection and thought, just as it is impossible to draw it in the objective basis of sensory and rational knowledge, i.e., between the external and internal properties and relations of things, between the accidental and the necessary, etc.

Generalized knowledge, resulting from social practice, is included in sensory perception by means of language, which takes part in all processes of knowledge. In thought, man proceeds from sensory reflection and is imbued with it. The objective basis of the unity of sensory and rational knowledge, as well as of the qualitative differences between them, is the real unity and difference of the external and internal sides of existence, phenomenon and essence, form and content, etc. Dialectical materialism thus overcomes the limitations both of *sensationalism* and *intuitionism*, which underestimate the role of logical thought, and of *rationalism*, which underestimates the role of sensory knowledge.

Human thought is a historical phenomenon which presupposes the transmission of knowledge acquired from generation to generation and consequently the possibility of its fixation by means of language with which thought is inseparably linked. The knowledge of the world by an individual man is closely conditioned by the knowledge of the world by the whole of mankind. The thought of modern man is a product of history, and the specific peculiarities which it has were historically formed on the basis of the development of human practice, which is also a historical phenomenon. The practice of modern society is radically different, for instance, from that of slave-owning society and the thought based on these levels of practice is profoundly different.

Like its foundation, practice, thought is a social phenomenon. Nature disclosed and is disclosing its "mysteries" to human thought not "privately" but through forms of social relations which are becoming more and more complex. The need for the historical method, which is in dialectical unity with the logical method, originates in the historical character of human knowledge and primarily in the historical character of the object of knowledge.

The essential methods of knowledge are *comparison, analysis, synthesis, generalization, abstraction, induction*, and *deduction*. They manifest themselves in different ways at the different levels of the historical and logical movement of thought as it progresses into the depths of the knowledge of the object. All these methods of knowledge develop out of the depths of the practical operation of man with objects, and function in inseparable unity in the process of knowledge. The starting point of knowledge, i.e., the sensory datum, is their terminal point; but it is such no longer in its summary wholeness, but in its analyzed unity, in the exposed interconnection of its parts; and it is in this that concrete knowledge consists. . . .

Thinking, as the process of reflecting the world, has as its result determinate thoughts which are logically interrelated. The various ways of connecting the thoughts or the various types of thought-structure lead to various forms of thinking.

The study of the formation and of the laws of development of the forms of thought, the disclosure of their objective content and of their dialectical interrelation in the process of knowledge are included in the theory of knowledge.

Knowledge is the process of the penetration of human consciousness into the object, and the cognitive aim of this process is the comprehension of *the truth*, i.e., of the right reflection of the object. The results of the process of knowledge, insofar as they are an adequate reflection of things, their properties and relations, always have an objective content and constitute the *objective truth*, which is not the reality itself but is the objective content of the results of knowledge. The epistemological unity of consciousness and of the objective world receives its most condensed expression in the concept of objective truth.

Human consciousness cannot at once and entirely reproduce and exhaust the content of an object. Any theory is historically conditioned and therefore includes not full but *relative truth*. Human thinking, however, can exist only as the thinking of past, present, and future generations, and in this sense the possibilities of knowledge are limitless. Knowledge is the development of truth and truth is the resultant expression of a historically determined level of the endless process of knowledge, a process which is composed of separate links. Truth as a process can only be endlessly accumulating knowledge. Truth as historically emergent and developing knowledge successively passes in its development through determinate levels. Dialectical materialism, proceeding from the recognition of the relativity of knowledge, in the sense of the historical conditionality of the degree of approximation to full knowledge, rejects the extreme views of *relativism*, according to which the character of human knowledge excludes the recognition of objective truth.

Each object, side by side with its common traits, has also its unique peculiarities, its specific "life context"; every social phenomenon is conditioned by specific circumstances of place and time. Therefore, a concrete approach to the object of knowledge is necessary, concurrently with generalization. This is expressed in the principle: there is no abstract truth; *truth is concrete*, and the multiform nature of knowledge requires the examination of the object in connection with the conditions on which it depends. . . . Lenin, warning against the error linked with a non-concrete approach to truth, wrote that "every truth, if overdone . . . if exaggerated, if carried beyond the limits of its actual applicability, can be reduced to absurdity, and, under the conditions mentioned, is even bound to become an absurdity."

(*Works*, 4th edition, Vol. 31, p. 44 [*"Left-Wing" Communism, an Infantile Disorder*, Ch. 7; *Selected Works (The Essentials of Lenin in Two Volumes)*, London, 1947, II, 603].)

The truth of the results of human knowledge is confirmed and verified by social practice, which is in substance the final goal of human knowledge and which is the criterion of the truth of the content of knowledge. The dialectical materialist teaching regarding the knowledge of the world is one of the most important principles of the world outlook and method of the working class and its party.

VI. *Dialectic as Logic and Theory of Knowledge*

Dialectic as the science of the general forms and laws of development of the objective world constitutes an indissoluble unity with logic and the theory of knowledge. This unity has as its objective basis the unity of the laws of being and thought. Dialectic, developed on a materialistic basis, provides scientific solutions to problems which previously were isolated in fields separated from dialectic, i.e., logic and epistemology. Lenin, proceeding from Engels' theories and characterizing the subject matter of the philosophy of dialectical materialism, wrote that dialectical materialism has no need of any philosophy standing above the other sciences: "Of former philosophies there remains 'the science of thought and its laws—formal logic and dialectics.' Dialectics, as the term is understood by Marx in conformity with Hegel, includes what is now called theory of knowledge, or epistemology, which, too, must regard its subject matter historically, studying and generalizing the origin and development of knowledge, the transition from *non*-knowledge to knowledge." (*Works*, 4th edition, Vol. 21, p. 38: "Karl Marx"; [Karl Marx, *Selected Works*, ed. V. Adoratsky, New York, n.d., p. 28].)

Lenin emphasized many times that dialectics is, indeed, the Marxist theory of knowledge and that the latter is logic representing "the science not of external forms of thought, but of the laws of development 'of all material, natural, and spiritual things,' i.e., of the development of the entire concrete content of the world and of its cognition, i.e., the sum-total, the conclusion of the *history* of knowledge of the world." (*Philosoph-*

ical Notebooks, 1947, p. 66; [*Collected Works,* Moscow, 1961, Vol. 38, pp. 92-93].) [1] The very nature of the materialistic interpretation of thought as always correlated with the object necessarily implies that the development of the theory of knowledge, of dialectical logic, is possible only in connection with the study of the material world. Dialectical logic has as its subject matter not thought by itself but the forms and laws of thought, filled with generalized content, in their relation to the objective world, or the basic forms of existence, and the laws of the development of the objective world in its relation to thought. The necessity of a historical examination of the content, forms, and laws of thought on the basis of the development of social practice results from the very nature of thought as *dialectically* understood. The concern of dialectical logic is the study of how the dialectic of being (of nature and society) is reflected in the dialectic of thought, i.e., in the expression, in the logic of concepts and categories, of the motion and development of objects and phenomena of the objective world, and of contradiction as the motive force of development. Dialectical logic is the application of all the basic theses of dialectical materialism to thought as the scientific reflection of reality in the human mind. From the dialectical interpretation of thought it necessarily follows that the content, the forms, and the laws of thinking must be examined concretely and historically on the basis of the development of social practice, in order to elucidate how some

1. There are two points of view among Soviet philosophers regarding these theories of Lenin's. Some consider that Lenin had in mind the *identity* of dialectic, logic, and the theory of knowledge. Others affirm that Lenin had in mind the *unity* of dialectic, logic, and the theory of knowledge; this presupposes their difference insofar as their object and content are concerned. The first point of view proceeds from the premise that dialectical materialism is dialectics, dialectical logic, and theory of knowledge. The second point of view proceeds from the premise that the concept of "dialectics" is broader than the concepts of "logic" and "theory of knowledge"; that dialectics teaches about the most general laws of the development of nature, human society, and thinking, while dialectical logic teaches about the laws of the *development of thinking;* theory of knowledge, being broader in its scope, has as its specific field the study of the relationship of subject to object, the study of the origin of sensations, of sensory knowledge, of the transition from sensation to thought, etc.

concepts emanate from others, what relationship obtains among the laws, categories, etc. . . . Dialectical logic is nothing but the history and process of knowledge in their logical treatment. Side by side with dialectical logic there is formal *logic*, which has as its subject matter the laws of the connection between premises and conclusions and the laws of demonstration.

Dialectical logic represents the theory of the origin and historical development of the logical forms of thought in their unity with their content, and therefore discloses their internal contradictions; on the other hand, formal logic abstracts from the historical development of thought, taking it as something ready-made, as a given, and abstracts from the internal contradictions of the object of knowledge as the motive force for the development both of the world and of knowledge. In formal logic, contradictions are conceived as occurring successively and as incompatible with their opposites; on the other hand, dialectical logic studies a way of thought in which contradictions are given simultaneously, i.e., in the way in which they exist in the object of thought. Dialectical logic studies the whole process of the development of knowledge in its entirety, and formal logic only a specific side of it. Thus formal logic is not abolished by dialectical logic, but is only limited by it. In the process of knowledge the laws of dialectical logic and the laws of formal logic operate simultaneously. The laws of formal logic, however, are insufficient for the scientific knowledge which spontaneously or consciously is governed by the materialist dialectic.

VII. *Categories and Laws of the Dialectic*

The materialist dialectic is a doctrine concerning the general laws of the development of both the external world and of human consciousness. These laws are reflected and fixed in the system of the categories. The categories are the most general, basic concepts and at the same time the essential determinations of the forms of the being and relations of things; the categories express the universal forms of the generalization of being and knowledge. Since all the categories are interdependent and are constantly developing, and since, in their development, they are subjected to the basic laws of the dialectic, the laws of the dialectic in their turn express the relations obtaining among the categories insofar as they are general aspects and relations of things. Thus, for instance, the relations between content and form, essence and appearance, necessity and contingency are, apart from their specificity, manifestations of the action of the law of the unity and struggle of opposites. The categories, appearing as a result of the knowledge of the objective world, become a premise and, in combination, a general method of scientific research. . . .

Insofar as they are a result of generalization, the categories express past practice and, insofar as they are an implement of knowledge, they serve present and future practice. The categories develop in conformity with the movement of reality and the development of man's knowledge of it. The categories, reflecting changing reality, undergo a development consisting in the enrichment, deepening, and concretization of their content.

In the objective sense, taking into account the world as a whole, a successive formation of the categories is inconceivable, since they are the basic and general properties and relations of things. Quality, quantity, causality, law, etc., exist from eternity and do not occur in succession, one from another or one after another. Only an idealistic logic can be constructed on the premise that the origin and development of logical categories are at the same time the very creation of things and of their relations. . . .

Dialectical materialism, in opposition to objective idealism, proceeds from the recognition of the *unity* of being and consciousness; this presupposes the community of the laws of the objective world and of those of consciousness, as well as their difference. . . . In the analysis of the categories, dialectical materialism adopts the principles of the Marxist-Leninist theory of reflection and dialectic. The study and formulation of the categories and of the laws of dialectical materialism must originate from the unity of the logical and historical methods, which in its turn reflects the objective logic of the relations of things and of their development, and reflects the unfolding in them of an ever greater wealth of determinations in connection with the complexity of their relations, because ". . . the course of abstract thought, proceeding from the most simple to the complex, corresponds to the real historical process." (K. Marx, see K. Marx and F. Engels, *Works,* 2nd edition, Vol. 12, pp. 728-729.) At the same time, the interconnection and the reciprocal transitions of the categories in logical form reflect (very conditionally, of course, and with unavoidable crudeness) the historical course of the development of the knowledge of the object and the logical sequence of the dialectical phases of the process of knowledge.

Since each category is a generalized expression of the corresponding level of the development of the knowledge of the world, in the system of the materialist dialectic each category occupies a more or less historically and logically determined place. Lenin considered the categories as the levels, the points of juncture of the knowledge of the world: "The history of thought from the standpoint of the development and application of the general concepts and categories of the Logic—*voilà ce qu'il faut!* (That's what is needed!)." (V. I. Lenin, *Philosophical Notebooks,* 1947, p. 152; [*Collected Works,* Moscow, 1961, Vol. 38, p. 177].)

The logical course of thought reproduces the movement of the historical process of knowledge from the direct perception of the properties of things to the knowledge of regular connections, which is arrived at by means of thought. The basis of the development of the categories is human social practice in the process of its historical development. The most abstract categories of thought have "earthly roots" and in the last instance grow on the ground of social practice and are products of the practical relations of men with the real world through their relations one with another at a specific level of social production. At the same time, the history of social experience through the ages shows that the categories, which arose on the basis of social practice in the process of its further development, suffer changes, are confirmed, enriched, corrected by practice. Consequently, as a result of the development of practice, the categories and concepts are developed as expressions of practice.

The category which forms the basis of the historically developing system of dialectical materialism must be one which has no need of any premise and which by itself is the premise for the study of all the other categories. Such a category is the category of matter. After the category of matter come the fundamental forms of the existence of matter: *motion, space,* and *time.* Such a successive study of given categories corresponds in a general way to the history and logic of knowledge. The multiform states of matter are conceived only through motion. Motion is the obvious fact first encountered by man in his practical activity and knowledge. Representations and concepts about space and time occur as a result of the knowledge of the properties and forms of ⌐moving matter.

Matter really exists as the infinite variety of forms of its manifestation. Man has to deal with subject matters and phenomena which appear as objects for his action and knowledge. . . . Every object appears to the practically acting man in its qualitative aspect, the knowledge of which, at first very superficial, represents a very important level of the knowledge of the object. Knowledge of material things begins directly with perception "and included in it is unavoidably *quality.*" (V. I. Lenin, *ibid.,* p. 215.) *Quality* is the specificity of the given object, its singularity, its difference from other objects. For the subject, the determinate being of the concrete object is first of all some qualitative determination enabling him to tell the given object from others and at the same time to find a likeness among them. The quality of the object appears only in the relations of the given object with other objects, but before manifesting itself the quality has first to be. Quality is linked with the being of the given object in such a way that in losing its quality the given object becomes another object.

The course of knowledge takes place in such a way that the awareness of quality comes before the knowledge of *quantity.* "First, *fleeting* impressions, then *something* appears, later the concepts of *quality* and *quantity* occur." (V. I. Lenin, *ibid.,* p. 214.) To realize, for instance, the operation of counting, man must first of all know what he is counting. To determine quantity it is necessary to abstract from quality. This is possible because quality and quantity are relatively independent from one another, so that change of quantity up to a certain point does not imply change of quality. . . . Any object represents by itself a unity of quantity and quality, i.e., a quantitatively determined quality. This unity provides the *measure*, the concept of which implies as its condition the perception of quality and quantity. In disclosing the qualitative and the quantitative determinateness of things, man at the same time determines their *difference* and *identity*, which make up one of the elementary levels of knowledge.

All objects have external aspects apprehended immediately by sensation and perception, and internal aspects the knowledge of which is acquired mediately by abstract thought. This diversity of the levels of thought is expressed in the categories of *external* and *internal*. The formation of these categories in human consciousness precedes and prepares for the understanding of *causality*, or the relation of cause and effect, a relation which was previously understood only as the succession of phenomena in time. Knowledge proceeds "from coexistence to causality and from one form of connection and reciprocal dependence to another, deeper, and more general form." (V. I. Lenin, *ibid.*, p. 193; [*ibid.*, p. 222].) Purposeful practical human activity is impossible without an elementary representation of causality. Man began to realize, in a further development of knowledge, that the cause not only produces the effect but also presupposes it as a reaction. Cause and effect, while differing from each other, are not two different and independent aspects of existence. Any action is *interaction*. In this way the relation of cause and effect is conceived by man as interaction, i.e., as a universal link of things and processes expressed in their mutual changes. . . . Interaction is the substance of cause and effect which are only its dialectical phases. . . .

The universal ground of the change and *development* of objects lies in their interaction and in the interaction of those various aspects, phases, within the object which are expressed in contradictions, in the struggle of opposites. This ground is based in the nature of things, and the change and development of objects occur not in consequence of an external push as a unilateral action, but because of interaction and *contradiction*. Development is the transition of the object from one quantitative state

into another, from lower to higher, from simple to complex. The
formation of the category of development in man's consciousness—a category which became one of the most important component parts of the methods of dialectical materialist thinking—
marked a huge conquest in the history of knowledge. Notions
concerning the development of reality, of its concrete objects,
as for instance, man, animals, and plants, had already arisen at the
dawn of human history. But in the beginning there was as yet
no concept of development in general, and concepts of development were applied only to singular and isolated instances: this
was bound up with narrowness of practice and underdevelopment
of thought. The further development of knowledge is tied to the
discovery that this process consists of a chain of phenomena, each
link of which is a starting point for the successive link and at
the same time the result of the preceding one, and that any link
in the chain of phenomena includes in itself its own negation, i.e.,
the possibility of transition into another object, into a new form
of existence of the initial object. Thus it becomes clear that the
being of things is not limited to their existence, that things
include in themselves a hidden, potential, or "future being," i.e.,
a possibility, which, until its transformation into existence, remains
in the nature of things as a tendency of their development.

The social and working activity of man transformed into reality
what in nature exists only as a possibility. On this basis these
categories were formed in human consciousness. It turns out
in this connection that various possibilities are included in reality
[deystvitelnost], but only those which possess the conditions
necessary for their realization are brought into existence.
The distinction between the possible and the actual being
of things enabled man better to understand that behind the external side of things there is hidden an internal side, and to
establish the connection between *form* and *content*. While originally the external and the internal could be considered as isolated,
in connection with the further extension of knowledge, in connection with the rise of the concepts of form and content, the
principle of their interrelation was established. As man discovers
deeper connections he is led to higher and higher generalizations.
The practical interaction of men with a multitude of similar and

different things led to the discovery of singular, particular, and general signs of things, and these served as a basis for the development of the categories of *singular*, *particular*, and *general*.

Continuous observation of objects and phenomena in nature on the one hand, and productive activity on the other, led men to the understanding that not all connections of things are repeated in the same manner, that some connections have a stable, constantly recurring character, and that other connections occur only very seldom. This served as a basis for the formation of the categories of *necessity* and *contingency*. In this case, the connection between them remained originally undiscovered. Further, deeper scientific knowledge showed that what is separate in its particular, immediate being is on the one hand something accidental and on the other hand something necessary, insofar as it contains in itself the general as the essence of the singular. The understanding of essence and, at a higher level of development, of the order of essences, signifies the discovery of the internal basis, included in the object, of all the changes occurring in it as it interacts with other objects. Knowledge of phenomena means the discovery of how essence is revealed. Essence and phenomenon are revealed as phases of *reality* presenting objectively, independently of consciousness, the existing unity of the laws of the development of objects and processes and their manifestations. Reality is the resulting expression of the process of the development of objects and of the processes of nature and of social life, a given level in the development of phenomena, the result of the emergence of existence from real possibility. Possibility is the manifestation of the internal, potential being of the object. Reality is richer than possibility because the latter is only one of the phases of reality. Each of them contains the other in itself. The real possibility has its basis, the conditions of its emergence, in reality and is itself part of reality. The knowledge of reality shows that the necessary is the genuinely real, i.e., is that which expresses its essence (for instance, the normal physical and intellectual development of man); what does not correspond to this is contingent. Consequently, not all that exists is genuinely real in the sense of the development of essence according to laws of the given system of phenomena. The necessary is that which is conditioned in its origin and development by the internal nature of things, provided that the corresponding external conditions are available. The contingent is all that is conditioned by external conditions not originating in the internal nature of things. But necessity and contingency are opposites which can pass into each other. The knowledge of the difference between the necessary and the contingent is the avenue leading to the knowledge of *law*, since necessity is one of the essential characteristics of law.

In the process of the development of knowledge, the categories are filled with an ever greater content, reflecting the world in its essential and regular interrelations. Thus, for instance, if at an early level of the development of knowledge, space and time were conceived as limited, then, during the further development of scientific knowledge, such properties of space and time were established as the unity of *discontinuity* and *continuity*, finiteness and *infinity*, actual and potential infinity, etc. By this the categories of matter, motion, space, and time were rendered concrete. . . .

Law is the essential relationship, the internal, indispensable connection between phenomena. It expresses, on the one hand, the essential recurring connection of coexisting objects in space, and, on the other hand, the necessary *tendency*, *direction* of the development, the order of succession of phenomena in time. Insofar as law is steadfast, enduring, and identical in a phenomenon, insofar as it is a relation of essences or among essences (see V. I. Lenin, *Philosophical Notebooks*, 1947, pp. 126-128; [*ibid.*, pp. 151-153]), to that extent is the knowledge of laws possible only on the condition of sufficiently developed scientific thinking. The category of law is the product of mature thinking and was formed, as history shows, only at a given, rather high level of the development of human society.

The material world, for instance, within the limits of our planet, presents itself as a series of successive historical levels of the development of the forms of the motion of matter, these levels being subjected both to general laws and to special laws for each such level. All these successive forms of the motion of matter (mechanical, physical, chemical, biological, and social) are arranged in the order of their complexity and of the transformation of the lower form into the higher. Such an arrangement expresses their reciprocal connection on the structural as well as on the historical plane, the general laws of the lower forms of the motion of matter retaining their force at each higher level, but also subject to the laws of the higher level and having no longer a leading role. The laws of the preceding levels of the motion of matter, retaining their force in the following levels of this movement, modify the result of their appearance in that they operate in other conditions. . . . Specific laws are the subject of concrete science, while the general laws of the development of being and thought are the subject of dialectical materialism. *Generality* is the law of the existence, change, and development of all singular things and phenomena in their connection, expressing the unity of the world. General laws were discovered as a result of the generalization of laws of a more particular order. The most general laws of dialectical materialism are: the *transition from quantity to quality*, the *unity and struggle of opposites*, the *negation of negation*. These laws express the universal forms, the ways, and the driving forces of the development of the material world and of its knowledge, and are the general method of dialectical thinking. The basic categories in their historical formation and relation are rendered concrete in these laws of the dialectic. The discovery and the scientific substantiation of the laws of the dialectic have enriched the understanding of the content and connection of previously known categories whose development is subject to these general laws. The laws of the dialectic represent the logical expression of what is essential in development.

Development as the movement from simple to complex, from lowest to highest, from an old qualitative condition to a higher, new quality, is at the same time both a continuous and a discontinuous process. In these circumstances, the quantitative changes of a phenomenon up to a certain limit have the character of the relatively uninterrupted growth of an object which remains the same in terms of its quality. The object, while changing quantitatively within the limits of a specific measure, does not cease to be what it is. The object loses its previous quality and becomes a new object only at a determined level of its development and in determined circumstances. Development is thus the unity of discontinuity and continuity, of revolutionary changes by leaps and of evolutionary changes of phenomena.

The law of the transition of quantity into quality shows how the new originates. But it does not disclose all the essence of the process of development, it does not answer the question, what is the driving force, what is the source of the development?

The driving force of the development is expressed by the law of the unity and struggle of opposites. The essence of this law is that the objects and phenomena of the objective world, during the process of their development which derives from the interaction and the contradiction among various objects and phenomena and among various aspects within the objects and phenomena, pass from the state of unnoticeable, unessential differences among the aspects and tendencies composing the given phenomenon to essential differences of the elements of the whole and to contrasts which among themselves enter into contradiction, struggle, thus constituting the internal source of the development of the given phenomenon. Each object contains its opposite in itself. The internal opposition of any object consists in that in each single object there is at one and the same time interpenetration and interexclusion of opposites. Development is only possible because of contradiction, i.e., because of the springing up of an active interaction, collision, struggle of opposites. The struggling opposites are in unity among themselves in the sense that they pertain to the same object or phenomenon. The source of development is a contradiction expressing itself in the struggle of opposites within the framework of a given unity.

This law, reflected in the system of theoretical knowledge, becomes the essential pivot or nucleus in the dialectical method of scientific knowledge. "Dialectics in the proper sense is the study of contradiction *in the very essence of objects*." (V. I. Lenin, *ibid.*, p. 237; [*ibid.*, pp. 253-254].) Dialectics thus provides the possibility of considering the stimuli of the development of the world within the world itself.

Any development is a process directed in a certain way. The law of the negation of negation expresses this aspect of development. Every phenomenon is relative and, because of its finite nature, passes into another phenomenon, which, under certain conditions, might become the opposite of the first and play the part of its negation. Negation is a necessary condition of development, insofar as it is not only the negation of the old but the confirmation of the new. But the process of development does not stop at that. The newly manifested quality in its turn passes into another quality. Negation is canceled by a second negation, and the entire chain of development is a process of the negation of negation. The transition of the object from simple to complex, from lower to higher, with elements of repetition of what has already been, of temporary regression, is a result of this growing negation of negation. The law of the negation of negation provides a generalized expression of development as a whole, disclosing the internal link, the gradual character of development. It expresses a transition of phenomena from one qualitative state into another in which the new quality reproduces on a higher level some aspects of the quality at the previous level. In a word, this law expresses both the process of the radical change of the previous quality and the repeating link between various different stages of development, i.e., the essential tendency of development and the succession between the old and the new. The development occurs in such a way that the highest stage of the development appears as the synthesis of all the preceding movement in its transcended form. Every phase of development, regardless of its difference from the preceding, is the result of the preceding development, and therefore includes it and keeps it in itself in a modified form. In essence, it is the first object which has become a different object. An important demand of scientific knowledge as a method results from this, namely, that only that historical knowledge can be fruitful which considers every stage of historical development as a result of the preceding stage and as being in organic connection with it.

In their origin, historical development, and correlation, the internal reciprocity of the categories and laws of the subjective dialectic present the logical expression of the objective dialectic of the world and of its knowledge in the dynamics of their development.

VIII. *Dialectical Materialism and Modern Scientific Knowledge*

Dialectical materialism, more than any other previous or existing philosophy, is internally and inseparably linked with the concrete sciences; it rests firmly on their achievements and provides the scientists with a unique scientific method of thinking, a method of knowledge adequate to the laws of the objective world. Dialectical materialism is a complete generalization of the achievements of all the natural and social sciences, but, at the same time, it is developing as a philosophical science on its own. This relation is mutual. Dialectical materialism has its own objective foundation. Besides specific laws for any field, more general laws characteristic of being and knowledge as a whole operate in every field. The subject matter of dialectical materialism is the most general laws of the motion and development of being and of thought. If the general laws of the development of the world and of knowledge and the concrete forms of their manifestations can be studied only on the basis of and in close relation with the study and the generalization of the particular laws, then the knowledge of the general laws in its turn will provide a basic guide for the study of the particular laws. Once discovered, these general laws become a powerful instrument of orientation in the complicated labyrinth of the infinite multitude of variously qualified things and phenomena. Every science, therefore, is based on the results of the knowledge of the general laws of development as methodological principles. The unique scientific method for the knowledge and transformation of reality is the materialist dialectic, "because it alone provides an analogy and consequently a method of explanation for the developments taking place in nature, for the general links in nature, for the changes from one field of research to another." (F. Engels, *Dialectics of Nature*, 1955, p. 22.)

The knowledge of the universal properties of the laws of the motion and development of the world as a whole appears in every concrete scientific research as the sole scientific method. However, the universal properties and relations of things present themselves differently depending on the specificity of the field which is studied by one or another science. . . .

When one recognizes the need of a variety of distinct methods generated by the knowledge of the specificity of one or another phenomenon, then it is impossible to ignore that there is only a single philosophical method of knowledge among all the particular methods of knowledge, i.e., dialectical materialism.

A correct dialectical materialist solution of the fundamental problem of philosophy has an enormous methodological significance for scientific knowledge. . . . Idealists in biology, professing vitalism, are unable to give a scientific explanation of the laws of the development of living organisms or to produce effective methods for the conscious influence of man on the formation of new species. Biology became a genuine science when Charles Darwin discovered the objective laws of the development of the organic world and rejected the idealistic inventions of a "vital force." The physiology of the brain and psychology became genuine sciences when I. M. Sechenov and I. P. Pavlov rejected the fables of the idealists regarding the *soul* and discovered the material basis of psychic phenomena. The number of such examples in various fields of scientific knowledge could be increased, but it appears clearly from the examples provided that the dialectical materialist solution of the fundamental problem of philosophy liberates science from innumerable idealistic speculations, from meaningless searches for "vital forces," "will impulses" in electrons, from the search for any kind of supernatural principles in nature.

The development of scientific knowledge and philosophy leads to an ever more thorough discovery of the world. The dialectical method as a first principle in the conception of the world permits the accurate reflection of the laws of the objective world in thought. Dialectics directs constructive efforts to the study of the processes of change and development, of interconnection and interchange, of contradictions in natural phenomena. All this makes possible the discovery in maximum depth of the essence of the things and processes under study. The knowledge of the general relations of things and of their development presupposes the possession of a scientific method, of logical categories, of theoretical thinking without which it is impossible to comprehend these relations and developments.

But theoretical thinking is only an innate property of the

human brain in the sense of being a faculty which must be developed and improved. This faculty is developed by the assimilation of the laws of dialectical thought, of logical categories, which reflect the general forms and laws of being and which have been historically worked out by practice and the history of philosophy and science. Philosophy, the highest achievement of which is dialectical materialism, has played and is playing an enormous role in the conscious understanding of these categories and their theoretical working out. Man, therefore, even in an uncomplicated action of theoretical thinking—whether conscious of it or not—is compelled to use the results of philosophical research; for the development of the faculty of theoretical thought "there is not, up to the present, any other means than the study of all previous philosophy" (F. Engels, *ibid.*), and primarily of dialectical materialism as the highest stage in the development of modern philosophical thought. Concrete research will use the notions peculiar to a given science as well as the general notions and laws of thought worked up by dialectical materialism. Because of this, concrete research cannot—without detriment to its own interests—ignore the results of the development of the theory of scientific thought which studies the laws and categories that express the most general connections and relations of things, without which human knowledge of reality is wholly impossible.

Emphasizing the significance of philosophy for scientific knowledge, Engels stated that "natural scientists believe that they free themselves from philosophy by ignoring or abusing it. They cannot, however, make any headway without thought, and for thought they need thought determinations. But they take these categories unreflectingly from the common consciousness of so-called educated persons, which is dominated by the relics of long obsolete philosophies, or from the little bits of philosophy compulsorily listened to at the university . . . or from uncritical and unsystematic reading of philosophical writings of all kinds. Hence they are no less in bondage to philosophy, but unfortunately, in most cases, to the worst. . . ." (*Ibid.*, pp. 164-165; [*ibid.*, trans. Clemens Dutt, with a Preface and Notes by J. B. S. Haldane, New York, 1940, pp. 183-184].)

Marx pointed out that the importance of dialectical materialism lay primarily in the fact that it provided the possibility of
free orientation in factual material. (See K. Marx and F. Engels,
Selected Letters, 1953, p. 239.) Dialectical materialism embodies
all the historical experience of the development of science and
therefore must be used as a compass for science, warning scientists
of the principal errors and deviations from the right course, not
a few examples of which are known to history. Dialectical
materialism helps the representatives of various sciences in the
understanding of the methodological essence of their discoveries,
in the struggle against idealistic and metaphysical distortions of
the results of scientific research. Referring to the necessity of a
close relationship between dialectical materialism and the concrete sciences, Lenin wrote that "without a solid philosophical
basis no scientific knowledge, no materialism of any kind can
sustain the struggle against the impact of bourgeois ideas and
the restoration of the bourgeois world outlook." (*Works*, 4th
ed., Vol. 33, p. 207 ["On the Importance of Militant Materialism,"
Under the Banner of Marxism, March 12, 1922, No. 3, signed:
N. Lenin].)

The very logic of the development of the sciences—dealing
with material objects and processes of nature which are full of
internal contradictions and which develop dialectically—itself
pushes scientists towards materialism and dialectic, though in
bourgeois countries this trend must often take roundabout ways
for a series of social, economic, and ideological reasons. For
instance, some important scientists (Heisenberg and others) passed
from a subjective and idealistic position to the point of view
of objective idealism, taking at the same time a step toward
materialism.

Soviet scientists, as well as some scientists abroad, have arrived
at the philosophical interpretation of the theoretical problems of
science in accordance with dialectical materialism. Such is the
unavoidable course of any progressive, unprejudiced scientist
who, in his research, is compelled consciously or unconsciously
to adopt dialectical materialism if he does not want to enter into
a contradiction between the philosophical foundations of his
world outlook and the objective content of concrete knowledge.

IX. *The Unity of Dialectical and Historical Materialism*

The use of materialism and dialectic in the study of human society is a very important expression of the fundamental principles of dialectical materialism as a total and fully consistent world outlook and method. The expansion, the application of dialectical materialism to the development of society is *historical materialism*. Historical materialism is an organic part of the philosophy of Marxism-Leninism. Dialectical materialism considers that being determines consciousness, that men are adapted to know the world and its laws. Historical materialism, in full accord with this, considers that social being determines social consciousness, that men are adapted to know society and the laws of its development. Dialectical materialism considers that the world develops because of its internal contradictions. Historical materialism, in full accord with this, approaches social phenomena dialectically, disclosing their internal contradictions as the sources of the development of society. Historical materialism, in line with the general laws of development proper to the whole world, discovers particular laws, motive forces proper only to society: forces of production, relations of production in the interaction of their elements, etc. The general laws of reality, which are the subject matter of Marxist philosophy, are established from the analysis of the phenomena not only of nature but of social life. Historical materialism cannot be separated from dialectical materialism and is incompatible with any other philosophical theory or method. The position of dialectical materialism regarding the primacy of matter and the derivative nature of consciousness differs from the materialism prior to Marxism in that it includes the idea that social being is primary and social consciousness secondary. By social being Marxism has in mind the real course of the life of men, labor, the production of goods, the relations among men in the course of production, etc. By social consciousness Marxism has in mind political, philosophical, legal, artistic views, morals, science, and religion.

The fundamental philosophical problem finds its final consistent solution in the materialistic explanation of the history of society: a change of human social consciousness depends on a change of social being. Only on the basis of historical materialism has it become possible to understand that consciousness is a socially produced function of the human brain, that it is the result of the social and labor activity of men, of the conditions of social life. Without historical materialism, the essence of practice as the basis of consciousness cannot be understood. All the fundamental problems of the theory and of the history of knowledge can be correctly solved only on the basis of the scientific solution of the central problems of the study of society. Therefore, the theory of knowledge of dialectical materialism is entirely unthinkable without historical materialism. Moreover, without the scientific understanding of society, i.e., without historical materialism, there can in principle be no philosophy of dialectical materialism.

Critics of Marxism, revisionists of various kinds, are striving to tear historical materialism away from dialectical materialism, declaring that the economic and sociological teachings of Marx can be completed or combined with Machism, neo-Kantianism, and other idealistic bourgeois views. Denouncing these endeavors, Lenin emphasized that there can be no historical materialism without dialectical materialism, and therefore that it is not possible to support historical materialism without adhering fully to dialectical materialism.

X. *Dialectical and Historical Materialism as an Ideological Weapon of the Marxist Party*

Any world outlook reflecting in one way or another nature and social reality is at the same time the reflection of the interests of definable classes and parties. Every class and its party, in a class society, has its world outlook, in which the notions of a given class about nature, man, and social relations are generalized into one whole by the ideologists of this class. The world outlook in this sense is a partisan outlook. As long as there are classes and class struggle there is not and there cannot be a non-partisan philosophy indifferent to the situation and the interests of one class or another. A class philosophy not only reflects the class struggle but is by itself an instrument of class struggle.

The bourgeois ideologists, and in their trail the revisionists of Marxism, praise non-partisanship in world outlook and philosophy, affirming that partisanship is irreconcilable with objectivity, with science. Partisanship in philosophy, indeed, does not correspond with science when it expresses and defends the position and the interests of such classes as are disappearing from the stage of history and are slowing up the development of society. Indeed, this kind of philosophy, representing the interests of disappearing classes, really does diverge from real life, from the objective approach to it, from its scientific appraisal. But philosophy is objective and scientific when it correctly represents life, expresses the interests of the forward-looking classes of society, contributes to the society's advancement. For instance, the materialist philosophy of the seventeenth and eighteenth centuries expressed the interests of the rising bourgeoisie which was at the time the progressive class of society struggling with the religious and idealistic world outlook of feudalism. This philosophy was partisan, but simultaneously, with all its limitations, it was objective and scientific. It contributed to the development of science and society as a whole. But the situation radically changed when the bourgeoisie, from being a progressive class, became a reactionary class. The interests of this bourgeoisie require the perpetuation of the exploitation of man by man, the resistance to and the struggle against the revolutionary labor and national-liberation movement. Contemporary bourgeois philosophy, expressing the interests of the imperialist bourgeoisie, is also partisan, but this partisanship no longer coincides with scientific objectivity, because the reactionary bourgeois idealistic philosophy presents a distorted reflection of reality and is slowing up the development of society. This philosophy expresses the narrow, egoistic class interests of the reactionary bourgeoisie, and these interests do not represent the objective course of history: on the contrary, they obstruct it. The partisanship of bourgeois ideologists, struggling against a change from capitalism to a more progressive social order, i.e., socialism, thus clearly contradicts the objective laws of history and distorts its course and its development.

The scientific world outlook, on the other hand, which correctly reflects the laws of the development of natural and social phenomena, defends the interests of the classes which are the bearers of progress and to which the future belongs. In present conditions such an outlook is Marxism, the outlook of the most progressive class, the proletariat, and of its vanguard, the Communist party. Marxism has proclaimed and consistently applies the principle of partisan philosophy, and considers the philosophy of dialectical and historical materialism as a scientific weapon in the hands of the proletarian masses struggling for their liberation from capitalism, for the victory of the most equitable, most human, most progressive social order, i.e., communism.

A revolutionary theory is necessary for the revolutionary, practical transformation of society on the road to communism. Such a theory is Marxism-Leninism, and its philosophical foundation is dialectical and historical materialism. The principle of communist partisanship requires that after the struggle of ideas in the field of philosophy, there should, in the end, occur the struggle of opposing classes, of their interests and aspirations. Materialism and idealism are, in the course of the whole history of the development of philosophy, the two main opposing currents, struggling with each other. Materialism and idealism are the two parties in philosophy. A bitter struggle has always taken and is still taking place between them. The newest philosophy, Lenin emphasized, is as partisan as two thousand years ago. The struggle between materialism and idealism always reflects the struggle of classes inside society. As a rule the struggle between these currents in philosophy reflects the struggle between the progressive and the reactionary classes.

Some bourgeois ideologists, and revisionists after them, declare that the Marxists simplify the problem, as it were, when they divide modern philosophers into materialists and idealists. Marxists, however, make this division in theory because it has also its place in life. It is a fact of reality itself.

Idealism and religion are enemies of science. They reflect the world incorrectly, distortedly. The metaphysicians profess the immutability of the existing order in the capitalist world. They consider this order permanent. This philosophy is profitable for them. It is clear, consequently, that the working class and its party cannot be reconciled with idealism, religion, and meta-physics. Religion, for the working class, is one of the kinds of spiritual oppression which weighs heavily everywhere on the working people crushed by exploitation, and idealism is but a more refined form of religion.

Only dialectical and historical materialism provide the possibility of liberating humanity from all the empty illusions of a paradise beyond the grave.

Marxist philosophy is the world outlook of the working class, and of its vanguard, the Communist party. It is the theoretical foundation of their revolutionary policy, strategy, and tactics. The political line of Marxism is always and in all problems "linked with its philosophical foundation" (V. I. Lenin, *Works*, 4th Edition, Vol. 15, p. 374 ["Concerning the Attitude of the Workers' Party toward Religion," *The Proletarian*, No. 45, 13(29), May, 1909].) No party aside from the Marxist party represents so objectively and subjectively the interests of all working mankind. Just as the interests of the working class coincide with the objective requirements of social development, with the interests of the overwhelming majority of working mankind, so precisely the working class is first of all interested in the scientific knowledge of nature and society, in the working out of a scientific world outlook and method, this being the necessary condition for its successful struggle against capital and for the construction of communism.

The partisanship of Marxist philosophy consists in the systematic carrying out of the materialistic line in philosophy, in the unmasking of all kinds of attempts of mixing materialism with idealism, dialectic with metaphysics, and in the unmasking of the reactionary political conclusions drawn from them. Only an honest study of reality answers to the interests of the working class and provides it with the possibility of basing all its practical and political activities on the solid foundation of science. Marxist-Leninist partisanship, therefore, not only does not contradict scientific objectivity, but is generated by it. The Communist party's concern regarding the observation and implementation of the principle of partisanship *is* the concern of keeping and developing an honest relationship with life.

XI. *Dialectical Materialism and Contemporary Bourgeois Philosophy*

A new epoch began in history when Marxism came to life and dialectical materialism opposed bourgeois ideology. Lenin established two fundamental stages in the bourgeois ideologists' struggle against Marxism. The first stage is the stage that precedes the victory of Marxism over that world outlook which influenced the working-class movement; the second stage is when Marxism won the victory in the working-class movement by eliminating the teachings opposed to it. As Lenin wrote, "the progress of Marxism and the fact that its ideas are spreading and taking firm hold among the working class, inevitably tend to increase the frequency and intensity of these bourgeois attacks on Marxism. . . ." (*Works*, 4th edition, Vol. 15, p. 17; ["Marxism and Revisionism," *The Essentials of Lenin in Two Volumes*, I, 67].) Contemporary bourgeois philosophy is the philosophy of a dying class. It reflects the deep crisis of capitalist society, the bourgeois fear of the masses and of communism.

Contemporary bourgeois philosophy is characterized by a great diversity of schools and trends. They are all unified by one fundamental problem, i.e., the direct or indirect struggle against communist ideas and their philosophical foundation, dialectical and historical materialism.

Attacking dialectical materialism, bourgeois philosophers at the same time make every effort to defend theoretically a dying capitalism. The bourgeois ideology has as its aim to divert the working masses from the revolutionary transformation of society, to educate them in the spirit of religious submissiveness and slavery, to lead them to a world of vain illusions. Proceeding on Lenin's principle of the peaceful coexistence of the two systems, the socialist and the capitalist, Marxist philosophers can nevertheless not abstain from fighting the bourgeois ideology. The relaxation and, even more, the cessation of this ideological struggle would inevitably entail a strengthening of the pernicious influence of the bourgeois ideology on the minds of the people.

Contemporary bourgeois philosophy is characterized by idealism and *agnosticism, irrationalism,* by the depreciation and misinterpretation of the role of science in the world outlook, by a false philosophical interpretation of its achievements, by a close relationship of philosophy and religion, by the denial of the social laws of nature and by eclecticism. The idea of the eternity of capitalism, the denial of the class composition of society, etc., are preached in sociology. The ideologists of the reactionary bourgeoisie are guided in their assertions either by the teachings of the most reactionary philosophers of the past, or by the weakest aspects in the philosophical teachings of the classical philosophers; at the same time they omit all that is most rational in these teachings, or construct eclectic combinations of separate theses of various teachings.

The ideologists of the rising bourgeoisie fought for the victory of reason, expressing an unshakable belief in its power, and led science to penetrate into the laws of the connections and relations of things. The ideologists of the reactionary bourgeoisie, however, are on the one hand compelled to contribute to the development of science because of the requirements of contemporary production, of technical development in general and of military development in particular; but, on the other hand, insofar as science ever further undermines the foundations of idealism and religion which are the main weapons for oppressing the masses, they carry on a war against reason and are that much the more interested in demonstrating the impotence of reason and in establishing the limits of knowledge.

There are idealistic-subjective as well as idealistic-objective trends among the great diversity of the trends of contemporary bourgeois philosophy. There are also varieties of vulgar materialism, for instance the *neo-materialism* of the French philosopher Ch. Meyer. However, the prevailing trend is the idealistic-subjective one represented by *neo-positivism, pragmatism,* and *existentialism.* Neo-positivism in its various forms is prevalent in England and the United States of America, but it is also widespread in other lands because of its relation to the natural sciences, mathematics, cybernetics, etc. A characteristic peculiarity of neo-positivism is its denial of the possibility of understanding the causes and laws of the real world, its reduction of the problems of science to the mere external description of the results of direct observation, and the reconciliation of science and religion.

Bordering on neo-positivism is pragmatism, one of the characteristic philosophical trends of the social reality of the United States of America. Pragmatism considers all theoretical constructions from the point of view of their practical advantage for the individual, independently of their relation to reality.

A characteristic peculiarity of contemporary bourgeois philosophy is the revival of medieval conceptions. The class meaning of this phenomenon was disclosed by Lenin, who stated that the "bourgeoisie, out of fear for the growth and increasing strength of the proletariat, is supporting everything backward, effete, and medieval." (*Works*, 4th edition, Vol. 19, p. 77 ["Backward Europe and Advanced Asia," *Pravda*, No. 113(317), May 18 (31), 1913; *The Essentials of Lenin in Two Volumes*, I, 562].) The wave of mysticism, open bigotry, and superstition grows higher and higher in bourgeois ideological life, slowing up the development of science and of all culture. Idealistic philosophy and religion enmesh science in reactionary conceptions and enter into sharp contradiction with the objective results of scientific investigations. *Neo-Thomism* and *personalism* are classified as trends of this kind. . . .

A fashionable trend in western Europe is existentialism. This view brings to the foreground the concept of "existence," meanwhile reducing the latter to the existence of the self-consciousness of the person, the fundamental content of which is the fear of death, the feeling of solitude, etc.

Despair is the last word of bourgeois philosophy. . . .

In this ideological situation only Marxist philosophy is loyal to natural science and firmly opposed to any superstition or mysticism. Marxist philosophy liberates the human mind from the opium of religion, from any kind of superstition and prejudice. Dialectical materialism recognizes the possibility of knowing the objective world and its laws. This inspires science, opens before it limitless prospects, raises in man a proud awareness of his power, belief in the indestructible might of human reason as able to penetrate the limitless expanse of the cosmos and the inexhaustible depths of the atom.

Bourgeois ideology, recognizing in dialectical materialism its main enemy and the greatest obstacle in the propagation of reactionary ideas, has recourse more and more frequently and intensely to falsification and criticism of dialectical materialism. If in the past the critics of dogmatic materialism tried to prove that materialism had already long ago been refuted and that it had no significance, now they are compelled under the pressure of facts to admit that dogmatic materialism is getting more and more widespread and influential. Quite a few works have recently been published whose authors are specialists in the falsification of the basic theses of dogmatic materialism and in its criticism. These authors, interpreting materialism in the spirit of mechanism, come to the false conclusion that dialectical materialism is applicable only to the explanation of natural phenomena and is unfit for the right understanding of the more complicated phenomena of social life.

Other critics misinterpret dialectical materialism in the spirit of the Hegelian idealistic philosophy and even of Platonic idealism.

Some bourgeois ideologists make efforts to falsify the substance of dialectical materialism by substituting for it Thomistic "dialectic" (called analectic) with its denial of contradictions. They admit the existence of supposedly peacefully coexisting opposites, i.e., social classes, but ignore the real contradictions among them and attack the Marxist teaching that the solution of these contradictions lies in social revolution. . . . Most of the critics of dialectical materialism, attaining to complete absurdity, try to interpret it as a variety of religious faith, to deny its scientific character, and to find common features between Catholic philosophy and dialectical materialism.

The fundamental "accusations" brought against dialectical materialism by bourgeois ideologists have found their expression in contemporary *revisionism*. The revisionists in their criticism of dialectical materialism try to use the "arguments" of bourgeois criticism, concealing them in Marxist phraseology. As a trend hostile to Marxism-Leninism, revisionism comes forward under the banner of a "correction," a "supplement," and a "creative" development of Marxism-Leninism, becoming in fact a champion of bourgeois ideology, of bourgeois philosophical views in the working-class movement. The theoretical roots of contemporary revisionism, repeating in essence the fundamental theses of the old revisionism, must therefore be found in contemporary bourgeois philosophy.

In imperialistic countries the struggle between progressive and reactionary world outlooks, between champions of materialism and idealism, becomes more and more heated. Marxist philosophers, members of the communist and labor parties, are in the foreground of the fighters for social progress and the scientific world outlook. Pre-eminent scientists give more and more support to the materialistic world outlook. Natural science, since it has to deal with nature, unavoidably leads to dialectical materialist conclusions. This has been deeply understood by such notable scientists as Paul Langevin, F. Joliot-Curie, John D. Bernal, J. B. S. Haldane, and others. They became conscious supporters of dialectical materialism.

In the struggle for the scientific world outlook in capitalistic countries, even people from among the bourgeois intelligentsia are coming forward in its favor. They are, for instance, M. Bouvier-Agen and Alfred Sauvy (France), Josué de Castro (Brazil), Corliss Lamont, John Davis, Barrows Dunham (United States of America), Kenjuro Yanagida (Japan), and others. Such notable scientists as Leopold Infeld and Louis-Victor de Broglie, who formerly were neo-positivists, have finally taken the side of materialism. The notable contemporary physicists N. Bohr and W. Heisenberg have come forward with criticism of a series of positivist theses (although not from the materialistic point of view).

XII. *Dialectical Materialism and the Present*

We are living at a time when Marxism-Leninism is winning one victory after another on an international scale. Marxism-Leninism is not simply a theory. It has impregnated the revolutionary practice of millions and millions of fighters against imperialism and war, of fighters for peace, national liberation, of fighters for communism. The victory of the Great October Socialist Revolution, having proved in practice the truth of the Marxist-Leninist teaching, has opened to all peoples the wide avenue to socialism and communism. The creation of popular democracies in a series of European and Asiatic countries, the full and final victory of socialism, the successes of the development of communist construction in the U.S.S.R., mean a new triumph for Marxism-Leninism and its philosophical foundation. Not a single philosophical teaching in the entire world has received such a glorious and thorough confirmation as dialectical materialism.

The Marxist-Leninist world outlook is all-powerful because it rightly reflects the general laws of being and thought, the objective tendencies of the progressive development of society; because it expresses most fully the interests of the working classes fighting for their liberation from capitalism and for the building of a new society, i.e., communism. As a giant oak penetrates deep into the ground with its powerful roots, dialectical materialism has its solid roots in the life of the working people whose interests and expectations it expresses. It is because of this that Marxist-Leninist philosophy is winning the struggle for the minds and hearts of the people, as, by the way, is recognized by many bourgeois ideologists who are awakening to the disturbing feeling of the superiority of socialism and the vitality of its theoretical foundation.

Dialectical materialism teaches that everything in the world is in flux, everything is changing, everything is in constant motion and development. Social life is also in perpetual motion in the course of development from lowest to highest. Every social and economic structure, including capitalism, is historically transitory. This means that in the history of mankind a social system which is growing obsolete unavoidably gives way to a new, progressive system. To replace capitalism a new, higher system is coming and in a series of countries has already arrived. This system, socialism, corresponds to the contemporary forces of production. Capitalist society is penetrated by deep internal contradictions of an antagonistic character which increase daily, shaking it from top to bottom and destroying its very foundations. Lenin, in analyzing the course of development of society, wrote that "the suppression of capitalism and of its vestiges, the building of the foundations of the communist system are the content of the new period of world history which has now begun." (*Works*, 4th edition, Vol. 31, p. 365 [*Concerning the*

Internal Struggle of the Italian Socialist Party, December 11, 1920].)

The contradictions in the theses and phenomena of the material world, in social life, get their deep reflection and their theoretical foundation in dialectical materialism which bends down before nothing and which, by its own essence, is critical and revolutionary. Dialectical materialism is the most reliable and tested spiritual weapon in the struggle of the Marxist party against reactionary bourgeois ideology, against revisionism, against *dogmatism.*

Where the dialectical materialist requirements of a thoroughgoing examination of animate life with all its contradictions and peculiarities, with all the fundamental tendencies of its development are disturbed, dogmatism unavoidably appears. . . .

Dialectical materialism teaches that there is no abstract truth, that truth is always concrete, that any fact of natural and social reality must be approached historically. This means that in order to solve present social problems in all fields of social life, and particularly in politics, one must look forward, take notice of the changes which occur in the distribution of social forces, and take into account the steady growth of the forces of the solid socialist camp.

Concrete scientific analysis, the historical approach to facts or to one or another theoretical thesis, have their objective bases in the changes of life itself. Since our knowledge is a reflection of reality, it is natural that, with the development of this reality, our knowledge about it must unavoidably grow. The only correct scientific criterion of truth is practice, life in its uninterrupted development. The creative character of dialectical materialism results from its own essence, which originates from the unity of revolutionary theory and revolutionary practice. Emphasizing the creative character of Marxism, Lenin wrote: " 'Our teaching,' said Engels about himself and his illustrious friend, 'is not a dogma but a guide to action.' An aspect of Marxism which is very often neglected is' emphasized with remarkable force and significance in this classical statement. By neglecting it, we make Marxism one-sided, deformed, dead, we take out of it its living soul, we undermine its basic theoretical foundations, i.e., the dialectic, which is the teaching that historical development is many-sided and full of contradictions; we undermine its connection with practical specific problems of the epoch which can change with every turn of history." (*Works*, 4th edition, Vol. 17, p. 20 ["Concerning Some Peculiarities of the Historical Development of Marxism," *Zvezda*, No. 2, December 23, 1910, signed: V. Ilyin].) . . .

It is not sufficient simply to memorize the fundamental theses of the dialectic in order to apply it rightly in knowledge and in practice, i.e., in politics. To do this a serious and thorough study of facts, of life in its developments is necessary. The manifestation of the laws of the dialectic in a given field of nature, society, or thinking can be understood only after a thorough study of facts, of life. This makes it possible thoroughly and correctly to project the line of practical action and so to obtain the necessary effect in the defense of the interests of the workers. The knowledge of dialectical materialism has a tremendous significance for the development of the theoretical and practical thinking of man: it sharpens the mind, gives it flexibility, perspicacity, receptivity to new, sometimes hardly perceptible phenomena of life. The dialectic liberates the mind from dogmas, prejudices, preconceived opinions, subjectivism, sophistry, and the pressure of imaginary "eternal truths" which fetter the mind and slow up the pace of the development of science and practice. Thus, for instance, in the field of the present international situation, dialectical materialism requires a comprehensive analysis of those contradictory developments which determine the basic direction of the evolution of contemporary society. . . . Under the entirely changed conditions of the alignment of social forces, many problems are solved anew, including those of war and peace in the international field. Under these new historical conditions the XXth Congress of the Communist party, guided by the principles of dialectical materialism, came to the conclusion that war can be prevented. The XXIst Congress of the Communist party came to the profound conclusion that world war could be excluded from among the instruments of international policy. All this is directed to the mobilization of popular masses for an active struggle for peace. In the last instance all depends on a consistent struggle for peace against the aggressive forces of imperialism.

The gigantic victories won by the Communist party of the Soviet Union and by other Marxist-Leninist parties are indicative of the fact that these parties are guided in all their actions by the theory and the method of the dialectic, while in turn developing them creatively. Deviation from dialectical materialism leads in the end to mistakes in theory, in practice, in policy.

The following is stated in the Declaration of the Conference of Representatives of Communist and Workers' Parties of Socialist Countries which took place in Moscow from 14th to 16th November, 1957: "If a Marxist political party did not proceed from dialectics and materialism in examining questions, this would lead to one-sidedness and subjectivism, stagnation of thought, isolation from practice, and loss of ability to make the necessary analysis of things and phenomena, revisionist or dogmatic mistakes and mistakes in policy." [*The Current Digest of the Soviet Press*, New York, 1958, Vol. 9, No. 47, p. 5.]

Dialectical materialism is not only a method of knowledge of the world, it is also a method of its revolutionary transformation. . . . Dialectical materialism demands an active, efficient, creative relationship with the world, with life. The blade of the dialectical method is checked, brought to use, and sharpened in work, class struggle, scientific activities, creations of art, and in the development of the construction of communism. Our great scientific discoveries and technical inventions which have astonished all the world (sputniks and space vehicles), the superiority of Soviet science in many fields, are the result of the socialist social system and at the same time the result of the superiority of the dialectical materialistic world outlook and method, which are the guiding star of Soviet scientists. . . .

One of the most important aspects of the Marxist-Leninist philosophy is its genuine *humanism*. It is incompatible with any manifestation of misanthropy, with any humiliation of human dignity, which are so characteristic of the ideology of contemporary imperialism, especially in its relations with the people of colonies and semi-colonies. Marxism-Leninism is profoundly imbued with faith in the limitless power and capacity of mankind to transform the surrounding world and its own nature. The problem which Marxist-Leninist philosophy brings forward is that of the theoretical preparation of practical means to create for the people of the earth genuinely human living conditions, i.e., those of communism, satisfying the highest humanitarian ideals.

Such an important feature of the Marxist-Leninist philosophy as its *optimism* is linked with its scientifically founded faith in the revolutionary possibilities of man. This philosophy opposes from beginning to end the bourgeois world outlook with its preaching of despondency, slackness, weakness and sorrow, pessimism, despair, lack of faith in the future.

Marxist philosophy, in contrast to the bourgeois world outlook, sets human reason on the solid foundations of science and practice and fills man's heart with noble feelings and aspirations; it gives man enormous spiritual forces: the force of ideological conviction, faith in the might of reason, strength of feeling and strength of will, confidence in the future, revolutionary aspirations in his outlook on life. The Marxist-Leninist philosophy is a bright, cheerful world outlook. The more it penetrates into the consciousness of the masses, the more actively, intelligently, and with the more inspiration will those masses take part in the struggle against exploitation and colonial oppression, the struggle for socialism and the construction of the communist system. . . . The Communist party and the Soviet government, proceeding from the humanitarian principles of the Marxist-Leninist world outlook, make every effort in the struggle for the peaceful development of society, for a peaceful coexistence of socialism and capitalism.

Marxist-Leninist philosophy unites all peoples without racial or national discrimination, and raises in them an aspiration for exalted and noble goals to serve the welfare of mankind. It makes it possible to size up the great vocation of man: to create a happy life on earth for all working people.

The developed construction of communism presupposes the formation of a new man, of the man of the communist system, thoroughly developed, armed with the most advanced scientific world outlook, i.e., with dialectical materialism. The Communist party paid and is paying enormous attention to the propagation of dialectical materialism among the working masses, and to its creative development. . . . The Communist and workers' parties lead their peoples with confidence of the radiant future of communism, basing their practical and ideological work on the teachings of Marxist-Leninist philosophy, the foundation of which is dialectical materialism.

Index

12; *The Question of Brotherhood or Relatedness*, 13, 16-54
Gagarin, P. I., Prince, 11
Gay Science, The. See Nietzsche.
Genius, 199-200, 202-203
Gentlewoman, The. See Dostoevsky.
Geographical Factor, 354, 355, 363-365, 387-388
Gilson, Étienne, 222
Gnosticism, 56, 312
God, nature of, 62-84
Godmanhood, 3, 58, 62-84
Goethe, Johann Wolfgang von, 205, 296
Grün, Karl, 465

Haldane, J. B. S., 501
Happiness, 32, 381
Hartmann, Nicolai, 188
Harvey, William, 360
Hegel, Georg Wilhelm Friedrich, 4, 56, 63n, 65n, 68n, 80n, 157, 162, 168, 183, 192, 193, 198, 230, 231, 232, 233, 234, 235, 236, 237, 238, 239, 240, 241, 243, 244, 246, 284, 356, 358, 359, 360, 361, 366-367, 373, 380-381, 387, 388, 389, 407, 408, 417, 430, 437-454, 457n, 462, 466, 475, 479; *Encyclopedia of the Philosophical Sciences*, 234, 435, 445, 464; *Lectures on the History of Philosophy*, 233, 447-450; *Philosophy of History*, 387; *Philosophy of Religion*, 233, 235; *Philosophy of Spirit*, 389; *The Science of Logic*, 437-447; and Thomas Aquinas, *see* Thomas Aquinas
Hegelianism, 183, 236, 239, 349, 500
Heidegger, Martin, 185-186, 187-188, 210, 213, 292
Heisenberg, Werner, 491, 501
Hell, 206, 210-211
Helmholtz, Hermann Ludwig Ferdinand von, 407, 459n, 460
Heraclitus, 291, 450, 453
Herzen, Alexander Ivanovich (1812-1870), 345
Hess, Moses, 465

Hieroglyphics, theory of, 348, 355, 373n, 386, 400-402, 403, 422, 455, 456, 459-460
Hinduism, 273, 274
History: individual in, 355, 368-370; philosophy of, 146-147, 204-208, 217-220, 306-314, 366-367, 368-370, 387-388, 389, 440, 492-496
History of Philosophy. See Hegel.
History of Russian Philosophy. See Lossky.
History of the Communist Party of the Soviet Union (Bolshevik) Short Course, 350
Hobbes, Thomas, 386
Holbach, Paul Henri Thiery, 358, 372, 373, 375, 382, 395, 453; *Système de la Nature*, 382
Humanism, 26, 205-208, 306-314, 505
Humanitarianism, 506
Hume, David, 281, 324, 334, 335, 378, 379, 411, 412, 413, 416, 420, 431, 435, 439, 453, 457; *Treatise of Human Nature*, 281n, 335n
Humeians, 413, 426
Husserl, Edmund, 188-189, 193, 222, 223, 224, 225, 248-276; *Ideen zu einer reinen Phänomenologie*, 235; *Logische Untersuchungen*, 249, 250, 251, 252n, 254-255, 258, 259, 263; *Philosophie als Strenge Wissenschaft*, 254

Ibsen, Henrik, 169
Ideal Man, 76, 77
"Ideal Realism," 319
Idealism, 193, 196, 349, 358, 366-367, 372, 377, 382-386, 389, 407, 415, 420, 422, 426, 429, 430, 435, 436, 454, 495; absolute, 445, 447; critique of, 410-436; German, 181, 182, 183, 188, 283, 360; Hegelian, 430, 500; Kantian, 140, 277; objective, 478; Platonic, 500; subjective, 376, 378
Ideen zu einer reinen Phänomenologie. See Husserl.
Identity, Law of, 337
Idiot, The. See Dostoevsky.

This is one of three volumes of RUSSIAN PHILOSOPHY.

VOLUME I

The Beginnings of Russian Philosophy
The Slavophiles
The Westernizers

VOLUME II

The Nihilists
The Populists
Critics of Religion and Culture

VOLUME III

Pre-Revolutionary Philosophy and Theology
Philosophers in Exile
Marxists and Communists

The University of Tennessee Press